# Fukushima and the Arts

The natural and man-made cataclysmic events of the March 11, 2011 disaster, or 3.11, have dramatically altered the status quo of contemporary Japanese society. While much has been written about the social, political, economic, and technical aspects of the disaster, this volume represents one of the first in-depth explorations of the cultural responses to the devastating tsunami, and in particular the ongoing nuclear disaster of Fukushima.

This book explores a wide range of cultural responses to the Fukushima nuclear calamity by analyzing examples from literature, poetry, manga, theatre, art photography, documentary and fiction film, and popular music. Individual chapters examine the changing positionality of post-3.11 northeastern Japan and the fear-driven conflation of time and space in near-but-far urban centers; explore the political subversion and nostalgia surrounding the Fukushima disaster; expose the ambiguous effects of highly gendered representations of fear of nuclear threat; analyze the musical and poetic responses to disaster; and explore the political potentialities of theatrical performances. By scrutinizing various media narratives and taking into account national and local perspectives, the book sheds light on cultural texts of power, politics, and space.

Providing an insight into the post-disaster Zeitgeist as expressed through a variety of media genres, this book will be of interest to students and scholars of Japanese Studies, Japanese Culture, Popular Culture, and Literature Studies.

**Barbara Geilhorn** is a JSPS-postdoctoral fellow based at Waseda University, Tokyo, Japan. Her publications include *Enacting Culture: Japanese Theater in Historical and Modern Contexts* co-edited with Eike Grossmann (2012).

**Kristina Iwata-Weickgenannt** is an Associate Professor of Japanese modern literature at Nagoya University, Japan. Her recent publications include *Visions of Precarity in Japanese Popular Culture and Literature*, co-edited with Roman Rosenbaum (Routledge, 2015).

# Routledge Contemporary Japan Series

*For a complete list of titles in this series, please visit* www.routledge.com/Routledge-Contemporary-Japan-Series/book-series/SE0002

54 **Religion and Psychotherapy in Modern Japan**
*Edited by Christopher Harding, Iwata Fumiaki and Yoshinaga Shin'ichi*

55 **Party Politics in Japan**
Political chaos and stalemate in the 21st century
*Edited by Ronald J. Hrebenar and Akira Nakamura*

56 **Career Women in Contemporary Japan**
Pursuing identities, fashioning lives
*Anne Stefanie Aronsson*

57 **Visions of Precarity in Japanese Popular Culture and Literature**
*Edited by Kristina Iwata-Weickgenannt and Roman Rosenbaum*

58 **Decision-Making Reform in Japan**
The DPJ's failed attempt at a politician-led government
*Karol Zakowski*

59 **Examining Japan's Lost Decades**
*Edited by Yoichi Funabashi and Barak Kushner*

60 **Japanese Women in Science and Engineering**
History and policy change
*Naonori Kodate and Kashiko Kodate*

61 **Japan's Border Issues**
Pitfalls and prospects
*Akihiro Iwashita*

62 **Japan, Russia and Territorial Dispute**
The Northern delusion
*James D.J. Brown*

63 **Fukushima and the Arts**
Negotiating nuclear disaster
*Edited by Barbara Geilhorn and Kristina Iwata-Weickgenannt*

64 **Social Inequality in Post-Growth Japan**
Transformation during economic and demographic stagnation
*Edited by David Chiavacci and Carola Hommerich*

65 **The End of Cool Japan**
Ethical, legal, and cultural challenges to Japanese popular culture
*Edited by Mark McLelland*

# Fukushima and the Arts
Negotiating nuclear disaster

**Edited by
Barbara Geilhorn and
Kristina Iwata-Weickgenannt**

LONDON AND NEW YORK

First published 2017
by Routledge
2 Park Square, Milton Park, Abingdon, Oxon OX14 4RN

and by Routledge
711 Third Avenue, New York, NY 10017

First issued in paperback 2018

*Routledge is an imprint of the Taylor & Francis Group, an informa business*

© 2017 Barbara Geilhorn and Kristina Iwata-Weickgenannt

The right of the editors to be identified as the authors of the editorial matter, and of the authors for their individual chapters, has been asserted in accordance with sections 77 and 78 of the Copyright, Designs and Patents Act 1988.

All rights reserved. No part of this book may be reprinted or reproduced or utilised in any form or by any electronic, mechanical, or other means, now known or hereafter invented, including photocopying and recording, or in any information storage or retrieval system, without permission in writing from the publishers.

*Trademark notice*: Product or corporate names may be trademarks or registered trademarks, and are used only for identification and explanation without intent to infringe.

*British Library Cataloguing in Publication Data*
A catalogue record for this book is available from the British Library

*Library of Congress Cataloging in Publication Data*
Names: Geilhorn, Barbara, editor. | Iwata-Weickgenannt, Kristina, editor.
Title: Fukushima and the arts : negotiating nuclear disaster / edited by Barbara Geilhorn and Kristina Iwata-Weickgenannt.
Description: Milton Park, Abingdon, Oxon : New York : Routledge, 2016. | Series: Routledge contemporary Japan series ; 63 | Includes bibliographical references and index.
Identifiers: LCCN 2016002255| ISBN 9781138670587 (hardback) | ISBN 9781315617589 (ebook)
Subjects: LCSH: Japanese literature–Heisei period, 1989–History and criticism. | Fukushima Nuclear Disaster, Japan, 2011, in literature. | Fukushima Nuclear Disaster, Japan, 2011, in motion pictures. | Fukushima Nuclear Disaster, Japan, 2011–Influence.
Classification: LCC PL726.87.F87 F85 2016 | DDC 895.609/358520512–dc23
LC record available at https://lccn.loc.gov/2016002255

ISBN 13: 978-1-138-60670-8 (pbk)
ISBN 13: 978-1-138-67058-7 (hbk)

Typeset in Times New Roman
by Wearset Ltd, Boldon, Tyne and Wear

*To those who were lost,
continue to struggle,
and will be born into a landscape forever changed
by the triple disaster of 11 March 2011*

# Contents

List of figures ... ix
Notes on contributors ... x
Acknowledgements ... xiv
Editors' note ... xvi

1 Negotiating nuclear disaster: an introduction ... 1
KRISTINA IWATA-WEICKGENANNT AND
BARBARA GEILHORN

2 Literature maps disaster: the contending narratives of 3.11 fiction ... 21
RACHEL DINITTO

3 *Summertime Blues*: musical critique in the aftermaths of Japan's 'dark spring' ... 39
SCOTT W. AALGAARD

4 Subversion and nostalgia in art photography of the Fukushima nuclear disaster ... 58
PABLO FIGUEROA

5 Uncanny anxiety: literature after Fukushima ... 74
SAEKO KIMURA

6 Problematizing life: documentary films on the 3.11 nuclear catastrophe ... 90
HIDEAKI FUJIKI

7 Gendering 'Fukushima': resistance, self-responsibility, and female hysteria in Sono Sion's *Land of Hope* ... 110
KRISTINA IWATA-WEICKGENANNT

## Contents

8 Antigone in Japan: some responses to 3.11 at Festival/Tokyo 2012    127
M. CODY POULTON

9 Poetry in an era of nuclear power: three poetic responses to Fukushima    144
JEFFREY ANGLES

10 Challenging reality with fiction: imagining alternative readings of Japanese society in post-Fukushima theater    162
BARBARA GEILHORN

11 *Oishinbo*'s Fukushima elegy: grasping for the truth about radioactivity in a food manga    177
LORIE BRAU

12 The politics of the senses: Takayama Akira's atomized theatre after Fukushima    199
KYŌKO IWAKI

Index    221

# Figures

| | | |
|---|---|---|
| 4.1 | 'Shinmachi Street' Jun. 12, 2011 by Watanabe Toshiya | 64 |
| 4.2 | 'Shinmachi Street' September 16, 2012 by Watanabe Toshiya | 65 |
| 4.3 | 'Photo Studio' Jun. 12, 2011 by Watanabe Toshiya | 66 |
| 4.4 | '#01' by Imai Tomoki | 68 |
| 4.5 | '#02' by Imai Tomoki | 68 |
| 4.6 | '#12' by Imai Tomoki | 69 |
| 4.7 | '#21' by Imai Tomoki | 69 |
| 4.8 | '#25' by Imai Tomoki | 70 |
| 10.1 | *Unable to See* by Okada Toshiki | 165 |
| 10.2 | *Current Location* by Okada Toshiki | 169 |
| 12.1 | The van used for *The Referendum Project* by Takayama Akira | 201 |
| 12.2 | *Tokyo Heterotopia* by Takayama Akira | 211 |
| 12.3 | A Cambodian restaurant, which was one of the visiting sites of *Tokyo Heterotopia* by Takayama Akira | 215 |

# Contributors

**Scott W. Aalgaard** (aalgaard@uchicago.edu) is a PhD candidate in the Department of East Asian Languages and Civilizations at the University of Chicago, where he engages with music, literature, and social critique in order to investigate ambiguous conceptualizations of community and belonging that are held by individual social actors amid conditions of precarity. Previous publications have appeared in the *Journal of Asian Studies*, *Bungei*, and *The Asia Pacific Journal: Japan Focus*. His translation of Nakano Shigeharu's *The Role of the Writer as National Citizen* is forthcoming in a compilation from Lexington Books.

**Jeffrey Angles** (jeffrey.angles@wmich.edu) is an associate professor of Japanese and translation at Western Michigan University. He is the author of *Writing the Love of Boys* (University of Minnesota Press, 2011) and the award-winning translator of dozens of Japan's most important modern Japanese authors and poets. His most recent translation is Orikuchi Shinobu's modernist classic *The Book of the Dead* (University of Minnesota Press, 2016). He believes strongly in the role of translators as social activists, and much of his career has focused on the translation into English of socially engaged, feminist, or queer writers. He is also a poet, and his first book of poetry written in Japanese, titled *Hizuke henkō sen (International Date Line)*, is forthcoming.

**Lorie Brau** (lbrau@unm.edu) is an associate professor of Japanese in the Department of Foreign Languages and Literatures at the University of New Mexico. She received her MA in Japanese Literature from the University of Michigan and her PhD in Performance Studies at New York University (1994). To research her dissertation and book, *Rakugo: Performing Comedy and Cultural Heritage in Contemporary Tokyo* (Lexington, 2008), she became a disciple of the storyteller Kokontei Engiku, and is an amateur performer of Japanese comic storytelling. She has published on the manga, *Oishinbo* (The Gourmet) as well as on *rakugo*, and is presently at work on a monograph on the discourses of culinary manga titled *Gourmanga: Reading Food in Japanese Comic Books*.

Contributors xi

**Rachel DiNitto** (rdinitto@uoregon.edu) is an associate professor of Japanese literature at the University of Oregon. She works on the literary and cultural studies of Japan's pre-war (1910s–1930s), and post-bubble eras (1990–2000s). In addition to her monograph, *Uchida Hyakken: A Critique of Modernity and Militarism in Prewar Japan*, her publications include articles on depictions of the Asia-Pacific War in the work of *manga* artist Maruo Suehiro; Kanehara Hitomi, the young female writer whose controversial novel *Snakes and Earrings* won Japan's most prestigious literary award in 2004; and cult director Suzuki Seijun's return to the cinema in the 1980s. Her chapter in this volume is part of a book project on the literature written in response to the March 11, 2011 triple disaster in Japan.

**Pablo Figueroa** (pablofigueroa@outlook.com) is an assistant professor in the Center for International Education at Waseda University. In this position, he teaches semester courses on globalization and social change in Japan, perspectives of leadership, natural and man-made disasters, and narratives in the construction of cultural identity. A social anthropologist specializing in Japanese studies, his research interests include *burakumin* and *zainichi* Korean minorities, public perceptions of nuclear energy, citizen participation, and the communication of risk during catastrophic accidents. Pablo is currently doing fieldwork on nuclear risk governance and photographic discourses of the 2011 Fukushima triple disasters.

**Hideaki Fujiki** (hfuji@lit.nagoya-u.ac.jp) is professor in cinema and Japanese studies at Nagoya University. His publications include *Making Personas: Transnational Film Stardom in Modern Japan* (Harvard University Asia Center, 2013) and *The Japanese Cinema Book*, co-edited with Alastair Phillips (British Film Institute, forthcoming). He is currently working on cinema and ecology.

**Barbara Geilhorn** (barbara.geilhorn@fu-berlin.de) is a JSPS-postdoctoral research fellow based at Waseda University, Tokyo. Her research interests include classical and contemporary Japanese theater, post-3.11 Japanese culture, gender studies, and cultural sociology. From 2009–2014 she worked as lecturer at the Institute of East Asian Studies of Freie Universität Berlin. She received her PhD in Japanese Studies with a thesis on professional Noh and Kyogen actresses from the Meiji period to the present. Barbara participated in international projects on Noh theater and held doctoral scholarships from the German Institute of Japanese Studies Tokyo (DIJ) and the German Research Foundation (DFG). Her publications include *From Private* zashiki *to the Public Stage – Female Spaces in Early 20th Century Nō* (*Asian Theatre Journal*, 2015) and *Enacting Culture – Historical and Contemporary Contexts of Japanese Theatre* (co-edited with Eike Grossmann, iudicium 2012).

**Kyōko Iwaki** (info@kyokoiwaki.com) is a PhD researcher and a visiting lecturer based at the Theatre and Performance Department of Goldsmiths, University of London. Her thesis focuses on the social, political, and aesthetic language of the post-nuclear catastrophe theatre in Japan. Before commencing scholarly research, she has worked for over a decade as a theatre journalist contributing to *The Asahi Shimbun*. Her recent media and festival appearances include, Radio SRF (Switzerland), Festival La Bâtie (Geneve), and LIFT Festival (London). Kyōko was appointed Associate Creative Partner of Kanagawa Arts Theatre in 2010. Recent publications include *Tokyo Theatre Today: Conversations with Eight Emerging Theatre Artists* (Hublet Publishing, 2011), *Ushio Amagatsu: Des rivages d'enfance au bûto de Sankai juku* (Actes Sud, 2013), 'Japanese Theatre after Fukushima: Okada Toshiki's Current Location' (*New Theatre Quarterly*), and an *Interview with Oriza Hirata* (in *A History of Japanese Theatre*, Cambridge University Press, 2016).

**Kristina Iwata-Weickgenannt** (kristina.iwata@lit.nagoya-u.ac.jp) is an associate professor of Japanese modern literature at Nagoya University. She received her PhD from Trier University, Germany for a thesis on performative constructions of gender and ethnicity in the work of *zainichi* Korean writer Yū Miri. Her thesis was given Trier University's Best Dissertation Award and received the European Association for Japanese Studies Book Prize in 2008. Before coming to Nagoya, Kristina worked as a research associate at the Japanese Studies Department of Trier University and spent six years at the German Institute for Japanese Studies Tokyo (DIJ) as a senior research fellow. She has widely published on *zainichi* Korean minority literature, precarity culture, and cultural representations of Japan's 3.11 disaster. Her recent publications include Kristina Iwata-Weickgenannt and Roman Rosenbaum (eds), *Visions of Precarity in Japanese Popular Culture and Literature* (Routledge, 2015).

**Saeko Kimura** (skimura@tsuda.ac.jp) is a professor in the Department of International and Cultural Studies at Tsuda College, Tokyo. She received her PhD from Tokyo University. Her books include *Homosexuality and Love Tales: Court Society and Authority* [*Koisuru monogatari no homosekusharitī: kyūtei shakai to kenryoku*] (Tokyo: Seidosha, 2008), and *Breasts for Whom?: Sexuality and Authority in Japanese Medieval Tales* [*Chibusa wa dare no mono ka: Nihon chūsei monogatari ni miru sei to kenryoku*] (Tokyo: Shinyōsha, 2009), which jointly received the Japanese Women's History Studies Prize in 2009. Her English publications include *A Brief History of Sexuality in Premodern Japan* (Tallinn: TLU Press, 2010). She recently published *Literatures after Fukushima* [*Shinsaigo bungakuron: atarashī nihon bungaku no tameni*] (Tokyo: Seidosha, 2013), and *Women in Heian court* [*Onna tachi no Heian kyūtei: eiga monogatari ni yomu kenryoku to sei*] (Tokyo: Kōdansha, 2015).

**M. Cody Poulton** (cpoulton@uvic.ca) is professor of Japanese literature and theater in the Department of Pacific and Asian Studies at the University of Victoria, Canada, where he has taught since 1988. Active as a translator of Japanese fiction and drama, he is the author of *Spirits of Another Sort: The*

*Plays of Izumi Kyōka* (2001) and *A Beggar's Art: Scripting Modernity in Japan, 1900–1930* (2010). He is also co-editor (with Zdenka Svarcova) of *Dreams and Shadows: Tanizaki and Japanese Poetics in Prague* (2007); (with Katsuhiko Endo and Richard King) of *Sino-Japanese Transculturation: From the Late Nineteenth Century to the End of the Pacific War* (Lexington Books, 2011); and (with Mitsuya Mori and J. Thomas Rimer) of *The Columbia Anthology of Modern Japanese Drama* (2014). A current Fellow of the Interweaving Performance Cultures International Research Center at Berlin Free University, he is preparing a book on the non-human in Japanese theatre.

# Acknowledgements

### "Nuclear power—energy for a bright future"

On the cover of this book, we see two people standing in front of a gate bearing the abovementioned slogan. The gate was built in the spring of 1988—eighteen years after the Fukushima Daiichi Nuclear Power Plant was first commissioned, two years after Chernobyl, and twenty-three years before 'Fukushima' became global shorthand for the latest large-scale nuclear disaster. The gate is located in central Futaba, one of the host towns of the crippled Fukushima plant. Like other host municipalities throughout Japan, Futaba had also received large amounts of central government subsidies and generous donations from utilities for decades, and eventually became entirely dependent on nuclear power. Until March 11, 2011, almost everyone from the local government to schools and local businesses had been promoting nuclear power as a matter of course. On March 12, one day after the earthquake and tsunami hit, all 6,520 residents were hastily evacuated to faraway locations while their hometown was declared a no-entry zone. The ban has subsequently been lifted in some areas, but the vast majority of Futaba is still designated as a 'difficult to return' zone.

The cover photograph was taken on November 9, 2013. It shows Ōnuma Yūji and his wife Serina, who are wearing a combination of mourning clothes and protective gear. Weeds are growing wild on both sides of the street, breaking through the asphalt here and there. We see a Geiger counter dangling around Serina's neck. Standing next to her, Yūji is holding an urn with his aunt's ashes in his arms. Their family was dispersed all over Japan after the Fukushima explosions, and no one was able to attend the funeral except Serina and Yūji, who used a self-timer to record the event. For Yūji, it must have been a moment of particular bitterness. He was born and raised in Futaba, and as a sixth grader won a town-wide competition, which his teacher had made the class participate in, for the best promotional slogan. "Nuclear Power—Energy for a Bright Future" is his composition, and he recalls that the gate filled him with pride every time he saw it.

After 3.11/'Fukushima,' Yūji has returned to Futaba numerous times and taken photographs of the gate on every occasion, often using a self-timer to include himself. At times, he altered the slogan by holding up cardboard signs so that it variously read "Nuclear Power—Uncontrollable Energy," "Nuclear Power—Energy for a Devastating Future," "Renewables—Energy for a Bright Future." In our communication with Yūji, he stressed that being the originator of this slogan, he feels a strong sense of sensibility and an urge to 'correct' it while admitting his past indoctrination.

As is apparent from the photograph, the gate has seen better days. It appears old and a bit run down, but probably it is the now embarrassing slogan itself that led to the decision to dismantle the gate. Yūji had been running a preservation campaign that attracted a lot of attention from the media and on the Internet, but it was in vain: On December 21, 2015, the demolition work began. The sign will be kept somewhere in storage, out of public sight.

We wish to express our deep gratitude to Ōnuma Yūji and Serina for readily letting us use their photograph as the cover image for this volume. Hopefully, we will be able to make a small contribution to what they have been fighting for—the preservation of the memory of an inconvenient past.

An edited volume is always the product of cooperation. Therefore, we would like to thank our contributors, whose amazing commitment has made this book possible. Thank you all for keeping a number of tight deadlines, and for diligently addressing our many requests for revisions.

We have received moral support and constructive criticism along the way from numerous friends and colleagues, among them (in alphabetical order) Peter Eckersall, Andrea Germer, Nathan Hopson, Marilyn Ivy, Satoko Kakihara, Livia Monnet, Ulrike Wöhr, and many others. Phan Thi Thu Ha has been a great help with editing.

Our editors at Routledge have been continuously helpful and understanding. In particular, we would like to thank Stephanie Rogers for her ability to read through the lines, and Rebecca Lawrence for her patient support.

We would like to extend our gratitude to the Japanese Society for the Promotion of Science and Nagoya University, which provided the essential funding and support that allowed the editors to realize this project. Last but not least, we gratefully acknowledge the permission granted by all artists to reproduce their work.

# Editors' note

Japanese names are given according to the East Asian convention of family name first unless in cases in which Japanese authors are writing in a language other than Japanese.

The Hepburn system of romanization has been employed throughout except in cases where an established convention exists for corporate or individual names.

Unless specifically acknowledged, all translations included in this volume are attributable to the author of the respective chapter.

# 1 Negotiating nuclear disaster

## An introduction

*Kristina Iwata-Weickgenannt and
Barbara Geilhorn*

**The 'unexpected' disaster—a scenario**

March 11, 2011, was a chilly and profoundly cloudy day in northern Japan (Tōhoku) that felt nothing like spring.[1] In the early afternoon, at 14.46, the region was struck by what was later termed the Great East Japan Earthquake, a gigantic 9.0 magnitude quake that could be felt all the way down to southern Kyushu.[2] The temblor unleashed several equally enormous tsunamis, devastating six prefectures, and triggered the second INES level-seven accident in history at Fukushima I, the country's fourth oldest nuclear power plant, which was first commissioned in 1971.[3]

Even now, the sheer facts of the March 11 triple disaster are dizzying—*sōteigai*, or 'exceeding all expectations,' was one of the most frequently repeated adjectives used to describe the quake and tsunami, both of which were classified as occurring once in a thousand years.[4] The quake shoved portions of northeastern Japan by as much as 5.3 meters closer to North America; the seabed near the epicenter shifted around fifty meters horizontally toward the southeast and was elevated by up to ten meters (JAMSTEC 2011). Water, gas, and electricity supplies were knocked out for days if not weeks in the affected areas, and telecommunications were severely disrupted. Even several hundred kilometers from the epicenter, more than 1.2 million books fell off the bookshelves in Tokyo's National Diet Library; the capital's skyscrapers swayed visibly, and with much of the public transportation system paralyzed until the next day, millions had to walk home. Nonetheless, thanks to Japan's strict building standards, most buildings in the disaster area remained standing and the overall damage caused by this largest quake ever recorded in Japanese history was remarkably small (Earthquake Report.Com 2012).

Not so the damage caused by the tsunamis. A 500 km stretch of coastline was destroyed within minutes as the water rose up to 10 km inland, reaching a maximum run-up height of more than forty-three meters at an island off Onagawa Town in Miyagi Prefecture (*Sankei Shimbun* 2012). The tsunamis engulfed entire towns, dragged houses across rice fields and onto highways, and tossed around cars, trucks, and boats like toys, creating an estimated 20 million tons of debris as approximately 1.2 million buildings were damaged or completely destroyed.[5] Due to an earthquake-induced blackout, the tsunami warning system did not function properly in many coastal areas, and even where it did, the tremendous size and speed of the tsunami were underestimated by many. According to the National Police Agency, the tsunamis left almost 16,000 confirmed dead and, exactly four years later, 2,584 people are still missing (Keisatsuchō Kinkyū Saigai Keibi Honbu 2015).[6]

The nuclear dimension of the 3.11 disaster is less easily circumscribed. One year after the meltdowns, Jeff Kingston attempts the following summary:

> The long-term health effects are uncertain, but the costs of the nuclear crisis have been enormous and are mounting. The reckoning includes displacement of some 80,000 residents within the 20 km evacuation zone around the crippled reactors, many of whom will probably never return to their homes, loss of livelihoods suffered by local farmers, fishermen, and various businesses in Fukushima, together with anxiety about radiation and even the stigma of radiation that confronts the people of the prefecture. This stigma follows those who leave to restart lives elsewhere and raises concerns among young people concerning marriage prospects and raising families. In addition, there has been a wider economic fallout as bans on Japanese products were imposed overseas and overall in-bound tourism declined by 25% in 2011. Moreover, the nuclear crisis tarnished the Japan-brand, eroding the nation's reputation for technological prowess. Restoring what people and the nation lost will be costly and take considerable time. Compensation for losses are mounting while the costs of decontamination, disposal of tainted debris and decommissioning nuclear reactors will boost the final reckoning immensely. The Japanese will be paying for the folly of Fukushima for generations to come.
>
> (Kingston 2012a)

Obviously, there is no shortage of incident-related facts. Quite the contrary, the Fukushima I explosions were followed by an information tsunami and a staggering amount of incessant international data generation. However, most of this data is difficult for laypeople to assess and few 'facts' are undisputed even among experts. Some things simply remain unknown. For instance, to this day there is no agreement regarding the cause and course of the triple meltdown in reactors 1–3, nor on the amount of radiation released into the air and the ocean either back in 2011 or up to the present. The same holds true for the risk of recriticality, and, for that matter, the current shape and precise location of the molten fuels. Even if it is eventually located,[7] the technology to remove what is left of the reactor cores still needs to be developed. The question of human responsibility, let alone that of personal accountability, has not been properly addressed at any level. Above all, experts from the opposing camps assess the present and possible future health effects of the incident in disturbingly different ways.

The above shows that although undeniably linked, the three components of Japan's March 11, 2011 disaster are of a clearly different quality. Comparing the visual impact, deadliness, and time-frame of the natural and man-made[8] disasters, it becomes clear that the destruction caused by the former was massive, immediate and undeniable. As seen in the multitude of widely circulated images of untouched villagescapes next to total destruction, whether or not an area had been affected was not a matter of debate, but is obvious even to the untrained eye. On the other hand, the visual impact of the nuclear catastrophe was limited at best. The invisibility of radiation and the absence of *immediate* casualties meant that much of the terror of 'Fukushima'[9]—the global shorthand for the latest major nuclear catastrophe—originated in the realm of imagination. By this, we certainly do not mean to question the effects and dangers of radiation. However, it is important to note that due to both the perceived opacity and the fundamentally different temporality of nuclear issues, 'Fukushima' involves a psychological dimension missing from the earthquake and tsunami disasters. While the tsunami caused instant death, 'Fukushima' unfolds over time. Moreover, the nuclear contamination extends the time of catastrophe into the distant future. The uncertainty surrounding the implications of 'Fukushima' inevitably opened up space not only for debate, but also for denial. More than the far deadlier (at this point) tsunami, the nuclear catastrophe exposed deep fault lines running through Japanese society. It is for this reason that this volume puts a stronger emphasis on 'Fukushima' rather than on the calamity caused by the tsunami.

## March 11, 2011 as 'Japan's 9.11'?

In an obvious analogy to the 9.11 terrorist attacks in the USA a decade earlier, the triple disaster of March 11 was soon referred to as 3.11, suggesting that both catastrophes made a comparable impression not only on the respective societies, but also internationally. In Japan, 3.11 was frequently compared to the country's defeat in World War II in the immediate aftermath of disaster. This view, seen as a historical turning point, was most poignantly expressed by Mikuriya Takashi, who suggested that 3.11 would finally put an end to *sengo*, 'Japan's long postwar' (Harootunian 2000) and mark the beginning of a new paradigm he termed *saigo*, or 'after the catastrophe' (Mikuriya 2012).[10] Mikuriya's perception was shared by many, if only because *saigo* was synonymous with hopes for a better, more democratic future—a future that a surprising number of people set out to take in their own hands. With the notable exception of Okinawan protests against the US military bases, Japan had not been a country known for mass demonstrations in the decades after the violent street protests of the 1960s. Yet this changed after 3.11. In the months following the March disasters, tens of thousands of people across the country took to the streets peacefully—and often playfully—demonstrating against nuclear power (Manabe 2015; Ogawa 2013). Along with long-standing social activists such as Matsumoto Hajime of *Shirōto no ran* (Amateur Revolt),[11] a considerable number of artists, including Nobel Prize laureate and post-war moral institution Ōe Kenzaburō, feminist writer Ochiai Keiko, musician Sakamoto Ryūichi and many others, derived from their role as *hyōgensha*—an all-encompassing term that includes all who 'express themselves' through any type of art—a sense of responsibility to speak out, on the streets, through workshops, and through their art.

Regarding the international dimension of the March 2011 disasters, the foreign media's strong focus on 'Fukushima' (NHK Broadcasting Culture Research Institute 2012) rather than on the tsunami confirms that it was the nuclear incident that made 3.11 globally significant. Its impact can also be seen in the negative outcome of a number of referendums on nuclear power held in European countries, such as Italy and Lithuania, in the aftermath of 'Fukushima,' and most clearly by the conservative and initially pro-nuclear German government's decision to immediately shut down eight of its oldest reactors and phase out nuclear power completely by 2022, immensely speeding up the transition to renewable energy. Switzerland, too, quickly stopped the planned construction of new reactors and decided not to replace its existing ones after 2034; even in France, where nuclear power by far represents the main source of energy, the 2012 elections were won on the promise of a partial phase-out (Kalmbach 2015; Sahm 2015).

However, five years after 'Fukushima' and in the midst of worsening relations between the EU and its main gas supplier Russia, the impetus for a radical change of power supply systems is appearing to subside, not only in Eastern Europe, but also in the UK, where new reactors are slated to be built. Outside Europe, the nuclear renaissance first proclaimed around the turn of the millennium seems unchecked. Moreover, as evidenced by the US$22 billion nuclear deal sealed between Japan and Turkey only two years after the Fukushima I debacle (as well as Japanese–Indian negotiations over a similar agreement), Japan continues to be a major player in the industry (*Japan Times* 2013).

Yet, while the export of nuclear technology remains a key element of pro-nuclear LDP Prime Minister Abe Shinzō's so-called *Abenomics* (Kingston 2014), at home popular support for nuclear power has dwindled (Takahashi and Masaki 2012). 'Fukushima' brought an abrupt end to what is now known as *anzen shinwa*, the myth of the absolute safety of Japanese nuclear power plants. This mantra had been repeated to the point that power companies believed in their own propaganda and became negligent on safety issues; mandatory inspections were skipped, repair data falsified, and pre-emptive measures were reduced to a minimum. In other words,

> there has been an institutionalized culture of complacency and deceit in the Nuclear and Industrial Safety Agency (NISA) and the Tokyo Electric Power Company (TEPCO), Japan's most powerful utility and operator of Fukushima Daiichi, that explains why Fukushima in particular and the nuclear industry in general, settled for inadequate safeguards and emergency procedures.
> 
> (Kingston 2012b)

The post-'Fukushima' Japanese public was flabbergasted to learn about the extent to which the so-called 'nuclear village' (*genshiryoku mura*) had controlled the Japanese energy sector for decades. The term refers to an intricate economic-political network of corruption linking nuclear advocates from the power companies, the financial sector, the bureaucracy, politicians, scientists, and, importantly, the mass media. While collaboration with the Village was requited with "access to vast resources and corridors of power," any opposition entailed prompt punishment.

> Researchers who don't support the Village consensus on the need, safety, reliability and economic logic of nuclear power don't get grants and are denied promotions. Journalists who criticize the nuclear village are denied access and other perks, while politicians seeking contributions, and media companies eager for a slice of the utilities' massive advertising budgets, trim their sails accordingly. Crossing the nuclear village carries consequences just as support has delivered benefits.
>
> (Kingston 2012b)

There was much unwelcome attention to the Village in the aftermath of the disaster, but the long-term effects of this public outcry remain questionable. Soon after the March meltdowns, the then Prime Minister Kan Naoto (DPJ) issued an order to shut down Hamaoka Nuclear Power Plant (NPP) in Shizuoka Prefecture, which due to its location in the subduction zone of two tectonic plates has long been considered Japan's most dangerous NPP. Kan also advocated a drastic reduction in Japan's reliance on nuclear power, and passed a bill to subsidize renewable energy. He introduced new safety stress tests that all utilities had to pass as a condition for restarting reactors after regular inspections. Kan was, however, ousted from office in the summer of 2011 as a result of what is widely believed to have been a concerted action on the part of the nuclear village (Kingston 2011). Still, apart from a brief stint of electricity production at the Ōi Nuclear Power Plant in Fukui Prefecture, the so-called 'nuclear Ginza' (*genpatsu Ginza*),[12] and the restart of two reactors in Kagoshima Prefecture in 2015, the country's fifty-four commercial nuclear reactors have largely been idle since the Fukushima I incidents.

While 'Fukushima' led to a radical turnabout in far away Germany, in Japan the DPJ-led government's plan to phase out nuclear power completely by 2040 barely survived one weekend. On Friday, September 14, 2012, the Noda administration announced the historic policy shift, but quickly dropped the proposal five days later amid massive pressure from the industry and business lobbies (McCurry 2012a, 2012b). In fact, the various post-'Fukushima' administrations have shown great interest in containing 'Fukushima' and bringing the idle reactors back online. The pro-nuclear momentum gained significant strength when the LDP and its right-wing nationalist frontrunner Abe Shinzō won the general elections in a landslide victory in December 2012. The first Japanese politician to be elected prime minister for a second term after a rather unsuccessful first term in 2006–2007, Abe sees nuclear power as indispensible to an economic upswing and notably does not rule out the construction of new reactors.

Opposition to these ambitions is not limited to public opinion, but in some cases comes from the judiciary as well. For instance, in 2014 the Fukui District Court ruled against the restart of two reactors at Ōi, which had been the first to be brought back online after the Fukushima I incidents (*Asahi Shimbun Asia & Japan Watch* 2014). Almost one year later, the same judge issued a provisional injunction against the restarting of two Takahama reactors due to safety concerns (*Japan Times* 2015b). Other courts have ruled in favor of the utilities (*Japan Times* 2015c). In addition to the legal uncertainty, the costs of maintaining aging nuclear power plants are soaring and may well diminish the nuclear fleet. A number of utilities have announced plans to scrap their oldest reactors due to the projected high costs involved with meeting the new safety regulations.[13] While the government has yet to draft a long-term energy policy, the economic and technological issues that emerge from tightened security regulations as well as continued public (and, in some cases, judicial) opposition to nuclear power raise doubts about whether nuclear energy can still play a major role in the future (Hobson 2014).

## Re-mapping northern Japan—between containment and reconstruction nationalism

Following 3.11/'Fukushima,' Japan's ranking in the international watchdog Reporters Without Borders' Press Freedom Index rapidly deteriorated. Whereas in 2010, the country was ranked eleventh, it has since fallen fifty places, ranking sixty-first out of 180 countries in 2015. The organization cited the severe limitations placed on independent coverage of the Fukushima nuclear disaster—freelance journalists, for instance, were not admitted to press conferences reserved for accredited press club members—as the primary reason for the massive downgrade (Reporters Without Borders 2015). The country's ranking further dropped after the December 2013 implementation of the controversial *Act on the Protection of Specially Designated Secrets* (SDS), a draconian law which provides for sentences of up to a decade of imprisonment for whistleblowers who leak (vaguely defined) state secrets and for journalists who report information obtained illegally (*Japan Times* 2014). In addition to the above, NHK's Director-General Momii Katsuto—hand-picked by Prime Minister Abe Shinzō in December 2013—gave up impartiality, stating his intention to follow the government's line: "It would not do for us to say 'left' when the government is saying 'right'" (cited in *The Economist* 2014).

The lack of independence on the part of the mass media (Uesugi and Ugaya 2011) led to generally uncritical coverage of the way the disaster was handled by TEPCO and the government:

> The Japanese mass media, regarded as the fifth column of the "atomic village," supported the official strategy of downplaying the nuclear disaster thereby showing themselves at the time, as little more than the mouthpiece of the government and TEPCO. The trouble is that they occupy the hugely

influential, if occasionally Kafkaesque role of the gatekeepers to information. [...] While for several weeks after 3.11, the mass media suspended investigative journalism on site, i.e. within the 50-km zone, they nonetheless promulgated the government's line that the risk of radiation escaping from the reactors and thus the risk of irradiation to the population of Fukushima and the Tōhoku and Kantō areas were "minimal."

(Liscutin 2011)

Instead of critical journalism, Japan saw a (media) proliferation of national appeals for perseverance best represented in the widely popularized reconstruction slogans 'Hang in there, Japan!' (*ganbarō Nippon*) and its variations (*ganbarō Tōhoku, ganbarō Fukushima*). Similarly, *kizuna*, meaning bonds of love and solidarity, was elected *kanji* of the year 2011 (Nihon kanji nōryoku kentei kyōkai 2011). Solidarity with the disaster victims was also writ large in the Eat and Support (*tabete ōen*) campaign launched by the Ministry of Agriculture, Forestry, and Fisheries together with the Consumer Affairs Agency to encourage people to consume agricultural produce from the disaster areas.[14] The so-called reconstruction nationalism (*fukkō nashonarizumu*) was all about and often went hand in hand with downplaying the possible health risks and other potential dangers—a tendency that could be most clearly seen in Prime Minister Abe Shinzō's September 2013 speech before the International Olympic Committee prior to the decision on the 2020 host city when he stated: "Some may have concerns about Fukushima. Let me assure you, the situation is under control. It has never done and will never do any damage to Tokyo" (Prime Minister of Japan and His Cabinet 2013).

At the same time, however, post-disaster Japan also saw a resurfacing of a decades-old discourse on regional disparities and persistent structures of internal exploitation—a discourse that implicitly or explicitly challenged the notion of *fukkō* as nothing more than the restoration of the pre-disaster state and instead demanded a re-mapping of post-disaster Japanese power relations. Historians and economists alike have long argued that northern Japan's position within the Japanese nation state corresponds to that of a domestic colony, exploited for rice, cheap labor, and, in fact, electricity since the modernization rush of the Meiji period. The post-3.11 flare-up of this discourse had a particular focus on energy issues, exemplified by historian Kawanishi Hidemichi's explicit description of Tōhoku as Japan's "nuclear power colony" (Kawanishi 2011: 20; see also Hopson 2013).[15]

Arguably, NPPs all over the world tend to be built in structurally weak regions such as Fukushima. In the same way, the host municipalities' precarious financial dependence on NPP-related subsidies and donations from utilities can hardly be called a uniquely Japanese phenomenon (*Japan Times* 2012). Perhaps more of a peculiarity is that not a kilowatt of the electricity produced at Fukushima's two nuclear power plants was consumed locally; all of it was sent to Tokyo instead.[16] Obviously, the metropolis' ever-growing hunger for energy was not satisfied by the NPPs in Fukushima alone, nor was there *formal* pressure to sign the location agreements. The fact remains, however, that Tokyo does not have its own NPP, but outsourced the production of energy, including all related risks, to its rural periphery.[17]

Emerging from the renewed awareness of structural inequalities were numerous competing narratives effecting a precarious political re-contextualization of the whole disaster area, and in particular Fukushima. However, Fukushima's position within Japan was also called into question on a much more practical level. Quite unsurprisingly, the prefecture's agriculture and fishing industry were particularly hard hit by the disaster; the tourism industry almost collapsed (Zenshakyō saigaichi shien, saigai borantia jōhō 2012); the number of volunteers remained relatively low (*Asahi Shimbun* 2011). Especially during the first months after the incident, there was a lot of media talk about damage caused by baseless rumors, or *fūhyō higai*. This expression obviously works to shift the blame for accident-related damage to the consumers and thus obscures the true locus of responsibility. Used in connection with food issues, slogans such as *fūhyō higai* and the widely popularized Eat and Support campaign mentioned above, it disregarded many consumers' hunger for reliable information; they simply ignored the immense insecurity caused by the lack of agreement regarding the dangers of low-level exposure to radiation. In the end, it is the Fukushima farmers who suffer through no fault of their own.

However, the damage caused by rumors was not limited to agricultural produce. There have been numerous media reports about evacuees from Fukushima being stigmatized and discriminated against, ranging from a refusal to allow them to get gasoline refills to the non-acceptance of evacuated children in nurseries outside Fukushima (*Asahi Shimbun* 2012). The stigma remains even as people move. Moreover, fears of a recurrence of the marriage discrimination experienced by the victims of the 1945 atomic bombings were everywhere.

Arguably, post-3.11 Fukushima is experiencing serious stigmatization which reinforces the already existing marginalization of this aging, rural prefecture. Several cultural initiatives have sprung up to counter this trend, among them *Project Fukushima!* Through a variety of cultural events held in the prefecture, the project seeks to spread a positive image of Fukushima and thus help balance the incident-related negative headlines. On the project's official website, the initiators describe their objective as follows:

> FUKUSHIMA became known to the world as a dishonorable place. But we will not give up Fukushima. Even now that we are in danger of losing our hometowns, we want Fukushima to keep its ties to the outside world. We are filled with the hope that we will be able to go on living in Fukushima, and are eager to imagine a future for Fukushima.
>
> (*Project Fukushima!* "About")

Filled with determination and a fighting spirit, the quote also reads as a precarious expression of fear of isolation and exclusion. The yearly festivals clearly reflect this spirit. In 2011, for instance, the joint production of a giant quilt was one of the main events. Participants sewed together small pieces of cloth contributed from all over Japan, producing a quilt of more than 6,000 square meters and symbolically reconnecting Fukushima to the rest of Japan. Similarly, the initiators successfully reached out to Japan and the world, calling for the organization of synchronized events to be held on the same day.[18] The festival in general and this activity in particular can thus be read as an attempt not to let Fukushima be equated with and reduced to 'Fukushima,' and as such may be read as precarious resistance against Fukushima's symbolic exclusion from the imagined community called Japan.

## 'Fukushima' and the arts

The earthquake, tsunami, and nuclear meltdowns on 3.11 were followed by an unprecedented collection of data, the analysis of which is expected to give a clearer picture of past events as well as improve future disaster management. However, as writer Shigematsu Kiyoshi points out, Big Data does not allow us to understand the socio-cultural dimension of disaster. "If one forgets that 'big' results from the accumulation of 'innumerous smalls,' it can easily happen that something important is missed in the analysis" (*Shūkan Gendai* 2013: 118). While not denying the usefulness of scientific data collection, Shigematsu insists that the arts in general and literature in particular are indispensible when it comes to analyzing the human experience of disaster: "'Big data' is of no help when it comes to tracing the memories of the dead. It cannot record the voices of the deceased. But isn't that what humans have their imagination for?" (*Shūkan Gendai* 2013: 118). The author, whose own work on 3.11 clearly follows this trajectory (see DiNitto, Chapter 2), then goes on to discuss a novel by Itō Seikō titled *Imagination Radio* (*Sōzō rajio*, 2013). Written from the perspective of a drowned radio host who, hanging dead on a treetop in the highly irradiated evacuation zone, nevertheless keeps broadcasting his popular show, which is now audible only to those who allow their imagination to wander the wastelands.

With this novel, Itō addresses a number of questions that are key to this volume, first and foremost that of representation. The 3.11 disasters triggered a tsunami of images that flooded the news and social media, but despite the overwhelming amount of visual and textual information, the question of representation remained an immensely difficult one. How could, how should the arts react to the gigantic dimension of the disaster? What sort of language in the wider sense could adequately express grief and trauma, and capture the profound socio-political implications of the disaster? There can be no doubt that 'Fukushima' not only meant a crisis for the nation and the environment, but it also gave rise to an artistic crisis in the arenas of language and artistic representation.

Wagō Ryōichi, a Fukushima-based poet who was probably the first to react to the nuclear disaster using his art (Odagiri 2014; Iwata-Weickgenannt 2015; Angles Chapter 9)—he became instantly famous when he started a poetic Twitter feed just five days after the initial quake—recalls the paralysis of the first days:

So far in my life, I had been quite certain that I had something to say, as a poet, a teacher, a father. If I found something crucial to contemplate, I would put my thoughts into words – that is what I had done all the time, but in that moment I had reached a point where there was nothing left for me to say, neither as a poet, nor teacher, nor father. It felt like everything had just been washed away, as if I had completely lost my personality.

(Sano and Wagō 2012: 32–33)

Numerous others testified to similar experiences: 'Fukushima' forced artists across the genres to reconsider of the relationship between art, representation, and lived experience. Itō Seikō's novel, for instance, insists that the trauma of 3.11 is only accessible if approached from an individualized, personal level: "Your imagination turns into radio waves, into a microphone, into a studio, into a radio tower, in other words, it becomes my voice" (Itō 2013: 8). Towards the end, 'imagination' is replaced by 'sadness,' supporting the novel's claim that the full range of human empathy is needed to gain a deeper level of understanding.

*Imagination Radio* also touches upon a second issue that loomed large in the post-3.11 disaster discourse, and is also of direct relevance for this volume, namely the problem of positionality. Who has the right to speak about 3.11 and 'Fukushima'—as a victim, as researcher, or otherwise? In the past one or two decades, the experience of the so-called *tōjisha*—someone who is directly affected—has been radically re-evaluated. It was largely thanks to Ueno Chizuko's publication *Tōjisha shuken* (The Sovereignty of the *Tōjisha*, 2003) that in the area of elderly care, attention turned to the needs of those receiving it. However, in post-3.11 Japan, the privileging of the *tōjisha* experience had an intimidating if not silencing effect on 'outsiders.' Needless to say, the strictly geographical definition of evacuation zones—taken ad absurdum in Sono Sion's 2012 film *Land of Hope* (*Kibō no kuni*; see Iwata-Weickgenannt Chapter 7), where a property is divided in halves—and a finely graded system of state/ TEPCO compensation puts a particularly destructive spin on the question of who may or may not call himself or herself a *tōjisha*. Telling his story from the perspective of a drowned tsunami victim, Itō Seikō exposes the irrationality of this race for 'authenticity.' Itō reminds us that while the ultimate *tōjisha* are dead and thus unable to speak, any individual can engage with the disaster if only she/he is willing to be led by imagination and human empathy.

Moreover, by raising the issue of the rights of dead people, *Imagination Radio* is in line with the work of a considerable number of post-'Fukushima' theater makers whose performances explore the relationship between the living and the dead, fathoming the potential of theater as a space of mourning. Hirata Oriza's short android theatre play *Sayonara II* (2012), for instance, asks how to pray for the many dead in an area no longer accessible for human beings. Indeed, Hirata's android may well be described as a "bridging figure who reimagines the exclusion zone as a space of bardo, a Buddhist limbo, painfully lying between the experiences of life and death" (Eckersall 2015).

Appeasing the dead (*chinkon*) is also a key issue in Okada Toshiki's *Ground and Floor* (*Jimen to Yuka*, 2013).[19] Ghostly spirits haunt the living, who ultimately become entrapped in an incessant and ever-repeating cycle of grief work. Extending the endlessness of mourning into a lamentation for the country's future, Okada not only alludes to the temporality of nuclear issues, but also places the disaster in a national framework, implicitly questioning the unity of 'Japan.'

This volume includes discussions on artwork from a wide spectrum of geographical, political, and aesthetic perspectives, and covers an equally broad range of genres. All analyses are based on an understanding of disaster as constructs. In his seminal study on the social aspect of disaster, Robert A. Stallings suggests that "new ways of looking at objective conditions [...] *precede* rather than follow the 'discovery' of new aspects of those objective conditions" (1995: 142, emphasis in the original). In other words, neither the 'disaster' itself nor its implications are in any way self-evident, but rather are the outcome of social interpretation. The perception of an event as 'disaster' hinges on the various stakeholders' claims about conditions, their causes and consequences, which must be publicly promoted to become socially and politically meaningful (Stallings 1995: 193–95). Needless to say, artists participate in shaping perceptions about 'disasters' through their very work. Cultural responses to calamities "are likely to shape people's knowledge about disasters and how they respond to them—not just members of the public but also those working in emergency management, law enforcement, and other governmental agencies" (Webb 2006: 435).

The essays in this book explore the ways in which Japanese novelists and poets, manga artists, theater makers and performers, musicians, art photographers and film directors engage in the socio-cultural work of making sense of the 3.11/'Fukushima' calamity. Investigating the role of the arts in post-3.11 Japan, individual chapters explore the changing positionality of post-3.11 Tōhoku and the fear-driven conflation of time and space in near-but-far urban centers such as Tokyo; uncover political subversion and nostalgia surrounding the Fukushima disaster; expose the ambiguous effects of highly gendered representations of fear of nuclear threat; analyze musical and poetic responses to disaster; and explore the political potentialities of theatrical performances. By scrutinizing various media narratives and taking into account national and local perspectives, the chapters shed light on cultural texts of power, politics, and space, thereby making a contribution to the research of the cultural dimension of disaster, which is a still developing field in Japan and beyond.

## The structure of the book

In Chapter 2, Rachel DiNitto examines how fictive writing attempts to grasp the transformation of real and imagined spaces of northeastern Japan that were triggered by the triple disaster. The analysis focuses on Shigematsu Kiyoshi's *Map of Hope: The Tale of 3.11* (*Kibō no chizu: 3.11 kara hajimaru monogatari*, 2012) and Taguchi Randi's *In the Zone* (*Zōn ni te* and *Zōn ni te II*, 2013) as two prominent examples among the many artists who traveled to the disaster area immediately after March 11 in an effort to detail their experiences in later work. The texts aim at a narrative mapping of the disaster zone and emerge from the interstice of documentary and fiction: Shigematsu's story centers on the earthquake and tsunami damage along the coast, while Taguchi shows life in and around the exclusion zone surrounding the plant. DiNitto argues that by opening up a space for people living in the afflicted areas to communicate their stories and for the readers to relate to them, Shigematsu and Taguchi engage in the cultural work to transform the specific event of 3.11 into collective trauma memory. The study shows how the different temporality of the earthquake, tsunami and nuclear disaster is mirrored in the antithetic nature of their stories: While Shigematsu creates images of disaster relief and recovery, such a narrative is not possible in Taguchi's irradiated zone.

Scott Aalgaard, in Chapter 3, follows up on DiNitto's discussion, exploring the competing and contradictory re-evaluations of the position of 'Fukushima' within the broader entity of 'Japan' by drawing the reader's attention to the field of music. Aalgaard's comparative examination of Saitō Kazuyoshi's *It Was a Lie All Along* (*Zutto uso datta*) and Nagabuchi Tsuyoshi's *One* (*Hitotsu*) offers vital insights into the work of two prominent figures in Japanese popular music, both noted as critical voices after 3.11, but also before it. Although both works critically question the concept of 'Japan,' they do so from contrasting perspectives. Arguing that Saitō's song destabilizes fixed terms such as 'Japan' and its nuclear village, Aalgaard views Nagabuchi's work as constructing a narrative of 'Japan' as a new entity that has overcome the alienation of remote areas such as the disaster zones. By situating these works of musical critique in the broader socio-political context of capitalist modernity, the essay discloses the ambiguous political potentialities of musical critique between revolutionary promise and fascistic danger.

Elaborating on photographic discourses related to the Fukushima disaster, Chapter 4 delves deeply into the dilemma of how to visualize the invisible of the nuclear threat. Pablo Figueroa focuses his analysis on the works of two art photographers to critically examine the representations of 'Fukushima' in photography and situate them in the socio-political landscape of post-disaster Japan. Studying works by Watanabe Toshiya, originally from Namie, a town heavily affected by the nuclear disaster, and Imai Tomoki, a Tokyo resident, Figueroa scrutinizes the positionality of the artists' positions. Owing to the extensive ethnographic fieldwork conducted in Iwaki, Nihonmatsu, and Tamura, Figueroa takes the reader one step closer to daily life in the disaster zone. He suggests that photographic discourses engaged in negotiating space and memory have created images of political subversion and nostalgia. These images have the potential to counter hegemonic narratives on reconstruction and revival, narratives that obscure residents' hardships in the ongoing crisis.

In Chapter 5, Saeko Kimura examines the ambiguity of the boundaries determining affected areas and persons facing the invisibility of the nuclear threat in order to address the global dimension of the disaster. She analyses how the works of Tawada Yōko and Sekiguchi Ryōko, two Japanese writers living in Berlin and Paris respectively, reflect the paradox of simultaneously experiencing physical distance and strong emotional ties to their homeland and how this allows for their specific positionality in literary discourses on 3.11. While the geographic distance facilitated Tawada's and Sekiguchi's immediate response, since they were unhampered by taboos on radioactivity and the lack of information in Japan, as Japanese writers in Europe they were soon regarded as spokeswomen on the subject by European media. Kimura's thoughtful evaluation studies the vital importance of writing on radiation as an act of resistance that counters the government's efforts to downplay the impact of the nuclear disaster and the tendency in human nature to suppress unsettling anxieties. Besides offering a literary review, Kimura provides revealing insights into related sociopolitical issues of contemporary Japan that reaches far beyond the immediate context of 3.11.

Chapter 6 provides an overview of a wide range of documentaries, which account for the majority of filmic material dealing with 'Fukushima.' Hideaki Fujiki's investigation is based on the instructive observation that, by forcing residents to choose between staying or 'voluntarily' evacuating (*jishu hinan*), the nuclear disaster has imposed an artistic split between "(biological) life" (*inochi, seimei*) and "livelihood" (*seikatsu*). Exploring documentary films addressing this matter, he takes a twofold approach combining an overview of a broad range of cinematic materials with a close reading of Kamanaka Hitomi's *Surviving Internal Exposure* (*Naibu hibaku o ikinuku*, 2012) and Ian Thomas Ash's *A2-B-C* (2013). Both films counter pro-governmental works downplaying the conflict between life and livelihood by raising the concern for children's health problems. In so doing, they address the risk of low-level radiation, a topic of highly controversial debates in Japanese media. While all of the documentary films and other media have constituted a contested terrain for the imagination of the catastrophe, Fujiki reveals *A2-B-C* as particularly effective due to its unique integration of filmic narration in tandem with the non-authoritative and therapeutic potential of a documentary.

Kristina Iwata-Weickgenannt's in-depth analysis of Sono Sion's *Land of Hope* (*Kibō no kuni*, 2012), the first of very few feature films dealing with the Fukushima nuclear disaster, proceeds with Fujiki's discussion of the conflict between life and livelihood. Although set in the near future, Sono's film is clearly modeled after the events of March 11 and exhibits strong documentary traits. Centering on the fate of two families after a serious incident at a nearby nuclear power plant, *Land of Hope* confronts the audience with the inescapability of the nuclear threat by exposing the absurdity of demarcations such as concentric evacuation zones. In so doing, the film addresses one of the most serious consequences of the post-3.11 Japanese reality, namely the deterioration of public trust in government institutions. However, in exposing Sono's critique as a highly gendered one, which ties in with misogynist undertones in post-'Fukushima' discourse on nuclear power, Iwata-Weickgenannt shows that it is precisely the film's gender-biased nature which at least partly subverts its critical potential.

In Chapter 8, M. Cody Poulton draws our attention to the deep inner conflict in trying to find a reasonable balance between the necessity to mourn versus that to go on living, a topic which was addressed in various performances soon after the triple disaster, but which has still not been discussed in a broad range of scholarly works to date. He instructively investigates recent productions by two cutting-edge Japanese directors based on Sophocles' *Antigone* and applying its subject—the inability to mourn—to contemporary Japan: Matsuda Masataka's *Record of a Journey to Antigone* (2012) and Takayama Akira's *Kein Licht II* (*No Light*, 2012). Matsuda shows a group of young people preparing a performance of *Antigone* in Fukushima, combining live performance with material provided by social media. Poulton situates this intricate work in the artist's development towards increasing experimentation with dramatic form and a growing interest in the realm of dreams and ghosts; he reveals the play's proximity to Noh, a genre that is known for fathoming the borderlands between life and death. Takayama based his production on a text by Elfriede Jelinek (originally titled *Epilog?*), who used Sophocles' *Antigone* as one of her source texts. Poulton reveals how the site-specific performance in Tokyo's Shinbashi succeeded in communicating a sense of the disaster zone with an immediacy that was rare among the numerous post-3.11 plays.

Jeffrey Angles, in Chapter 9, discloses the post-3.11 shock waves running through the Japanese poetic world to scrutinize the crisis of language and representation brought about by the Fukushima calamity. Examining Wagō Ryōichi's *Pebbles of Poetry* (*Shi no tsubute*, 2011), he refers to one of the most striking examples of disaster poetry which the Fukushima native first posted on Twitter in real-time as the calamity unfolded. Furthermore, Angles gives close readings of works by Tokyo poets less known to non-Japanese readers, such as Takahashi Mutsuo, a well-established and highly prolific writer, and Arai Takako, author of some of the most original poems on the social implications of the nuclear disaster. Comprising poetic voices close and far from the stricken areas, the essay looks at aspects of positionality and its impact on artistic work, alternating between the call for socio-political change and the strong expression of the poet's love for his homeland. Angles implies that the Fukushima crisis provoked the poetic world to raise questions about the interrelationship between crisis, art, and lived experience that will continue to affect and shape Japanese poetry in the near future.

Chapter 10 reveals the political potentialities of theatrical space through an in-depth evaluation of two post-'Fukushima' plays by Okada Toshiki, who gained a reputation in Japan and abroad for his socially engaged theater. Barbara Geilhorn elaborates on two performances that take an entirely opposite approach: while *Unable to See* (2012) is a harsh satire, written for a foreign audience in an informal setting, that looks at the precarious situation at the molten reactor from the short-term perspective, *Current Location* (*Genzaichi*, 2012) takes a more long-term view, addressing the fear of nuclear threat from the perspective of Tokyo inhabitants in the form of science fiction. Ultimately, the systematic repression of the anxiety and anguish caused by looming disaster seems as absurd as leaving the planet to escape to another world. Dwelling on the dispute of *fūhyō higai* (harmful rumors), the play reveals the deep fault lines running through post-disaster Japan. Geilhorn scrutinizes the significance of Okada's recent concept of fiction as 'recessive reality' in his attempt to encourage audiences' critical thinking and argues that there has been a major turning point in Okada's work, triggered by the catastrophe.

Lorie Brau, in her discussion on the resources of popular culture to represent and critique the multifaceted implications of the Fukushima meltdown, follows up on Geilhorn's by pondering the issue of *fūhyō higai*. Chapter 11 elaborates on *The Truth about Fukushima* (*Fukushima no shinjitsu*, 2014), a recent episode of Kariya Tetsu's long-running culinary manga *Oishinbo*, which set off heated debates in Japanese media. The manga blends elements of fiction and documentary by depicting journalists doing research into the aftermath of the triple disaster at Fukushima Prefecture and interviewing residents. Its suggestion of a correlation between the protagonist's nosebleed and radioactive exposure triggered accusations of causing additional harm to afflicted areas and even led to a formal complaint by the Fukushima prefectural government. Brau's study is an inquiry into the startling question of how a culinary manga created such a stir in the media and among government officials, thereby addressing topics such as the continued muzzling of freedom of expression and the stamping out of criticism practiced in contemporary Japan. Along with addressing the implications of *Oishinbo*'s contentious reception, she offers a close examination of how the manga's interweaving of documentary, polemic, and elegy harnesses the resources of the medium in an effort to critique the mishandling of the accident and mourn the serious losses that resulted.

In the final chapter, Kyōko Iwaki addresses the intricate problem of how art and particularly theater can address an imperceptible catastrophe such as the nuclear threat in order to promote change in a society of over-stimulated consumers in which political apathy and indifference have been pervasive for decades. The analysis focuses on Takayama Akira's ongoing *The Referendum Project* (*Refarendamu Purojekuto*, 2011), which was first presented a few months after the Fukushima meltdown, and *Tokyo Heterotopia* (2013). Implementing the artist's socio-political engagement and transferring performance into the cityscape, both are exemplary of Takayama's work. While *The Referendum Project*, as evoked by its title, explores the possibilities of a national referendum on nuclear power in a rather indirect fashion, *Tokyo Heterotopia* takes Takayama's approach to performance one step further by sending audiences on a tourist-like trip to challenge familiar places with new perspectives. Iwaki reveals how Takayama's 'atomized theatre' that sensorially blurs the boundary between fiction and reality, successfully involves audiences in the political by creating more subtle strategies than direct action, which may easily end up being rejected as outrageous (*fukinshin*) in post-3.11 Japan.

## Notes

1 A number of passages in the introductory part of this chapter have been reproduced here verbatim from Kristina Iwata-Weickgenannt's "Precarity beyond 3/11 or 'Living Fukushima': Power, politics, and space in Wagō Ryōichi's poetry of disaster," in Kristina Iwata-Weickgenannt and Roman Rosenbaum (eds), *Visions of Precarity in Japanese Popular Culture and Literature* (London and New York: Routledge 2015), 187–211.

2  For a map indicating the seismic intensity, see Tenki.jp 2011.
3  Japan's first commercial nuclear power reactor went online in 1966; nuclear power has been a national strategic priority since 1973. In 2011, Japan's fifty-four nuclear reactors provided 30 percent of the electricity. Plans for further expansion have been under reconsideration since the incident at Fukushima I. The 7-level International Nuclear Event Scale (INES) was introduced in 1990 by the International Atomic Energy Agency (IAEA) to enable prompt and consistent communication of nuclear incidents and accidents. Defined as a major accident, INES 7 implies a massive release of radioactive material with widespread health and environmental effects requiring the implementation of extended countermeasures. The 1986 disaster at Chernobyl was retrospectively categorized as INES 7.
4  The term also tended to be used to obscure or at least relativize human responsibility for the Fukushima meltdowns.
5  On the amount of debris, see Prime Minister of Japan and His Cabinet (n.d.); on the overall scale of the damage, see Earthquake Report.Com 2012.
6  In April 2012, the Ministry of Health, Labour and Welfare published details regarding the so-called *kanrenshi*, disaster-related deaths mostly caused by disease or suicide. The number of acknowledged *kanrenshi* amounts to a third of all casualties in Fukushima; see *Mainichi Shimbun* 2012.
7  Hopes are pinned on muon tomography, a technique that uses cosmic ray muons to generate three-dimensional images of volumes and may thus help pinpoint the uranium from a safer distance; initial results yielded at the No. 1 core in spring 2015 were detailed but incomplete. See Normile 2015 and *Japan Times* 2015a.
8  It is argued that even the tsunami can at least partly be regarded as a man-made disaster because of the dense human settlement in coastal areas. More of an issue was, however, the question whether or not the nuclear calamity was man-made (*jinzai*). Several fact-finding commissions quickly found that the meltdowns could have been prevented and thus qualified the disaster as man-made. It took more than one and a half years for Tokyo Electric Power Company (TEPCO) to come to the same conclusion; see *Asahi Shimbun Digital* 2012.
9  In order to differentiate between the geographical place and the event, the nuclear catastrophe soon became frequently referred to as 'Fukushima' written in *katakana* instead of *kanji* (similar differentiations are used for the atomic bombings at Hiroshima and Nagasaki, and the Minamata disease). In the transcription, this differentiation is rendered through the use of inverted commas.
10  Mikuriya first used this neologism in a column published in the *Yomiuri Shimbun* newspaper on March 24, 2011 (reprinted in Mikuriya 2012: 7–9) and later elaborated on this notion; see Mikuriya 2012.
11  On Matsumoto and his artistic and social activist collective *Shirōto no ran*, see Mōri 2007 and Richter 2012. Matsumoto organized the large-scale first anti-nuke demonstration in Kōenji, Tokyo, on April 10, 2011.
12  The name is derived from Fukui's extraordinary high number of nuclear power plants—Wakasa Bay is host to a total of fourteen reactors, including the controversial fast breeder Monju—which makes it comparable to the concentration of wealth and prestige in Japan's most luxurious shopping street. Due to new safety regulations introduced after the Fukushima I meltdowns, reactors were not allowed to restart after regular inspections until they passed safety tests. As a result, following the shutdown of Tomari II (Hokkaido) on May 5, 2012, Japan was nuclear-free until the reactors III and IV at Ōi were restarted in July 2012 amid widespread public protests. The reactors were taken offline again for inspection in September 2013, and not allowed to go back online following an injunction by a Fukui district court issued in May 2014 citing safety concerns (*Asahi Shimbun Asia & Japan Watch* 2014).

13 A 2014 Reuters survey suggests that only fourteen of Japan's fifty-four commercial reactors are likely to be restarted; twenty-three are expected to be decommissioned, and the future of seventeen of them is undecided (Saito et al. 2014).
14 Notably, questions of food safety were completely ignored in this campaign. Masami Yuki argues that by attaching a moral tinge to the consumption of (possibly irradiated) Tōhoku produce, open dissent became difficult; she therefore assesses the campaign as being totalitarian (Yuki 2014: 41).
15 For an overview of the pre- and post-3.11 debates on the exploitation of Tōhoku, see Hopson 2013.
16 Fukushima's electricity is instead provided by Tohoku EPCO. Similarly, all the electricity produced at the world's largest NPP, Kashiwazaki-Kariwa, in Niigata Prefecture, also a part of Tōhoku and thus served by Tohoku EPCO, is sent to Tokyo.
17 Playing with this fact, the 2004 anti-nuclear fiction movie *Tōkyō genpatsu* (Tokyo NPP) features a charismatic governor who proposes building a NPP in the center of Tokyo.
18 For a list of sister events, see Project Fukushima! "Sekai dōji tahatsu ibento 2011". Note that the organizers of the Fukushima festival were heavily criticized on Twitter and other social media for holding the event outdoors despite the still high radiation levels. The official news coverage was far more favorable.
19 For an insightful analysis of the play, see Eckersall 2015.

## References

*Asahi Shimbun*. 2011, "Fukushima no onsenchi, kukyō – ukeire hinansha gekishō, kyakuashi ga modorazu." September 28, at: www.asahi.com/national/update/0927/TKY201109270233.html (accessed June 5, 2012).

*Asahi Shimbun*. 2012, "Fukushima kara hinan no kodomo, nyūen kotowarareru – Yamanashi-ken no hoikuen." March 2, at: www.asahi.com/national/update/0302/TKY201203020761.html (accessed May 10, 2012).

*Asahi Shimbun Digital*. 2012, "Genpatsu jiko 'taisho kanō datta' – Tōden tasukufōsu ga kenkai." October 12, at: www.asahi.com/national/update/1012/TKY201210120529.html (accessed October 22, 2012).

*Asahi Shimbun Asia & Japan Watch*. 2014, "Fukui court deals setback to Kansai Electric bid to restart Oi reactors." May 21, at: http://ajw.asahi.com/article/behind_news/social_affairs/AJ201405210079 (accessed June 15, 2015).

Earthquake Report.Com. 2012, "Japan – 366 days after the Quake … 19000 lives lost, 1.2 million buildings damaged, $574 billion." March 10, at: http://earthquake-report.com/2012/03/10/japan-366-days-after-the-quake-19000-lives-lost-1-2-million-buildings-damaged-574-billion (accessed March 1, 2014).

Eckersall, Peter. 2015, "Performance, mourning and the long view of nuclear space." *The Asia-Pacific Journal* Vol. 13, Issue 6, No. 2 (February 16), at: www.japanfocus.org/-Peter-Eckersall/4278/article.html (accessed June 20, 2015).

*The Economist*. 2014, "My country right or righter: The ghosts of the past once again embrace Shinzo Abe." February 8, at: www.economist.com/news/asia/21595983-ghosts-past-once-again-embrace-shinzo-abe-my-country-right-or-righter (accessed June 20, 2015).

Harootunian, Harry D. 2000, "Japan's long postwar: The trick of memory and the ruse of history." *The South Atlantic Quarterly* Vol. 99, No. 4 (Fall): 715–39.

Hobson, Christopher. 2014, "What role for nuclear power in Japan's future?" *The Asia-Pacific Journal* Vol. 11, Issue 27, No. 2 (July 7), at: www.japanfocus.org/-Christopher-Hobson/4146/article.html (accessed June 10, 2015).

Hopson, Nathan. 2013, "Systems of irresponsibility and Japan's internal colony." *The Asia-Pacific Journal* Vol. 11, Issue 52, No. 2 (December 30), at: www.japanfocus.org/-Nathan-Hopson/4053/article.html (accessed June 10, 2015).
Itō Seikō. 2013, *Sōzō rajio*. Tokyo: Kawadeshobō shinsha.
Iwata-Weickgenannt, Kristina. 2015, "Precarity beyond 3/11 or 'Living Fukushima'— Power, politics, and space in Wagō Ryōichi's poetry of disaster," in Kristina Iwata-Weickgenannt and Roman Rosenbaum (eds), *Visions of Precarity in Japanese Popular Culture and Literature*. London and New York: Routledge, 187–211.
JAMSTEC [Japan Agency for Marine-Earth Science and Technology]. 2011, "Press releases: Seafloor displacement caused by the 2011 Tōhoku-Oki Earthquake," at: www.jamstec.go.jp/e/about/press_release/20111202 (accessed June 7, 2012).
*Japan Times*. 2012, "Municipal Nuclear Addiction." November 26, at: www.japantimes.co.jp/opinion/2012/11/26/commentary/municipal-nuclear-addiction (accessed March 11, 2014).
*Japan Times*. 2013, "Japan, Turkey ink $22 billion nuclear plant deal." May 4, at: www.japantimes.co.jp/news/2013/05/04/national/politics-diplomacy/japan-turkey-clinch-nuclear-energy-deal (accessed May 8, 2015).
*Japan Times*. 2014, "Press freedom ranking falters due to secrecy law." February 12, at: www.japantimes.co.jp/news/2014/02/12/national/press-freedom-ranking-falters-due-to-secrecy-law (accessed April 15, 2015).
*Japan Times*. 2015a, "Muon scan gives detailed, but incomplete, look at meltdown of No. 1 reactor." March 20, at: www.japantimes.co.jp/news/2015/03/20/national/tepco-confirms-nearly-fuel-melted-sank-vessel-fukushima-1-unit (accessed April 8, 2015).
*Japan Times*. 2015b, "Fukui court forbids Takahama nuclear plant restart." April 14, at: www.japantimes.co.jp/news/2015/04/14/national/crime-legal/critical-case-fukui-court-rule-takahama-nuclear-plant-restart (accessed June 15, 2015).
*Japan Times*. 2015c, "Kagoshima court rejects injunction against Sendai reactor restarts." April 22, at: www.japantimes.co.jp/news/2015/04/22/national/crime-legal/looming-ruling-sendai-reactor-restart-injunction-embolden-nuclear-foes (accessed June 15, 2015).
Kalmbach, Karena. 2015, "From Chernobyl to Fukushima: The impact of the accidents on the French nuclear discourse," in Thomas Bohn, Thomas Feldhoff, Lisette Gebhardt, and Arndt Graf (eds), *The Impact of Disaster: Social and Cultural Approaches to Fukushima and Chernobyl*. Berlin: EB Verlag, 67–95.
Kawanishi Hidemichi. 2011, *"Tōhoku" o yomu*. Akita: Mumyōsha shuppan.
Keisatsuchō Kinkyū Saigai Keibi Honbu. 2015, "Kōhō shiryō: Heisei 23nen (2001nen) Tōhoku chihō taiheiyō-oki jishin no higai jōkyō to keisatsu sochi." March 11, at: www.npa.go.jp/archive/keibi/biki/higaijokyo.pdf (accessed April 7, 2015).
Kingston, Jeff. 2011, "Ousting Kan Naoto: The politics of nuclear crisis and renewable energy in Japan." *The Asia-Pacific Journal* Vol. 9, Issue 39, No. 5 (September 26), at: http://japanfocus.org/-Jeff-Kingston/3610/article.html (accessed May 6, 2015).
Kingston, Jeff. 2012a, "Mismanaging risk and the Fukushima nuclear crisis." *The Asia-Pacific Journal* Vol. 10, Issue 12, No. 4 (March 19), at: www.japanfocus.org/-Jeff-Kingston/3724/article.html (accessed May 6, 2015).
Kingston, Jeff. 2012b, "Japan's nuclear village." *The Asia-Pacific Journal* Vol. 10, Issue 37, No. 1 (September 10), at: www.japanfocus.org/-Jeff-Kingston/3822/article.html (accessed May 6, 2015).
Kingston, Jeff. 2014, "'Abe-genda': nuclear export superpower." *Japan Times*, January 25, at: www.japantimes.co.jp/news/2014/01/25/world/abe-genda-nuclear-export-superpower/#.U3moW17rXfY (accessed January 31, 2014).

Liscutin, Nicola. 2011, "Indignez-Vous! 'Fukushima,' new media and anti-nuclear activism in Japan." *The Asia-Pacific Journal* Vol. 9, Issue 47, No. 1 (November 21), at: www.japanfocus.org/-Nicola-Liscutin/3649/article.html (accessed June 20, 2015).

*Mainichi Shimbun.* 2012, "Shinsai kanrenshi: 1tto 9ken de 1618 nin – 'Hanshin' ōhaba ni uwamawaru." April 27, at: http://mainichi.jp/select/news/20120427k0000e040181000c.html (accessed May 17, 2012).

Manabe, Noriko. 2015, *The Revolution Will Not Be Televised: Protest Music after Fukushima.* New York: Oxford University Press.

McCurry, Justin. 2012a, "Japan plans to end reliance on nuclear power within 30 years." *The Guardian*, September 14, at: www.theguardian.com/world/2012/sep/14/japan-end-nuclear-power (accessed June 15, 2015).

McCurry, Justin. 2012b, "Japan drops plans to phase out nuclear power by 2040." *The Guardian*, September 19, at: www.theguardian.com/world/2012/sep/19/japan-2040-nuclear-power-exit (accessed June 15, 2015).

Mikuriya Takashi. 2012, *'Sengo' ga owari, 'saigo' ga hajimaru.* Tokyo: Chikura Shobō.

Mōri Yoshitaka. 2007, "Sutorīto ga sayoku wo torikaesu." *Ronza* (April): 45–50.

NHK Broadcasting Culture Research Institute. 2012, "The Great East Japan Earthquake in overseas media: Survey of eight news programs in seven countries." September, at: www.nhk.or.jp/bunken/english/reports/pdf/report_12090101-2.pdf (accessed April 10, 2012).

Nihon kanji nōryoku kentei kyōkai. 2011, "2011 nen 'kotoshi no kanji' dai-ichi I wa 'kizuna'," at: www.kanken.or.jp/project/edification/years_kanji/2011.html (accessed June 15, 2015).

Normile, Dennis. 2015, "Nuclear disaster—Muons probe Fukushima's ruins." *Science* Vol. 347, No. 6226 (March 6): 1052–53, at: www.sciencemag.org/content/347/6226/1052.full (accessed April 8, 2015).

Odagiri, Takushi. 2014, "The end of literature and the beginning of praxis: Wagō Ryōichi's Pebbles of Poetry." *Japan Forum* Vol. 26, Issue 3: 361–82.

Ogawa, Akihiro. 2013, "Young precariat at the forefront: Anti-nuclear rallies in post-Fukushima Japan." *Inter Asia Cultural Studies* Vol. 14, Issue 12: 317–26.

Prime Minister of Japan and His Cabinet. 2013, "Presentation by Prime Minister Shinzo Abe at the 125th Session of the International Olympic Committee (IOC)." September 7, at: http://japan.kantei.go.jp/96_abe/statement/201309/07ioc_presentation_e.html (accessed May 6, 2015).

Prime Minister of Japan and His Cabinet. n.d., "Seisaku kaigi," at: www.kantei.go.jp/jp/singi/kaiyou/hyouryuu/qanda_eng.html (accessed May 1, 2014).

Project Fukushima! "About," at: www.pj-fukushima.jp/about/2022.php (accessed May 31, 2012).

Project Fukushima! "Sekai dōji tahatsu ibento 2011," at: www.pj-fukushima.jp/2011/ (accessed May 15, 2014).

Reporters Without Borders. 2015, "Japan," at: https://index.rsf.org/#!/index-details/JPN (accessed April 15, 2015).

Richter, Steffi. 2012, "Das Ende des 'endlosen Alltags'? Post-Fukushima als Japan-Diskurs," in Steffi Richter and Lisette Gebhardt (eds), *Japan nach "Fukushima": Ein System in der Krise.* Leipzig: Leipziger Ostasien-Studien, 91–134.

Sahm, Astrid. 2015, "Germany's energy turnaround after Fukushima: Outsider or trendsetter in Europe?," in Thomas Bohn, Thomas Feldhoff, Lisette Gebhardt, and Arndt Graf (eds), *The Impact of Disaster: Social and Cultural Approaches to Fukushima and Chernobyl.* Berlin: EB Verlag, 97–132.

Saito, Mari, Sheldrick, Aaron, and Hamada, Kentaro. 2014, "Japan may only be able to restart one-third of its nuclear reactors." *Reuters*. April 1, at: www.reuters.com/article/2014/04/01/us-japan-nuclear-restarts-insight-idUSBREA3020020140401 (accessed June 15, 2015).
*Sankei Shimbun*. 2012, "Miyagi-oki no shima de sojōkō 43 mētoru ka – shinsai tsunami de saidai no kanōsei." March 23, at: http://sankei.jp.msn.com/affairs/news/120316/dst12031619280011-n1.htm. (accessed March 29, 2012).
Sano, Shin'ichi and Wagō, Ryōichi. 2012, *Kotoba ni naniga dekiru no ka – 3.11 o koete*. Tokyo: Tokuma Shoten.
*Shūkan Gendai*. 2013, "Rirē dokusho nikki—Shigematsu Kiyoshi." April 13, 118–19.
Stallings, Robert A. 1995, *Promoting Risk: Constructing the Earthquake Threat*. Hawthorne, NY: Aldine de Gruyter.
Takahashi, Kōichi and Masaki, Miki. 2012, "Higashi nihon daishinsai de nihonjin wa dō kawatta ka. 'Bōsai, enerugī, seikatsu ni kansuru seron chōsa' kara". June, at: www.nhk.or.jp/bunken/summary/research/report/2012_06/20120603.pdf (accessed April 10, 2013).
Tenki.jp. 2011, "Jishin jōhō: 2011–3–11, 15:01h happyō." at: http://tenki.jp/earthquake/detail-3611.html (accessed May 17, 2012).
*Tōkyō Genpatsu*. 2004, Dir. Yamakawa Gen.
Ueno, Chizuko. 2003, *Tōjisha shuken*. Tokyo: Iwanami.
Uesugi, Takashi and Ugaya, Hiromichi. 2011, *Hōdō shinsai, genpatsu-hen – jujitsu o tsutaenai media no daizai*. Tokyo: Gentōsha shinsho.
Webb, Gary R. 2006, "The popular culture of disaster: Exploring a new dimension of disaster research," in Havidán Rodríguez, Enrico L. Quarantelli, and Russell R. Dynes (eds), *Handbook of Disaster Research*. New York: Springer, 430–40.
Yuki, Masami. 2014, "Post-Fukushima discourses on food and eating: Analysing political implications and literary imagination," in Lisette Gebhardt and Masami Yuki (eds), *Literature and Art after "Fukushima": Four Approaches*. Berlin: EB Verlag, 37–51.
Zenshakyō saigaichi shien, saigai borantia jōhō. 2012, "Saigai borantia sentā de uketsuketa borantia katsudōsha-sū no suii (kashūkei)," at: www.saigaivc.com (accessed June 5, 2012).

# 2 Literature maps disaster
## The contending narratives of 3.11 fiction

*Rachel DiNitto*

The disaster of March 11, 2011 was one of the worst in post-war Japan, with close to 16,000 dead, over 330,000 displaced, and large swaths of land in three northeastern prefectures devastated by massive structural damage from the earthquake and tsunami.[1] The level-seven meltdowns at the Fukushima Daiichi Nuclear Power Plant rendered many towns uninhabitable, and threatened the health and safety of Japan and neighboring countries, as radiation spread through the air and water contaminating food sources. This triple disaster transformed the spaces of Tōhoku, remapping them to the concentric circles of disaster zones, evacuation zones, and exclusion zones, and redefining them along new vectors of tidal waves, aftershocks, radiation exposure, and debris fields.

The disaster and these reconfigurations have also altered the imagined spaces of Tōhoku. Fiction writers attempted to grasp these new configurations as they, along with artists and film-makers, poured into the disaster area in the days and months after March 2011. This chapter takes up the works of two authors, Shigematsu Kiyoshi (b. 1963) and Taguchi Randy (b. 1959), and their fictional texts detailing the travels of their protagonists into the disaster zone. Both texts attempt a narrative mapping, but focus on different aspects of the 3.11 disaster: Shigematsu's *Map of Hope: The Tale of 3.11* (*Kibō no chizu: 3.11 kara hajimaru monogatari*, 2012), a fiction-cum-documentary novel, centers on the earthquake and tsunami damage along the coast, while Taguchi's more strictly fictional short stories *In the Zone* and *In the Zone II* (*Zōn ni te* and *Zōn ni te II*, 2013) depict life in and around the 20 km nuclear exclusion zone surrounding the plant.

In the aftermath of the disaster, various narratives began to contend for interpretative power. It is not clear that any one narrative has become dominant, but in order for the events of 3.11 to remain relevant and rise above the specifics of the immediate victims of Tōhoku—in other words, to be successfully transformed into a collective representation—they must be narrativized as trauma. This narrative is not that of individual psychological trauma, but of cultural trauma, a representation of the event that establishes significant meaning for the social group. As the sociologist Jeffrey Alexander argues: "It is by constructing cultural traumas that social groups [...] 'take on board' some significant responsibility for it." The participation in this process is crucial because "if social groups restrict solidarity," they isolate the victims, who are left to "suffer alone" (Alexander 2004: 1).

While the disaster was initially perceived as a national one, narratives like Prime Minister Abe Shinzō's speech to the International Olympic Committee regarding Japan's successful bid for the 2020 Olympics have regionalized the disaster, geographically and socially isolating Tōhoku.[2] In his speech, the prime minister emphasized the safety of Tokyo and the fact that the situation in Fukushima is "under control. It has never done and will never do any damage to Tokyo."[3] Despite government assurances about their ability to handle the ongoing nuclear crisis, this narrative is far from hegemonic. Abe's speech met with outrage from the affected communities, but it clearly indicated the central government's plans for containing Tōhoku, a region that has long been considered one of Japan's "internal colonies," seen as backward and peripheral.[4] The 3.11 disaster washed away any "veneer of prosperity" in Tōhoku and laid bare its subordinate status to Tokyo, the region's payment of tribute having historically shifted from soldiers and rice to nuclear powered electricity (Hopson 2013; Jinno 2011: 87–88).

It is not just government narratives, but the realities of life on the ground in the wake of 3.11 that have also fractured and isolated Fukushima. Forced evacuation has broken up communities and the stigma of being labeled a nuclear victim (*hibakusha*) has kept some from self-identifying as such (Haworth 2013; Aoki 2013). However, Alexander argues that successful narratives of cultural trauma require that victims be identified, related to a wider audience, and responsibility be attributed—steps that are both difficult and controversial. The process of identifying victims is fraught due to a number of factors, including the multifaceted nature of the disaster and the spread of radiation beyond the exclusion and evacuation zones. Identifying victims via the designated disaster zones may focus relief efforts, but it can also isolate those victims and hinder the process of relating them to a wider audience. This can lead to a mindset that 3.11 is solely a problem of Fukushima, in other words, a problem that can be forgotten by those on the outside.

The question of blame, Alexander's third step, was a critical component of the discourse in Japan, but one that the government and Tokyo Electric Power Company (TEPCO) have virtually avoided through a characterization of the disaster as "beyond expectation" (*sōteigai*). TEPCO did eventually take some responsibility for the accident in March 2013 (Associated Press 2013). Additionally, the discourse of national self-reflection and self-blame made on both the international and individual scale arguably shifted some of the responsibility, as Japanese citizens questioned their own culpability in allowing the advancement of nuclear power.[5] The disaster did give birth to a new citizen activism, but it is questionable how effective the anti-nuclear campaign will be in the face of Prime Minister Abe's plans to restart the reactors (Tabuchi 2014).

Both Shigematsu and Taguchi's texts engage in the work of narrating cultural trauma, and both regionalize the disaster to Tōhoku: their stories take place almost exclusively in the disaster area and the problems and solutions of 3.11 are found therein. Yet the authors work to different purposes. Shigematsu resists various framing devices that would turn the local experience into a larger narrative that risks losing meaning. Instead, through his dogged emphasis on the specifics of the local, he makes the reader identify with the local struggle and, in doing so, expands the circle of solidarity. The end result is that the Tōhoku victims do not suffer alone, but are also not subsumed within a larger framework that would erase their identity. Taguchi also expands the circle of solidarity, making room for outsiders such as her Tokyo-based protagonist, but in the end her story is about her protagonist and not the disaster area or its victims. Taguchi also depicts an environment in which narratives clash and contend, leaving the story of "Fukushima as disaster area" unresolved, and her protagonist unwilling to commit to any narrative. I argue that the difference between the two texts—the consensual or polarizing nature of their narratives of cultural trauma—emanates primarily from their foci. Shigematsu constructs hopeful stories of disaster relief and recovery along a coast afflicted by the earthquake and tsunami, but given the realities of life in the irradiated zone, such a narrative is not possible in Taguchi's writing.

## Mapping the disaster as local

Shigematsu Kiyoshi's *Map of Hope* tells the story of Tamura Akira, a freelance writer who travels around the disaster area conducting interviews and collecting information for a series of newspaper articles. The book starts six months after the 3.11 disaster struck northeastern Japan, as Tamura invites Kōji, a middle-school boy, to join him on his trip. Shigematsu sets the travels of his fictional protagonists against the realities of the earthquake- and tsunami-ravaged coastline, as Tamura seeks out hopeful stories of residents coping with the disaster and rebuilding their lives. The chapters are set in specific locales within the three affected prefectures of Fukushima, Miyagi, and Iwate, including towns that were heavily damaged or made uninhabitable by radiation, such as Iitate, Ishinomaki, Kamaishi, Kesennuma, Minamisanriku, and Rikuzentakada. The story is told in third person, with the exception of Chapter 4 and the Epilogue that are in the form of letters from Tamura to Kōji. The book is a record of Tamura's travels to collect material, but the reader never sees the articles he produces.

Shigematsu builds a level of the documentary into his fictional story. The *obi* band on the book describes it as a "documentary novel" (*dokyumento noberu*), and Tamura Akira is one of Shigematsu's pen-names. Many of the initiatives and people he features in the story are real, as the author lays a thin veil of fiction over the historical facts of the disaster. In the opening pages of the book is a map of northeastern Japan, on which are marked disaster towns, the epicenter of the earthquake, and the location of the Fukushima Daiichi Nuclear Power Plant. The map comes after a series of photographs (fourteen pages) taken in the aftermath of 3.11 that, although they cannot all be readily tied to specific chapters, reinforce for the reader the reality of the disaster in Shigematsu's semi-fictional setting.

My analysis focuses on Shigematsu's mapping of the disaster area through this semi-fictional approach, his positioning of Kōji as the intermediate victim, and his nostalgic characterization of Tōhoku. By zeroing in on the local towns, Shigematsu rejects the tendency to view the tsunami and earthquake damage along the coast as homogenous, in other words as a disaster that exceeded prefectural bounds to decimate the northeastern seaboard. Shigematsu's emphasis on the specifics allows him to champion the local, to position Tamura and Kōji as intermediaries that facilitate the reader's identification with the disaster area, to write a counter-narrative to the national story of recovery, and to critique the mass media coverage.

Chapter 1 highlights three local attempts to use the media to aid in the disaster relief effort. Tamura speaks with Takahashi Atsushi, well-known television personality and the force behind Apple Radio (*ringo rajio*), the emergency radio he established in Miyagi Prefecture. Tamura also takes Kōji to meet Takeuchi Hiroyuki, the managing director of the *Ishinomaki Daily Press* (*Ishinomaki Hibi Shimbun*), and Tsuda Yoshiaki, Ishinomaki local and NHK announcer for the program *Voices from the Disaster Area* (*Hisaichi kara no koe*) that features interviews with residents in the affected zones. These men are not fictional creations, but real people known to Shigematsu's readers.[6]

Chapter 5 is set in Iwaki, south of the nuclear power plant, as Tamura and Kōji visit the well-known Aquamarine Fukushima Aquarium and Spa Resort Hawaiians, both damaged in the disaster, but both able to reopen. In Chapter 6, Tamura speaks with a representative of the local Sanriku Railways, which opened their train lines to residents free of charge after the disaster. He and Kōji also interview workers at a hotel that sheltered victims and rescue workers in Jōdogahama in Miyako, the famous coastal tourist site in Rikuchū Kaigan National Park.

As part of Shigematsu's emphasis on the local, both Tamura and those he interviews critique the mass media, either for the lack of coverage of the disaster, or for their overemphasis on recovery (*fukkō*) and the need for victims to keep their chins up (*ganbaru*).[7] Tsuda Yoshiaki argues that behind news of the progress in structural repairs are people in shelters who feel depressed that they have been left behind. The continual calls for recovery and moving forward can seem overwhelming to those not in a position to act (Shigematsu 2012: 71).

Shigematsu's championing of the local also extends to a critique of the government. The local representatives in Kamaishi felt strongly that it was better to have residents submit plans for the rebuilding of the town, rather than leave it to Tokyo politicians, who although they can garner mass media attention, are cold-hearted with regard to the victims (Shigematsu 2012: 97–98). Businessmen, who were trying to protect their workers, expected more help from the government, but the process for getting financial assistance was slow and complicated, and the unemployment office could offer no solution other than lay-offs (219–20). Tamura remarks with chagrin that the predecessor of Spa Resort Hawaiians was born of the shift from coal to oil, but that half a century later nuclear power had plunged the resort back into trouble, despite the fact that the energy it produced did not benefit the local area (Shigematsu 2012: 158). The local organizations he features stand in stark contrast to the picture he paints of an ineffectual, cold-hearted, negligent government and mass media. The mention of the *Ishinomaki Daily Press* recalls local efforts to resist an oppressive wartime government, portraying the locals as the underdogs fighting the good fight.

Tamura resists larger framing devices that distance us from the local experience of 3.11. In Chapter 4, he travels to Fukushima alone, not wanting to expose Kōji to the radiation. The chapter is in the form of a letter to Kōji in which Tamura states his dislike for the new convention of writing Fukushima in the phonetic *katakana* script, used for emphasis or to mark a foreign loan word, rather than in the traditional Sino-Japanese characters. There are only two other cities that are regularly written this way—Hiroshima and Nagasaki—and when Fukushima is added to the list, Tamura argues that it becomes subsumed under the heading of "nuclear power" and the "atomic."[8] Tamura explains that those in favor of *katakana* emphasize both the international nature of the problem and its historical significance (Shigematsu 2012: 123). This is certainly the case for atomic-bomb literature specialist Kuroko Kazuo, who unequivocally states his reasons in the opening of his book *Writers on the Nuclear and Fukushima: Yoshimoto Takaaki, Ōe Kenzaburō, Murakami Haruki* (*Bungakusha no "kaku, Fukushima ron": Yoshimoto Takaaki, Ōe Kenzaburō, Murakami Haruki*, 2013). Kuroko argues that he writes Fukushima in *katakana* because the nuclear accident was a global event on the order of Hiroshima and Nagasaki, one which affects the future of humanity and easily exceeds national bounds (Kuroko 2013: 7).

Despite Tamura's support for expanding the boundaries beyond Japan, he fears that such action can turn into wordplay that allows for responsibility to be shirked. Additionally, he argues that this large scale makes it harder to see the actual pain, anger, and sadness borne by the residents of Fukushima. Tamura suspects there are those who would prefer to avert their gaze from the harsh realities, but once you face these realities and try to find ways to help, the *katakana* Fukushima reverts back to the actual locale (Shigematsu 2012: 124–25).

This struggle over script encapsulates the larger debate about how the disaster and Fukushima are perceived within a national versus global consciousness. For atomic-bomb specialists, the need to tie the nuclear to the atomic is vital given the historical struggles of anti-atomic movements to protest against nuclear weapons, and of atomic-bomb victims to gain recognition and health benefits from a reluctant government.[9] For Shigematsu, this elevation to the global risks diluting his emphasis on the local, but in rejecting the global he leaves himself open to a discourse that seeks to regionalize Tōhoku and contain the disaster, to move it off the national stage.

## Mediating the experience of victim

Through Tamura's interviews, the reader encounters and hears about many victims of the 3.11 disaster. Shigematsu addresses the issue of victim through two strategies: a documentary-like focus on the actual state of victims' lives in the disaster areas, as seen above, and the use of Kōji as an intermediary, yet immediate, victim. Kōji, Tamura's friend's son, lives in Tokyo and was not directly affected by 3.11, however, he is a victim nonetheless. Bullied at school, he has become a virtual shut-in, who is deeply affected by his failure in the entrance exams to place into a better middle school. Kōji is a familiar type in contemporary Japanese society, and is the one constant victim in the shifting line-up of victims the reader meets in the book.

Kōji experiences a range of responses as he slowly comes to terms with the disaster. In the prologue, Tamura takes Kōji and his father to Akihabara to show them the Fuji Film Photography Rescue Project. When Tamura asks Kōji's opinion of 3.11, the boy is flummoxed. As a middle-school student living far away from the disaster area, Kōji does not feel it is his place to comment (Shigematsu 2012: 26). When a moment of silence is observed at 2:46 pm, Kōji does not know how to mourn, not having known any of the victims (35). After they visit Apple Radio, Kōji remarks to himself that the plight of the victims has nothing to do with him (Shigematsu 2012: 52).

Kōji slowly starts to come to terms with his own problems, but both Tamura and Kōji are sensitive to the fact that it would be inappropriate and disrespectful to the victims for Kōji to use the disaster as a motivation to pick himself back up again (Shigematsu 2012: 108). Nevertheless, Kōji does take heart from the various interviews and starts his own recovery. Toward the end of the book, Kōji begins to feel a sense of relief, a lifting of the heavy uncertainty that plagued him. He also starts attending school again (267–68).

What does it mean for Shigematsu to use a character like Kōji, a pariah grown out of contemporary Japan's social problems, as not only Tamura's travel companion, but as the book's point of contact for readers? In setting up Kōji as a victim, is Shigematsu equating or drawing parallels between Kōji's situation and that of the 3.11 victims? At no point does the book encourage the reader to equate Kōji's victimhood with that of the people in the disaster area, in fact, as mentioned above, it discourages it. As a victim, Kōji serves as an intermediary point of contact between the actual 3.11 victims and readers who are not victims. Kōji is confused about how he should react to what he sees in the disaster zone, but since he is immature and fragile, the reader is less inclined to criticize him than if had he been a socially well-adjusted adult. Through Kōji readers can explore their own anxieties about how they as outsiders should relate to, understand, and act in the face of the disaster, without having to come up with answers or be embarrassed about their own confusion. Shigematsu uses Kōji to widen the circle of solidarity for his narrative of cultural trauma, allowing readers to process their feelings about the disaster. Shigematsu does not dictate how readers should emotionally respond to the plight of the 3.11 victims, just as Tamura does not dictate Kōji's response, but Shigematsu does reinforce the importance of local experience and community, and a criticism of both the central government and the mass media.

Shigematsu's strategy of using Kōji as an intermediary is effective, but is not without its problems. Given Kōji's age and mental state, Tamura makes an effort to shield him from the worst of the disaster. Tamura tells Kōji's father that he will not let Kōji meet people who are truly in despair: those who have lost family members, are searching for missing people, isolated in temporary housing, displaced from their homes by the nuclear accident, or damaged by harmful rumors (Shigematsu 2012: 234).[10] But in protecting Kōji, Shigematsu insulates the reader, who is never forced to deal with the more troubling, unresolved issues of the ongoing crisis, especially the nuclear crisis.

Shigematsu portrays the plight of the victims, the conflicted feelings of an outside observer like Kōji, and Tamura's own crisis about his position as a writer. In the Epilogue, Tamura admits to his own doubts concerning his right to narrate the disaster, wondering if an outsider such as himself has the qualifications to turn it into a news story. He is also worried that he was profiting from the disaster by using it as material for his work, but ultimately he decides that the work is too important to abandon (Shigematsu 2012: 281). Through the character of Tamura, Shigematsu affirms the value of outsiders for crafting narratives about the disaster area. Both Tamura and Kōji voice the concerns and anxieties of outsiders, be they Japanese from areas beyond the disaster zones or non-Japanese living elsewhere. This is one important function of Shigematsu's book as he builds a narrative of cultural trauma that speaks to a wide audience, a technique he uses in other of his 3.11 writings as well.[11]

The book ends with Tamura's letter to Kōji in which he struggles with his depictions of the disaster areas, and expresses his concern that it is too soon to confine the disaster to history (Shigematsu 2012: 278). He explains that he wanted to show the disaster area to someone like Kōji whose life was just beginning, because there would be a chance that those landscapes could belong to the future and not just the past (284–86). Ultimately Tamura decides that he must keep visiting Tōhoku, and that the involvement of young people like Kōji, whose lives will overlap with the recovery period for the disaster area, is critical for any future the area might have (Shigematsu 2012: 292).

## Turning back the clock on Tōhoku

Despite Tamura's emphasis on the future, the picture he paints of Tōhoku is heavily based in the past, as he creates a nostalgic narrative of Japan that predates the economic crisis of the early 1990s. The local communities of Japan's northeastern coast that Tamura lauds are held together by strong bonds and shared traditional values. The business leaders he interviews are reluctant to lay off their employees, treating them as family. Despite financial worries, one company president says he does not want to cut his bonds (*kizuna*) with his employees, using one of the key words in post-disaster Japan.[12] Since his employees lost everything, he feels that the company must care for them (Shigematsu 2012: 221). Yet the reality is that this traditional, company-as-family model has lost currency in a Japan of neoliberal reforms (North 2014).[13]

Tamura rejects media images of the Tōhoku dialect as being always linked to country bumpkins and the rural poor. At one point, Tamura and Kōji interview the president of a company that printed a version of the Bible in the local dialect, called *Kesengo* (Shigematsu 2012: 192). Tamura argues strongly that we can only accept Tōhoku speech as a dialect if we accept Tokyo speech as the standard, something he is unwilling to do. Rather than present us with stereotypical images of Tōhoku as a place of dwindling towns, Tamura emphasizes the 'disaster returnees' (*shinsai U-tān*). These are people in their twenties and thirties, who left lives and jobs in Tokyo because they felt compelled to help rebuild their local towns (Shigematsu 2012: 99, 103). Tamura presents vibrant communities, but many of the disaster towns were aging centers of depopulation.[14] As Daniel Aldrich argued in *Site Fights: Divisive Facilities and Civil Society in Japan and the West* (2010), research shows that the towns likely to end up with nuclear power plants are places with weak local bonds, shifting populations, and atomized societies. In Shigematsu's eyes, Tōhoku is a place that once held all that has been lost in the rest of Japan. For other commentators on 3.11, this Japan is gone, but Shigematsu still sees a future for Tōhoku.[15]

Yet, Shigematsu would not have been able to emphasize recovery and hope in the same way had he set his story amidst the nuclear disaster in Fukushima. Tamura recalls Fukushima via a poorly attended Obon festival he saw last August; the town is now abandoned and the residents scattered due to high radiation levels.[16] He also notes the mercy killing of the local specialty, the Iitate cows; families that have been split up into temporary housing; the skepticism that residents will be able to return in two years as per government predictions, since 75 percent of the area is mountainous and hard to clean up; overgrown rice paddies, shuttered businesses, and abandoned towns (Shigematsu 2012: 126–27).[17] Tamura fears the negative effects on the minds of the local children should this disaster landscape become normalized (139). In many ways it has become normalized; three years after the disaster, many towns are still unpopulated or, where they have been repopulated, it is with tremendous controversy (Fackler 2014).

## Mapping radiation *In the Zone*

Taguchi Randy's short story *In the Zone* (*Zōn ni te*) Parts I and II are about Hatori Yōko, a 39-year-old writer from Tokyo who travels to Fukushima twice to tour the disaster area.[18] The story is written in the first person from Hatori's perspective, and in many ways the trip is really about her and not the victims. Unlike in Shigematsu, there is no indication that the stories are anything other than a fictional imagining of the disaster area; however, Taguchi did travel to the exclusion zone four months after 3.11, and the reader may wonder if she is basing her stories on the landscapes she saw during that trip (Shiotsuka 2013).

On Hatori's first trip, she is guided inside the 20 km nuclear exclusion zone (*keikai kuiki*) around the Fukushima Daiichi Nuclear Power Plant by a local, Kudō Ken'ichi, who is living in a shelter because his farm is within the zone. Taguchi does not attempt to record the stories of local victims in order to narrate a map of hope, as does Shigematsu. Hatori does, however, metaphorically map the zone as she travels closer and closer to the nuclear power plant, passing through the concentric circles of evacuation and exclusion zones and taking repeated readings with her Geiger counter. Her travels into the zone fall somewhere between disaster tourism and scientific data gathering, as she wavers between palpable fear of radiation exposure and false reassurances of safety. Hatori shows none of Tamura's commitment to giving voice to the local concerns, and the text at times seems inappropriately lighthearted and foolish, even describing Hatori's romantic crush on Kudō.

Hatori's confusion and lack of commitment draw a picture of an outsider who is unwilling to take sides in a highly polarized debate. Hatori does not have Kōji's excuse of being young and inexperienced, and the reader may be less likely to forgive her. Taguchi, as author, also seems to want to stand to the side. When discussing her work in an interview with *MSN Sankei nyūzu* (Sankei News) Taguchi said, "Everyone has a different position, and there is no correct answer to be found" (Shiotsuka 2013). She sought to write something that would be easy to read, would appeal to a wide readership, and would not leave readers with a sense of desperation. Yet for all the naivety her statements seem to imply, the reader should not take it to mean that Taguchi is ignorant of the dangers of nuclear and atomic disaster. She wrote on the atomic bombs and the Chernobyl nuclear accident long before the Fukushima disaster struck.[19] Yet her comments and portrayal of Hatori raise questions about how Taguchi views the disaster, her relation to it as an outsider, and her desire to consign it to easy reading.

Kudō picks up Hatori at the Fukushima train station and takes her to the Minamisōma city hall for a permit to enter the 20 km exclusion zone, an area in which entry is forbidden (*tachiiri kinshi kuiki*). This is the closest of the concentric circles to the plant. Since his ranch is between the 10–20 km radii of the plant, he is allowed limited access to the zone. In order to get Hatori inside, he lies on the permit they file at city hall, pretending she is his wife. They enter the zone in Minamisōma, and make stops in Namie (13 km), and Ōkuma (10 km), eventually coming within 2 km of the plant itself.

Kudō confirms the seriousness of their endeavor: entering a forbidden zone with very high levels of radiation (Taguchi 2013a: 10). He thinks Hatori is crazy to want to expose herself. His actions continue to confirm the gravity of the threat. Even outside the exclusion zone on their drive to Minamisōma, they sweat inside Kudō's red Audi, because the air conditioning is not working and they are afraid to open the windows. On their way, Hatori takes out a Geiger counter she borrowed from a friend; the machine keeps beeping due to the high levels and the low threshold at which her friend had set the machine. She shuts it off in frustration and embarrassment that she cannot even use this machine she thought so necessary to bring (Taguchi 2013a: 11–12).

Despite his warnings, Kudō sends Hatori conflicting messages. Hatori is surprised to find that she cannot get protective clothing from city hall, as she expected. He insists that she can enter the zone wearing regular clothing (*heifuku*), and he procures some cheap vinyl rain gear for her (Taguchi 2013a: 20–21). He wears regular clothing, saying that the residents cannot obsess about exposure; since they cannot tell where or if the levels are high or low, they are tired of having to worry about it (31). Hatori suspects Kudō has been secretly entering the zone more than he is officially allowed, exposing himself to higher and higher doses.

Once inside the zone, Hatori starts to question its meaning. She wonders how these seemingly arbitrary circles drawn on a map can protect people from radiation that is floating in the air (Taguchi 2013a: 25–26). Her Geiger readings confirm that proximity to the plant does not necessarily indicate higher radiation levels.[20] The readings that Hatori takes in *In the Zone* range from 0.75 to 20 microsieverts/hour. However, in Part II of the story, she tells the friend who lent her the Geiger counter that some readings went as high as 80 microsieverts/hour. When he jumps out of his chair in shock at the number 80, Hatori remarks to herself that in reality some of her readings were over 100 (Taguchi 2013b: 71).

When the machine keeps going up and down, suddenly spiking when she is in the zone, she begins to question whether it is working properly (Taguchi 2013a: 32). Yet once she exits the zone through the checkpoint, she removes her protective gear and relaxes in the "safety" of the area beyond the 20 km concentric circle (Taguchi 2013a: 60–62). The urge to both question the exclusion zone and to take comfort in her location outside of it seems contradictory or even foolish, but given the uneven, shifting nature of the zones and the unpredictable spread of radiation, perhaps the reader cannot criticize her.[21] The exclusion zone was established to indicate proximity to high levels of radiation, yet the zone does not map neatly to the spread of radiation, and the characters in the story cannot effectively negotiate this danger.

## Visitor or victim?

Kudō would seem to be Taguchi's natural choice for examining the effects of the 3.11 nuclear disaster on residents. Early in the story he is identified as a victim (*higaisha*), living the reality of life in the shelters, knowing his ranch has been contaminated (Taguchi 2013a: 11). Hatori imagines he must lose his patience with day-trippers from Tokyo, like herself, who come as tourists. Kudō is also a returnee; after having spent many years in Tokyo, he came back to farm in Fukushima. But unlike the "disaster returnees," Kudō came back before 3.11 because he ran out of employment options in Tokyo. His father died and he inherited the land (15). At one point Hatori asks if he offers himself as a guide for city folk like herself in order to spread the word to outsiders about the fate of the irradiated areas; some places are destined to become nuclear dumpsites never to be repopulated.[22] He denies this, saying he likes to see people's reactions when they encounter radiation (Taguchi 2013a: 34). Taguchi does not present any heroic stories of the victims, rather she shifts away from characters like Kudō to her real focus: Hatori and *her* experience of the zone.[23]

Ultimately Hatori's willingness to enter the zone, even the most highly irradiated areas, is underwritten by her status as a temporary visitor. At the end of their trip, Kudō plans to take her to his ranch, but warns that the radiation there will be high since they are so far into the zone (Taguchi 2013a: 47–49). She finally agrees to go when she realizes that she will not be in the zone very long. Since, as she says, "It's not like I'll be here forever" (*zutto iru wake ja nai*), the short-term exposure to high doses is not a major concern (50).[24] Kudō wryly echoes her comment, revealing his precarious situation as a long-term resident (Taguchi 2013a: 50). These comments she makes to Kudō about her temporary status in the zone is indicative of her position as an outsider. She clings to her role as an observer, refusing to interview anyone and shrinking away from the opportunity to use her literary skills to help the residents publicize the plight of their children. Unlike Tamura, Hatori claims she is only there to observe (*mi ni kita dake*) (Taguchi 2013a: 38). Later Komori, an editor for a women's magazine and the friend who had introduced her to Kudō, offers to help Hatori find appropriate venues to publish something about her trip, but Hatori deflects the question, saying that she has no plans to write because she is not a reporter (Taguchi 2013b: 74–75). This comment undermines the value of 3.11 fiction, including Taguchi's own work.

Despite her purported desire to keep her distance and to remain merely a visitor, the area holds a strange attraction for Hatori. Kudō's use of the term "zone" (*zōn*) intrigues her. The word sounds so new and fresh that she feels as if she is in a science fiction movie (Taguchi 2013a: 23). She echoes the comment in Part II of the story when she returns for a second trip to Fukushima; she remarks that the daily reporting of radioactivity levels on the weather forecast is like something out of a movie. When Kudō wryly asks if she returned to Fukushima to join the cast, she admits he may be right. She talks about her "radiation exposure anniversary" (*hibaku kinenbi*), and when she is mistaken for a resident of the shelter, she runs to share the news with Kudō (Taguchi 2013b: 79, 103–105). Hatori plays the role of victim with a vicarious thrill.

Hatori further identifies with the disaster area through the nostalgia she exhibits for Tōhoku, or as she sees it, old Japan, thereby repeating widespread stereotypes about Japan's presumably less developed north (Taguchi 2013b: 75). She talks about the vast, verdant landscapes that are so easy on the eyes of city dwellers like herself, and appreciates the abandoned beauty of the place (Taguchi 2013a: 11, 26). Beyond the appeal of exoticism, the zone represents something deeper for Hatori. It becomes a way for her to deal with the grief she still feels from her sister's death. The sister was a stewardess who died in an airplane crash, and Hatori still has nightmares of falling from the sky. For Hatori the zone represents absolute bottom. She finds comfort in a place from which she can fall no further (Taguchi 2013b: 78). She maps the zone by projecting her own personal tragedies onto the disaster site. The zone is incorporated into Hatori's own trauma narrative. Like Kōji, Hatori is a victim and she uses the disaster as a way of healing her own psychological wounds. Yet unlike Kōji, Hatori has no reservations about using the zone for her own purposes. Hatori seeks to be both an insider and an outsider, to have the freedom to walk away from the disaster zone, yet to also feel deeply connected to it. Taguchi does not identify victims of 3.11, rather she makes Hatori the victim and Fukushima a mere backdrop for her trauma narrative.

## Refusing to take sides

Unlike Tamura in *Map of Hope*, Hatori shies away from blaming either TEPCO or the government and, in doing so, she omits one of the crucial components of a successful trauma narrative, the need to attribute responsibility. She makes a number of remarks that can be taken as veiled criticism, but Taguchi chooses instead to show the pressure Hatori feels to take sides in the debate and her reluctance to do so, perhaps as a means to connect to readers who feel this way. We see her make a number of contradictory comments including her remarks about the atomic bombs. Hatori comments that when she sees maps with concentric circles radiating out from the Fukushima Nuclear Power Plant, she cannot help but remember similar maps for Hiroshima and Nagasaki. In her opinion these mappings are meaningless because they place too much emphasis on the location of victims at the time of the bomb and not enough on the experience of those who were irradiated. She is disturbed to see the same thing happening in Fukushima (Taguchi 2013a: 26). Yet in Part II when she talks to Kudō about the scientists who developed the atomic bomb, she excuses them of any blame by claiming that they had no way knowing how the technology would be used (Taguchi 2013b: 83).[25]

Part II contains a passage in the first person that stands apart from the rest of the text in which Hatori relates her visit to an irradiated town in Belarus on the twentieth anniversary of the Chernobyl disaster. She was part of a study tour by an NGO that aided child victims. In relating this story, Hatori focuses on a group of Italians who were also on the tour. Unlike the Japanese, the Italians wore protective clothing in the zone and refused the souvenir of strawberry jam. In comparison, the Japanese dressed in regular clothes and ate the same food as the locals (Taguchi 2013b: 100–01). Based on her experiences in Belarus, Hatori thought the Italians were "cowards" (*okubyōmono*), until she saw a group of Italians doing relief work at the shelters in Fukushima (Taguchi 2013b: 101). She revises her opinion of the Italians, but in Fukushima she is the one who chooses to remain detached, taking on the attitude she so readily critiqued in the Italians earlier.

When visiting a shelter, Hatori meets a woman who critiques the government, saying that the levels they have set for radiation exposure are unacceptable. She argues that children are more susceptible and many will die, but the government does not care about them (Taguchi 2013b: 102).[26] When she begs Hatori to use her writing skills to help this cause, Hatori declines. She silently criticizes the woman, arguing that "what she wanted was a tool that would work for the sole purpose of her own righteousness" (Taguchi 2013b: 103). Hatori feels she is the wrong choice to be this tool, because she has no use value for such a task. Hatori's desire not to get involved translates into a rebuke of anti-nuclear activists.

Hatori also reacts negatively when Komori gets angry at Hatori's nostalgia for Tōhoku's natural beauty and charm (Taguchi 2013b: 75). Komori, a Fukushima native, disabuses Hatori of her romantic ideas about Fukushima, impressing upon her the reality that nobody can live there anymore (*hito wa sumemasen*), her own family having fled to Okinawa (Taguchi 2013b: 75). Hatori knows there are people living in Fukushima, however by this she can only mean life in the shelters, which hardly qualifies as living (Taguchi 2013b: 76). Hatori wonders if Komori was mad at her, at TEPCO, or at the government. As readers, we never get an answer.

Hatori admits to feelings of unease since leaving the zone. The news is full of reports of radiation levels, but residents must measure the radiation themselves in order to locate the hotspots. People are living in these areas even though the radiation levels differ little from those in the exclusion zone. Hatori wonders how the residents figure out when to feel safe and when to be scared. A friend with children lambasts Hatori for her "irresponsible" (*musekinin*) comments about radiation and the zone; she accuses Hatori of only thinking about herself, a luxury that people with families do not have (Taguchi 2013b: 77). Back in Tokyo, Hatori's friends treat her trip to the zone with morbid curiosity (Taguchi 2013b: 70, 74). She feels she cannot talk about the zone, because everyone has their opinion and everyone thinks they are right. She wants to run away from the chorus of fearful voices (Taguchi 2013b: 77).

Taguchi shows Hatori as torn between the various debates on 3.11, conflicted by what she sees, and ultimately unable or unwilling to take sides. Given the realities and uncertainties of radiation, the reader should not be surprised, for narratives of cultural trauma do not always gain consensus and rectify damages. Alexander, in his work with Elizabeth Butler Breese, shows a reevaluation of their early theories of cultural trauma, a shift from the progressive narratives of a post-Cold War world, which imagined consensual narratives of cultural trauma that offered social reconciliation, to the harsh realities of the twenty-first century strife in which "trauma construction so frequently crystallizes polarizing narratives, exacerbates conflict, and leads to more suffering in turn" (Alexander and Breese 2011: xxxiii). This exacerbated conflict is apparent in Fukushima; the nuclear crisis drags on for residents of the contaminated zones, but they have to contend with a nation who may be ready to move on and put the disaster behind them. Caught in the middle of an unresolved situation, Hatori confronts the reader with an uncomfortable struggle. Taguchi widens the circle of solidarity by making space for conflicted outsiders like Hatori, but she relegates Fukushima to a backdrop. This precludes not only the hopeful, yet somewhat false, ending in Shigematsu's book, but also any real engagement with the actual victims of 3.11.

## Conclusion

Both Shigematsu Kiyoshi and Taguchi Randy question the new configurations and narratives that are meant to make sense of Tōhoku in the aftermath of 3.11. Shigematsu moves beyond the maps of the battered coastline to focus on specific towns, organizations, and individuals who make a difference, and in the process, he creates a means for the victims to tell their own stories and for readers to relate to them. He successfully crafts a narrative of cultural trauma that identifies victims, widens the circle of solidarity, and places some blame for the areas affected by the earthquake and tsunami. But the irradiated areas are still characterized by exclusion zones, shifting maps, and before-and-after photos that make hopeful stories of recovery virtually impossible. Hatori's inability to navigate the zone speaks to the reality of the situation and the contending narratives of cultural trauma that continue to plague the disaster areas of 3.11. Taguchi does create a link to the outsider, yet in regionalizing the nuclear disaster as Fukushima's problem, she makes that link one that can easily be severed. Although contending narratives of cultural trauma may polarize, they still bring visibility. As the five-year anniversary of 3.11 has passed, the real fear is that the disaster will cease to be a matter of importance and the government will be successful in writing it off the map, relegating it to the periphery of Tōhoku.

## Notes

1 The National Police Agency of Japan reported 15,889 dead as of November 10, 2014; as of March 11, 2012, the BBC reported over 330,000 in temporary accommodation. Citing figures from the National Police Agency of Japan, the BBC further reported that "almost 300,000 buildings were destroyed and a further one million damaged, either by the quake, tsunami or resulting fires. Almost 4,000 roads, 78 bridges and 29 railways were also affected" (*BBC News* n.d.).
2 See DiNitto (2014) for more on the perception of the disaster as a national one.
3 See "Presentation by Prime Minister Shinzo Abe at the 125th Session of the International Olympic Committee (IOC)," *Speeches and Statements by the Prime Minister*, 2013.
4 For criticism of Abe's speech, see "Local leaders criticize Abe for saying radioactive water leaks 'under control,'" 2013; for more on Tōhoku's "colonial" status, see Hopson 2013.
5 The English language version of *The Official Report of the Fukushima Nuclear Accident Independent Investigation Commission*, characterized 3.11 as a man-made disaster with fundamental causes in the "ingrained conventions of Japanese culture" (Kurokawa 2012: 9). Murakami Haruki, in his acceptance speech for the International Catalunya Prize, also laid blame on the nation for having embraced nuclear power (Murakami 2011). The writers Kawakami Hiromi and Nosaka Akiyuki have also questioned their own complacency (Kawakami 2012; Nosaka 2012).
6 This local Ishinomaki paper was lauded internationally for its *kabe shimbun*, a handwritten newspaper they posted in the local town when the newspaper offices were damaged. The paper got the idea from World War II, when they resisted the government order of one paper per prefecture, which was meant to shut them down. Unable to produce a newspaper due to restrictions on paper stock, their reporters posted articles around town on handwritten sheets. See Ōta Keisuke (2012) and Ishinomaki Hibi Shimbunsha (2011).
7 For more on the slogans encouraging Fukushima and Japan to keep their chins up, see DiNitto (2014: 3–4), Hopson (2013), and Samuels (2013: 39–41).
8 The term translated as atomic is *kaku* as in "nuclear weapons." The term for nuclear, as in "nuclear power," is *genshi*.
9 For more on the struggles of atomic-bomb victims and her hopes for the new nuclear victims of 3.11, see Hayashi 2013.
10 For more on the "harmful rumors" (*fūhyō higai*), see Slater *et al.* (2014: 497–501).
11 Shigematsu's short story *The Charm* (*Omajinai*) is also about an outsider, a woman from Tokyo who once lived in one of the disaster towns and who struggles with her feelings of helplessness as she watches the disaster unfold on the television. See *Mata tsugi no haru e*, and *March Was Made of Yarn* for an English translation.

*Literature maps disaster*  35

12  For more on the term *kizuna* as a metaphor for social solidarity and its conflicts with the various social realities on the ground, see Samuels (2013: 39–45).
13  In his article on proposed labor rules that would encourage the expansion of "limited regular employment," North (2014) provides an overview of neoliberal reforms in Japan starting after the collapse of the bubble economy in the 1990s that increased contingent employment, as companies sought (and still seek) to "dismantle costly traditions of employment security."
14  Shigematsu mentions this in reference to evacuated towns within the nuclear exclusion zone (2012: 137). He worries that if the evacuation orders are lifted and youth do not return, then the current rate of aging (25 percent) will double. See also, Stallings:

> The average age of the more than 9,000 dead is 68-years-old [...] The areas hit by the earthquake and tsunami encompassed many smaller port and fishing towns and villages [...] with significantly older populations. People 65 or older accounted for 21% of the total population in 2005. By 2010 that figure increased to 23.07%.
>
> (Stallings 2014)

15  For a discussion of nostalgia for Tōhoku in Fujiwara Toshi's documentary film *No Man's Zone*, see DiNitto (2014).
16  This town sounds similar to the one described in Shigematsu's fictional short story "To the Next Spring—Obon" (Mata tsugi no haru e—urabone). For the original and an English translation, see *Shinsai to fikushon no 'kyori': Ruptured Fiction(s) of the Earthquake*. It was later reprinted in Shigematsu's *Mata tsugi no haru e* as *Homecoming (Kikyō)* (2013).
17  Google set up two websites as part of their Street View Mapping Project in Fukushima: *Memories for the Future* (English) and *Mirai no kioku* (Japanese). These sites have before and after photos of the damaged and abandoned towns.
18  Taguchi does not give dates for Hatori's trips to Fukushima, but due to the characters' comments on the hot weather, the reader may assume that the first trip is in the summer. *In the Zone II* is about the protagonist's second trip to Fukushima, two months after the first, when she visits shelters just outside the 20 km exclusion zone and a debris field along the coast 25 km from the plant.
19  See Taguchi's *Hiroshima, Nagasaki, Fukushima: The Japan that Accepted Nuclear Power* (*Hiroshima, Nagasaki, Fukushima: Genshiryoku o ukereta Nihon*, 2011) and her work on Chernobyl, *Hope in the Age of No Resort* (*Yorubenaki jidai no kibō*, 2006). For more on Taguchi's nonfictional engagement with the nuclear, see Masami (2014: 45–47). Taguchi has visited towns downwind of Chernobyl, as has her semi-autobiographical protagonist, who also wrote a book on Hiroshima.
20  In *In the Zone*, Hatori measures Namie as 10 microsieverts/hour (Taguchi 2013a: 35), Ōkuma 20 microsieverts/hour (42), Kudō's ranch 8.5 microsieverts/hour (54), and the plant at 5.5 microsieverts/hour (58). The plant is ground zero, but the readings there are some of the lowest she takes.
21  In the early days of the disaster, residents were getting conflicting information about whether to evacuate or shelter indoors (Makinen 2011). However, as time passes, the government has re-evaluated the status of certain areas. See, for example, the Ministry of Economy, Trade, and Industry (METI) website for more on the disaster, specifically for nuclear victims, and METI reports on reconsidering the evacuation zones, such as "Hinan shiji kuiki no minaoshi ni tsuite." See also the maps made by the citizen action group Safecast and the Fukushima Prefecture Radioactivity Measure Map for up to date radiation levels.
22  There is no indication that Kudō is working in any capacity as a formal tour guide or is being paid to show people like Hatori around the disaster area. The question of disaster tourism for Fukushima is a controversial one. Companies like Bridge for Fukushima run tours to educate people about the disaster area and encourage them to think about the future of these areas. The cultural critic Azuma Hiroki has been working to

create Fukushima as a site of dark tourism akin to Chernobyl, so as to guarantee that the disaster is not forgotten (Azuma 2013; Fukui 2013).
23 For example, Hatori presents a critical view of the residents in the shelters: residents bicker and engage in turf wars; victims cannot agree on whether they like or dislike the press coverage; and one older female resident scandalously has sex with some of the younger men (Taguchi 2013b: 90, 96, 105–106). Along these lines, see Ogino Anna's depiction of corruption in the shelters in *The Great Disaster: Desire and Duty (Daishinsai: yoku to jingi*, 2011). For a critique of Ogino's work, see Kawamura (2013: 26–28).
24 All translations are my own unless otherwise noted.
25 Hatori's desire to absolve the scientists of guilt is questionable in light of comments like the following from Albert Einstein, made when the plans were announced to manufacture hydrogen bombs: "annihilation of any life on earth has been brought within the range of technical possibilities" (Treat 1995: 4).
26 On the health effects of radiation exposure in children in Fukushima eighteen months after the disaster, and their mothers' frustrations with the government and medical system that does not seem to care, see Ian Thomas Ash's film *A2-B-C* (2013; discussed in Chapter 6). Also see Slater *et al.* (2014.)

## References

*A2-B-C*. 2013, Dir. Ash, Ian Thomas. Film.
Aldrich, Daniel P. 2010, *Site Fights: Divisive Facilities and Civil Society in Japan and the West*. 1 edition. Ithaca, NY; Bristol: Cornell University Press.
Alexander, Jeffrey C. 2004, "Toward a theory of cultural trauma," in Jeffrey C. Alexander, Ron Eyerman, Bernhard Giesen, Neil J. Smelser, and Piotr Sztompka (eds), *Cultural Trauma and Collective Identity*. Berkeley, CA: University of California Press, 1–30.
Alexander, Jeffrey C. and Breese, Elizabeth B. 2011, "On social suffering and its cultural construction," in Ron Eyermen, Jeffrey C. Alexander, and Elizabeth B. Breese (eds), *Narrating Trauma: On the Impact of Collective Suffering*. Boulder, CO and London: Paradigm Publishers, xi–xxxv.
Aoki, Mizuho. 2013, "Fukushima activist fights fear and discrimination based on radiation." *The Japan Times Online* May 9, at: www.japantimes.co.jp/news/2013/05/09/national/fukushima-activist-fights-fear-and-discrimination-based-on-radiation/ (accessed December 12, 2014).
Associated Press. 2013, "Japanese utility takes blame for nuclear crisis." *The Washington Post*, March 29, at: www.washingtonpost.com/world/japanese-utility-takes-blame-for-nuclear-crisis/2013/03/29/45a53462-98bb-11e2-97cd-3d8c1afe4f0f_story.html (accessed December 4, 2014).
Azuma, Hiroki. 2013, *Cherunobuiri dāku tsūrizumu gaido*. Tokyo: Genron.
BBC News. n.d., "Japan quake: Loss and recovery in numbers," at: www.bbc.com/news/world-asia-17219008 (accessed December 4, 2014).
Bridge for Fukushima. n.d., at: http://bridgeforfukushima.org/ (accessed December 12, 2014).
DiNitto, Rachel. 2014, "Narrating the cultural trauma of 3.11: The debris of post-Fukushima literature and film." *Japan Forum* Vol. 26, Issue 3: 340–60.
Fackler, Martin. 2014, "Forced to flee radiation, fearful Japanese villagers are reluctant to return." *The New York Times* April 27, at: www.nytimes.com/2014/04/28/world/asia/forced-to-flee-radiation-fearful-japanese-villagers-are-reluctant-to-return.html (accessed May 28, 2014).

Fuji Film Photography Rescue Project. n.d., at: http://fujifilm.jp/support/fukkoshien/about/ (accessed December 12, 2014).
Fukui, Yohei. 2013, "Cultural critic Azuma wants to turn Fukushima Nuclear Plant into tourist spot." *AJW by The Asahi Shimbun*, at: http://ajw.asahi.com/article/0311disaster/fukushima/AJ201310070075 (accessed December 2, 2014).
Fukushima Prefecture Radioactivity Measure Map [*Fukushima-ken hōshanō sokutei mappu*]. n.d., at: http://fukushima-radioactivity.jp/ (accessed December 2, 2014).
Haworth, Abigail. 2013, "After Fukushima: Families on the edge of meltdown." *The Guardian* February 24, at: www.theguardian.com/environment/2013/feb/24/divorce-after-fukushima-nuclear-disaster (accessed December 12, 2014).
Hayashi, Kyōko. 2013, "Futatabi Rui e." *Gunzō* 4: 7–25.
Hopson, Nathan. 2013, "Systems of irresponsibility and Japan's internal colony." *The Asia-Pacific Journal* Vol. 11, Issue 52, No. 2, at: http://japanfocus.org/-Nathan-Hopson/4053/article.html (accessed December 16, 2015).
Ishinomaki Hibi Shimbunsha (ed.). 2011, *6-mai no kabeshimbun : Ishinomaki Hibi Shimbun Higashi Nihon Daishinsaigo 7-nichikan no kiroku*. Tokyo: Kadokawa Magajinzu.
Jinno Toshifumi. 2011, *Sekaishi no naka no Fukushima: Nagasaki kara sekai e*. Tokyo: Kawade Shobō Shinsha.
Kawakami, Hiromi. 2012, "God bless you, 2011," in Elmer Luke and David Karashima (eds), *March Was Made of Yarn: Reflections on the Japanese Earthquake, Tsunami, and Nuclear Meltdown*. New York: Vintage, 37–53.
Kawamura, Minato. 2013, *Shinsai genpatsu bungakuron*. Tokyo: Inpakuto Shuppankai.
Kurokawa, Kiyoshi. 2012, *The Official Report of the Fukushima Nuclear Accident Independent Investigation Commission*. Tokyo: National Diet of Japan, at: http://warp.da.ndl.go.jp/info:ndljp/pid/3856371/naiic.go.jp/en/report/ (accessed August 18, 2014).
Kuroko Kazuo. 2013, *Bungakusha no "kaku, Fukushima ron": Yoshimoto Takaaki, Ōe Kenzaburō, Murakami Haruki*. Tokyo: Sairyūsha.
"Local Leaders Criticize Abe for Saying Radioactive Water Leaks 'under Control.'" 2013, *AJW by The Asahi Shimbun*. September 21, at: http://ajw.asahi.com/article/0311disaster/fukushima/AJ201309210057 (accessed December 8, 2014).
Luke, Elmer and Karashima, David (eds). 2012, *March Was Made of Yarn: Reflections on the Japanese Earthquake, Tsunami, and Nuclear Meltdown*. New York: Vintage.
Makinen, Julie. 2011, "Japan steps up nuclear plant precautions: Kan apologizes." *Los Angeles Times* March 25, at: http://articles.latimes.com/2011/mar/25/world/la-fgw-japan-nuclear-plant-20110326 (accessed December 4, 2014).
Masami, Yuki. 2014, "Post-Fukushima discourses on food and eating: Analyzing political implications and literary imagination," in Lisette Gebhardt and Yuki Masami (eds), *Literature and Art after "Fukushima": Four Approaches*. Berlin: EB Verlag, 37–51.
Memories for the Future. n.d., at: www.miraikioku.com/en (accessed September 12, 2013).
METI. "Genshiryoku saigaisha shien," at: www.meti.go.jp/earthquake/nuclear/kinkyu.html#shiji (accessed December 12, 2014).
METI. "Hinan shiji kuiki no minaoshi ni tsuite," at: www.meti.go.jp/earthquake/nuclear/pdf/131009/131009_02a.pdf (accessed December 12, 2014).
Mirai no kioku. n.d., at: www.miraikioku.com (accessed September 12, 2013).
Murakami, Haruki. 2011, "Speaking as an unrealistic dreamer." *The Asia-Pacific Journal* Vol. 9, Issue 9, No. 29, at: http://japanfocus.org/-Murakami-Haruki/3571/article.html (accessed December 16, 2015).
National Police Agency of Japan. 2014, "Damage situation and police countermeasures associated with the 2011 Tōhoku district – off the Pacific Ocean earthquake." November 10, at: www.npa.go.jp/archive/keibi/biki/higaijokyo_e.pdf (accessed December 12, 2014).

*No Man's Zone*. 2011, Dir. Fujiwara, Toshi. Film.
North, Scott. 2014, "Limited regular employment and the reform of Japan's division of labor." *The Asia-Pacific Journal* Vol. 12, Issue 15, No. 1.
Nosaka, Akiyuki. 2012, "Tachidomaru no wa ima," in Nihon Pen Kurabu (ed.), *Ima koso watashi wa genpatsu ni hantai shimasu*. Tokyo: Heibonsha, 471–74.
Ogino, Anna. 2011, *Daishinsai yoku to jingi*. Tokyo: Kyōdō Tsūshinsha.
Ōta, Keisuke. 2012, "Senjichū no densetsu ga unda kabe shimbun." *Spork* November 30, at: http://spork.jp/?p=4065 (accessed August 20, 2014).
Safecast. n.d., at: http://blog.safecast.org/ (accessed September 13, 2013).
Samuels, Richard J. 2013, *3.11 : Disaster and Change in Japan*. Ithaca, NY: Cornell University Press.
Shigematsu, Kiyoshi. 2012, *Kibō no chizu: 3.11 kara hajimaru monogatari*. Tokyo: Gentōsha. Print.
Shigematsu, Kiyoshi. 2013, *Mata tsugi no haru e*. Tokyo: Fusōsha.
Shiotsuka, Yume. 2013, "Hon no hanashi o shiyō: Inochi ni taisuru kokoro no mochikata ga towareteiru 'Zōn ni te' sakka Taguchi Randisan." *MNS Sankei Nyūzu* October 6, at: http://sankei.jp.msn.com/life/news/130610/bks13061014310000-n1.htms. (accessed March 10, 2014).
Slater, David H., Rika, Morioka, and Haruka, Danzuka. 2014, "Micro-politics of radiation: Young mothers looking for a voice in Post–3.11 Fukushima." *Critical Asian Studies* Vol. 46, No. 3: 485–508.
*Speeches and Statements by the Prime Minister*. 2013, "Presentation by Prime Minister Shinzo Abe at the 125th Session of the International Olympic Committee (IOC)." September 7, at: http://japan.kantei.go.jp/96_abe/statement/201309/07ioc_presentation_e.html (accessed November 20, 2014).
Stallings, Michael. 2011, "Japan's aging population: What emergency response lessons will we learn from the Tōhoku earthquake and tsunami?" *University of Maryland Center for Health and Homeland Security*, March 24, at: www.mdchhs.com/japan-s-aging-population-what-emergency-response-lessons-will-we-learn-from-the-tohoku-earthquake-and-tsunami/ (accessed August 18, 2014).
Tabuchi, Hiroko. 2014, "Reversing course, Japan makes push to restart dormant nuclear plants." *The New York Times* February 25, at: www.nytimes.com/2014/02/26/world/asia/japan-pushes-to-revive-moribund-nuclear-energy-sector.html (accessed December 4, 2014).
Taguchi, Randy. 2006, *Yorubenaki jidai no kibō: hito wa shinu no ni naze ikiru no ka*. Tokyo: Shunjūsha.
Taguchi, Randy. 2011, *Hiroshima, Nagasaki, Fukushima: genshiryoku o ukeireta Nihon*. Tokyo: Chikuma Shobō.
Taguchi, Randy. 2013a, "Zōn ni te." *Zōn ni te*. Tokyo: Bungei Shunjū, 7–65.
Taguchi, Randy. 2013b, "Zōn ni te II." *Zōn ni te*. Tokyo: Bungei hunjū, 69–112.
Treat, John Whittier. 1995, *Writing Ground Zero : Japanese Literature and the Atomic Bomb*. Chicago, IL: University of Chicago Press.
*Voices from the Disaster Area*. n.d., at: www.nhk.or.jp/sendai/hisaichikara/ (accessed December 12, 2014).
Yoshikawa, Yasuhisa, ed. 2012, *Shinsai to fikushon no "kyori": Ruptured Fiction(s) of the Earthquake*. Tokyo: Waseda Bungakukai.

# 3 *Summertime Blues*
## Musical critique in the aftermaths of Japan's 'dark spring'

*Scott W. Aalgaard*

### Introduction[1]

On December 31, 2011, much of Japan sat glued to its television sets and radios, watching, listening as the 62nd annual NHK *Kōhaku uta gassen* (Red & White Song Contest) unfurled its glittering pageantry from NHK Hall in Tokyo. The *Kōhaku* is a yearly, five-hour, live-broadcast popular music extravaganza, showcasing some of the most noteworthy (in NHK's eyes, at least) musical acts and artists of the concluding year, and presenting its audience with an opportunity to consume, in digest form, 'Japan's music' from the year gone by—music that, compiled as it is by Japan's public broadcaster, is usually ensconced in some wider message about the state of Japan, or of Japan's place in the world.

And on this particular New Year's Eve, there was plenty to talk about, much to be addressed. The 2011 installment of the *Kōhaku* was particularly highly anticipated because of the multiple tragedies of March 11: many eagerly tuned in to see how the venerable broadcast(er) would respond to Japan's triple (and ongoing) disasters. From a video montage of children born on March 11, to an onstage reproduction of major Tōhoku-area (the region most impacted by 3.11) festivals set to *enka*[2] performances by Hosokawa Takashi and Fuji Ayako, to Mori Shin'ichi's sad warbling about Japan's port cities (including several lost to 3.11's tsunami), Japan's devastated northeast took center stage throughout. The seemingly ubiquitous and, by then, already rather worn-out mantra of *Ganbarō Nippon* (Chin Up, Japan!)—so oft heard in the days and weeks immediately following 3.11, and which continues to haunt many of those affected to this day[3]— could be detected throughout the *Kōhaku*, undergirding its theme of 'Sing of Tomorrow' and all but demanding that Tōhoku pull itself up by its bootstraps and get on with things. Nowhere was this more apparent than in the performance of the Funky Monkey Babys [*sic*], who sang their stirring *Soredemo shinjiteru* [I Still Believe] backed by a hyper-energized university cheer squad clad in starched black student uniforms and armed with fluttering flags and pumping fists, both groups performing against the almost palpably hot glare of a digitized mock-up of a shimmering rising sun.

The 2011 *Kōhaku* seemed, in other words, to insist upon presenting a particular vision of a unified 'Japan,' one girded by the experience of shared tragedy and a common resolve to move toward the future. This is no surprise—indeed, as Brunt (2003) teaches us, the *Kōhaku* has long demonstrated a commitment to presenting certain conceptualizations of 'community' and 'unity.' But if we pause to consider 2011's *Kōhaku* with a slightly more critical eye, it soon becomes apparent that, for all of its emphasis on the events of 3.11, the 'unity' and 'community' conjured by NHK that evening were not outcomes of the triple disasters of Japan's dark spring at all, but rather a supposed 'original reality' that was understood as having *pre-dated* the crises, and that demanded a restoration of sorts. In other words, the crises seemed, in this important musical statement on the state of 'Japan,' to be rendered a momentary sideswipe, a blip, a harbinger of heartbreak, and death, and pain, to be sure, but ultimately something that could not disturb the predestined nature of 'Japan'-as-community, or, as I will suggest below, as History.[4] Catch-phrases like *Ganbarō Nippon* and its successor, *kizuna* (bonds, emotional ties), were granted the mystique of magical words, capable of healing hearts and earth, of making the crises go away and returning the nation to its regularly scheduled programming. What these magic words managed (and continue to manage) to conceal, in other words, was any consideration of just how deep the tectonic fissures revealed by 3.11 may actually run.

In the immediate aftermath of the triple disasters of March 11, Karatani Kojin (2011) suggested that: "[i]t is not Japan's demise that the earthquake has produced, but rather the possibility of its rebirth. It may be that only amid the ruins can people gain the courage to stride down a new path." It seems to me that Karatani may have sensed "amid the ruins" a way to disturb 'Japan' as History, manifested in that universalized narrative of preordained (capitalist) belonging lamented by Harry Harootunian as "Japan's Japan" (Miyoshi and Harootunian 1993: 196). What his hopeful vision seems to invoke is the revolutionary potential of what Bergson (1911: 324), Deleuze and Guattari (1987: 238), and others have called *becoming*, that constant, situationally-specific, affect-driven process of turning-into, a process that both informs and that is key to any meaningful understanding of the social context(s) in which it unfolds. "Becoming," of course, "produces nothing other than itself. [...] What is real is the becoming itself, the block of becoming, not the supposedly fixed terms through which that which becomes passes" (Deleuze and Guattari 1987: 238). But "supposedly fixed terms" like 'Japan' cannot simply be ignored: they are in fact vital to the whole equation. Post-3.11 Tōhoku is a potential hotbed for unpredictable becoming *precisely because* the sheer violence of the upheavals there has shaken the dust off of assumptions concerning the nature of things like 'community,' 'belonging,' and 'Japan,' and has rendered these "supposedly fixed terms" susceptible to radical rearrangement and redefinition. It is exactly these "fixed terms" which, as the constituting agents of the conceptual corridors through which we pass, are always already in a position of impacting—*affecting* (Massumi 2002: 23–45)—the one-becoming. In a sort of feedback loop (Novak 2013), the ways in which "fixed terms" like 'Japan' are confronted can provide a framework by which one's actual experiences living therein can be gauged, and the nature of that affective experience prompts one, in turn, to critique those terms (or not), destabilizing them, and sometimes driving a fluidity of becoming that can propel a positing of 'Japan' according to new and different terms. This becomes nothing less than a critique of History itself—and it was precisely such a critique that was disavowed amid the fervent assertion of originary reality that permeated the 2011 *Kōhaku*.

As scholars have repeatedly shown us, music and becoming are inextricably intertwined; NHK was thus ultimately attempting an impossibility when it tried to posit an originary 'Japan' that could be returned to by overcoming 3.11 through music. But what the attempt serves to highlight is precisely that which evades capture, and there seems much to be gained by directing our critical gaze toward the very fluidity and context (DeNora 2004; Finnegan 2003) that the *Kōhaku*, intentionally or not, disavowed. I thus want to respond to NHK's (static) deployment of music on the 2011 *Kōhaku*, and to address different forms of *musical critique* that have been amplified—though not engendered—by the upheavals of 3.11. What I refer to as 'musical critique' herein should be understood as the critical reassessment, through music, of some of the constitutive elements and assumptions—the "supposedly fixed terms"—that inform this realm called the social, a praxis whose end result can involve bouncing the one-becoming into radically new directions. 'Japan' as History, through such critique, can be thoroughly destabilized, and re-envisioned according to new and different terms—and this, it seems to me, is simultaneously one of the great promises and lurking dangers of the events of 3.11, and speaks directly to what Karatani had in mind when he wrote of "new paths." With this in mind, the purpose of this chapter is to consider how the events of March 11, 2011, situated firmly within historicity, provided an impetus for the amplification of a (musical) critique that had little to do with the restoration of the sort of dubious 'community' and 'unity' implied in fuzzy and imprecise terms like *kizuna* and *Ganbarō Nippon*, and apparently insisted upon by NHK in the 2011 installment of the *Kōhaku*. I want to step back and consider, via the medium of the voices themselves engaged in ongoing processes of becoming, what sort(s) of "new paths" these sorts of critique may lead us down.

My aim here is not to add to the literature describing the ways in which musicians have critiqued nuclear power (for example) in works released in the aftermaths of 3.11. Rather, I want to adopt a stance that is ultimately *critical* of the tendency to privilege 3.11 as the defining criterion driving cultural production in the wake of the crises (an approach that threatens the very sort of contextual isolation and dehistoricization for which I've already critiqued NHK), and explore how we might *peer through* specific musical responses in order to pick up the traces of longer critical praxes concerning the fixed terms of 'Japan.' Such praxes may have been altered, enhanced, or clarified by the historical specificities of 3.11, but they always represent longer, always-unfurling paths of critical 'becoming': situating 3.11 as a key *waypoint* on the critical paths of the artists to be discussed below also allows us to envision post-3.11 musical critique as more than a simple pushing back against some of the entities viewed as perpetuators of the ongoing misery of Japan's dark spring—the state, for example, or TEPCO, the power utility responsible for operations at Fukushima Daiichi—and in fact demands that we view critique as an intensely ambiguous enterprise, capable of, despite the best intentions of the artists involved, fostering structures of feeling that threaten to steer 'Japan' straight back into the conditions that helped to potentiate this crisis in the first place. With this caveat in mind, then, let us commence our journey by engaging one of contemporary Japan's most intriguing musical minds—Saitō Kazuyoshi.

## Rattling cages: Saitō Kazuyoshi and the nuclear village

Saitō Kazuyoshi (b. 1966), a singer-songwriter from Tochigi Prefecture (which borders Fukushima Prefecture), made his debut onto the professional Japanese music scene with the release of his 1993 single, *Boku no mita Beatles wa TV no naka* [The Beatles I saw were on the TV]. Saitō started playing the guitar in sixth grade, and the guitar has remained his primary medium ever since—becoming a singer was never something that Saitō had envisioned, but it is hard to imagine him today without his trademark smooth-but-raspy tenor, giving voice to the experiences and frustrations of (his) everyday. In 1992, prodded and encouraged by family members, Saitō, having by then dropped out of university to pursue music in Tokyo, submitted an audition to a TBS 'star search' program, and the rest, as they say, is history.

Since 3.11, Saitō's name has become synonymous with what is perceived as a new emergence of so-called 'protest songs,' largely understood as dealing specifically with the crises that have been focused upon the Fukushima Daiichi Nuclear Power Station in the wake of the meltdowns there. Indeed, Saitō's *Zutto uso datta* [It was a lie all along] has proven to be a foundational contribution to this musical trend, and we will examine this song in some detail below. In order to conceive of Saitō's work more productively, however, we must first understand that music, for Saitō Kazuyoshi, is more than a means of responding to specific events—it is an *extension of his engagement with daily life* (Tsumabaki *et al.* 2014: 143). Despite his current reputation as a so-called 'message singer,' the artist insists that it is self-expression that is of the utmost importance in his musical praxis (Tsumabaki *et al.* 2014: 134). Indeed, in conversation with Tsumabaki Satoshi in 2012, Saitō explained how he is unable to "sing fiction" (Tsumabaki *et al.* 2014: 144), by which he seems to mean the sort of bubbly, feel-good songs which tend to dominate Japan's popular music charts. Rather, for Saitō, the process of composition is a form of therapy, a means by which he can grapple with the stresses and frustrations of the world.

In a November 2011 interview with the online news service *livedoor*, Saitō alluded to his more blatantly critical works—including *Zutto uso datta*—as habitual sorts of "gripes" (*guchi*; *livedoor NEWS* 2011) on his part, which must be understood as being situated along an arc of dissatisfaction with the world that both precedes and follows the crises at Fukushima Daiichi. In the interview, Saitō seems to bristle at the suggestion that he is the writer of 'message songs':

"I've never so much as listened properly to a so-called 'message song'," he says. "I don't really like those sorts of preachy, formalistic (*kata-kurushii*), fist-pumping things anyway. On the other hand, though, asked if I preferred songs with no message at all, that wouldn't be the case either" (*livedoor NEWS* 2011). It seems that Saitō is pointing here to the importance of a critique that does not rely on an established theme or form or structure, but that is rather directly related to the artist's own engagement with the world, and that serves to give voice to his "gripes." In the end, according to Saitō, the best that he can hope for is for as many people to commiserate with him on those points of complaint as possible (Tsumabaki *et al.* 2014: 144–45). It is this sort of critique as lived experience that seems to have informed Saitō Kazuyoshi's artistic expression from the outset, and realizing this is precisely what allows us to move beyond seeing his post-3.11 musical commentary as an isolated reaction to a single set of events, and to begin to sense a more expansive critical praxis lurking behind and informing his responses to 3.11—one that cannot be defined as abiding solely within the moment of the onset of the crises itself.

Although Saitō Kazuyoshi resists being identified as a writer of 'message songs,' then, we can sense that this may have more to do with a desire to distance himself from (what he sees as) a sort of musical medium called the 'message song' that hovers somewhere above the plane of everyday life than with a reluctance to engage with social questions per se. Indeed, one need not look much farther than many of Saitō's musical influences and engagements to get a sense of the artist's stance vis-à-vis the role of music in society. Along with bands like the Rolling Stones and the Beatles, for example, Saitō lists heavy-hitting social commentators like Tom Waits, Izumiya Shigeru, and Bob Dylan among his key inspirations (Isaka and Saitō 2007: 95). He has also been a regularly invited performer in the annual (from 2001–2013, at least—the event was on temporary hiatus in 2014) *John Lennon Super Live*, a charity event organized by Lennon's widow Yoko Ono and held on December 8, the anniversary of Lennon's death (Isaka and Saitō 2007: 76). The names of some of the other performers in this concert series read like an A-list of artists variously engaged with social questions in Japan: notable are personalities like Inoue Yōsui, Yuzu, Sakamoto Ryūichi—and Imawano Kiyoshirō. Kiyoshirō, who died in 2009 at the age of fifty-eight, bringing a too-early end to a thirty-nine-year performance career, was one of contemporary Japan's most powerful and influential musical voices, a razor-sharp social critic in his own right, and was much loved by Saitō Kazuyoshi (musical elegies to him appear in albums such as 2011's *45 Stones*). Kiyoshirō is particularly well known as having a sharp critical tongue vis-à-vis matters of the Japanese social (and the nuclear village itself),[5] and is "tied to a revolutionary becoming that is not to be confused with the history of revolutions" (Endo 2012: 1032). There seems, in short, to be something that this disciple of Kiyoshirō wants to say—but we must move *beyond* the contextual moment of 3.11 to hear his voice (and indeed his response to 3.11) clearly.

It may be helpful to revisit here Saitō's concept of *guchi*, or "gripes," touched upon briefly above. As we have already seen, "gripes" in Saitō Kazuyoshi's compositional praxis seem to arise from a dissatisfaction with the world, a nagging, haunting sense that something is wrong. This dissatisfaction seems to be the result of a direct critical engagement with the world that Saitō apparently works hard to maintain,[6] and it is, I want to suggest, precisely this sort of dissatisfaction that has constituted the foundational condition for the writing of *Zutto uso datta*. What Saitō is encountering in his engagements with the world are, it seems, precisely the terms and conditions of life in contemporary (capitalist) Japan,[7] and the choices that are made in the quest to secure 'survival' and 'shelter.'[8] Although we are unable to review Saitō's library in any detail here, brief mention might be made of the 1997 album *Jirenma* [Dilemma], which sports an intriguing cover photo featuring Saitō dressed as a samurai, wielding a guitar instead of a sword (an image inviting an interpretation of the artist as "taking on the world with just a guitar" [Isaka and Saitō 2007: 57]). From the first track of the album, a rushed, noisy, and somehow angry song[9] that berates Tokyo, the center of 'Japan' as "fixed terms," as a "developing *zoo* [my emphasis]" in which abide characters such as an elderly individual (we do not know whether s/he is male or female) sleeping in the shade of a tree with flies crawling upon his or her eyes (clearly suggesting homelessness or even death), to the eighth (intriguingly titled *Susume Namakemono* [Press On! O Lazy One]), which seems simultaneously to cite the precarity and struggle faced by those unwilling or unable to match the pace of the terms of survival in contemporary Japan[10] and to voice a determination to reject those very terms in favor of pursuing what Harootunian (2006) might call 'other histories' (an optimism reflected in the work's gentle-yet-steady rhythmic flow and smooth vocal delivery), this album appears to present several indictments of the consequences of capitalist unevenness. By no means do I intend to suggest that Saitō Kazuyoshi's artistic priorities abide in the promotion of tired ("preachy and formalistic," in his words) attempts at 'revolution' (a problematic term at best) or in the overturning of 'capitalism,' and we know from the artist's own comments that he would vigorously resist being hemmed in as a so-called message singer of any stripe. But we also know that, for Saitō, music is about embeddedness in lived experience, and that his critique comes from engagement with the world. Put somewhat differently, perhaps, the object of Saitō's critique seems very much to be the History of 'Japan' as "fixed terms"—and, as Endo teaches us, History is nothing but capitalism itself (Endo 2012: 1032).

This, then, is Saitō Kazuyoshi's stance (Berger 2009), and it is only with this stance in mind that we can productively consider the first of the artist's specific responses to 3.11 (more would come later, particularly in the aforementioned *45 Stones*). Saitō's thirty-sixth single, released in April 2010, was titled *Zutto suki datta* [I loved you all along], and it was this song that Saitō, clad in sunglasses in a sly nod of sorts to the stealth with which critique must often assert itself (no doubt informed at least in part by an awareness of the difficulties faced by Kiyoshirō's band RC Succession when that group attempted to release its own critique of nuclear power in the form of a revamped version of Eddie Cochrane's *Summertime Blues* [Manabe 2012]), revamped in a bitingly critical self-cover and unleashed via the Internet on April 7, 2011. The song has since earned wide recognition as a symbol of post-Fukushima angst, but there is more at stake here than the simple vocalization of anger and dismay on the part of the artist. As a "gripe" borne of a dissatisfaction with the world, *Zutto uso datta* clearly takes its place on the longer arc of Saitō's critique, but also, as I will suggest below, seems to extend this critique toward a praxis of action, aimed at clearing a space for change. As such, the work constitutes musical critique par excellence—and it sets its sights squarely on destabilizing the "fixed terms" Japan's so-called nuclear village, which we might now view as the definitive representation of 'Japan' as History.

The crises of 3.11 have, if nothing else, served to strip this chameleon-esque nuclear village of its camouflage and throw it into high relief. An incestual sort of "network [that] includes the scientific establishment, mainstream media, think-tanks and advisory bodies [to say nothing of the state itself]" (Matanle 2011: 838), the nuclear village has had a profound influence on post-war Japanese society through its hegemonic generation of what Valentine (Valentine and Sovacool 2010: 7971–79) calls a "prevalent ideology of self-sacrifice," rooted in a nationalized narrative of working as a unified communal body—under the leadership of the state—to support Japan's economic growth through enduring the "necessity" of nuclear power (Karatani 2011). It has been, in short, one of the great "supposedly fixed terms" of the (capitalist) Japanese social since the 1970s or so, and particularly in the northeast, where it was implicated in a devil's bargain of sorts for survival itself. With its bitter condemnation of power officials as "assholes," direct attacks on government, and descriptions of a life disrupted, however, *Zutto uso datta* has set out to demolish the credibility of the nuclear village itself, thus disrupting the "fixed terms" of History and positing an "exhilaratingly damaged" (Gilroy 1993: 101) conceptualization thereof through which new directionality might be envisioned. Even the manner in which Saitō initially chose to unleash this work on the world—via a disguised Internet appearance, as opposed to through the usual channels of the mainstream media, itself a part of the nuclear village—is evidence of this. Though the move is likely symbolic (the artist has gone on to release more singles and albums via major labels), Saitō seems to present himself in this particular instance as no longer trusting the media apparatus of which he himself has been a part. It is no longer credible.

Saitō's critique of the nuclear village as a critique of History writ large is set up in the very opening line of this work. While the crisis at Fukushima may have provided the impetus for *Zutto uso datta*, that is not where the artist starts his journey—and in fact, 'Fukushima' is never isolated for exclusive mention in the song at all. Rather, the problem is one of "this country": "[s]trolling through *this country*, you'll come across 54 nuclear reactors," Saitō sings, already situating his critique as extending beyond the specific context of Fukushima itself. He further sets up the scope of his criticism by placing "[t]he textbooks and the commercial messages" side by side on the very next line, indicting the complicity of education and the state in capitalism, and furiously lamenting the manner in which "they deceived us." And this is, ultimately, the point of the song: as its title insists, "it was a lie all along." Many of the proponents of the "fixed terms" of 'Japan' since around-1970 are lined up for explicit indictment here: education, "[t]he government of this land," and multiple utility conglomerates ("Tokyo Electric, Hokkaido Electric, Chubu Electric, and Kyushu Electric, too"—the list changes depending on performance) all face Saitō's wrath. But I wish to stress here once again that Saitō's project in *Zutto uso datta* seems to exceed the fact of finding fault in a specific historical instance: rather, through this work, the artist seems interested in rewriting (= critiquing) History itself. The officials have been "assholes," after all, and the narrative of nuclear safety itself has been a lie, *all along*. By rattling the cages of 'Japan' as History, in short, Saitō prepares the ground for imagining it according to different terms.

In an extended 2007 round-table discussion with author Isaka Kōtarō, Saitō Kazuyoshi voiced a disdain for the "promotional videos" (PV) that are, in his view, a necessary evil of music promotion in Japan (Isaka and Saitō 2007: 95). Rather than relying upon the visual, he insists, the music should "speak for itself." This disdain was in plain sight in the release of *Zutto uso datta*—the initial video release of the work (a second version, incidentally, would stream online the very next day, when Saitō worked it into his weekly post-3.11 charity Internet broadcast, hosted on UStream) was sparse and simplistic, grainy and exquisitely unprofessional, and one could not even be sure in this first version that the figure singing was in fact Saitō Kazuyoshi himself (there was no mistaking his identity in the UStream version, although it was equally sparse and simple, if less grainy). All attention, in other words, was directed to the voice and the guitar. By deflecting attention from both himself and the general distractions of slickly-polished promotional videos, Saitō seems to be deploying his music as a medium that can "speak for itself" through mixing with the experiences of the world endured by individual actors engaged in their own processes of 'becoming' in the post-3.11 moment—and particularly by those in Fukushima. While *Zutto uso datta* may be a *guchi* on the part of Saitō Kazuyoshi, in other words, it certainly appears to be one that he hopes will be commiserated with by individual social actors as the music trickles into and mixes with their own realities. In the process, the music, perhaps, becomes *corrosive*, damaging assumptions over the nature of History that may have been held by those who deploy it in their own daily lives.

Although Saitō's original video was removed from the sharing site shortly after it was posted, at the request of Victor, the artist's record label, both it and the UStream version have since found their way onto YouTube and various other video hosting sites, and the song has become something of a protest anthem (though a controversial one) amidst the ongoing nuclear crisis in Fukushima. And as a musical critique, it is busily rearranging and undermining Deleuze and Guattari's "supposedly fixed terms" of the social—here, the 'givenness' of the nuclear village—realigning them in ways that may bring us closer to a realization of Karatani's vision. The work's real potential, perhaps, lies in its ability to produce what Grossberg (1997) has called 'affective alliances' among individuals involved in their own destabilizing praxes—*Zutto uso datta* served as a theme song for the mass Kōenji (Tokyo) rally against nuclear power held on April 10, 2011, and continues to galvanize audiences at concerts and rock festivals nationwide (including at emotionally-charged performances within Fukushima itself). It perhaps goes without saying, then, that Saitō Kazuyoshi was most definitely not invited to perform on the 2011 installation of the *Kōhaku*.

Composition, Saitō Kazuyoshi once said, is nothing exclusive. Mothers, for example, do it all the time, humming and whistling tunes as they put dinner together in the kitchen for their families, and so on (Tsumabaki *et al*. 2014). This assertion—with Saitō's views on the importance of the embeddedness of music and its messages in daily life, and his resistance toward being cast as "messenger," in mind—demands our attention. For if Saitō Kazuyoshi can riff off of his own work to spin up new levels of critique in *Zutto uso datta*, then individual voices engaging with his work can do the same. What happens when a housewife in Iwaki (just down the coast from Fukushima Daiichi), or a truck driver in Satsumasendai (home to Kyushu Electric Power Co.'s Sendai Nuclear Power Plant, currently [as of December, 2015] the only online nuclear power station in Japan) hums *Zutto uso datta* under their breath as they go about their daily routine? What sorts of alternate 'Japans' might be envisioned in those moments of composition, unfolding amidst specific historic and geographical contexts? If post-3.11 musical critique was for Saitō Kazuyoshi about rattling Japan's cages in the form of a demolition of the credibility of the nuclear village, it has been more specifically re-constitutive of 'Japan' for others. It is to this form of musical critique that I shall now turn—and I will appeal to one of Japan's heaviest-hitting rock voices to do so.

## Becoming 'one': Nagabuchi Tsuyoshi and the (ambiguous) potentials of alternative 'Japans'

Nagabuchi Tsuyoshi (b. 1956) is one of contemporary Japan's most influential and important artists. Known primarily for his prowess as a singer-songwriter and, contemporarily, as a hard-driving rock star, Nagabuchi has also been a prolific calligrapher and painter, an actor on both the big and small screens, and more recently, a martial artist. Born and raised in Kagoshima Prefecture, Nagabuchi worked to hone his own acoustic guitar and harmonica styles amidst the folk boom of the late 1960s and early 1970s, and became active as a composer and performer in the bars and 'live houses' of Kyushu in the middle years of the decade. After successful showings at the 1976 and 1978 installments of the Yamaha Popular Song Contest (known as *Popukon*, a competition in composition that ran from 1969 through 1986, and that would prove to be pivotal to the establishment of the careers of many of Japan's premier musical names), the artist who would be known in history as Nagabuchi Tsuyoshi[11] made his official debut onto Japan's professional music scene with the release of the ballad *Junrenka* [Roundabout Love] in October 1978.

During the more than thirty years which have passed between *Junrenka* and the release of the post-3.11 *Hitotsu* [One], to be discussed below, Nagabuchi has consistently refused to be artistically pinned down. He started his career as a wispy, long-haired (folk) singer of love and heartbreak, but it didn't take long for his art to take on a much sharper edge. By 1983, Nagabuchi's sound was beginning to shift toward pop-rock, and individual works featuring commentary on broader historical and social issues were beginning to creep into his LPs.[12] By 1987, as Japan's bubble economy was beginning to run white-hot, Nagabuchi had fully embarked upon what might be called his 'inward turn,' which was characterized by critical meditations on the status of 'Japan,' his own home (*furusato*) of Kagoshima, and the position(s) of himself and his compatriots vis-à-vis each. This 'inward turn' seems to have been fully established by around 1990 (crucially, just as Japan's bubble economy was reaching its zenith): musically, it is characterized by a coupling of the (often harsh) grain of Nagabuchi's voice with a thrumming, high-powered acoustic-guitar-and-harmonica combination, a sound that has become one of Nagabuchi's trademarks and that is extremely effective at transmitting a certain angst or frustration, which often targets particular conceptualizations of 'Japan.' Indeed, though his artistry has continued to evolve, Nagabuchi has persisted in a critical engagement with the concept of 'Japan' that is probably unparalleled in its complexity in contemporary Japanese popular music, and this critique presents significant implications for the ways in which we might understand the artist's responses to the crises in Tōhoku.

Nagabuchi's engagement with 3.11 shares with Saitō's, then, a pre-existing sense that there is something amiss in 'Japan.' In order to grapple effectively with *Hitotsu*, we must first reach beyond 3.11 for hints revealing what this 'something' might be. Notable works such as 1990's *O-uchi e kaerō* [Head on home], for example, explicitly deride a "shitty Japanese-style capitalism" and consumerism (presented in the form of a Seven-Eleven convenience store), as its chorus sings of an intent to literally "piss on" the National Diet Buildings at Nagatachō as the narrator "head[s] on home." In 1991 *Oyashirazu* [Wisdom teeth], meanwhile, pleads with "Japan, my homeland" to not (literally) "melt into America." "Money? Sure, I want money!" howls Nagabuchi in this work. "But no matter how much we make, no matter how much piles up, there are some things that I just won't give up." Musically, both of these works are characterized by precisely the 'angry' sort of guitar-harmonica-voice triad that I have already introduced above, helping to lend a strong sense to these works that there is something seriously wrong with the "fixed terms" by which 'Japan' had come to be defined in the 1980s and 1990s. That something, it seems, has much to do with (global) capitalism, and the way(s) in which it is seen (by the artist) as alienating Japan(ese) not from a mythical lost moment of purity, but rather from alternative potentials for life and belonging as 'Japan[ese].' Remedying this, for Nagabuchi, does not lie solely in destabilizing the "fixed terms" of 'Japan,' the strategy pursued by Saitō Kazuyoshi. As I've already suggested, there is a strongly *reimaginative* aspect to Nagabuchi's musical critique—and the artist relies upon the discursive concept of 'Japan' itself (the dominant conceptual apparatus of Nagabuchi's historical moment, as Harootunian [1993] teaches us) to pursue this. It is precisely such a re-imaginative project that seems to present itself in *Hitotsu*.

*Hitotsu* was the first new work to be released by Nagabuchi in the aftermaths of 3.11, and were it not for our intertextual understanding of his priorities and past artistic endeavors, we may find ourselves hard-pressed to see this work as a musical critique per se. Indeed, with its gentle piano-and-strings framework and tender delivery (though punctuated in key spots—such as the lead-in to the chorus—with a strained grain of voice that has remained an important indicator of critique over the course of Nagabuchi's career), *Hitotsu* seems, at first listen, to be a simple song of love: and on many levels, it is. The lyrics of the work have the narrator searching for *kimi* (an affectionate form of 'you'), a vague object of longing who is neither male nor female and who is (importantly) never explicitly identified, but whose name is not difficult to reveal, especially in the context of the song's promotional video, which foregrounds footage of a booted Nagabuchi walking across a vast, snowy landscape into mountainous terrain clearly meant to represent Tōhoku. The search, apparently, was a long one ("I walked on and on"), and unfurled through the dark, "as the stars fell from the sky." When *kimi* (Tōhoku) is finally found, however, Nagabuchi/the narrator apparently has little interest in dwelling upon the difficult questions concerning the "sadness" of the initial separation—"No matter how much I think, I can't find an answer [for where the sadness comes from, or where it goes]," sings the narrator. "So, I've decided just to embrace it." Crucially, the emphasis here is on feeling and sentiment as the ointments suturing the scars of separation (we shall revisit the concept of sentiment briefly below). *Hitotsu*, in short, is a work about overcoming *alienation*: the artist, it seems, aims to achieve this by "[b]ecoming one" with Tōhoku within the discursive confines of 'Japan,' and there to "be together always, living side by side." Indeed, it is none other than Tōhoku itself that Nagabuchi addresses when he sings: "I'm sorry to have left you/All alone/ Never again will I let you go, or leave your side."

*Hitotsu* is multi-layered and challenging to read. On one hand, Nagabuchi is clearly singing to the historical specificity of 3.11. But on the other, his call to become-One cannot be disentangled from the longer threads of his critique, which, as we have seen, has targeted the "fixed terms" of History and posited a praxis of re-imagining an alternative 'Japan' that can no longer be subjected to the pain of alienation from itself. The very vagueness of the *kimi* constituting the object of Nagabuchi's love in this work allows the artist's hail to reach far and wide, throughout Tōhoku—and beyond. And perhaps paradoxically, when we abandon our fixation on the supposed generative conditions of 3.11 itself on this work, we begin to see how the myriad facets of the crisis—specifically, for our purposes, the meltdowns at Fukushima Daiichi—may have affected Nagabuchi in terms of his broader critique of the alienating capacities of capitalism, and thus how the work may fit into a broader critical narrative aimed at challenging History.

*Hitotsu* is not a Fukushima-specific work—as we have seen, it seems to address Tōhoku as a whole, even as the object of its hail is left vague. Its fixation on sentiment and the wide net that the work casts open interesting (though ambiguous) possibilities for individuals responding thereto in locales far beyond the northeast. But the nature and implications of the One that the artist imagines can only be approached by attending to the manner in which Fukushima haunts both this work, and (retrospectively) Nagabuchi's broader critical praxis. The situation in Fukushima has been particularly troubling to Nagabuchi: he was among the first public figures to deliver critical commentary from the very edge of the exclusion zone itself (on a March 2012 live broadcast of the news program *Hōdō Station*, he declared that the crisis had led him to "feel betrayed by Japan" [*Nikkan Sports* 2012]), and has released songs grieving the displacement of individuals from their homes in affected areas such as Namie (mere kilometers from the plants). Perhaps most telling, however, were the comments made by the artist during a concert in his hometown of Kagoshima in 2012, where he declared that "what is generated by those nuclear power plants is not energy. What is generated there is *money*" (Yukawa 2012). Here we can see the manner in which Nagabuchi's response to 3.11 ties into his pre-existing critique of capitalism, and we begin to glimpse the possibility that the long search for *kimi* may be as much about rescuing Tōhoku (yet not only Tōhoku) from the alienation/precarity attending global capitalist modernity as it is about finding fellowship in times of natural disaster.

*Hitotsu*, it seems, fits into a broader project aimed at bringing about change through attempting to jump-start a communal sort of intentional becoming (an integral part of the project pursued by Nagabuchi since at least 2004, though something not really possible in Bergson's [1911] formulation) and delegitimizing the "fixed terms" of 'Japan' as History—and this project has often traversed Kagoshima. I have already mentioned the important (and ambivalent) role played by Kagoshima in Nagabuchi's artistry: it lurks as an important site (both physical and conceptual) informing and potentiating the change that the artist envisions. Despite its ambivalence, in other words, Kagoshima has persisted as a site of alternative possibilities, a place from which a critique of the wider space of 'Japan' might be potentiated. Indeed, other key works, such as *Kibai-yanse* (Fight It Out; the only work by Nagabuchi has composed entirely in the Kagoshima dialect) offer a vision of community that is potentiated precisely through an embracing of a certain 'decadence' (Sakaguchi 2010) (marking an important contrast with conservatives and their concern for 'morality' [Kaihara 2009]) and a rejection of many of Japan's "fixed terms," thereby inviting a certain becoming-Kagoshima that promises to displace the fixed terms of 'Japan' with a new Kagoshima nation. Crucially, this project has been pursued through the mounting of massive "musical events" (DeNora 2003: 57) such as the artist's then career-topping, all-night concert on Kagoshima's Sakurajima in 2004, thus revealing the way in which Nagabuchi sees coming together in a sort of 'affective alliance,' or becoming-One, as a key vehicle for change. Nagabuchi, it seems, aims to overcome precarity—including consequences of capitalist modernity—by tying 'Japan' together in structures of sentiment.

As Wedeen (2008) has pointed out, national sentiment does not simply 'exist'—it is always *performed*, and the nature of this performance and the imagining that informs it is of great interest here. But it is also a matter of great ambiguity. On the one hand, as we have already noted, Nagabuchi's critique has revolved around indictments of capitalist modernity and of the state itself. While there are clearly some echoes of conservative thought in Nagabuchi's work—especially in his critique of political economy (Kaihara 2009: 358)—the artist's stance is quite the reverse of that of the conservative: despite appearances,[13] he does not seek a return to "monuments of the past" (Boym 2001: 41) in the form of lost moments of purity or morality. Rather, it is forward movement, a constantly-unfurling communal "becoming" that can lead somewhere new, that characterizes Nagabuchi's vision ("I am neither right nor left," the artist [2005] once said—"I go straight ahead!"). The 'nation' obviously lurks herein (not necessarily surprising, since, as Boellstorff writes, "resistance [to hegemonic state narratives] often takes the form of transformation rather than rejection" [Boellstorff 2005: 154–55]), but its implications depend entirely upon how it is imagined and performed, and this has yet to be played out. As Karatani (2014) teaches us, the 'nation,' as a structure of feeling that arises as surrogate form of (imagined) community when actual community is destroyed at the hands of the coupling of capital-state, is certainly complicit in solidification of the hegemony thereof (conceived of as the triad capital-nation-state). But it also represents an important form of resistance to capital-state's terms, and it may be precisely from here—from a troubling of the narratives of [H]istory precisely where they appear to be left untouched—that Karatani's "higher form" of belonging emerges (Karatani 2014: 27).

In recent years, the conceptual and physical locus of Nagabuchi's critical project has shifted more explicitly from Kagoshima to 'Japan' itself, as was vividly illustrated through the massive, all-night outdoor concert mounted by the artist at the base of Mount Fuji in August 2015. And as the emphasis on critique and "other histories" at this event helped to clarify, Nagabuchi's interest lies not in the promotion of a closed sort of nationalism, but rather in the formulation of what I have elsewhere termed an "alternative collective," one that continues to deploy the national pronoun and symbolism, but that is in fact radically open and inclusive, and intentionally toxic to "Japan's Japan," or 'Japan' as History. This is an exceedingly tricky line to walk, however, and indeed, alongside this intriguing critique, we must also grapple with the fact that a number of Nagabuchi's support activities in the aftermaths of 3.11 have been directed toward *agents of the state itself*, despite his critique of the state on other fronts, and despite its culpability, as we have noted above, in the nuclear village. Along with launching programs aimed at supporting children in Fukushima and hosting a Tōhoku regional radio program intended to voice a sort of moral support for those in the affected regions, for example, Nagabuchi also mounted live performances in hard-hit regions such as Iwate that were intended to encourage the Self-Defense Forces troops (whom he has publicly lauded as the 'pride of Japan') involved in recovery duties there. On December 20, 2011, he accepted an official Special Commendation from Japan's Ministry of Defense at a ceremony in Tokyo, the first musician in modern history to receive such recognition. Now, as I hope that the preceding comments have made clear, Nagabuchi's position vis-à-vis 'Japan' is highly complex, and not definable in simplistic terms of right-versus-left. He does not see himself as "political" in those terms, or in terms of party affiliation and so on. It is also unlikely that the artist would see any contradiction between his condemnation of nuclear power and his support for what are ultimately apparatuses of state violence—SDF personnel appear to be disassociated from state policy in his formulation, and hailed as vital contributors to an organic, naturalized familial community—helpers, not fighters. But here, in this very disavowal of politics and appeal to a 'natural' (if alternative) collective called 'Japan,' we can already sense the potential danger that attends Nagabuchi's critique taking shape.

The lack of clearly-enunciated destination in Nagabuchi's quest for an alternative collective is what allows it to remain radically open and inclusive, and sidestep the trap of a reanimated national phantasm (Ivy 1995)—but this openness also renders the artist's 'Japan' vulnerable to commandeering by visions that are less critical and less re-imaginative, not unlike the restorative visions of an originary 'One-ness' that permeated NHK's *Kōhaku* on New Year's Eve, 2011. It is precisely this ambiguity that demands our attention now, if we are to have any hope of considering where Karatani Kojin's 'new paths' may lead. The deployment of a narrative of a communal Japanese body that is always and already the Same (Endo 2012: 1020)—and here we can hear again the echoes of overused and obfuscating catchwords like *kizuna*—can become, in the end, a critical tactic that has the effect of concealing (and normalizing) the very unevenness that has been so key to Japan's capitalist development, thereby priming conditions for its persistence, and potentially foreclosing the possibility of its critique.[14] It was, after all, precisely such a becoming-One (or, becoming-Japanese) that served as the building blocks for the nuclear village itself, and that fueled Valentine's aforementioned "prevalent ideology": the nuclear village was built upon a narrative of a singular community called 'the Japanese' working to make the nation prosperous, even as it was in fact founded in fundamental unevenness between rural areas (such as Fukushima, but also Kagoshima) and urban industrial centers. I must stress that Nagabuchi Tsuyoshi's project lies in the pursuit of a critical, constructive sort of *solidarity*: his determination to debut *Hitotsu* on 2011's Kōhaku, in a live performance out of the grounds of devastated Kadonowaki Elementary School in Ishinomaki (a town particularly hard-hit by 3.11's tsunami) is indicative enough of this. But the line separating the fascistic from the critical is agonizingly thin and easily breached, especially, it seems, in the context of crisis; and the attempt to banish difference and generate even alterative conceptualizations of the 'nation' under a banner of One-ness carries with it a danger that cannot be ignored. For as Harootunian teaches us, the disavowal of unevenness, which itself constitutes an "ideological promise of [...] even development everywhere" (Harootunian 2000a: 115) can be a brooding harbinger of fascism, as attempts are made to draw the fragments together in a national identity devoid of difference, an authentic folk. The quest to disturb History, in other words, can lead to unintended destinations.

## Conclusion

Nagabuchi Tsuyoshi's *Hitotsu* is no less a critique than Saitō's *Zutto uso datta* and yet the former's vision for rearranging Deleuze and Guattari's "supposedly fixed terms" of the social is much different from that of the latter. While Saitō seems interested mainly in rattling cages and clearing a space for change, Nagabuchi's quest is to "become-One." If music *is* the social, as DeNora (2003), following Adorno, suggests, then in these two musical responses to 3.11 we can sense the manner(s) in which both the crises and these responses themselves are firmly situated within the socio-historical experience (= historicity) of modern 'Japan,' and the ways in which both might serve to disturb or reinforce History— or to do both simultaneously. And if we listen carefully, we can discern how these voices locate the events of 3.11 as a waypoint on longer paths of critique— critiques whose effects can end up being highly ambiguous. As I've tried to stress in the preceding pages, critique did not start with 3.11 for either Saitō Kazuyoshi or Nagabuchi Tsuyoshi; we lose much, I think, by isolating their voices to the moment of March 11, 2011, and its immediate aftermaths. Shifting tactics and attending to the ways in which such philosophers are embedded in history along with crises like those of 3.11 can provide valuable hints not only into the ways in which the events of Japan's dark spring may impact the "becoming" that unfurls in Japan in the years to come, but also into the forms that critiques of 'Japan' as "fixed terms" may take—and as such, afford an important window into some of the very ambiguous ways in which individual actors may poke around at the roots of those terms. This, it seems, provides an important key to at least beginning to conceive of the myriad of possibilities that abide in Karatani's (2011) declaration that "it may be [...] only amid the ruins [that] people gain the courage to stride down a new path," a vision whose promise abides in the realization that becoming is the very antithesis of History itself.

A good friend of mine in Fukushima once told me that, for all of its infamy and significance as both the source and symbol of so much of the ongoing heartache and upheaval that started on that cold afternoon in March, the Fukushima Daiichi Nuclear Power Station is, in the final analysis, something akin to a dandelion. In so saying, my friend by no means intended to belittle the enormous challenges and heartbreak that have been visited upon so many tens of thousands along Fukushima's Hamadōri coastline, who have found their lives uprooted and their livelihoods destroyed by the meltdowns at the facility. Rather, she wanted to point to something vital that has been missed in much of the impassioned commentary aimed at shuttering Japan's remaining nuclear plants permanently. You can cut off the head of the dandelion, was her point—but the roots remain. The weed will simply grow back next year, or sooner—perhaps with a slightly different hue, or smaller, or larger, but make no mistake: it will be back. What my friend was pointing to, I think, was the need for systematic change, the sort of social re-imagining that Saitō and Nagabuchi (with the ghost of Imawano Kiyoshirō, for whom this chapter is named, always hovering nearby) appeal to in musical artistry that addresses 3.11, to be sure, but that does so through an engagement with the social that simultaneously transcends and encompasses that specific event. But I have written here only of possibilities, of a small number of ways in which these critical voices may be understood. For if 'Japan' has meant different things to Saitō Kazuyoshi and Nagabuchi Tsuyoshi, then how much more true must this be for the millions of social actors uprooted, rendered homeless, and otherwise impacted by the ongoing disasters of March 2011? How might the artistry that Saitō and Nagabuchi (among others) produce be deployed by such individuals in the unearthing and modifying of the 'roots' (= "fixed terms") of their own specific historical circumstances? To come full circle, then, it seems that we must attend to what community and belonging, *furusato* (home) and 'Japan' actually *mean* to these disparate actors, each rooted in his or her own historically- and geographically-specific context. But that, of course, is a song that is still being written.

## Notes

1 This chapter constitutes an expanded version of a paper originally presented at a conference at the University of Chicago in April 2012. I would like to thank the mediator of the panel in which this paper was presented, Hoyt Long, for the constructive and insightful feedback that has made this expansion possible. I would also like to thank my colleague, Nick Lambrecht, for sharing with me his much valued and incisive insights on music, and for rekindling my esteem for the artistry of Saitō Kazuyoshi.
2 *Enka* is a genre of Japanese popular music that is strongly associated with discourses of 'home' and 'Japan,' and that has long been a mainstay (though less so in recent years) of the Kōhaku. For more on *enka*, see Aalgaard 2011.
3 In revealing discussions with a prominent broadcast personality in Fukushima in 2012 and 2015, I learned that terms like '*ganbaru*' (fight, persevere) are carefully avoided in interviews with affected persons, at least by this particular broadcaster. The term tends to "stop the discussion," he said: implicit in his comments seems to be a critique of a disavowal of ongoing movement and flow in favor of an urging of the restoration of fixed conditions, conditions which may no longer be desired, helpful, or even possible.
4 What I mean to invoke here is the sort of (conjured) "true, unchanging history" critiqued by Harry Harootunian in his essay, "Japan's long postwar: The trick of memory and the ruse of history" (Harootunian 2006: 116–19).
5 For a brief backgrounder on the difficulties faced by Imawano's RC Succession when it attempted to release its own musical critique of nuclear power in 1988, see Manabe 2012.
6 In his conversation with Isaka Kōtarō, Saitō specifically stated that he finds "too much information" (by which he seems to mean the passive input, from television, or music, or other textual sources) to be detrimental to his musical work, preferring instead to get a sense of the realities of the world through interaction therewith—being exposed to music while walking the streets, seeing what's on television at the local diner (rather than watching television at home), having the radio on in the background while driving, etc.
7 These terms and conditions are addressed by Yoda Tomiko in her conceptualization of the "enterprise society," envisioned as having been dominated since around 1970—which is, of course, precisely Saitō Kazuyoshi's own historical moment (Yoda 2006).
8 For more on the ambiguous forms that the quest for shelter under capitalism can take, see Virno 2004.
9 Indeed, the work seems composed in a manner that serves to communicate tension and consternation.

10 The deployment of the term 'lazy' here makes it difficult to avoid approaching this work in terms of the commodification of labor power. For more on the desperation that can lie behind the quest to ensure that one's own labor power is valued under capitalism—and that one thus has the means to survive—see, for example, Tomiyama 2000.
11 An earlier debut, under the quasi-pseudonym Nagabuchi Gō, sputtered.
12 The 1983 release *Heavy Gauge* (the title is in English), for example, featured the song *Tsumetai Gaikokujin* (Cold-Hearted Foreigner), which addressed the brutalities visited upon war prisoners by Japan's notorious Unit 731.
13 Nagabuchi has in the past released works that appear to glorify Japan's militarist past, such as his 2007 controversial release *Kamikaze Tokkōtai*, though the point of such songs seems not to glorify this history as much as to call attention to how the ways in which individual actors grappling with it at the time may offer lessons for the present/future.
14 In this respect, Nagabuchi's project bears certain resemblances to that of Yanagita Kunio, who sought to fill in "the crevices of unevenness [wherein] lay the real possibility for antagonism and social conflict that would demand change and transformation" (Harootunian 2000b: 313).

## References

Aalgaard, Scott W. 2011, *Gimme Shelter: Enka, Self, and Society in Contemporary Japan.* MA Thesis, University of Victoria, at: https://dspace.library.uvic.ca/handle/1828/3385 (accessed 14 March 2015).
Berger, Harris M. 2009, *Stance: Ideas about Emotion, Style, and Meaning for the Study of Expressive Culture.* Middletown, CT: Wesleyan University Press.
Bergson, Henri. 1911, *Creative Evolution.* New York: The Macmillan Company.
Boellstorff, Tom. 2005, *The Gay Archipelago: Sexuality and Nation in Indonesia.* Princeton, NJ: Princeton University Press.
Boym, Svetlana. 2001, *The Future of Nostalgia.* New York: Basic Books.
Brunt, Shelly. 2003, "The Kohaku Song Contest: A community in performance." *Context: A Journal of Music Research* Vol. 25 (Autumn): 5–15.
Deleuze, Gilles and Guattari, Felix. 1987, *A Thousand Plateaus: Capitalism and Schizophrenia.* Trans. Brian Massumi. Minneapolis, MN: The University of Minnesota Press.
DeNora, Tia. 2003, *After Adorno: Rethinking Music Sociology.* Cambridge: Cambridge University Press.
DeNora, Tia. 2004, "Musical practice and social structure: A toolkit," in Eric Clarke and Nicholas Cooke (eds), *Empirical Musicology: Aims, Methods, Prospects.* Oxford: Oxford University Press, 35–56.
Endo, Katsuhiko. 2012, "A unique tradition of materialism in Japan: Osugi Sakae, Tosaka Jun, and Uno Kozo." *positions*, Vol. 20, No. 4: 1009–39.
Finnegan, Ruth. 2003, "Music, experience and the anthropology of emotion," in Martin Clayton, Trevor Herbert, and Richard Middleton (eds), *The Cultural Study of Music: A Critical Introduction.* New York: Routledge, 181–92.
Gilroy, Paul. 1993, *The Black Atlantic: Modernity and Double-Consciousness.* London: Verso.
Grossberg, Lawrence. 1997, *Bringing it All Back Home: Essays on Cultural Studies.* Durham, NC: Duke University Press.
Harootunian, H.D. 1993, "America's Japan/Japan's Japan," in Masao Miyoshi and H.D. Harootunian (eds), *Japan in the World.* London: Duke University Press.

Harootunian, Harry. 2000a, *History's Disquiet: Modernity, Cultural Practice, and the Question of Everyday Life*. New York: Columbia University Press.
Harootunian, Harry. 2000b, *Overcome by Modernity: History, Culture, and Community in Interwar Japan*. Princeton, NJ: Princeton University Press.
Harootunian, Harry. 2006, "Japan's long postwar: The trick of memory and the ruse of history," in Yoda Tomiko and Harry Harootunian (eds), *Japan after Japan: Social and Cultural Life from the Recessionary 1990s to the Present*. Durham, NC: Duke University Press, 98–121.
Isaka, Kōtarō and Saitō, Kazuyoshi. 2007, *Kizuna no hanashi*. Tokyo: Kōdansha.
Ivy, Marilyn. 1995, *Discourses of the Vanishing: Modernity, Phantasm, Japan*. Chicago, IL: University of Chicago Press.
Kaihara, Hiroshi. 2009, "Contemporary conservative thoughts in Japan: Conservative views on morality, history, and social issues." *International Relations of the Asia Pacific* Vol. 9, No. 2: 339–64.
Karatani, Kojin. 2011, "How catastrophe heralds a new Japan." Trans. Seiji M. Lippitt. *Counterpunch* 24 March, at: www.counterpunch.org/2011/03/24/how-catastrophe-heralds-a-new-japan/ (accessed March 14, 2015).
Karatani, Kojin. 2014, *The Structure of World History: From Modes of Production to Modes of Exchange*. Trans. Michael K. Bourdaghs. Durham, NC: Duke University Press.
*livedoor NEWS*. 2011, "Intabyū: Saitō Kazuyoshi 'Ongaku baka no kakko yosa wo kurai-yagare!' " 22 November, at: http://news.livedoor.com/article/detail/6052175/ (accessed March 14, 2015).
Manabe, Noriko. 2012, "The No Nukes 2012 Concert and the role of musicians in the anti-nuclear movement." *The Asia-Pacific Journal* Vol. 10, Issue 29, No. 2 (16 July), at: www.japanfocus.org/-Noriko-MANABE/3799 (accessed March 14, 2015).
Massumi, Brian. 2002, *Parables for the Virtual: Movement, Affect, Sensation*. Durham, NC: Duke University Press,
Matanle, Peter. 2011, "The Great East Japan Earthquake, tsunami, and nuclear meltdown: Towards the (re)construction of a safe, sustainable and compassionate society in Japan's shrinking regions." *Local Environment: The International Journal of Justice and Sustainability* Vol. 16, No. 9 (October): 823–47.
Miyoshi, Masao and Harootunian, H.D. (eds). 1993, *Japan in the World*. London: Duke University Press.
Nagabuchi, Tsuyoshi. 1978, *Junrenka*. October 5. Tokyo: Toshiba EMI. LP single.
Nagabuchi, Tsuyoshi. 1983, *Tsumetai gaikokujin*, from the album *HEAVY GAUGE*. Tokyo: Toshiba EMI. June 21. LP.
Nagabuchi, Tsuyoshi. 1990, *O-uchi he kaerō*, from the album *JEEP*. August 25. Tokyo: EMI Music Japan. CD Album.
Nagabuchi, Tsuyoshi. 1991, *Kibaiyanse*, from the album *JAPAN*. December 14. Tokyo: EMI Music Japan. CD Album.
Nagabuchi, Tsuyoshi. 1991, *Oyashirazu*, from the album *JAPAN*. December 14. Tokyo: EMI Music Japan. CD Album.
Nagabuchi, Tsuyoshi. 2006, Promotional website commentary pertaining to the release of the concert DVD *YAMATO/Yamato-damashii*. May 31, at: www.nagabuchi.or.jp/post_discography/1038/ (accessed March 14, 2015).
Nagabuchi, Tsuyoshi. 2012. *Hitotsu*. 1 February. Tokyo: Universal Music. Maxi-single. at: www.dailymotion.com/video/xoeqj4_長渕剛-ひとつ-pv_music (accessed March 14, 2015).

Novak, David. 2013, *JAPANOISE: Music at the Edge of Circulation*. Durham, NC: Duke University Press.
*Nikkan Sports*. 2012, "Nagabuchi 3.11 'Hō-sute de Tōhoku kara nama shin-kyoku. March 12, at: www.nikkansports.com/entertainment/news/p-et-tp0-20120310-915150.html (accessed December 6, 2015).
Sakaguchi, Ango. 2010, "Discourse on decadence," in James Dorsey and Doug Slaymaker (eds), *Literary Mischief: Sakaguchi Ango, Culture, and the War*. Trans. James Dorsey. Lanham, MD: Lexington Books, 175–96.
Saitō, Kazuyoshi. 1993, *Boku no mita Beatles wa TV no naka*. August 25. Tokyo: Funhouse. CD single.
Saitō, Kazuyoshi. 2008, *Jirenma* [Dilemma]. September 17. Tokyo: JVC Music Japan. CD Album.
Saitō, Kazuyoshi. 2011a, *Zutto uso datta*, original version. Uploaded to YouTube April 7, at: www.youtube.com/watch?v=FZ2-vE6PqAg (accessed March 14, 2015).
Saitō, Kazuyoshi. 2011b, *Zutto uso datta*, UStream version. Live-streamed via UStream on April 8, at: www.youtube.com/watch?v=B1AxzZdKp2Y (accessed March 15, 2014).
Tomiyama, Ichiro. 2000, "'Spy': Mobilization and identity in wartime Okinawa." *Senri Ethnological Studies* (National Museum of Ethnology) Vol. 51 (March 27): 121–31.
Tsumabaki, Satoshi, Saitō, Kazuyoshi, *et al.*, 2014, *Otona elebētā*. Tokyo: Fusōsha.
Valentine, Scott Victor and Sovacool, Benjamin K. 2010. "The socio-political economy of nuclear power development in Japan and South Korea." *Energy Policy* Vol. 38, No. 12 (December): 7971–79.
Virno, Paolo. 2004, *A Grammar of the Multitude*. New York: Columbia University Press.
Wedeen, Lisa. 2008, *Peripheral Visions: Publics, Power, and Performance in Yemen*. Chicago, IL: The University of Chicago Press.
Yoda, Tomiko. 2006, "A roadmap to millennial Japan," in Yoda Tomiko and Harry Harootunian (eds), *Japan after Japan: Social and Cultural Life from the Recessionary 1990s to the Present*. Durham, NC: Duke University Press, 16–53.
Yukawa, Reiko. 2012, "*Nagabuchi Tsuyoshi san ga senjitsu okonawareta Kagoshima Shimin Bunka Hall no konsāto no sutēji de katatta kotoba desu.*" (July 2), at: https://twitter.com/yukawareiko/status/219680068333608960 (accessed December 6, 2015).

# 4 Subversion and nostalgia in art photography of the Fukushima nuclear disaster

*Pablo Figueroa*

The March 11, 2011 Great East Japan Earthquake and ensuing tsunami left a death toll of more than 15,000 in the Tōhoku region (National Police Agency of Japan 2014). This tragedy was compounded by the Fukushima reactor meltdowns; the authorities' poor handling of the nuclear crisis, the release of radiation into the environment, and the forced evacuation of local residents caused widespread anxiety among Japanese citizens. Four years on, the attitudes of the government and the nuclear industry fail to address public concerns about radiation as well as the psychological hardships affecting the displaced populations. The official stance to this day has been to downplay the seriousness of the 3.11 events. This chapter will argue that the Fukushima nuclear disaster has generated photographic discourses of political subversion and nostalgia among Japanese art photographers. In doing so, it will attempt to situate and discuss those discourses against the backdrop of wider cultural texts of power, politics, and space. The research will draw upon ethnographic fieldwork, scholarly analysis of the Fukushima disaster, and cultural criticism.

## Introduction

An increase in the frequency and scope of disasters would appear to characterize the post-industrial society of the early twenty-first century (Oliver-Smith 2002: 43). The Haiti and Sichuan earthquakes, the South Asian tsunami, and typhoon Haiyan are painful reminders of the sheer magnitude of destruction that accompanies such events of nature. In this context, Asia's urban transition has exacerbated the vulnerability of the poor: at present, nearly 50 percent of Asia's population lives in cities. This rapid urbanization has taken place in countries with enormous deficits in urban infrastructure. By 2010, there were 470 million people living in slums across Asia (Douglas 2013: 9).

Although disasters are frequently labeled 'natural' or 'man-made,' no contemporary disaster can be seen only as the result of natural causes. To a significant extent, anthropogenic factors such as prevention and response determine how disasters will unfold. Moreover, disasters are highly contested political events. The socio-cultural anthropologist Gregory Button points out that:

Disasters highlight the asymmetrical distribution of power and foreground the struggle of the state, corporations, and human agency for the redistribution of power. The control of information in public discourse, as well as the attempt to control the social production of meaning, is an attempt to define reality. It is, therefore, a distinctly ideological process that we cannot afford to ignore.

(Button 2010: 16)

Despite having patterns in common with other catastrophes such as inefficient government response, lack of disaster preparedness, and the official denial of the seriousness of the crisis, 3.11 stands out in a class of its own: it is a paramount example of a compound disaster, one that is haunted by memories of devastation after the atomic bombings. The scars of that trauma have left a deep social imprint. Scholars have argued that post-war Japanese pop culture can be seen as a creative response to that cataclysm (Tsutsui 2011: 138).

The 2011 triple disasters have torn the social fabric of Fukushima communities. A Japanese newspaper reported that nearly half of the households that were forced to evacuate following the nuclear crisis are split up (*Asahi Shimbun* 2014). Often, this is due to fears over radioactive contamination as well as locations of schools and workplaces. Adding to this disruption, ongoing stress affects Fukushima residents. A recent large-scale survey conducted by the prefectural government shows that 1,656 people in Fukushima Prefecture died from stress-related illnesses, surpassing the 1,607 people who died from injuries related to the disasters. More than a thousand residents were similarly affected in the Iwate and Miyagi Prefectures. In addition, there is mothers' anxiety about the cancer risk for their children. According to a medical report—the first of its kind since the nuclear accident—the lifetime risk of cancer for children in Fukushima has increased (*Japan Times* 2014). However, the construction and interpretation of this radiological data is a matter of bitter dispute. While the Fukushima medical authorities assert that the effects of radiation will be insignificant, concerned mothers believe the exact opposite. Given the government's shortcomings in communicating risk (Figueroa 2013: 54) and the scientific uncertainty surrounding the effects of radiation, it should come as no surprise that local residents are distrustful of the official standards of safety. Idogawa Katsutaka, the former mayor of Futaba Town which co-hosted the Fukushima plant along with Okuma Town, thinks that despite what the government says, it is by no means safe to return to Fukushima. According to Idogawa, radiation maps reveal that the levels of contamination in certain areas are so high and widespread that it is impossible to avoid exposure if one lives there (Idogawa 2014).

Idogawa feels that the government has neglected Futaba's nuclear evacuees, an issue enhanced by the perceived lack of proper housing and psychological support:

We are refugees living inside of Japan. We are like forgotten people, who cannot be seen. Wasted people. [...] We are treated without regard. We have nowhere to go. We need houses and places. But it has not happened.

(Greenpeace 2014)

My own observations among Fukushima residents in Iwaki, Nihonmatsu, and Tamura in August 2014—which are consistent with the previous fieldwork I carried out in Iwaki, Soma, Minamisōma, and Fukushima in September 2011— suggest that people's anxieties are ongoing and include: (a) concerns related to health, food, and the environment; (b) distrust toward the government and the nuclear industry; and (c) future work and housing worries. So far, the use of reconstruction budgets, the creation of employment, check-ups for radiation, and the treatment of contaminated soil has been anything but satisfactory. Especially for those whose former residential areas have become inhabitable as a result of the nuclear contamination, trust toward the government and the nuclear industry will be hard to regain.

In this context of deep uncertainty, how have Japanese art photographers reacted? I argue that photographic discourses of political subversion and nostalgia surrounding the nuclear accident have emerged. To illustrate this I will look into the works of two photographers, Watanabe Toshiya (b. 1966) and Imai Tomoki (b. 1974). Both men have a trajectory in art photography, and their images will serve as a way to engage in a critical discussion of photographic representations of the Fukushima disaster and the wider socio-political landscapes.

My position is that the meaning of a photograph is created by cultural context. Meaning in photography refers to images as social discourses that embody information exchange in systems of relations. Communication is tendentious, and messages are the "embodiment of an argument" (Sekula 1982: 85). In addition, following Burgin (1982: 144) I will argue that photographs can be understood as texts that gain sense in the broader photographic discourse, and these texts interact in complex ways with other texts in a phenomenon known in semiotics as intertextuality. With the abovementioned notions in mind, this research will aim to draw upon ethnographic fieldwork, scholarly analysis of the Fukushima disaster, and cultural criticism in an interdisciplinary manner.

## Negotiating the visual maze: practical and theoretical considerations

Much in the same way as the 1923 quake, when visual images inundated the public sphere (Weisenfeld 2012: ix–x), a mind-boggling amount of images was rendered in response to the Fukushima catastrophes. In the beginning, most of the images published nationally were representations pertaining to photojournalism. Special issues focusing on the disaster were released by news agencies in Tōhoku and Tokyo. These include publications by the main newspapers and magazines such as the *Asahi Shimbun*, the *Mainichi Shimbun*, *AERA*, *Friday*, Kyodo News, the *Yomiuri*, and the *Sankei* Publishing Company among others.

In addition, international photojournalists covered 3.11. But the views sustained by domestic and foreign media have been dissimilar. Japanese critics point out that the foreign press was after the 'photographic effect.' This refers to the creation of images that accentuate tragedy and fear such as people wearing anti-radiation suits, small children taking body scans, Geiger counters, post-tsunami debris, landscape destruction, and survivors searching for their loved ones in the rubble (differently from other historical disasters, photos of human corpses in Tōhoku were not prominently displayed in the official outlets of information). In the ultra-fast, highly competitive media environment, news agencies crave for images that shock viewers in order to sell.[1]

The images I chose for this study differ from the above in that they fall into the category of art photography: they were made by Japanese art photographers, displayed in exhibitions at art galleries, and compiled in the form of photo books. By discussing art photography of the Fukushima nuclear disaster, I aim to explore how two Japanese photographers deal with representations of the catastrophe, and how their works may be inscribed in the broader cultural and political landscape. The reason for choosing art photography over other genres is methodological. For instance, a meaningful analysis of journalistic representations would have implied the use of resources that are beyond the possibilities of this study. In contrast, art photography is comparatively limited in size as a body of work and easier to narrow down for the purposes of ethnographic research.

My interest in art photographers Watanabe and Imai is twofold. First, I wanted to work with photographers whom I could interview. Given that Watanabe is originally from Namie, one of the towns affected by the nuclear accident in Fukushima, and that Imai is from Tokyo, I was able to meet with them several times and discuss how they conceived their images in the context of the Fukushima disaster. A second personal motive relates to the classic distinction between *studium* and *punctum* formulated by Roland Barthes. Barthes defines *studium* as the average feeling one gets when looking at a picture. It provokes on the viewer an interest which is half-detached; one may like or dislike the image but always with a semi-desire that is dispassionate. Thus, in Barthesian terms *studium* is a kind of rational activity that one engages politely in. *Punctum*, on the other hand, is a disturbing feeling that pricks, bruises the viewer. It ruptures the element of *studium* by piercing the observer and stirring a kind of emotional response that is absent in images characterized by *studium* (Barthes 2010 [1980]: 25–60). This element of *punctum* which is mainly a personal experience is what made me choose these photographers and their photos. When I first came across Watanabe's and Imai's Fukushima photographs, the response that took place within me went beyond the detached state of *studium* that Barthes refers to. I was moved in a way that closely resembled *punctum* in that I felt disturbed, pierced by the images—they were no longer inert shapes and colors under my gaze. The photographs forced me to think about them way after I had seen them. They lingered in my mind with unexpected force, and this was the reason that compelled me to choose those particular photographs.

As Susan Sontag has argued, no photographer can determine the meaning of a photograph, which will be read in very different terms depending on political loyalties, nationality, and how the image is identified by the viewer (Sontag 2003: 29–38). Furthermore, the veracity of photography in absolute terms (its immediacy of representation and transparency) has been questioned over the years by a number of theorists (Tormey 2013: 32). Tagg (1988: 64) argues there is no neutrality in photography because photographic images are highly coded and its power is dependent on cultural context. Sekula points out that the meaning of a photograph is determined by cultural definition and that all communication is tendentious. Therefore, photographs are manifestations of interest (Sekula 1982: 84). Victor Burgin also stresses the need to inscribe photographic texts within the social discourses that have produced them:

> A fact of primary social importance is that the photograph is a *place of work*, a structured and structuring space within which the reader deploys, and is deployed by, what codes he or she is familiar with in order to *make sense*. Photography is one signifying system among others in society which produces the ideological subject in the same movement in which they 'communicate' their 'ostensible' contents.
> (Burgin 1982: 153)

In line with the above, rather than understanding photographs as transparent representations of truth I adopt the viewpoint that the meaning of a photograph is subject to cultural definition. Photographic discourse as utilized here is based on the notion proposed by Sekula that a discourse is an arena of information exchange defined by a system of relations between parties engaged in communicative activities (Sekula 1982: 84). The photographic message is the embodiment of an argument that can never be neutral. The photograph becomes a message, albeit an incomplete one: it depends on external conditions that confer its sense.

It is useful to clarify here the idea of 'Japanese art photography.' I assume that photography *is* an art, and that it has been so for at least a hundred years. Japanese art photography in this paper will simply refer to the photographic representations produced by Japanese photographers without assuming a priori that there is something 'essentially' Japanese in their ways of seeing. Photographic discourses in Japan developed in a complex interplay with ideas and images of the West. Native responses were perhaps unique insofar as how they made sense in a national context but photographers' modes of seeing were not essentially different from those developed in other countries.

## Art photography of the Fukushima disaster: discourses of nostalgia and subversion

I argue that art photography of the Fukushima disaster has produced texts of subversion and nostalgia. The forced evacuation of Tōhoku residents generated an overwhelming sense of loss and anger among those who felt betrayed: state narratives of technological safety that had been meticulously crafted for fifty years clashed with the harsh realities of nuclear catastrophe.

Looking at the role of photography in bearing witness to disaster, Barbie Zelizer stresses that photography plays a key function in helping individuals and

*Subversion and nostalgia* 63

collectives articulate the painful process of going from trauma to recovery. In the aftermath of a catastrophe, personal response rather than group action is what rebuilds the lost sense of self. The relationship between the individual and the collective is interdependent but it is the individual meanings that first help to facilitate the establishment of moral accountability and the transition to a normal life (Zelizer 2002: 698).

I shall first discuss three photographs made by Watanabe Toshiya that belong to a photo book titled *18 months*. Watanabe was already a promising photographer during his student days at the reputed Tama Art University, where he majored in graphic design. Now a Tokyo-based professional art director and fine art photographer with several exhibitions and international awards to his credit, Watanabe was born and raised in the town of Namie in the Fukushima Prefecture. Although Watanabe moved to Tokyo upon graduating from high school, he kept in touch with Namie through friends and relatives; his mother was still living there in March 2011. During the nuclear crisis, Namie residents were forced to evacuate and the town was declared off-limits due to the high levels of radioactive contamination brought about by the nuclear fallout. Gradually, residents who wanted to recover their personal belongings were allowed to enter the no-go zone for short periods of time. Since the accident, Watanabe has visited Namie in many occasions and has photographed the town during those trips.

Watanabe's photos were shown in a solo exhibition titled *18 months* that took place at the Poetic Scape gallery in the Tokyo neighborhood of Naka Meguro, from March 9–31, 2013. The images were compiled into a photo book that carries the same title as the exhibition, and I selected three of those photos for discussion. There is no text in the book other than details of the edition. The first image I refer to is *Jun. 12. 2011, Shinmachi street* (Figure 4.1). Taken from the center of the road—an unusual location to place the camera during the daytime when cars would normally be running—it provides the spectator with a rare point of view. The structure of the composition is symmetric, balanced—lines converge in the horizon. The traffic lights appear to be off and no vehicles can be seen. On the right there is a collapsed house, its fallen roof tiles spread pathetically on the pavement. A lighting pole is badly distorted. The date of the photograph indicates that three months have passed since the disaster. Perhaps the element that stands out in the composition is the road sign: the reference to place here is unmistakable. The sign, written both in Japanese and in Roman letters, shows the directions to the station of Namie, the towns of Futaba and Katsurao, and the cities of Minamisōma and Iwaki. In terms of message these names carry a heavy emotional load for Fukushima evacuees and have become gloomy signifiers of nuclear disaster for those living outside the prefecture.

So how to 'read' this first photograph? I argue that the relevance of this image lies in its witnessing the present as much as in its evocation of the past. A town's main street represents the hub of activity; Shinmachi street is where the gathering of neighbors used to take place during festivals (*matsuri*). The scene is nostalgic. In the socio-political context in which the picture was taken, deep

*Figure 4.1* 'Shinmachi Street' Jun. 12, 2011 by Watanabe Toshiya (courtesy of the photographer)

uncertainty toward the future dominated the perceptions of Namie residents because, given the high levels of radioactive contamination, they did not know whether they might be able to return to their town ever again.

This interpretation is complemented by another picture taken from the very same spot, but fifteen months later, in September 2012 (*Sep. 16. 2012 Shinmachi street*, Figure 4.2). In the second take, little has changed since the nuclear accident; it may seem that this image is a mere replica of the first. With the exception of weeds that have grown on both sides of Shinmachi Street, the rest of the picture looks almost identical. However, a different message emerges here, and it is shaped by the temporal dimension of the photograph: two and a half years have passed since the disaster and yet there are no visible transformations in the landscape. It is as if time in Namie were put on hold, with no indication of the authorities' intended plans for the town's future.

The government's troubles in finding a direction for the future of Namie contributed to creating a deep sense of loss and nostalgia among its former

*Subversion and nostalgia* 65

*Figure 4.2* 'Shinmachi Street' September 16, 2012 by Watanabe Toshiya (courtesy of the photographer)

inhabitants. Would they ever be able to return home? What are the tangible health risks of radioactivity? Are those risks worth taking? At present, although Namie has been allowed to lift the evacuation orders and has been reclassified as 'safe,' its former residents are pressed to make very hard choices (NHK 2013) that will deeply affect the quality of their everyday lives.

The third photograph (Figure 4.3) is more complex than the previous two, because it operates simultaneously on a number of levels. Despite its deceptively simple caption title—*Jun. 12. 2011, Photo studio*—the image symbolically transcends its proposed reference to a town's shop. First, by means of the window's reflection the photographer is metadiscursively placed in the frame. We can guess there is a subject in the photograph but we do not know who it is. The features are indistinguishable due to a mask and a hazmat suit. However, personal identity holds secondary importance here. In a sense, the person in the photo is a phantom-like figure that iconically represents the tragedy of the nuclear evacuee: displaced and dispossessed, the nuclear refugee is in a liminal state.[2]

*Figure 4.3* 'Photo Studio' Jun. 12, 2011 by Watanabe Toshiya (courtesy of the photographer)

Furthermore, the photographer's silhouette appears in the middle of two portraits on the window. These portraits, a boy and two girls, and a young female can be interpreted as a metaphor of severed families and interrupted lives. The referents align in the center of the photograph and are interwoven through the personal identification with collective sorrow. This mirror-like reflection enables the photographer to seamlessly blend in with the background. The feel is phantasmagoric. There are no people, no animals, and no vehicles. The only trace of life is the displaced human-ghost, a temporary visitor into the no-go zone.

The second theme I want to discuss is subversion. For this, I shall examine five pictures made by art photographer Imai Tomoki that belong to a book titled *Semicircle Law* (Figures 4.4–4.8). A photo exhibition with the same name took place between January 26 and February 16, 2013 at the Taka Ishii Gallery in the Tokyo neighborhood of Roppongi. For the exhibition's flyer, Imai wrote:

From the mountaintop, the building was sometimes visible as a blurred white dot. Neither the building's enormous emission nor 20 km and 30 km radii could be seen. No transformation excepting the change of the seasons was visible. Not being an interested party in the strictest sense, I felt that I would eventually forget this tragedy as I had many others. To forget something is to become accustomed to it. I did not want to become accustomed to the idea that a semicircle of emptiness was just a four hour drive away. And yet, I probably will forget. As the memory slides gently into oblivion, my photographs allow me to recall not only visible, but also invisible things.

The photo book, published by MATCH and Company in 2013, contains two essays by curators and twenty-five photographs shot at multiple locations during a twenty-month period between April 2011 and December 2012. Imai started taking photographs in Fukushima in April 2011 and a few days later the Japanese government declared a 20 km area around the crippled Fukushima Daiichi Nuclear Power Plant a no-go zone. The new measure decreed that trespassers would be subject to fines of up to 100,000 JPY (about US$1,000) and possible imprisonment. Before the measure was enacted, people entering the off-limits area were not liable to criminal prosecution (*Aljazeera* 2011).

To put the *Semicircle Law* in better context, it is useful to remember Sekula's idea that the meaning of a photograph is determined by cultural definition. Without conceptual understanding of this project, and without historical knowledge of how nuclear power has played out in Japan during the past fifty years, one would perhaps conclude that these images are terse depictions of nature, subtle portraits of mountainscapes that change with the passing of seasons. However, although the referent of the images appears to be the natural environment, the thread of the narrative is to be found outside the photos. Imai told me that he felt puzzled at the idea of humans having to fight something as lethal as radiation, which cannot be seen. The photographer knew that given the official prohibition he could not enter into the evacuation area now, so he decided to continue making photographs by placing the camera on top of mountains, following the imaginary contour of the 20 km no-go zone. All the photographs have something in common: in each one of them, the camera lens is directed to the reactors at Fukushima Daiichi. Sometimes the nuclear plant is visible as a tiny object in the distance. Other times it cannot be seen due to the trees obstructing the views or the mountains covering the nuclear plant in the background; either we do not see the reactors or we see them from afar in a very small size. This material aspect of representation becomes a suitable metaphor for the veil that was cast upon Japanese citizens regarding the seriousness of the crisis and the real dimension of the issues at Fukushima. For more than two months after 3.11, TEPCO and the government maintained that there were no serious problems with the reactors, that people could expect no immediate threats to health as a consequence of exposure to radiation. Thus, the geographical place in the *Semicircle Law* becomes a metaphor of a political space, a realm in which citizens' perceptions are dismissed as irrational and considered irrelevant for nuclear policy.

*Figure 4.4* '#01' by Imai Tomoki (courtesy of the photographer)

*Figure 4.5* '#03' by Imai Tomoki (courtesy of the photographer)

*Figure 4.6* '#12' by Imai Tomoki (courtesy of the photographer)

*Figure 4.7* '#21' by Imai Tomoki (courtesy of the photographer)

*Figure 4.8* '#25' by Imai Tomoki (courtesy of the photographer)

I argue that these photographs can be read as a statement of political subversion. The way in which Imai visually addresses issues of nuclear radiation, people's right to know, and political responsibility is oblique yet compelling. Imai's work subverts roles and opens up the possibility of empowering viewers politically. Instead of narrating a catastrophe through literal depictions of destruction, the *Semicircle Law* positions spectators in a very different angle. Cognizant observers can critically dispute official discourses. The story is slow in its development and subtle in its contents but it carries unexpected force. By looking at the photographs in their narrative sequence, we see mountain landscapes that change over time with the passing of the seasons. But despite seasonal changes, mountains—like the Japanese government's stance toward nuclear power—remain unmoved. They stay largely unchanged in spite of the looming threat posed by the reactors in the background. Furthermore, we can also find hints as to what is hidden from us; we can sense a struggle for political power in the decreeing of a no-go zone. What is the broader agenda of this prohibition? Is it to enforce public safety? Or could it be that the issue at stake is control over the representations that will be transmitted to the public, to the world, and someday to history?

## The dynamics of power, politics, and space

As argued above, post-disaster scenarios become fertile grounds for the renegotiation of different actors' political agendas. To the disappointment of the anti-nuclear citizen groups, the Fukushima disaster did not generate a more inclusive political mindset that might have helped rebuild trust with the population at large.[3] Rather, the official response has been to further insulate the nuclear sector from public scrutiny. In line with national energy policies during the past fifty years, the governing LDP led by Prime Minister Shinzō Abe is admittedly in favor of nuclear energy. Ever since coming to office Abe has done everything within his reach to speed up the restart of idled reactors. Despite public opposition and lack of proper evacuation plans, the Abe administration is moving toward plugging reactors back online.[4] However, a too-hasty restart runs the risk of repeating the mistakes that triggered the 2011 Fukushima meltdowns.

In addition, the Abe administration has aggressively sought to increase its share of power. This is evidenced in its passing a state secrets protection law that has caused anger among citizens, academics, and journalists. The bill heavily punishes the so-called leaking of state secrets. Penalties for offenders are heavy and include imprisonment for up to ten years. A point of concern is the further empowering of the bureaucracies, which can lock documents for up to sixty years and then destroy those files. Thus, the public does not know what becomes a state secret, or why it is classified as such. Furthermore, the government has argued for the need to reinterpret the constitution so Japan can exercise the right to collective self-defense. For many citizens, the reasons behind this change are unclear at best, and opposition has been widespread. But people's dissatisfaction has not had a measurable impact on the government's mindset. On December 14, 2014 the ruling coalition seized a two-thirds majority in the Lower House election, giving the LDP the ability to push legislation through the Diet. Judging from the results, nuclear power was not a main concern for active voters. Ex-Prime Minister Naoto Kan, who built his election campaign around renewable energy, could barely retain his seat. At 52 percent, the December 2014 voter turnover was the lowest ever in Japanese politics (Hayashi and Schlesinger 2014).

In this shifting landscape of renegotiation of power, how do photographic discourses of the Fukushima disaster make sense into larger cultural and political texts? A hint can be found in the construction of narratives of space and memory. Although this is an ongoing process, it is safe to say that there are two competing narratives. One is embodied by the dominant national discourse, which seeks to play down the ongoing issues related to the Fukushima disaster. The other narrative(s) is represented by people's views, among them, art photographers who see the disasters from the perspective of emotion and creativity. Intentionally or not, these narratives embody a social struggle to redefine space and memory after disaster.

The March 11, 2011 Fukushima triple disaster signals not a crisis in nuclear technology but a crisis of trust in society at large: the displaced populations feel betrayed and ignored by the government. Feelings of nostalgia abound within evacuees; such notions have been expressed by art photographers through their personal gaze. Imai wrote he does not want to forget the nuclear tragedy. His images, like those shot by Watanabe, are a way to build a transition to a future in which memory will not be completely lost. This personal and local struggle for memory is articulated through selection in wider political contexts. The emotional dimension of space in Fukushima is to be found, not in the official discourses, but in the individual and group counter-narratives that seek to make sense of place and disaster.

## Notes

1 It is not easy for photojournalists to escape this editorial bias if they want to remain in business, especially when the public has become accustomed to consuming others' sorrows. According to Japanese photojournalists I have spoken with, part of the problem lies in the fact that once the photographer sells the image to the photo agency, the photo agency in turn sells the image to newspapers, magazines, and other media. Thus, the photographer has ultimately no control over how the image will be used. Of course one could argue that the photojournalist could decide not to sell the image to stock photo agencies at all. But finances and the pressures associated with stepping up in the photographic career exert strong influence over such decisions.
2 Unable to return to their homes, evacuees now inhabit temporary housing complexes; these complexes consist of tiny wooden constructions that are placed on close to the other in spaces that look like huge parking lots. Deprived of the tasks they used to do in their former residences, they spend their days doing nothing much: they wake up late, they sleep late, and their general lifestyle has changed for the worst. In the afternoon, some residents gather to have conversation with neighbors. Discrimination against nuclear evacuees is sometimes rampant as people in the towns hosting temporary housing feel "they are doing the refugees a favor" by having them in those areas.
3 People's perceptions do matter for effective risk management and risk communication. It is not enough to tell Fukushima residents that it is safe to return to their former houses. A variety of actors and stakeholders must co-participate in the construction of risk discourse.
4 Following the 2011 Fukushima disaster all fifty nuclear reactors in Japan were taken offline for security checks. Since then, the electric companies and the government have been trying hard to restart them for "economic" reasons. But the public is distrustful of the operators' abilities to prevent accidents. In 2012, NHK conducted a poll in 142 communities in the vicinity of Japan's nuclear power plants. NHK concluded that only 14 percent of respondents were in favor of restarting idled reactors while 79 percent opposed the idea (Kingston 2012).

## References

*Aljazeera*. 2011, "Japan declares nuclear no-go zone". April 21, at: www.aljazeera.com/news/asia-pacific/2011/04/201142135957974110.html (accessed March 31, 2015).

*Asahi Shimbun*. 2014, "Survey: Half of Fukushima evacuee households split up; distress life in families." April 29, at: http://ajw.asahi.com/article/0311disaster/fukushima/AJ201404290046 (accessed February 23, 2015).

Barthes, Roland. 2010 [1980], *Camera Lucida: Reflections on Photography*. Trans. Richard Howard. New York: Hill and Wang.

Burgin, Victor (ed.). 1982, *Thinking Photography*. London: Macmillan Press.

Button, Gregory. 2010, *Disaster Culture: Knowledge and Uncertainty in the Wake of Human and Environment Catastrophe*. Walnut Creek, CA: Left Coast Press.

Douglas, Michael. 2013, "The urban transition of environmental disaster governance in Asia." *Asia Research Institute. Working Paper Series* No. 210: 1–25.
Figueroa, Pablo M. 2013, "Risk communication surrounding the Fukushima nuclear disaster: An anthropological approach." *Asia Europe Journal* 11: 53–64.
Greenpeace. 2014, *Fukushima 3rd Anniversary Case Studies Report*, at: www.green peace.org/international/global/international/briefings/nuclear/2014/Case-Studies/CS02-Idogawa/pdf (accessed February 24, 2015).
Hayashi, Yuka and Schlesinger, Jacob M. 2014, "Japan's Abe secures landslide election win." *The Wall Street Journal*. December 14, at: www.wsj.com/articles/japans-abe-poised-for-landslide-election-win-1418555237 (accessed March 31, 2015).
Idogawa, Katsutaka. 2014, Personal interview, June 11.
*Japan Times*. 2014, Editorial "Fukushima's appalling death toll." March 1, at: www.japantimes.co.jp/opinion/2014/03/01/editorials/fukushimas-appalling-death-toll/#.VOrNXSx8uAo (accessed February 23, 2015).
Kingston, Jeff. 2012, "Mismanaging risk and the Fukushima nuclear crisis." *The Asia-Pacific Journal* Vol. 10, Issue 12, No. 4 (March 19), at: http://japanfocus.org/-Jeff-Kingston/3724/article.html (accessed December 16, 2015).
National Police Agency of Japan. 2014, "Heisei 23nen (2011nen) Tōhoku chihō taiheiyōoki jishin no higai jōkyō to keisatsu sochi." December 10, at: www.npa.go.jp/archive/keibi/biki/higaijokyo.pdf (accessed March 31, 2015).
NHK documentary. *Yearning for Home: Fukushima Evacuees Face Difficult Choices*. (First aired August 24, 2013), at: www.youtube.com/watch?v=qkpBHHjsnY8 (accessed July 14, 2014).
Oliver-Smith, Anthony. 2002, "Theorizing disasters," in Susanna M. Hoffman and Anthony Oliver-Smith (eds), *Catastrophe and Culture*. Santa Fe, NM: School of American Research Press, 23–47.
Sekula, Allan. 1982, "On the invention of photographic meaning," in Victor Burgin (ed.), *Thinking Photography*. London: Macmillan Press, 84–109.
Sontag, Susan. 2003, *Regarding the Pain of Others*. New York: Picador.
Tagg, John. 1988, *The Burden of Representation: Essays on Photographies and Histories*. London: Macmillan.
Tormey, Jane. 2013, *Cities and Photography*. Abingdon: Routledge.
Tsutsui, William. 2011, "Soft power and the globalization of Japanese popular culture," in Holroyd C. and Coates K. Abingdon (eds), *Japan in the Age of Globalization*. New York: Routledge, 136–47.
Weisenfeld, Gennifer. 2012, *Imaging Disaster: Tokyo and the Visual Culture of Japan's Great Earthquake of 1923*. Los Angeles, CA: University of California Press.
Zelizer, Barbie. 2002, "Finding aids to the past: Bearing personal witness to traumatic public events." *University of Pennsylvania Scholarly Commons* 1–17, at: http://repository.upenn.edu/cgi/viewcontent.cgi?article=1086&context=asc_papers (accessed December 9, 2015).

# 5 Uncanny anxiety
## Literature after Fukushima

*Saeko Kimura*

The nuclear accident at the Fukushima Daiichi power plant in March 2011, widely referred to simply as "Fukushima," has had an incredible (and still ongoing) impact on the world, second only to the nuclear accident at Chernobyl. The world literary sphere quickly responded to the 3.11 disaster, not only the tsunami but also the nuclear meltdowns. The Nobel Prize winner Elfriede Jelinek (b. 1946), for example, who released three plays on the Internet in response to the disaster,[1] pointedly addressed the problem of radioactive contamination and the ensuing health risks it posed in her play *No Light* (*Kein Licht*, 2011):

> People are shipping their precious children abroad; do not stand in their way, they will clamber right over your heads, because rescue is the order of the day! And they are right to do so! They do exactly what is right! The only thing that is right. Those who do not do the right thing at the right time must die [...] You cannot smell the radiation on the skin; yes, you can tweet about it. But better than tweeting—the best of all—is to get yourself to safety. In these times, safety is the only way out. Safety before all else. Only safety helps over the long term. And when finally secured, it is expected to, unconditionally, be maintained.
>
> (Jelinek 2012: 37–38)

Considering how sharply Jelinek responded to the situation, the Fukushima nuclear accident clearly was not someone else's problem happening in faraway Japan, but her own concern as an intellectual living on the same planet. In the above passage, the narrator repeatedly calls for evacuation to safety. Of course, this assumes that there are still safe places on earth. And yet it is difficult to determine where one can really be safe, especially after what happened at Chernobyl, Three Mile Island, and the Marshall Islands. Jelinek's call for evacuation demonstrates not only her global sensibility but also speaks to what we all experience with each nuclear catastrophe—in one phrase: the uncanny anxiety caused by radiation. The main problem is that people largely remain uninformed of exactly how radiation affects the human body. This ignorance gives rise to an uncanny fear, leading people to doubt whether anyone understands the real situation of contamination, and to wonder whether the government is suppressing any information.

The impalpability of radiation also makes it difficult to determine who the victims are. Who counts as affected by the nuclear accidents, and how can the boundaries of affected areas and the extent of risks posed to people's health be determined? Such ambiguity of boundaries, paired with the impalpable nature of nuclear contamination, causes great unease. In the current situation in Japan, only those who received an evacuation directive by the government are considered victims—only these people can file claims to TEPCO.[2] However, there are also many radioactive hotspots today, both inside and outside of Fukushima. When the contamination spread to Tokyo's drinking water[3] two weeks after the explosions, the government issued an alert not to give the water to infants. Later that year, powdered milk made in a Saitama factory was found to contain cesium,[4] again putting the health of infants at risk. Moreover, also that year, tea leaves in Shizuoka Prefecture were found to contain cesium, bringing danger to a wider population.[5] The more reports of contaminated food are published, the deeper people's fear of exposure becomes. Consequently, many residents evacuated of their own accord from the Tōhoku and Kantō areas, including Tokyo. Since no relief funds were made available to people outside the official contamination zones, leaving was an option only for those with sufficient financial means. In this sense, Jelinek's call to "evacuate to safety" could be seen as a little cruel to those people who could not afford to leave. The Fukushima incident revealed the stark distinction between "protected" and "precarious" life circumstances according to both financial resources and the ability to access information. Those who are "abandoned" by the government can only fight for support in court, much like the victims of the Hiroshima and Nagasaki bombings, and the victims of Minamata disease, which was caused by environmental pollution. The suffering of the victims of Fukushima should therefore not be downplayed—as some have argued—in order to avoid anxiety from spreading further. Instead, the truth must be told in order to ensure that the victims receive rightful compensation.

Leaving questions of liability and compensation aside, there is still the issue of people's lives and health. In 1986, after the Chernobyl incident, the news reported that spinach and milk in Japan were contaminated. Even at such a great distance from Chernobyl, Japanese people were still exposed to radiation, making it clear that no matter where on earth people live, they cannot be entirely safe from radioactive contamination. It is thus quite natural that novelists living outside of Japan reacted quickly to the Fukushima accident, among them not only Jelinek but also Japanese writers living in Europe such as Sekiguchi Ryōko (Paris, France) and Tawada Yōko (Berlin, Germany), both of whom have published extensively on radioactive contamination. Their geographical position in Europe helped trigger their motivation for writing. Being interviewed by European media as Japanese writers residing in Europe, they inevitably became spokeswomen on the issue, not least because physical distance from Japan does not necessarily mean emotional distance. Both started their careers as writers in Japan and have strong connections there, familial and otherwise. Furthermore, the Fukushima nuclear disaster has raised the specter for them of never being able to return to Japan. It is a terrifying thought to imagine such a familiar destination suddenly becoming inaccessible. This fear could be compared to Fukushima evacuees being roped out of their homes as the matter still stands. Perhaps this explains why Sekiguchi and Tawada reacted so quickly. The simultaneity of physical distance and intimacy they experienced corresponds in many ways to the paradox of radioactive contamination itself. For most people around the world, Fukushima is a faraway place; however, as a consequence of the global trade system, radiation is a present danger for people worldwide, whether it be borne by air, water, or food. The following will discuss in detail how Sekiguchi Ryōko and Tawada Yōko strive to represent this paradox of radioactive contamination in their works.

## Collective and potential fear

Sekiguchi Ryōko (b. 1970) has lived in Paris since 1997, where she works as a poet, writer, and translator both in French and Japanese. She reacted quickly to the nuclear incident by publishing portions of her diary in October 2011 as *This is not an Accident* (*Ce n'est pas un hasard*, 2011). The work includes diary entries from the days leading up to March 11 through to the end of April. Since it begins one day before March 11, the diary effectively shows how easily and abruptly daily life can break down. The day before March 11, she chats with her friend living in Tokyo who asks Sekiguchi to purchase an Hermès scarf. This endearing episode shows how easily a promise (in this case, bringing a scarf to Tokyo) can become impossible to keep. After reading about the disaster through several Facebook postings, she attempted to call her parents, but could not get through. For the first several days after the earthquake, the degree of information available in Yokohama and Paris seemed similar, based on television and Internet reports. However, after the explosions at the nuclear plants, the information gap between Japan and France expanded. The nuclear crisis in Japan woke the French people up to the possibility of a similar disaster occurring in France, and led the Green Party to make significant headway in the presidential elections of April 2012.

Drawing on my own experience back in 2011, I received a call from a friend in Paris after the disaster, asking me to leave Yokohama and fly to Paris, or at least move to western Japan. I laughed off his suggestion because I was unable to leave the city until spring break began. This friend had already called his parents but had failed to persuade them to leave Tokyo—they instead reassured him that they were fine. Sekiguchi, based in Paris since 1997, similarly writes that she had tried to convince her parents to leave Tokyo but failed. Many people would or simply could not leave. In contrast, French nationals, for example, were quickly evacuated from Japan on government-chartered planes, and the French embassy was temporarily vacated.[6] I remember hearing that Chinatown in Yokohama was sparsely populated after the nuclear disaster because many Chinese nationals also left Japan, while various foreign brand-name shops such as Louis Vuitton had to be shut because merchants chose to return to their home countries. Thus, the impact of the nuclear accident seemed to effectively set in motion actions and responses in France and other countries, yet not in Japan. This gap had to do with access to information on the danger and extent of radiation leaks. At the time, the Japanese people were mostly unaware of the reality of radioactive contamination. It is not surprising that Japanese writers living in Europe first realized this information gap. For example, Japanese residents did not know of the information of SPEEDI (System for Prediction of Environmental Emergency Dose Information), an information source on where radiation is spreading and in what doses. Instead, Japanese people continued going to work as usual. It was left to those writers living in Europe to spark and lead the intellectual discourse of the Japanese literary sphere.

Sekiguchi Ryōko shows her knowledge of the intricacies of Japanese society when she writes about taboos surrounding radioactivity. She cites Hiroshima and the Tōkaimura nuclear accident of 1999, and also mentions the so-called Daigo Fukuryū Maru incident when a Japanese ship of that name accidentally ran into US thermonuclear device tests on the Bikini Atoll on March 1, 1954, and was contaminated by the nuclear fallout. It is the memories of these historical incidents of radiation exposure that have evoked fear in people and prompted them to avoid being contaminated at all costs. Such avoidance can easily lead to the discrimination of the people in Fukushima since it is assumed they have been exposed to radiation. Immediately following March 11, 2011, consumption of domestic produce decreased in Japan due to the cautious and even depressed state of the populace, but it was only when consumption rose again about one year later that the reality and extent of radioactivity began to be better understood. By this point, the focus had shifted to other matters as interest in the disaster abated.

As a culinary expert who also publishes on cooking in food magazines in France, Sekiguchi is sensitive to the safety of food. In an article on the food from Fukushima, titled *The Taste of Fukushima* (*Le goût de Fukushima*, Sekiguchi 2012a) and published on August 19, 2011, she describes how, when making *osekihan* (red rice with beans) by herself, she remembers her childhood and realizes that the memory of food is not only about taste, but also triggers cherishable memories of her grandmother, her house, and her own existence back then. This episode strongly evokes part of what was lost at Fukushima. The disaster destroyed not only the regional food but also the lives and memories connected to it. Since the details of local culinary culture and living are handed down as oral history within the community, they can easily be lost when the community is dispersed.

Thinking of the government's efforts to clean up the contaminated land around Fukushima, Sekiguchi is reminded of a performance by the avant-garde artist group Hi-Red-Center, who were active in the 1960s and 1970s. Just before the Tokyo Olympics in 1964, Hi-Red-Center organized a street cleaning event called the Campaign to Promote Cleanliness and Order in the Metropolitan Area. The members wore white doctor's smocks and surgical masks and polished the street in an oddly impossible response to the government's appeal to clean up

Tokyo before the Olympic Games. The performance expressed, with bitter irony, the impossibility of ever completely cleaning the streets. Today, a similarly vain effort to decontaminate irradiated land is in progress in Fukushima; yet, despite these efforts, the histories of people's everyday lives cannot be recovered.

Right after *This is not an Accident*, Sekiguchi published two texts: *Eating Ghost: A Practical Handbook of Vaporous Food* (*Manger fantôme: Manuel pratique de l'alimentation vaporeuse*, Sekiguchi 2012b) and *The Astringent* (*L'astringent*, Sekiguchi 2012c). In the latter, she talks about astringent dried persimmons, explaining: "Fukushima Prefecture is (was) one of the regions producing dried persimmons (more than 2,500 tons per year)" (Sekiguchi 2012c: 25). By writing "is (was)," Sekiguchi indicates that some of the rich specialties of the Tōhoku region such as dried persimmons (*kaki*) cannot be produced anymore in the radiation-contaminated area, since not only the trees but also the air is contaminated.[7] Before the disaster, Fukushima and other areas in Tōhoku were regions where farmers sold their own products, assuring both their safety and taste through organic farming. It is painfully ironic that such an area was contaminated by radiation.

Furthermore, the catastrophe of Fukushima brought about the loss of a long and rich heritage of regional cuisine.[8] Culinary traditions handed down within families suddenly disappeared after people relocated and/or families fell apart. In the text *Eating Ghost*, Sekiguchi argues that whenever we eat we inevitably end up ingesting things we cannot taste. She takes up the case of genetically modified products unidentifiable by smell, taste, or touch; and yet we know they might affect our bodies some day. She thus parallels the fear of genetically modified products with radiation-contaminated products, although she does so without using the word "radiation-contaminated" (Sekiguchi 2012b: 72–73). Rather, she inserts a note in the text mentioning that a golf course 45 km away from Fukushima showed radiation levels of 2–3 micro Sieverts per hour in August 2011, and uses the word "phantom" to explain this thing undetectable to human senses (Sekiguchi 2012b: 82). In summary, enjoying good tasting food is not the same thing as eating food that is good for one's health; and even though it is labeled as safe by the government, the obvious fact of contamination in the Fukushima area inevitably creates anxiety. Such fear might be unjustified, yet it persists in those areas where radiation is still being detected.

In June 2013, a politician of the Liberal Democratic Party, Takaichi Sanae, declared that no deaths had resulted from the incidents at the nuclear reactors; however, after much criticism, she retracted her words and apologized.[9] Her ignorance and failure to appreciate the extent of the damage are traits shared with not just a few other Japanese who continue to underestimate the extent of the crisis and the danger it poses. According to a Reconstruction Agency report of March 31, 2015, a total of 3,331 people have died of causes related to the 3.11 disaster (Fukkōchō 2015). In Fukushima Prefecture, the number of deaths by disaster-related causes is much higher than the number of people killed by the disaster itself. This is both because the reconstruction process is too slow, and because for some people from Fukushima, reconstruction has meant living with severe anxiety over their health. The government has already given up on complete decontamination of the land, and instead is encouraging people to return to their homes assuring them that their personal exposure doses will be monitored. With the passage of time, the problem is not the disaster itself, but the insecurity it has created, and the lack of hope.[10] As if she had predicted such a situation, Tawada dealt with life in a contaminated land in her novels written immediately after Fukushima.

## Writing on a radiation-exposed world

Tawada Yōko provides a telling assessment of Japan's future in her short story "The Island of Eternal Life" ("Fushi no shima," Tawada 2012a), which was included in a commemorative book titled *March was Made of Yarn* (*Soredemo sangatsu wa mata*, 2012b) published in March 2012 in both English and Japanese. The short story is set in 2017, following the explosion of another nuclear reactor in 2015. This second nuclear power plant explosion leads to Japan being completely isolated from the world. With no one entering or leaving Japan, information about the country is limited.

The story is ominous in its prediction of the post-Fukushima shift back to nuclear power: After the shutdown of the Ōi Nuclear Power Plant in September 2013, all the reactors in Japan were shut down. However, as of October 2015, the two reactors at the Sendai Nuclear Power Plant in the Kagoshima Prefecture have been restarted, and one of the reactors in the Ehime Prefecture is ready to restart. On April 14, 2015, a group of residents won a court ruling preventing two nuclear reactors of the Takahama Nuclear Power Plant in the Fukui Prefecture from restarting, hampering the government's efforts to rebuild the country's atomic industry. The judge ruled that the restart of reactors poses a definite risk of infringing on personal rights. On the other hand, on April 22, 2015, residents of Sendai lost their court battle, and two of the Sendai power plant reactors were restarted (Reactor 1 was restarted on August 11, 2015; Reactor 2 was restarted on October 15, 2015). Considering that the court of the Fukui Prefecture admitted the danger of nuclear power plants, there is no certainty about their safety. However, this judgment of April 14, 2015 was reversed by the court on December 24, 2015, thus clearing the way for the restart of two nuclear reactors at the Takahama Nuclear Power Plant.

Tawada published another short story in 2014, called "The Far Shore" ("Higan"), which is now available in English via the Internet. The story again depicts Japan in the near future after another explosion at a nuclear power plant, this time caused by a US military airplane accidentally crashing into the plant. The resulting explosion is much more devastating than those at Fukushima and even more than the nuclear bombs dropped on Hiroshima and Nagasaki. In our situation today, as nuclear plants prepare to restart one by one, Tawada's story also sounds like a prophecy.

In the story, the female protagonist and narrator—a nameless Japanese women who has been living in Germany for years—wonders, "Why were they so slow to act, when they knew another big earthquake was inevitable?" She recalls what she observed in Japan during a previous visit in early spring of 2013, a date that was still in the future at the time of publication. The protagonist's reflections point to the crux of the problem that Japanese society faced in the aftermath of the nuclear disaster. The protagonist now lives in Berlin but has made her way to Kyoto for a week where she awaited the appearance of a live broadcast on television by the emperor, scheduled for two years after March 11, 2011. As she watches, she first sees a close-up of the Rising Sun flag blowing in the wind. She then describes, "What came on next was not the face we had been expecting, but a man with a black gauze hood over his face" (Tawada 2012b: 5).

> The entire screen shook. The cameraman must have been trembling. Sticking his neck out toward the microphone like a turtle, the masked man said, "The emperor's wish is that all nuclear plants should be shut down immediately." Everyone in the hotel lounge froze. He went on reassuringly, "There is no need for concern. This is not a kidnapping. I am very closely related to the person who was to have spoken here today," then added, "And we are all in agreement with him."
>
> (Tawada 2012b: 5)

The man in the black gauze hood brings to mind an incident in 2004 when a 24-year-old Japanese man named Kōda Shōsei was killed by terrorists in Iraq. In late October 2004, terrorists masked in black claimed responsibility for kidnapping Kōda and demanded that the Japanese government withdraw the Self-Defense Forces from Iraq within forty-eight hours of the broadcast. The prime minister of the time, Koizumi Junichirō, refused to withdraw and the terrorists responded by distributing a videotape of the beheading of Kōda. Immediately after Kōda's death, the focus in Japan was on blaming the young man for his thoughtless act of visiting a war-torn area alone. Rather than attacking Koizumi for failing to provide support for a Japanese citizen abroad, the mass media was saturated with the neo-liberalist notion of self-responsibility (*jiko sekinin*), which has become the political mantra of all Japanese administrations since. In Tawada's story, the image of the black mask can be seen as symbolically representing the government's disengagement from assisting citizens and a shift toward prioritizing economic profit above all else. The hooded man in Tawada's story thus links the government's collusion with the nuclear industry, and their failure to protect citizens such as with the state response to Kōda's capture in 2004. Moreover, the Japanese commitment to send Self-Defense Forces to Iraq during the war in 2004 can be seen as the turning point in national preparations to revise or abandon the war-renouncing Article 9 of Japan's Constitution. In Japan, this kidnapping is remembered as a symbolic image of the insecurity of citizens' lives. Again, in 2015, ISIS kidnapped two Japanese men, an activist called Yukawa Haruna and a journalist Gotō Kenji, and made a ransom demand to the Japanese government. Again, the government refused to pay and the two Japanese were beheaded. This awakened the nightmare of 2004, now intensified by the experience of the government's irresponsible handling of the Fukushima incident.

In "The Island of Eternal Life," the prime minister suddenly appears on television and declares, "Next month, all nuclear power plants will be closed down. For good!" (Tawada 2012b: 6). He then disappears, seemingly kidnapped or assassinated.

> After a period of unrest following the prime minister's disappearance, in 2015 the Japanese government was privatized; an organization calling itself the Z Group became the major government shareholder and began running the thing as a corporation. Television stations were taken over, and compulsory education was abolished.
>
> (Tawada 2012b: 7)

The process of privatization fictionally described here can be linked to the postal service privatization carried out during the term of former Prime Minister Koizumi Junichirō (2001–2006). As Tawada describes, Japan was indeed rapidly shifting toward utilitarianism and materialism, with economic benefit taking priority over actual lives. Tawada's story reveals how this approach acts today as justification for continuing to operate nuclear power plants in Japan. Moreover, with the current mood that hails the economic growth enabled through the government promotion of so-called Abenomics—that is, the pro-growth, neo-liberal economic strategy implemented by Prime Minister Shinzō Abe—the voices demanding denuclearization and decommissioning of nuclear plants have been nearly completely silenced.

As the title "The Island of Eternal Life" suggests, this piece of fiction does not center on the fear of death but rather on the anguish of a life eternally affected by radiation. In this inverted world, the younger generation dies young, so that the older generation must take care of them. Although having eternal life has long been the dream of humankind, here life without death is described pessimistically and ironically. In the final part of the story, Japan is revealed to be isolated in the world due to radioactive contamination and has lost all connections with other countries. There is no electricity and people live in a primitive way. Although science fiction (SF) literature often imagines hyper-future to be a highly electrical world, this SF story describes it as a dark age. The only way to avoid this fate, the story implies, is by abandoning nuclear energy.

Tawada continues to depict future worlds in her fiction, worlds in which people live with genetic defects caused by radioactive exposure. The story, "The Ambassadors of Light" ("Kentōshi," Tawada 2014b), can be seen as the second installment of the story "The Island of Eternal Life." In this novel, the Japanese government and police are privatized and Japan has adopted the policy of seclusion. Learning English is prohibited. The story is set almost half a century in the future, and the world familiar to us today is described as long past. The protagonist, Yoshirō, is 108 years old, and could easily be us in the future. Yoshirō is living in an evacuation house, together with his great-grandson called Mumei, in an outer western suburb of Tokyo, because Tokyo's twenty-three wards are too contaminated for human habitation. Countless people have been extinguished in just a few decades. Those people who survive have to import vegetables and fruits from Okinawa because Japan's mainland has been contaminated. The notion that all living beings have been affected at the genetic level is suggested by the fact that in this society the term sudden mutation (*totsuzen hen'i*) has come to be thought of as discriminatory, so people use the euphemism environmental assimilation (*kankyō dōka*) instead. Old people live to an advanced age, over 100 years, and their great-grandchildren's generations have bodies like a soft-bodied octopus, bodies that make them look almost like aliens as the result of genetic mutation. Since the younger generations have to be taken care of by the older, the word nuisance (*meiwaku*) has fallen out of use, as an elementary school teacher in the story explains: "The word 'nuisance' is now obsolete. You should remember this. Long ago, in less civilized times, people made a distinction between useful and not useful people. You must guard against this way of thinking" (Tawada 2014b: 137–38).

As pointed out above, under the Koizumi administration, Japan shifted increasingly toward a highly competitive society and abandoned the traditional welfare system. Many people lost their jobs during the long economic slump and the ensuing lay-offs. These people were considered social losers, unworthy of pity or assistance. They were labeled as such not because they fell through the cracks of the social welfare system, but because they were seen as failing to take responsibility for themselves. Ironically, it is only when faced with a catastrophic situation such as 3.11, after all the electricity has run out, that the state abandons the loser–winner paradigm. On the other hand, a little later in Tawada's story, the elementary school teacher explains: "Japan did not become like this because of any earthquake or tsunami. If it were only the result of a natural disaster, we could have overcome it a long time ago" (Tawada 2014b: 143). Since the readers after 3.11 easily remember that the nuclear disaster was triggered by an enormous earthquake and tsunami, the world described in this novel can be read as a depiction of how radioactive contamination harms human bodies and the entire living world.

The story's title, "Kentōshi," has a double meaning, depending on the characters used to write it. It is typically written with characters meaning "Japanese envoys sent on missions to Tang Dynasty." These missions had stopped by the eighth century and the subsequent decline of Chinese influence made possible the flowering of a Japanese court culture different from the Tang. Tawada uses other Chinese characters to create a word with the same pronunciation, but meaning "The Ambassadors of Light." In this story, children who are deemed "suitable" are sent secretly to Chennai (formerly known as Madras) in India, where they are hospitalized for tests to enable medical advances for the rest of the world. Thus, the term "Ambassadors of Light" could refer to those who facilitate new knowledge ("light") through their radiation-induced genetically altered bodies. The young protagonist Mumei is selected as one such *kentōshi*. His name, Mumei, literally means "no name," which suggests the anonymity, and lack of agency, of the "ambassadors"—sent abroad as hopeless cases, only for the purpose of testing.

Is this image that Tawada depicts too pessimistic? Is such a world possible? Perhaps they are—but we do know that radiation affects DNA. We know that no one welcomes radioactive contamination. And it is common knowledge that Japan is an island where earthquakes and tsunamis are unavoidable. Knowing these things, the consequences of having nuclear plants in Japan should be clear. Although Tawada does not use the term radioactive in her story and never explains the cause of people's genetic defects, the reader cannot help but think of it—and even more so with the follow-up works of various writers.

One month after "Kentōshi," Tawada published a short story called "The Far Shore" ("Higan") in literary magazine *Waseda Bungaku* (Autumn volume, 2014). In this story, a US military airplane accidentally crashes into a recently restarted nuclear plant in Japan. All Japanese citizens evacuate abroad as refugees. When the government restarted the nuclear power plant, it had counted on the support of twenty-two countries. Experts made assurances that this nuclear plant was "absolutely safe." However, no one anticipated an airplane crashing into it. The plant had been online for only one month before the accident.

> The newspapers had stated, "Engineers have been working with an outstanding French company to employ the best technology to finally bring the nuclear reactor back online. Every effort was made to check on the safety of the reactor and earn the approval of the local citizens." But to tell the truth, no one could figure out whose approval the newspapers had been talking about. The reason was that there was only a single person left living in the area—a former poet named Sachio Yamano—and he was dead set against reactivating the reactor. Other families had lived in the area too, but the antinuclear movement had turned family members against one another, and eventually, everyone grew weary of the tension and left the area.
> (Tawada 2014a)

Today, this is a desperately familiar sight in Japan. After five years of catastrophe, the electric companies and the government are enthusiastically preparing to restart nuclear plants one by one. There are no signs of abandoning nuclear energy, even after such a shocking experience. The Japanese government and TEPCO tend to think of the Fukushima incident not as the result of human error but as the result of an unforeseeable natural disaster. Their conclusion: "It is absolutely safe to restart the reactors as long as nothing unforeseen happens," or "When one stops to think about it, it should be obvious that there is always a chance that something unforeseen might happen"—as described in "The Far Shore." In Tawada's interpretation, the decision of restarting the nuclear power plant is the result of a pressure to conform (*dōchō atsuryoku*). In such a situation, the possibility of something like the following evacuation scene is all too real.

The expression "there is more than one way to weather a crisis" had been popular at the time of the disaster, but afterward, the opposite was true.

> There was only one way to survive, and that was to leave Japan. It was no longer possible to live anywhere on the Japanese archipelago. The nuclear reactor was a monster whose brains had been bashed in, and in its fury, it burned the flesh of anyone that drew near. It would take millennia for its anger to subside.
>
> (Tawada 2014a)

If another nuclear plant exploded in Japan, the small archipelago could very well become uninhabitable. In Tawada's story, Russia and China accept the refugees from Japan. Among them is a former member of the upper house of the Diet named Sede Ikuo. He worries whether he will be accepted in China because of his past acts of hate speech toward China, statements he had made not out of a policy objective, but because he found that insulting China cured his erectile dysfunction. In reality, there is a tendency among some Japanese to vent their pent-up frustration by attacking China or Korea. Moreover, since the right-wing Liberal Democratic Party took control of the government after March 11, and the relations between Korea or China and Japan increasingly have got worse, Tawada's text can be read as a critique of the government. The title "Higan" literally means "the other shore," with the nearest "shores" to Japan being those of China and Korea. However, in Buddhist context, the word *higan* also means "the other realm after death." Thus, Sede Ikuo's fate hinges on whether he is accepted as a refugee in China or arrested as a political criminal. The ending of the novel can be read as black humor, or a kind of black realism.

In "The Far Shore," Tawada also writes in greater detail about radiation exposure, describing the long-term suffering caused by internal exposure:

> But those terrifying scenes lasted only a few seconds. After that came painful burns that inflicted great, lingering suffering on the victims. The skin itself did not look that different, but the burns hurt terribly. The victims felt like their arms and legs had been pierced all the way to the bone with long skewers, and their flesh was being roasted over hot coals. These were strange burns, unlike any that anyone had ever experienced before. Some people survived because their burns were less severe. Afterward, they said that the burns were not visible at first, but their flesh continued to cook from the inside over the course of days. Before long, the burned areas swelled and blistered until they looked like fish eggs pickled in red peppers. Fortunately, there was a type of Chinese medicine made of the roasted skin of a water snake that proved effective in treating the burns. People who applied it to their skin were saved, but it took years for the pain to disappear and the stretched, reddish purple, glistening skin to return to normal.
>
> (Tawada 2014a)

The victims of Hiroshima and Nagasaki fought for a long time for compensation for the effects of internal exposure. The government has only acknowledged external exposure as measured by the distance from ground zero. Irradiation is difficult to verify and quantify exactly. Irradiation is experienced less as a concrete phenomenon and more as anxiety, the cause of which is only retrospectively identified, after the disease becomes visible. The cause of irradiation can thus rarely be proven conclusively in court or even diagnosed at a hospital. In this sense, the real problem of irradiation has to do not only with the particular health problems it may cause, but also, and perhaps even more devastatingly so, with the way it plunges one into a lifelong state of precariousness and anxiety. According to Hayashi Kyōko (b. 1930), who has written novels as a survivor of Nagasaki, she was astonished to hear the expression "inner exposure" being used by the government after the Fukushima incident. Survivors had fought for compensation to make the government admit the fact of internal exposure, but in some cases failed in court. In Hayashi's view, the people of Fukushima share the same fate with the victims of Hiroshima and Nagasaki in their struggle for indemnities (Hayashi 2013). The victims of Minamata disease and other environmental disasters have also sued the government, and now the victims of Fukushima join their numbers.

In "The Far Shore," Tawada explicitly uses the image of Hiroshima and Nagasaki victims as follows:

> That day, tens of millions of victims stretched their burned arms before them and staggered toward the nearest rivers and lakes, trying to find relief in the water. They didn't notice if they lost their shoes along the way. Their bare, blood-soaked feet didn't feel pain when they stepped on the broken window panes scattered all over—they just kept tottering along as they searched for water, heads lowered and stuck out in front of them like fighting bulls. Countless people fell along the way. It was as if the roads were exerting some powerful force and sucking them down, face first. The dead lay motionless, kissing the asphalt. No one drove anywhere. All the cars had grown so hot that it was impossible to touch the metal on their doors. All the buses and trains had stopped, with the outlines of incinerated drivers and train conductors burned into the seats.
>
> (Tawada 2014a)

Hideously burned people walking toward the river is a well-known image from the aftermath of the atomic bombings of Hiroshima and Nagasaki. In "The Far Shore," the nuclear power plants explode with the same force as those bombs, and this terrifying image echoes as a possible future for Japan. Tawada's novels have a strong critical tone, and she is not isolated in the literary sphere.[11] Her works help us to imagine both the short- and long-term consequences of relying on nuclear power in this small archipelago.

## Conclusion

How can one write effectively about the dangers of radiation? Does such writing necessarily involve a warning or a prophecy? Sekiguchi Ryōko and Tawada

Yōko's works do not simply inflame people's fears, but rather work to close the gap between the facts and anxiety. Most Japanese people no longer think very much about the explosions at the Fukushima Daiichi Nuclear Power Plant. Indeed, most of them seem to have forgotten about them and remain unaware or, even worse, ignorant of the continuing effects. Somehow, they have convinced themselves that the danger has passed and the plants are now safe again. Yet the amount of radiation being released has not decreased after four years. Instead, the situation has gotten even worse as the present government sleepwalks its way back to the days before the disaster. Fears of radioactive contamination are mostly hidden in silence.

On the other hand, it is often reported that TEPCO is doing an abysmal job in its clean-up efforts at Fukushima. The *Asahi Shimbun* reported on December 31, 2014, that TEPCO had been using a radiation-suppressant dust that was so diluted as to be entirely ineffective. On February 25, 2015, it was reported that TEPCO had secretly allowed contaminated water to run into the sea for an entire year (see *Nihon Keizai Shimbun Web News* 2015). People subconsciously or consciously know that radioactive water is leaking into the environment, and they know that the threat of radiation will continue for many decades to come. In this situation, it is perhaps understandable that people simply decide to not think about radiation anymore. Many prefer to remain ignorant rather than spend every day and every moment worrying for their present and future. However, no matter how much they may try to forget, an uncanny anxiety persists.

People living with such uncanny anxiety are generally unaware of the full extent or effects of radiation exposure. However, the problem is not only that they cannot know the future but also the anxiety-laden atmosphere that prevents them from speaking up, even after certain facts and effects have come to light. In Tawada's story "Kentōshi," there is an episode in which Yoshirō cannot publish a children's story he wrote—a story about a girl whose mother makes boxed lunches to look like Japan's national flag. One day her mother is hospitalized and the girl prepares a lunch box by herself using seaweed on rice in the shape of a panda's face. Because this is perceived as an unpatriotic act, the girl is sent to reform school and her mother is arrested. The situation of people having to show their loyalty to the nation in the novel can be read as a vivid description of daily life in present-day Japan after the 3.11 triple disaster, especially in affected areas,[12] as showing loyalty to the nation too often means not speaking out about radiation. The rationale, it seems, is that to speak out is to spread fear of contamination and, possibly, to subvert Japan's plan to host the Olympic games in 2020. Meanwhile, Fukushima's farmers are suffering, unable to sell their products; and those people who speak out are accused too quickly and easily of worsening their situation. After Fukushima, people in Japan feel this kind of pressure to toe the party line of the government's reconstruction policies and not question its assurances of safety against radioactive damage. Most of the hesitation over voicing concerns over the danger of radiation results from this unspoken pressure. In this regard, writing on radiation can be identified as a crucial act of resistance against the government's efforts at covering up the truth. Those writings clear a path for acknowledging the reality of contamination and bring readers closer to understanding the suffering of the victims. Writings on radiation have the potential to jolt the community of mute spectators out of complacency, filling their empty jars of anxiety with words.

**Notes**

1 Another work worth mentioning is the novel *A Tale for the Time Being* (2013) by Japanese-Canadian Ruth Ozeki who lives on the coast of Canada. The novel is based on a diary of a Japanese high school girl who is driven away from Japan.
2 According to TEPCO's website (TEPCO n.d.), areas qualifying for compensation are within 20 km of the Fukushima Daiichi Nuclear Power Plant, as well as Iidate-mura, Kawamata-machi, Katsurao-mura, and part of Minamisōma-shi; the rest is part of Namie-machi. TEPCO also has said it will pay for the business lost due to the nuclear accident.
3 According to the *Nihon Keizai Shimbun* (March 24, 2011, morning edition), radio-iodine levels of 210 Bq/kg were detected, that is, over the temporal limit of 100 Bq/kg for infants.
4 According to the *Nihon Keizai Shimbun* (December 7, 2011, morning edition), cesium levels of 30.8 Bq/kg were detected in powdered baby milk. Although this is below the temporal limit of 200 Bq/kg, Meiji initiated a recall of the powdered milk.
5 According to the *Nihon Keizai Shimbun* (June 10, 2011, morning edition), cesium levels above the temporal limit of 500 Bq/kg were detected, prompting Shizuoka Prefecture to issue a cease shipment order.
6 The US Embassy decided on March 16, 2011, to support US nationals and their relatives' evacuation from within 80 km of the Fukushima Daiichi Nuclear Power Plant, including evacuation from Japan; the British Embassy also issued an evacuation advisory to UK nationals residing in Tokyo areas further north (*Nihon Keizai Shimbun Web News* 2011b). While, apparently, the French government had made the decision to offer support for evacuation earlier than any other country (*Nihon Keizai Shimbun Web News* 2011c). However, the paper also reports that although some people thought this was an overreaction, the French were most likely applying safety protocols by the book rather than responding to the actual situation on the ground.
7 On December 22, 2015, the *Tokyo Shimbun* reported that Date City in Fukushima Prefecture had restarted the production and selling of dried *kaki* fruits in 2015; they conducted intensive decontamination of the trees and land and are monitoring radiation levels before shipping.
8 The idea that the traditional foods of Fukushima are being lost is the main theme of the mangas *Oishinbo: Fukushima no shinjitsu* (*The Gourmet: The Truth of Fukushima*, Kariya and Hanasaki 2013). See Chapter 11 in this volume.
9 According to the *Nihon Keizai Shimbun Web News* (2013), Takaichi Sanae claimed at a press conference: "The accident at the Fukushima Daiichi nuclear plants did not cause any deaths. We have no choice but to restart the nuclear plants as we proceed with utmost caution."
10 According to the *Nihon Keizai Shimbun Web News* (2014), the Ministry of the Environment and the Fukushima Prefectural Government released an interim report that they had shifted from a policy of pursuing complete decontamination to one of individual dosimetry.
11 Kawakami Hiromi continues to write short stories with the common theme of genetic defects set in the near future. This theme resonates with the story in Tawada's story "Kentōshi" in that gender and sexuality are not determined as they are now, and human beings change sex once or twice in their lifetime.

12 This is the main theme of *Bollard Syndrome* (*Borado byō*, 2014) by Yoshimura Man'ichi. In this novel, people come back from an evacuation center and live in their home town of Umizuka, a presumably radioactive contaminated area. They are at risk if they eat the products from this area and yet they love this area. The protagonist Kyōko is a girl of elementary school age. Her fellow students die one after another. The story is narrated by Kyōko from her perspective as an elementary school girl until the end. Readers do not know what these episodes mean until the end, when the narration switches to a grown-up Kyōko, and readers learn that Kyōko has now been arrested and imprisoned for knowing that her town is contaminated and refusing to eat the food from the area.

## References

Fukkōchō, 2014, "Higashi nihon daishinsai niokeru shinsai kanrenshi no shishasū" 26 December, at: www.reconstruction.go.jp/topics/main-cat2/sub-cat2-6/20150630_kanrenshi.pdf (accessed November 27, 2015).

Hayashi, Kyōko. 2013, "Futatabi rui e." *Gunzō*, April, 8–27.

Jelinek, Elfriede. 2012, *No Light*. Originally published in German (*Kein Licht*. 2011, premiered at Schauspiel Köln), here translated into English from Japanese translation: Hayashi Tatsuki trans. *Hikari no nai*, Tokyo: Hakusuisha, 37–38.

Kariya, Tetsu and Hanasaki, Akira, 2013, *Oishinbo: Fukushima no shinjitsu 1*, No. 110, Tokyo: Kodansha. *Oishinbo: Fukushima no shinjitsu 2*, No. 111, Tokyo: Kodansha, 2014.

*Nihon Keizai Shimbun Web News*. 2011a, "Bei, seifu kankeisha kazoku no nihontaihi o shōnin, chātāki yōi mo." March 17, at: www.nikkei.com/article/DGXNASGM17015_X10C11A3000000/ (accessed May 19, 2015).

*Nihon Keizai Shimbun Web News*. 2011b, "Eigaimushō, Tōkyō ihoku kara no taihi kentō o kankoku." March 17, at: www.nikkei.com/article/DGXNASFK16022_W1A310C1000000/ (accessed May 19, 2015).

*Nihon Keizai Shimbun Web News*. 2011c, "Daishinsai, hinan isogu furansujin shūtōna manyuaru de kōdō." March 21, at: www.nikkei.com/article/DGXNASGM1806G_Z10C11A3000000/ (accessed May 19, 2015).

*Nihon Keizai Shimbun Web News*. 2013, "Takaichi shi 'Fukushima jiko, shisha detenai' yoyatō ga hihan." June 18, at: www.nikkei.com/article/DGXNASFS1803L_Y3A610C1PP8000/ (accessed May 19, 2015).

*Nihon Keizai Shimbun Web News*. 2014, "Josen, kojin senryō jūshi ni kuni nado chūkanhōkoku." August 2, at: www.nikkei.com/article/DGXLASDG0104U_R00C14A8CC1000/ (accessed May 19, 2015).

*Nihon Keizai Shimbun Web News*. 2015, "Osen mizu ryūshutsu, gyogyōsha 'shinrai yuragu' Tōden wo hihan." February 26, at: www.nikkei.com/article/DGKKASDG25H6J_V20C15A2CR8000/ (accessed May 19, 2015).

Sekiguchi, Ryōko. 2011, *Ce n'est pas un hasard: Chronique japonaise*. Paris: P.O.L.

Sekiguchi, Ryōko. 2012a, "Le goût de Fukushima," in Corine Quentin and Cécile Sakai (eds), *L'archipel des séismes*. Paris: Éditions Philippe Picquier, 274–85.

Sekiguchi, Ryōko. 2012b, *Manger fantôme or Eating Phantom*. Paris: Argol.

Sekiguchi, Ryōko. 2012c, *L'astringent*. Paris: Argol.

Tawada, Yōko. 2012a, "Fushi no shima." *Soredemo sangatsu wa mata*. Tokyo: Kōdansha.

Tawada, Yōko. 2012b, "The Island of Eternal Life," in Elmer Luke and David Karashima (eds), *March was Made of Yarn*. New York: Vintage Books, 3–11.

Tawada, Yōko. 2014a, "Higan." Trans. Jeffrey Angles. "The Far Shore," at: http://wordswithoutborders.org/article/the-far-shore (accessed March 27, 2015).

Tawada, Yōko. 2014b, "Kentōshi." *Kentōshi*. Tokyo: Kōdansha.
TEPCO. n.d., "Genshiryoku songai baishou ni tsuite," at: www.tepco.co.jp/fukushima_hq/compensation/index-j.html (accessed May 19, 2015).
*Tōkyō Shimbun*. 2015, "Fukkatsu mokuzen—Anpogaki no sato Date chihō shinsai mae no 75% shukka mezasu." December 22, at: www.tokyo-np.co.jp/article/feature/tohokujisin/fukushima_report/list/CK2015122202000171.html (accessed January 10, 2016).
Yoshimura, Man'ichi. 2014, *Borado byō*. Tokyo: Bungeishunjū.

# 6 Problematizing life

Documentary films on the 3.11 nuclear catastrophe

*Hideaki Fujiki*

The 3.11 nuclear catastrophe has imposed a split between life and livelihood on the residents and former residents of the stricken areas.[1] By 'life,' I mean biological existence and health in distinction to death and disease. 'Livelihood,' on the other hand, means modes of living, including eating, sleeping, working, shopping, and also encompasses familial relationships, kinship, friendship, culture (hobbies, arts, and crafts), and one's homeland, as well as the overall economy. The English word 'life' usually signifies these two meanings together, but the post-3.11 reality has forced the (exiled) residents to consider them separately and to value one over the other. A major part of this problem has resulted from the fact that scientists do not completely agree on the full extent and effect of the radioactive contamination. In its April 19, 2011 notification, the Japanese government defined 1–20 millisieverts (mSv) per year as the provisional standard by which to decide whether a school facility and playground will be allowed for children's use (Bandō *et al.* 2011).[2] However, although the government said this standard is based on a statement by the International Commission on Radiological Protection (ICRP), ICRP's 2007 Recommendations show that this range of radiation is normally reserved for "occupational exposure in planned situations" rather than the general public (Valentin 2007: 97). Moreover, even this international authority is often suspected of conspiring with the nuclear industry or at least of putting priority on the economic optimization (see, for instance, Yagasaki 2013; Kashimoto 2011: 515). In this critical yet ambiguous situation, the Japanese government and mass media have promoted the vision of safety in which the radioactive diffusion is not a fatal matter for the stricken areas and their adjacent areas, and people's anxiety about the contamination of air, water, and food has largely been caused by rumors (*fūhyō*). This has posed the following dilemmas. Should the residents overcome their anxiety about the radiation by believing this discourse of safety and focus on reconstructing the areas? Or, should they not prioritize protecting their and their children's biological lives over their livelihoods in consideration of any potential radioactive risk? From a standpoint of people who live in relatively safe areas both inside and outside Japan, should we leave the choice of whether they will remain in their hometowns to the affected residents or should we actively assist or even urge them to evacuate from the seemingly stricken areas without sticking to any part of the livelihoods they had enjoyed there? I argue that how to represent life and livelihood is a crucial point granting access to films and other media dealing with the aftermath of the nuclear catastrophe. This is inextricably linked with their stance vis-à-vis econo-political power: the network mockingly named *genshiryoku mura* or the 'nuclear power village' consisting of bureaucrats, politicians, the Tokyo Electric Power Company (TEPCO) and its affiliates, scientists labeled *goyō gakusha* (opportunist scholars), and mass media. The meltdowns of the Fukushima Daiichi Nuclear Power Station led to a surge of criticism of this econo-political power block for victimizing, exploiting, and deceiving citizens (see Fujiki: forthcoming). This chapter focuses on documentary films and will discuss how they deal with these two axes: their different stances vis-à-vis econo-political power and their representations of life and livelihood.

I will first briefly provide an overall perspective on documentary films concerning the 3.11 nuclear catastrophe in terms of the two main axes. Since March 11, 2011, a countless number of documentary films on the post-catastrophe have been made and are being made, and they have constituted a tendentious yet contested terrain for the imagination of the issue. Among them, whereas pro-government documentaries like *Living in Fukushima: A Story of Decontamination and Reconstruction* (*Fukushima ni ikiru: Josen to fukkō no monogatari*, 2013) de-problematize the split between life and livelihood, many other documentaries problematize either side of this division. While the former is freely accessible on the government's website, the latter are independent films that are privately financed (at times in combination with crowdfunding) and mostly shown at film festivals, independent film theaters,[3] and non-commercial venues such as independent screening events organized by citizens and schools, in addition to being released on DVD and online (for more details, see Fujiki: forthcoming). This overview is followed by a close examination of two documentary films: *Surviving Internal Exposure* (*Naibu hibaku o ikinuku*, 2012) and *A2-B-C* (2013). While many independent documentaries such as *Nuclear Nation* (*Futaba kara tōku hanarete*, 2012)[4] predominantly illuminate the issues of livelihood, these two films first and foremost are concerned with issues of life. Yet, they take markedly different approaches; in contrast with *Surviving Internal Exposure*, which tends to advise the self-management of children's health through a narrational reference to scientific proof, *A2-B-C* questions institutional practices for protecting children's health and illuminates the residents' struggle with the public sphere through a non-authoritative and therapeutic mode of filmic narration. Through these analyses, I will show how these two films are taking significant positions in a contested arena for the representation of life and livelihood, an arena that an increasing number of documentary films have constituted with regard to the post-3.11 nuclear catastrophe. Needless to say, the split between life and livelihood is not the only matter that the post-3.11 documentaries engage with. Nevertheless, combined with the issue of econo-political power, this, I believe, is an integral matter not only for films and other media but also for the overall complexity of the socio-political situation after 3.11.

## Mapping documentaries

Almost all documentary films concerning the 3.11 nuclear catastrophe take a stance on the econo-political power embodied by the national government, the nuclear industry, and their affiliated forces. We can see that some films are supportive of this power while many are critical of it. Although some films are ambiguous in their stance, this very ambiguity can be seen as a particular political stance. What then defines these stances vis-à-vis econo-political power? If a film propagates the government's policy, how does it represent its administrative and political ideas and practices? In what sense are some filmic representations critical of econo-political power? I argue that the difference between the pro-power films and anti-power films largely hinges on how they represent the issues of life and livelihood.

As noted, the 3.11 nuclear catastrophe has imposed a split between life and livelihood on residents. This split reminds us of Giorgio Agamben's divisions between *zoē*, *bios*, and 'bare life.' For Agamben, *zoē* is the biological fact of having life or existence whereas *bios* is the form of living. 'Bare life' lies between these two categories produced by the way 'life' has been split in the Western political tradition. On the basis of Carl Schmitt's conception of the 'state of exception,' Agamben traces the inclusive exclusion of bare life from the political. For him, typical examples in the modern age are refugees as well as the prisoners in Nazi concentration camps and in Guantanamo Bay, where these people are reduced to their bodily life or 'bare life' under conditions in which exception becomes the rule. In these cases, 'bare life', Agamben emphasizes, is included as a form of existence stripped of political rights at the limit point of politics (Agamben 1998; Murray 2010).

This idea of inclusive exclusion may be applicable to the Japanese government's designation of the post-3.11 'safe area' as areas affected by less than 20 mSv of radiation—a standard that ICRP advises only in exceptional cases. In this case, politics differentiates the residents of disaster areas with radioactive doses from 1–20 mSv from those who live in areas outside the designated disaster zone with less than 1 mSv of radiation, which is ICRP's normal standard. This state of exception, however, seems more complicated than Agamben's examples. While the national government deals with the post-3.11 residents as the object of protection rather than the object of surveillance, it does so only on the surface, while also focusing on minimizing financial costs. This is clear in the two directions that the government has taken. In the first place, rather than making efforts to evacuate the residents who are possibly jeopardized and to provide them with a comfortable environment elsewhere, the government has carried out a decontamination (*josen*) program that nudges the residents to choose to remain in the 1–20 mSv areas rather than to leave. In other words, the measure has defined the option of evacuating from the 'exceptionally safe' areas (and the nearby possibly dangerous areas) not as the matter of the government's administrative responsibility but as the matter of the residents' own decision or responsibility. Moreover, this neo-liberalist policy has gone hand in hand with the proliferation of a discourse of safety and human bonds (*kizuna*) promoted by the government and mass media. As a result, Japan has seen the emergence of a type of public sphere that clearly differs from that described by Jürgen Habermas (1996) (in which rational subjects are assumed to engage in candid discussions). Instead, this public sphere pressures the residents not to voice contrary opinions for fear of spoiling the friendly atmosphere and the popular groundswell toward reconstruction. Significantly, this tendency has taken hold while leading people to forget the original and fundamental responsibility of the government and TEPCO for the nuclear catastrophe.

Most documentary films on the catastrophe are concerned with these complexities, but their stances on econo-political power, as well as their ways of representing life and livelihood, vary. A few films are, explicitly or implicitly, supportive of government-corporate power. *Living in Fukushima* is a typical example. It was sponsored and planned by the Ministry of the Environment, produced by United Nations University's Institute for the Advanced Study of Sustainability, and supported by the giant advertising company Dentsū Inc. The resultant film allows for free access on the website of the Plaza for Information on Decontamination (*Josen jōhō puraza*), which was co-founded by the Ministry of the Environment and the Prefectural Government of Fukushima. Echoing the overall governmental logic, this film suggests that the affected areas are now safe thanks to the government's decontamination measures and therefore the residents' anxiety about the radiation is just caused by 'rumors' (*fūhyō*) and their own paranoia about radiation. According to this logic, the disbelief and rumor should be overcome by their effort to change their own feelings (*kimochi*) rather than putting demands on the government and TEPCO. Thus, *Living in Fukushima* de-problematizes life and livelihood altogether and depoliticizes the aftermath of 3.11 by beautifully representing the cooperation between the government, the industry, and the residents. A similar inclination can be seen in the academy-awarded short documentary *The Tsunami and the Cherry Blossom* (*Tsunami soshite sakura*, 2011), as well as in *Pray for Japan* (*Nihon eno inori: Kokoro o hitotsuni*, 2012), and *Beyond the Cloud* (*Kiri no mukō no Yonaoshi 3.11*, 2013). Even though official production notes do not list formal government backing, *The Tsunami and the Cherry Blossom*, for instance, cheers the mood of reconstruction while emphasizing Japanese traditions and 'soul' (*kokoro*) symbolized by the cherry blossom.

The majority of documentaries, however, are critical of the government and nuclear industry to a greater or lesser extent. Yet, the ways in which these films represent life and livelihood vary considerably. The films that can be positioned at the one end of this range exclusively highlight the (ex-)residents' livelihoods. A prominent example is Funahashi Atsushi's *Nuclear Nation*, which have been most remarkably shown at independent film theaters and screenings events organized by citizens' groups and schools both inside and outside Japan, in addition to its release on DVD. From the beginning toward the end, the film chronicles the seasonally changed livelihood of the former residents of Futaba District—which has the fifth and sixth reactors of the Fukushima Daiichi Nuclear

Power Station in its land, and more than 80 percent of the land of which is located within a radius of ten kilometers from the plant—with an emphasis on emotion and sentiment. This enables the film to narrate the post-3.11 nuclear catastrophe from a thoroughly bottom-up point of view. It follows that, although this documentary is not overtly a political film, the bottom-up telling of the story on the 'refugees' from Futaba necessarily leads to a both implicit and explicit critique of the econo-political power. However, because *Nuclear Nation* predominantly concerns the issues of livelihood, it does not really problematize the concept of life or the split between life and livelihood. This inclination, we could argue, reveals an unintentional co-optation by the logic of the government, which de-problematizes the issues of life and promotes the former residents' return to the town and its reconstruction. Other examples of this type of documentary include *The Will: If Only There Were No Nuclear Power* (*Yuigon: Genpatsu sae nakereba*, 2013), *Fukushima: We Won't Forget* (*Wasurenai Fukushima*, 2013), and *Fukushima 2011: A Record of People Exposed Radiation* (*Fukushima 2011: Hibaku ni sarasareta hitobito no kiroku*, 2011). Despite their different characteristics, each of them emphasizes certain elements of livelihood, including familial relationships, bi-national married couples, and cultural traditions.

At the other end of the spectrum, films such as *Women of Fukushima* (*Fukushima no joseitachi*, 2012), *Fukushima Never Again* (2012), and *Kakusei: The Fukushima End* (2013) illuminate health issues by interviewing and showing citizen-activists, critics, physicians, and/or scientists protesting the government's policies on nuclear energy and the spreading radiation. In these films, a conflict between life and livelihood often comes to the fore, as in the case of *Kakusei: The Fukushima End*'s poignant and lyrical depiction of the relationship between a mother and son. She wants to evacuate her high-school-aged son from the stricken area for the sake of his health, while he wants to stay there because of his affection for his hometown. As such, these films each show a certain tension between concerns about health and those about the economy of livelihood. I will discuss this type of documentary in more detail by analyzing *Surviving Internal Exposure* and *A2-B-C*.

Other films can be identified within this spectrum, but they tend to suggest the compatibility of life and livelihood. *Friends after 3.11* (2012) and *Welcome to Fukushima* (*Fukushima e yōkoso*, 2013), with the exception of certain scenes, both juxtapose the issues of life and livelihood, rather than problematizing their tension. In *Friends after 3.11*, its celebrated director Iwai Shunji himself shows up, going around interviewing famous anti-nuclear cultural figures including scientists, journalists, a film-maker, a physician, actors, and a social worker. *Welcome to Fukushima*, on the other hand, represents the issues by combining interviews with several residents and experts on radioactivity with poetic images of the landscape and traditional culture (such as a *shogun* riding a horse). In this vein, *Ordinary Lives* (*Futsū no seikatsu*, 2013) is an interesting case because it is more concerned about life; nevertheless, its tension with livelihood is still ambiguous. At times, this film does introduce some residents' psychological conflicts concerning life and livelihood through interviews and scenes of dialogue. Concurrently, however, the film regularly punctuates the story with shots of beautiful scenery like cherry blossoms and Mount Aizu-Bandai in Kōriyama City, Fukushima Prefecture, as well as chronicling residents' daily activities. In this way, it communicates their affection for their hometown and their desire to maintain their previous livelihoods. While these films have different points of emphasis and filmic styles, they all share a critical stance regarding the government and the nuclear industry.

It should be noted here that all of the films above, from the pro-government to the anti-government films and from those prioritizing livelihood to ones focusing on life, have several common features. First of all, most of them extensively use interviews, though their modes of interviewing differ. In addition, unlike the American National Geographic Channel's sensational docu-drama *Seconds from Disaster: Fukushima, Japan's Nuclear Nightmare* (2012), those films neither insert re-enacted scenes nor construct mystery plots (though *311* [2011] can be seen as a somewhat sensational mystery type of documentary). Equally important, the majority of the documentaries cannot be seen as environmentalist films.[5] Certainly, there are exceptions. They include: *Wind from Fukushima* (*Fukushima karano kaze*, 2011), which introduces an environmentalist theme through an interviewee's remark: "all the human beings are victimizers of nature"; *Fukushima: A Record of Living Creatures* (*Fukushima: Ikimono no kiroku*, 2013) and *Zone: The Life Did Not Exist* (2013), both of which pay primary attention to the impact on animals including livestock and pets; and Robert Stone's *Pandora's Promise* (2013), which argues that global warming is a far more imperative issue to be solved than nuclear energy.[6] However, the majority of documentaries on the nuclear catastrophe do not problematize the damage that human beings inflict on non-humans. Moreover, placed in the context of the history of Japanese documentary, they do not engage in what the film scholar Jane Gaines calls 'political mimesis' as much as, say, Prokino films[7] and Ogawa Shinsuke's films[8]; although some anti-nuclear films include footage of demonstrations, they do not dedicate central, long sequences to "the production of affect in and through the conventionalized imagery of struggle" such as "bloodied bodies, marching throngs, angry police" (Gaines 1999: 92). The documentaries on the nuclear catastrophe also depart from Tsuchimoto Noriaki's series of documentaries on mercury poisoning in Minamata and from documentaries on the aftermath of the Chernobyl catastrophe such as *Chernobyl Heart* (2003) and *Controverses nucléaires* (2004) in that they do not explicitly present visibly diseased bodies. They instead portray people who are struggling with invisible matters, such as radiation, internal exposure, and the impact of the crisis on social relations or the structure of feeling. Finally, none of the films mentioned above take as extreme a position as urging the residents to evacuate from the possibly contaminated areas. This is probably because of either filmmakers' own econo-cultural ideal of reconstructing the stricken areas or because they work from an ethical position that pre-emptively respects the decision made by those who have recently suffered this extraordinary calamity.

Positioned in this broad perspective, *Surviving Internal Exposure* and *A2-B-C* can be seen as simultaneously representative and unique films that counter econo-political power and problematize life in the wake of the 3.11 nuclear catastrophe. Below I will move on to close analyses of these two films.

## Advising the management of life: *Surviving Internal Exposure*

Kamanaka Hitomi's *Surviving Internal Exposure* and Ian Thomas Ash's *A2-B-C* both highlight the health or biological life of residents, and especially children. Kamanaka, after studying and practicing film-making in North America and then working for NHK briefly in the 1990s, has been engaged in making documentary films on nuclear issues since the early 2000s. In alliance with the independent media company Group Gendai/NPO TVE, she has worked as an independent film-maker as her reputation was boosted through awards at film festivals and other opportunities. Ash, on the other hand, was born in New York, but started making films while in graduate school in Bristol, UK, in the early 2000s. He then moved to Tokyo and has worked as an independent film-maker while also being employed at a private Japanese company unrelated to film-making, which has allowed him to continue living in Japan. *Surviving Internal Exposure* has been screened widely at events organized by citizens and schools mostly inside Japan (and occasionally elsewhere). Kamanaka and her team see these events as more important exhibition venues than film theaters and film festivals. *A2-B-C* has also been shown at citizens' and schools' screening events both inside and outside Japan. In addition, it played at many film festivals including Nippon Connection Film Festival (Frankfurt, 2013), Guam International Film Festival (2013), Yamagata International Documentary Film Festival (2013), STEPS International Rights Film Festival (Kharkiv, Ukraine, 2013), and International Uranium Film Festival (Rio de Janeiro, 2014).[9] During the early stages of its distribution, Ash aimed to build a reputation for the film by having it shown at film festivals in order to obtain theatrical distribution (Ash 2013). In any case, while the two film-makers' documentaries share concerns about life, they represent these concerns in significantly different ways. *Surviving Internal Exposure* advises the management of life through a narrational reference to scientific proof, whereas *A2-B-C* takes a non-authoritative and therapeutic narration. Narration here means not simply the voice-over narration, but the filmic narration, which is overall ongoing process of supplying audio-visual information (Bordwell 1985). The points that the two films emphasize regarding the residents' struggle with the issues of life are also characteristically dissimilar.

*Surviving Internal Exposure* deals with the immediate aftermath of the Fukushima disaster in 2011 and early 2012, and it was released in late 2012. And yet, it should be seen not only as a film on the nuclear catastrophe, but also as an important addition to the director Kamanaka Hitomi's series of critical documentaries on the nuclear industry and radioactive contamination—*Hibakusha at the End of the World* (*Hibakusha: Sekai no owari ni*, 2003), *Rokkasho Rhapsody* (*Rokkashomura rapusodi*, 2006), and *Ashes to Honey* (*Mitsubachi no haoto to chikyū no kaiten*, 2010). Indeed, clips from some of these films are inserted in the opening sequence so as both to position the film in her oeuvre and to place the 3.11 catastrophe in a wider global context related to the nuclear problems, including the use of depleted uranium during the Gulf War and protests against the Rokkasho Nuclear Fuel Reprocessing Facility. This is further emphasized in the course of the film through a comparison between the aftermath of the 3.11 catastrophe and those of the atomic bombing in Hiroshima and the nuclear accident in Chernobyl. In this contextualization, all these cases concern radiation's harmful effects on life and the human body.

This aspiration is, first, reflected upon the plot that is principally designed around three successive questions: how dangerous is the current situation in the stricken areas for the residents' health?; how are they surviving the situation?; and, what can they do in order to cope? The earlier sequence introduces four experts and their views on the current conditions in Fukushima and the risk of radiation on health. These experts are all physicians who have become involved with the issues of radiation: Hida Shuntarō who has engaged with the effects of radiation on human health in Hiroshima since the atomic bombing; Kodama Tatsuhiko, the Director of the University of Tokyo's Radioisotope Center, who led decontamination in and around Minamisōma City and became famous for criticizing the government's policy in the House of Representatives; Kamata Minoru, an honorable director of Suwa Central Hospital, Nagano Prefecture, who has committed himself to the medical care of the people harmed by the Chernobyl disaster and depleted uranium in Iraq; and Valentina Smolnikova, a pediatrician in Belarus who has observed children affected by the radiation from the damaged Chernobyl reactor. The central section of the film then shows how the residents (and one of the experts) are confronting the radioactive contamination of the soil and food, especially in terms of protecting children's health. Finally, the last sequence communicates the residents' efforts to minimize the risk of internal exposure as well as the experts' suggestions on how to handle it.

In this plot, demonstrating scientific proof and its limitations plays a key role in communicating the seriousness of these issues affecting life. Featuring the aforementioned four experts exactly matches this purpose. Kamanaka (2012) thought that employing the experts' different viewpoints would more convincingly prove the physical danger of the situation than using only one. Yet, obviously all of them are critical of the government's policies and share concerns about the effects of radiation on human health with the film-maker. They respond to Kamanaka's questions from this position of shared concern as well as from their own distinctive views based on their experience and knowledge. Over the course of the film, these interviews touch on the initial aftermath of the catastrophe, the radioactive contamination of the land and food, its influence on the human body, and how to cope with this condition. These experts' comments are of great value partly because the undetectable nature of radiation makes it difficult to recognize how hazardous it is for biological life and partly because this undetectable nature also probably upholds the discourse of safety and reconstruction.

The film further reinforces their views by another strategy: what the film scholar Sean Cubitt calls data visualization, which includes graphs, diagrams, and the CGI simulation of the body (Cubitt 2013: 282). In many scenes, such data visualization corresponds to an expert's statement; for example, a shot of Kamata explaining the aftermath of the Chernobyl accident is followed by a shot of a sequential graph indicating the relationship between the changing number of patients with thyroid cancer from 1986–2002 in Belarus and the World Health Organization's delayed acknowledgement of the cancers in 2005. This combination can be seen as a form of cooperation between the experts and the filmmaker, who inserts these non-diegetic data visualizations. Moreover, the data visualization serves to make visible what is invisible, for example radiation and its effect on the human body, through an inserted CGI shot of the mechanisms of the body. At the same time, every time the data visualization appears, it is accompanied by non-diegetic electronic music that sounds like dripping liquid, thereby enhancing the sense of scientific processes leading to proof. Cubitt notes that "data visualization aims to mobilize demands in the people by translating the empirical data of experts into visually legible symbols for the mass population, ostensibly to persuade through reason but actually to mobilize at an affective level" (Cubitt 2013: 282). Whether the information is accurate or not, *Surviving Internal Exposure* clearly uses audio-visual rhetoric in its positing of scientific proof.

However, the film also attempts to make clear that there are still many issues that the current science cannot verify. This scientific limitation surfaces twice. On one occasion, while following Kodama and his team working on decontamination in Namie District, Kamanaka points out in a voice-over: "once radioactive materials infiltrate an ecosystem, their flow and concentration move unpredictably. Moreover, it takes thirty years for the toxicity of radioactive cesium to fall by half. Decontamination thus involves a variety of problems." Hence, although Kodama insists on the need for decontamination, this series of scenes suggests that the government's measures are not an absolutely effective solution, but rather problematic in both practical and economical terms. This ambivalent representation clearly differs from the assertive representation of decontamination in the aforementioned pro-government film *Living in Fukushima*. Likewise, the cause of internal exposure is also presented as ambiguous. In the last sequence, the film shows Kodama, Kamata, and Hida agreeing that a low level of radioactive materials influences DNA directly or indirectly through epigenetic effects and the action of free radicals, and so can induce not only cancer but also arteriosclerosis, cerebral infarction, high blood pressure, myocardial infarction, cerebrovascular dementia, and many other diseases. Still, we cannot know from the film exactly what radioactive dose induces any of these illnesses. This stands in contrast with *Living in Fukushima* as well as the governmental policy in general, which somehow arbitrarily specifies a numerical standard of safety. *Surviving Internal Exposure* addresses the risk of radiation both by its scientific confirmation and by its scientific obscurity.

Integrating both proof and its limitation, the overall structure of the film operates according to a scheme of filmic narration that educates through explicitly referring to science, and the director's voice-over plays an integral part. As in *Living in Fukushima*, Kamanaka's voice-over functions as an authoritative translation of the scientific view of the post-3.11 situation. It interprets and explains these views, and clarifies and emphasizes some points. In this sense, she sounds very knowledgeable. Some other devices, however, make her seem less sober or removed than the voice-over narrator in *Living in Fukushima*. For one thing, her voice-over commentary is interlaced with inter-titles and subtitles so that its didactic sense is mitigated. An excellent example is commentary added via inter-titles in the ending shots: "Effects of low-level internal exposure appears after some time has passed. We still do not know what effects appear in many cases. Therefore, preventive actions [...] will protect life (*inochi*)." While this textual form of narration is more abstract than the human voice, narrating these lines in a voice-over would have sounded more ponderous. Moreover, whereas the voice-over in *Living in Fukushima* functions as a disembodied non-diegetic human agency throughout the film, Kamanaka is at times visible in the diegetic space on screen, and is thereby positioned at the same level as the experts and residents. Given that her consistent role is listening to and learning what the social actors say, her position is arguably even lower than that of the interviewees. Most importantly, as this device suggests, her voice-over can be interpreted as the voice of the specific individual, Kamanaka, possessing a unique body and mind, so that she creates a dialogue with her audience. At this point, *Surviving Internal Exposure* crucially differs both from *Living in Fukushima*, which is consistently narrated by the abstract voice-over and from *Nuclear Nation*, which limits the non-diegetic narration to inter-/sub-titles. Thus, Kamanaka's voice-over narration maintains its reference to scientific truth, but it presents itself in a nuanced way as moderately authoritative and highly individualized. As such it acts as an agent in something akin to a quasi-dialogic role.

This filmic narration (including the voice-over) makes clear that the film's primary concern is with biological life. This leads the places and landscapes in this film to develop different meanings from those in *Living in Fukushima* and *Nuclear Nation*. The setting of *Living in Fukushima* is Kōri District, Fukushima City, and Kawauchi Village in Fukushima Prefecture, apparently because of its focus on residents who cooperated with the government. *Nuclear Nation* tells the story of the (former) residents of the Futaba District, and is predominantly concerned with their livelihood. In contrast, *Surviving Internal Exposure* deals with Nihonmatsu City, Namie District, and Hirata Village in Fukushima Prefecture, precisely because it involves people who are confronted with the effects of radiation on children's health. Focusing on a family and their wider community in Nihonmatsu, Kamanaka records her interviews in their domestic environment, just as the film director Funahashi does in *Nuclear Nation*. This allows her to capture the interviewees' rich facial expressions and tones of voice, as in the scene in which a woman starts to cry, while remarking: "It is the most distressing to be told 'you could evacuate'." And yet, Kamanaka's interviews are less concerned with the residents' struggles for their livelihood than the conflicts between their livelihoods and lives. The woman above mentions that she wants to escape but she cannot due to reasons like schooling and work. The interviewer also speaks with a young mother about how carefully she chooses ingredients and cooks them in order to avoid internally exposing her children to radiation. More extensively, through interviewing this woman's husband, the film reveals many conflicts, including that he and other residents do not trust the governmental radiation safety standard, that many parents experience guilt about their children's health, and that they are in a quandary about how they can balance their children's health and their livelihood.

This tendency also can be found in the presentation of landscape. In fact, whereas *Living in Fukushima* celebrates the natural environment and *Nuclear Nation* sentimentalizes the ruined scenery, *Surviving Internal Exposure* includes very little landscape footage. One possible exception is a series of long shots of children playing in the snow. This, however, cannot be seen as a heartwarming scene because it is contextualized within the issue of children's health in relation to the kindergarten's efforts to decontaminate and to manage food safety. There is another moment of landscape footage in which the fields, houses, and woods of Namie District are shot from a moving car. Here again, however, over the landscape, Kamanaka's ongoing voice-over narrates the difficulty of decontamination rather than the beauty of the nature. In this film, the landscape signifies not pure nature, but contaminated land.

In this way, it operates as a mode of filmic narration constructed through direct reference to scientific proof. Like *Nuclear Nation*, this film offers a critical view of government policy from the residents' standpoint (although it departs from the former in also relying on the experts' advice). But, unlike *Nuclear Nation*, it is primarily concerned with the residents', especially children's, health. The two films end with sharply contrasted statements: the former calls for sufficient compensation whereas the latter advocates the need to protect life (*inochi*). Moreover, while the voice-over narration is somewhat authoritative, it is individualized as a form of dialogic agency. In this sense, *Surviving Internal Exposure* may be characterized as a truth-claim type of documentary (see Musser 2010: 175–94), like Michael Moore's *Fahrenheit 9/11* (2004) and *Sicko* (2007) insofar as it addresses 'the truth' to the public from the director's point of view. But, it is not a 'partisan film' like Moore's because it neither "reject(s) the ideal of objectivity" nor aims "to present subjective and politically charged representations of the world" (Kellner 2013: 59). Indeed, Kamanaka's film concludes not with a demand to the government but with the residents' self-management, which runs the risk of echoing the neo-liberalist idea of self-responsibility. Probably because of her democratic ethics as well as her fundamental respect for the residents, the film does not articulate their option to evacuate, much less recommend it. While questioning the governmental safety standard of 20 mSv as well as its overall policy, *Surviving Internal Exposure* does not offer any specific solutions. In the end, only by offering rather abstract suggestions and encouragements through the experts' comments, the social actors' statements and actions, and its overall filmic narration including the director's voice-over, the film ends up both empowering the residents and general citizens and hoping for the audiences' own power.

## Questioning the management of life: *A2-B-C*

Similar to *Surviving Internal Exposure*, *A2-B-C* puts the most importance on children's health. The title refers to the categories describing levels of radioactive damage to a human thyroid: A2 designates a nodule of 5.0 mm or smaller, or a cyst of 20.0 mm or smaller; B a nodule of 5.1 mm or larger or a cyst of 20.1 mm or larger; and C indicates the need for an immediate secondary examination. And yet, unlike *Surviving Internal Exposure*, this film does not adopt a mode of linking its filmic narration to scientific proof; instead, it opts for an unobtrusive and as-it-were therapeutic narration. In other words, while trying not to define the meanings of the situations it shows, the film—physically the camera, the microphone, and the film-maker as the interviewer—functions as a device for the residents (including children) to speak about the situation and themselves. In so doing, it reveals the psychological and social problems that the residents experience with regard to their children's health.

The film uses many tactics in order to avoid providing an authoritative and determining narration. In the first place, the overarching plot does not take the form of a recovery story (as in *Living in Fukushima*), a chronological account (*Nuclear Nation*), or a logical progression toward scientific proof (*Surviving Internal Exposure*). Rather, it consists of a series of episodes and questions, although its main theme roughly shifts from decontamination in the first half to thyroid examinations in the second. *A2-B-C* also does not provide any non-diegetic music. Nor does it have any voice-over narration. Although it does have inter-titles/subtitles, they are extremely limited, only appearing in three shots of an early sequence: two inter-titles on black backgrounds indicating time, and one superimposed subtitle stating that Dr. Yamashita Shun'ichi[10] is a "government adviser on radiation health-risk." The absence of voice-over narration and the minimization of superimposed explanatory titles further mean that the director does not present himself as authoritative or knowledgeable on the non-diegetic level. This is congruent with the extra-filmic context. Ash is not known for a long engagement with the problem of radiation as Kamanaka is, and his appearance in the diegetic space is limited to scenes where he plays with a child and where he and residents argue with a scientist and a school administrator. This style is consistent with his previous film, *In the Grey Zone* (2012), in which his self-representation as a non-authority is made more transparent. Indeed, this film includes footage of him telling a resident that he does not have sufficient knowledge about radiation.

In addition, in contrast with *Surviving Internal Exposure*, *A2-B-C* does not present any scientist who makes claims to scientific truth. Yamashita may be an exception, but even he states that: "science is not perfect." The non-diegetic insertion of data visualization is also absent in this film. Although we see a map of radioactive contamination on an iPhone in one scene, it is presented by Kanno Yoshiaki, a non-scientist assembly member of Kōriyama, in the diegetic space rather than on a non-diegetic meta-level. So are the Geiger counters, another device to audio-visualize the insensible radiation, which are also used by the residents in the diegetic space. Moreover, none of the people appearing in the film (except Yamashita) is introduced through non-diegetic narration, either through voice-over narration or inter-titles/subtitles. To be sure we learn some of their identities (like Kanno's), but only through their dialogue in the diegetic space. This is also the case for time and place. Only the aforementioned inter-titles provide two indications of the specific time: "12 days after the nuclear meltdown in Fukushima" when the director turns a microphone to Yamashita; and "18 months later" when the rest of the plot unfolds. Because no non-diegetic narration indicates the place, we only can extrapolate from the diegetic dialogue that Date City and Fukushima City are the main sites in the film. In all these multiple ways, *A2-B-C* counters any authoritative and determining narration.

Crucially, this combination of non-authoritative narration and the obscuring of personal, temporal, and geographical identities have two important functions. One is to prevent the audience from having political and spatial preconceptions about the film. The non-authoritative narration sharply distinguishes the film from the truth-claim type of political documentary like Michael Moore's and even Kamanaka's. These films tend to attract only people with the same political leanings, and have an impediment to drawing other people's interest. The tactic of non-authoritative narration echoes the obscuring of the identities of the citizen-activists who appear in the film. Although someone who is familiar with citizens' activism could probably identify them, the film presents them anonymously so that it can avoid alienating potential audiences who might perceive the film as 'political' prior to watching it. Moreover, the ambiguity of geographical identities is also worth noting. This tactic, Ash (2013) explains, was intended to prevent the audience both from viewing the film through certain preconceptions or stereotypes about 'Fukushima' and from constructing an imposed image of a specific place by watching this particular filmic representation. In fact, what is at stake for *A2-B-C* is not to inform audiences about a situation happening in a specific place distant from the rest of the world, but to make them think about the issue of life everywhere.

This tactic dovetails with the other prime function of the combination of non-authoritative narration and the obscuring of identities: getting the residents, including the children, to share their feelings and thoughts about biological life in an egalitarian and therapeutic way. The egalitarian aspiration can be observed most typically in the way the film does not explicitly indicate the social status of the people appearing on screen. Because the non-diegetic narration does not introduce the social statuses of all the actors—the residents, the assembly members, the physicians, and citizens-activists—the spectator is invited to pay more attention to what a person says than to who says it. The film gives equal value to all voices by refraining from privileging those with distinguished social status. This, albeit partly, even pertains to children. The film maintains a dual representation of children: innocent and insightful. Children are implied to be innocent especially in the sequences in which adults confirm children's descriptions of certain conditions. For instance, the scene in which children express their wish to return to the Fukushima of before 3.11 is juxtaposed with a scene in which two women agree that Fukushima cannot go back to how it used to be. Between these consecutive scenes, a sound-bridge—where we see the last part of the previous shot while hearing the voice of the person in the next shot on the soundtrack—occurs, thereby suggesting the relation between the children's innocence and adults' knowledge. On the other hand, however, children are also presented as no less insightful than adults. In one scene, children calmly articulate their recognition that, judged as A2 (which means their thyroids have lesions of a certain size), they are vulnerable to illnesses like leukemia and skin cancer. In another scene, answering the director's questions, a high school girl articulates keen insights into the wider situation, for example mentioning that children are more susceptible to radiation due to their smaller stature and faster cycles of cell division while asking a related question to a politician who has approved the government's uniform safety standard irrespective of the difference between the effects of radiation on adults and children. Here, her view is presented as equivalent to adults', while also being privileged as something unique that significantly differs from an adult point of view.

This egalitarian mode of narration predominantly concerns the issues of biological life and its conflict with livelihood. While the decontamination and the thyroid examination are highlighted as central issues with regards to how they serve (or do not serve) to protect children's health, the interviews with a wide range of residents also raise many other issues, such as health insurance, pregnancy, marriage, food, school policy regarding lunch and outdoor activities, and the recognition of the spread of radiation. All of these issues are problematized as instances of the conflict between life and livelihood. For instance, in an early scene a young woman and a man both suggest that more people in Fukushima are choosing to have abortions in the fear that the radiation will affect their babies.

Landscape, while only minimally presented, has a similar implication in this film. While many long shots of the environment include children playing or residents measuring radioactivity, only one empty landscape appears in the film. Here we see a slowly panning panoramic view over the city (the name of which is never indicated, although it seems to be Fukushima City as seen from Bentenyama Park). But this shot is presented in juxtaposition with two consecutive interviewees suggesting that the national and local governments are concealing the actual gravity of the radioactive contamination in order to avoid the evacuation of the whole population currently living in Fukushima. Clearly, in stark contrast with *Living in Fukushima*, *A2-B-C* problematizes the landscape, rather than celebrates it, in terms of an environment for residents' lives.

In this way the film raises many issues about life and its conflict with livelihood, but two socio-psychological problems are particularly noteworthy. One is the residents' anxiety about the deleterious effects of radiation on their children's health. It is for this reason that the film pays persistent attention to how the parents are managing the air and food in their immediate environment and how they react to the results of their children's thyroid examinations. On this point, *A2-B-C* parallels *Surviving Internal Exposure*. However, *A2-B-C* significantly departs from *Surviving Internal Exposure* in showing how the residents struggle with the public sphere and with institutions such as the national and local governments and the schools. The aforementioned high school student points to the incongruity between her family who cares about the radioactive contamination and most young people around her who do not. The two women who say that Fukushima cannot return to how it used to be also agree that people in Fukushima should get angry about the radioactive contamination of their land and the government's concealment of this fact, but they nevertheless hesitate to express this anger in the fear of seeming ungraceful. The woman who detects high levels of radioactivity with a Geiger counter on a site just next to a schoolyard describes her own psychological conflict when the school's response to her claim made her feel as if she was in the wrong. According to her, the school's answer was that the radiation emanates only from outside the school property; therefore sports events can be held inside the schoolyard. Later, the director, accompanied by the woman, is admonished by the vice-principal for filming in the schoolyard without permission. The director then argues that children's health should take precedence over school rules. This episode suggests that the residents are confronting the institutional pressure that overtly or covertly restrains their individual determination and action and that keeps the vice-principal from acting on his own thoughts and judgments. While these scenes are the most prominent examples of this kind of struggle, many similar cases of socio-psychological conflicts are embedded throughout the film.

In the interviews that draw out such conflicts, we can also see that the film often functions as a therapeutic device. The presence of the camera, the microphone, and the film-maker(s) is an invaluable opportunity for the residents to openly discuss the issue of radiation. Their dialogue suggests that such an articulation would otherwise be difficult because they are afraid that it may disrupt the friendly atmosphere and subject them to peer pressure based on the discourse of safety and reconstruction. Like a closed counseling room, each interview is held not only in their domestic environment, but also often in a space that protects the interviewees from the harsh public sphere. While of course the subjects of the film eventually ended up being watched by many people, the director has gained sufficient confidence to overcome their anxiety through his open-minded communication with them.[11] Moreover, the interview operates not simply as a succession of questions and answers, but as a catalyst that facilitates the interviewees' dialogue and conversation in an unpredictable way. Thus, in an early scene one interview leads to a lively conversation between ten or so office workers at work. Another interview leads to the expression of emotion, when two women in a later scene have tearful eyes and voice their anger about the radioactive contamination of their land. This kind of therapeutic interview may appear to be facilitated by the director's status as a 'foreigner' insofar as it serves to mitigate the interviewees' concern about their vulnerability to public criticism from other Japanese, but I would argue it is the tactics and efforts of Ash's filmmaking that enabled him to elicit the frank articulation of their feelings.

Using the combination of non-authoritative, highly reserved narration and egalitarian, therapeutic interviewing, *A2-B-C* devotes itself to eliciting the residents' feelings and thoughts. While this film echoes *Nuclear Nation* insofar as both thoroughly stand on the side of the (former) residents and offer critical views of the econo-political power, *A2-B-C* remains primarily concerned with children's health rather than those relating to livelihood. The film also shares *Surviving Internal Exposure*'s concern about life, but it does not end up portraying it as the matter of the residents' self-management. Rather, it interrogates the responsibility of the government and industry for the present crisis. In the very last scene, while measuring the levels of radioactivity around her home, the woman states that she is doing so because she intends to collect evidence to convince the government to prioritize the evacuation of children over decontamination. The option of collective evacuation is also mentioned in earlier interviews. In one, a woman insists that the principle of handling radiation is to isolate it in one place and move people away, rather than moving radioactive waste elsewhere. But these demands directed at the econo-political power structures are only suggested through interviewing, not directly urged by the non-diegetic narration. In effect, *A2-B-C* leaves further thinking and action to the audience and refrains from imposing the truth.

## Conclusion

The 3.11 nuclear catastrophe has challenged democratic ideas relating to the split between life and livelihood. Should we respect the residents' livelihood and their decision as to whether they will stay in or leave their hometown? Or, if we recognize even a low level of risk in human exposure to radiation, should we recommend that residents leave their hometown or demand that the government proactively facilitate this evacuation? At a screening event in December 2014, Ash suggested the government's current encouragement and financial support for the evacuees to return to their hometowns (Naikakufu genshiryoku hisaisha seikatsu shien team 2013) as a political trick, saying that any future health problems afflicting them or their children would be blamed on their choice to return. In essence, the government attempted to appropriate the former residents' nostalgia for their hometowns in order to avoid more costly forms of compensation—more precisely, compensation paid by TEPCO and backed up by the government—to support their relocation to safer areas, he said. Obviously, this is an extremely complicated matter with many concomitant scientific, economical, and political issues.

As I have discussed, the growing number of post-3.11 documentary films has confronted this matter and demonstrated a tendentious yet contested range of attitudes. Pro-governmental films like *Living in Fukushima* de-problematize the conflict between life and livelihood by emphasizing the progress of decontamination, an optimistic vision of reconstruction, and the glory of cooperation among the government, the industry, and the residents. Other films like *Nuclear Nation* counter such a representation by problematizing livelihood from a bottom-up viewpoint that is engaged with the lives of (former) residents. Yet other films like *Surviving Internal Exposure* and *A2-B-C* problematize life, but the two films represent it in markedly different ways: whereas the former illuminates the self-management of children's health through its somewhat authoritative narration, the latter questions institutional practices of protecting children's health and foregrounds the residents' struggle with the public sphere through its non-authoritative and therapeutic narration.

To be sure, despite these significant differences and contestation, all of the documentaries maintain a certain level of respect or soberness toward the (former) residents and their choice of whether they will remain or leave. None of the films pose a more extreme attitude toward this choice. This seems to have resulted both from the film-makers' democratic ethics and from a shared tenet characterizing a certain type of documentary: that "the documentary filmmaker must contact and respect social actors" (Nichols 1991: 109). This is particularly the case in *A2-B-C*. While this documentary suggests some conflicts in the public sphere as we have seen, it does not present them as explicitly as does the fiction film *Odayaka* (*Odayakana nichijō*, 2012).[12] The latter includes a scene in which one woman attacks another woman who is worried about the radiation. Whereas the fiction film audio-visually *presents* such a conflict by staging it, the documentary *represents* it only via interview clips suggesting it verbally and retrospectively in lieu of showing it. The documentary ethic demanding respect for the social actors partly restrains the director of *A2-B-C* from staging the problem and from directly intervening in the situations.

However, it is through this ethic that *A2-B-C* successfully conveys a sense of reality when the residents voluntarily address their feelings and thoughts to the camera despite having experiencing psychological pressure due to harsh public security. It would be difficult for a fiction film to show the very moment when the film—a mechanism made up of the camera, the microphone, and the film-maker—plays such a respectful therapeutic role for the interviewees. While all the documentary films and other media can be said to have significantly constituted a contested terrain for the imagination of the post-3.11 nuclear catastrophe, *A2-B-C* has made a particular contribution to it through its unique integration of filmic narration in tandem with the ethics requisite for documentary film-making.

## Notes

1 The Japanese article of Norma Field's interview (2014) inspired me to explore this idea. The article uses the two distinct Japanese terms, *seikatsu* and *seimei* (or *inochi*), which correspond to the distinction I make between 'livelihood' and 'life' throughout this chapter.
2 This notification was made in parallel with the government's designation of "the planned evacuation zone" (*keikakuteki hinan kuiki*) on April 22, 2011, where accumulated radioactive doses may reach 20 mSv within one year ("Hinan shiji tō no keii"

2012). On October 11, 2013, when the Ministry of Economy, Trade and Industry announced a reworked plan for zones, it designated the zone from 1–20 mSv as "the zone in preparation for having the evacuation order lifted" (*hinan shiji junbi kuiki*) (Naikakufu genshiryoku hisaisha seikatsu shien team 2013). In all these cases, "20 mSv" operates as a yardstick for estimating the safety.
3 They include Pore Pore Higashi Nakano (Tokyo), Uplink (Tokyo), and Nagoya Cinematheque. The films are distributed to these independent film theaters by small distribution companies like Uplink, Group Gendai, and ad hoc organized committees such as the Committee for Screening *A2-B-C*. (Yet, the Committee began to distribute *A2-B-C* to domestic exhibition venues only in May 2014. Before that, the director himself had done so since its opening release in April 2013 and this is still the case in its distribution outside Japan.)
4 The literal translation of the Japanese title is "moving away from Futaba," but the official released English version of the film is titled *Nuclear Nation*, which apparently foregrounds the disaster as a national matter, rather than a local one, so as to make a global appeal. Thereafter, all translations—except where the video and films already have English subtitles—are mine.
5 For environmentalism, see Gerrard (2011: 18–27). Yet, the environmentalism in this chapter is closer to what Gerrard calls "deep ecology" than what he calls "environmentalism."
6 It should be added that regarding the post-3.11 nuclear catastrophe, so far I have not found any documentary like *A Hard Rain* (Australia, 2007) and *Uranium: Is It a Country?* (Germany and Australia, 2008), both of which highlight the problem of nuclear energy vis-à-vis the issue of global warming. For these films, see Lynch (2012).
7 Prokino is an abbreviated name of the Proletarian Film League of Japan (*Nippon puroretaria eiga dōmei*) and the independent documentary film movement conducted by this left-wing organization in the late 1920s and early 1930s. Its central figures, Iwasaki Akira and Sasa Genjū, not only made their own films but also guided factory workers to make films on political issues such as labor disputes and strikes.
8 Ogawa Shinsuke (1935–1992) is a prominent documentary film-maker who is well known particularly for having made films on students' protests and the protests against the planned construction of Narita International Airport from the late 1960s through the 1970s.
9 Among them, *A2-B-C* was awarded at Frankfurt and Guam as well as STEPS.
10 Yamashita Shun'ichi is a professor in medical science at Nagasaki University. On March 19, 2011, upon request by the governor of Fukushima Prefecture, he was an advisor of Radiation Health Management as well as a part-time professor for a special mission at Fukushima Medical University. His repeated statements of safety have created a controversy among those who are concerned about the radioactive contamination.
11 According to Ash (2014), this is one of the reasons why he has refrained from releasing the film on DVD in order to protect them from possible public attack.
12 "*Odayaka*" literally means tranquility.

## References

Agamben, Giorgio. 1998, *Homo Sacer: Sovereign Power and Bare Life*. Trans. Daniel Heller-Roazen. Stanford, CA: Stanford University Press.
*A Hard Rain*. 2007, Dir. David Bradbury. Film and web, at: http://thoughtmaybe.com/a-hard-rain/ (accessed February 25, 2015).
*Ashes to Honey* [*Mitsubachi no haoto to chikyū no kaiten*]. 2010, Dir. Kamanaka Hitomi. Film and DVD.

Ash, Ian T. 2013, Personal interview. Nagoya University, November 11.
Ash, Ian T. 2014, Talk in Shintomiza, Ise, Mie Prefecture. December 21.
*A2-B-C*. 2013, Dir. Ian Thomas Ash. Film.
Bandō Kumiko, Yamanaka Shin'ichi, Aida Takashi, and Nunomura Yukihiko. 2011. "Fukushima kennai no gakkō tōno kōsha kōteitō no riyōhandan ni okeru zanteiteki kangaekata." *Ministry of Education, Culture, Sports, Science and Technology-Japan*, April 19, at: www.mext.go.jp/a_menu/saigaijohou/syousai/1305173.htm (accessed February 24, 2015).
*Beyond the Cloud [Kiri no mukō no Yonaoshi 3.11]*. 2013, Dir. Keiko Courdy. Film.
Bordwell, David. 1985, *Narration in the Fiction Film*. Madison, WI: University of Wisconsin.
*Chernobyl Heart*. 2003, Dir. Marion DeLeeo, Film and web, at: www.youtube.com/watch?v=Vhb5pCXMkxU (accessed February 26, 2015).
*Controverses nucléaires*. 2004, Dir. Wladimir Tchertkoff. Film and web, at: www.youtube.com/watch?v=oryOrsOy6LI (accessed February 26, 2015).
Cubitt, Sean. 2013, "Everybody knows this is nowhere: Data visualization and ecocriticism," in Stephen Rust, Salma Monani, and Sean Cubitt (eds), *Ecocinema Theory and Practice*. London: Routledge.
*Fahrenheit 9/11*. 2004, Dir. Michael Moore. Film and DVD.
Field, Norma. 2014, Interview. "Heiwa to han'ei no ato de." *Asahi shinbun* March 1. web: June 20, at: www.asahi.com/articles/DA3S11005077.html (accessed February 26, 2015).
*Friends after 3.11*. 2012, Dir. Iwai Shunji. Film and DVD.
Fujiki, Hideaki. forthcoming, "Networking citizens through film screenings: Cinema and media in the post-3.11 social movement," in Jason G. Karlin and Patrick Galbraith (eds), *Media Convergence in Japan*. Ann Arbor, MI: Kinema Club.
*Fukushima: A Record of Living Creatures [Fukushima: Ikimono no kiroku]*. 2013, Dir. Iwasaki Masanori. Film and DVD.
*Fukushima: We Won't Forget [Wasurenai Fukushima]*. 2013, Dir. Shinomiya Hiroshi. Film and DVD.
*Fukushima Never Again*. 2012, Dir. Steve Zeltzer. Film and web, at: www.youtube.com/watch?v=LU-Z4VLDGxU (accessed February 26, 2015).
*Fukushima 2011: A Record of People Exposed Radiation [Fukushima 2011: Hibaku ni sarasareta hitobito no kiroku]*. 2011, Dir. Inazuka Hidetaka. Film and DVD.
Gaines, Jane. 1999, "Political Mimesis," in Jane Gaines and Michael Renov (eds), *Collecting Visible Evidence*. Minneapolis, MN: University of Minnesota Press, 84–102.
Gerrard, Greg. 2011, *Ecocriticism*. London: Routledge.
Habermas, Jürgen. 1996, *The Structural Transformation of the Public Sphere: An Inquiry into a Category of Bourgeois Society*. Trans. Thomas Burger. Cambridge, MA: MIT Press,.
*Hibakusha at the End of the World [Hibakusha: Sekai no owari ni]*. 2003, Dir. Kamanaka Hitomi, Film and DVD.
"Hinan shiji tō no keii." n.d., *Fukushima Prefecture*, at: www.pref.fukushima.lg.jp/sec/11050a/hinanchiiki-kuiki.html (accessed February 24, 2015).
*In the Grey Zone [Gurē zōn no naka de]*. 2012, Dir. Ian Thomas Ash. Film.
*Kakusei: The Fukushima End*. 2013, Dir. Dion Tan. Film and web.
Kamanaka Hitomi. 2012, Personal interview. Nagoya University, August 1.
Kashimoto Yoshikazu. 2011, "ICRP kankoku no suii to kankoku ga motsu imi: Hōshasen hibaku bōgo no gensoku ni kakusareta mondaiten." *Kagaku* Vol. 81, No. 6: 513–15.

Kellner, Douglas. 2013, "On truth, objectivity and partisanship: The case of Michael Moore," in Brian Winston (ed.), *The Documentary Film Book*. London: BFI.
*Living in Fukushima: A Story of Decontamination and Reconstruction* [*Fukushima ni ikiru: Josen to fukkō no monogatari*]. 2013, Dir. Imafuku Kaoru. Film and web, at: http://josenplaza.env.go.jp/materials_links/index.html#Tab03 (accessed February 24, 2015).
Lynch, Lisa. 2012, "We don't wanna be radiated: Documentary film and the evolving rhetoric of nuclear energy activism." *American Literature* Vol. 84, No. 2, 327–51.
Murray, Alex. 2010, *Giorgio Agamben*. London: Routledge.
Musser, Charles. 2010, "Truth and rhetoric in Michael Moore's *Fahrenheit 9/11*," in Matthew Bernstein (ed.), *Michael Moore: Filmmaker, Newsmaker, Cultural Icon*. Ann Arbor, MI: University of Michigan Press, 167–201.
Naikakufu genshiryoku hisaisha seikatsu shien team. 2013, *Hinan shiji kuiki no minaoshi nituite*, October 11, at: www.meti.go.jp/earthquake/nuclear/pdf/131009/131009_02a.pdf (accessed February 24, 2015).
Nichols, Bill. 1991, *Representing Reality: Issues and Concepts in Documentaries*. Bloomington, IN: Indian University Press.
*Nuclear Nation* [*Futaba kara tōku hanarete*]. 2012, Dir. Funahashi Atsushi. Film and DVD.
*Odayaka* [*Odayaka na nichijō*]. 2012, Dir. Uchida Nobuteru. Film and DVD.
*Ordinary Lives* [*Futsū no seikatsu*]. 2013, Dir. Yoshida Taizō. Film.
*Pandora's Promise*. 2013, Dir. Robert Stone. Film and web, at: www.youtube.com/watch?v=kBMj-96hols (accessed February 26, 2015).
*Pray for Japan* [*Nihon e no inori: Kokoro o hitotsu ni*]. 2012, Dir. Stu Levy. Film and DVD.
*Rokkasho Rhapsody* [*Rokkashomura rapusodī*]. 2006, Dir. Kamanaka Hitomi. Film and DVD. "Seconds from Disaster 5: Fukushima, Japan's Nuclear Nightmare." 2012, American Geographic Channel. Television and web, at: www.youtube.com/watch?v=fyIBlygNlcc#t=90 (accessed February 26, 2015).
*Sicko*. 2007, Dir. Michael Moore. Film and DVD.
*Surviving Internal Exposure* [*Naibu hibaku o ikinuku*]. 2012, Dir. Kamanaka Hitomi. Film and DVD.
*311*. 2011, Dir. Mori, Tatsuya, Watai, Kenyō, Matsui, Yōju, and Yasuoka, Takuji. Film.
*The Tsunami and the Cherry Blossom* (*Tsunami soshite sakura*). 2011, Dir. Lucy Walker. Film and DVD.
*Uranium: Is It a Country?* 2008, Dir. Kerstin Schnatz. Film and web, at: www.youtube.com/watch?v=pnW0N_gJiTA (accessed February 26, 2015).
Valentin, J., ed. 2007, "The 2007 Recommendations of the International Commission on Radiological Protection." *Annals of the ICRP* 37, 2–4: 1–34.
*Welcome to Fukushima* [*Fukushima e yōkoso*]. 2013, Dir. Alain de Halleux. Film and web, at: www.youtube.com/watch?v=bjv1b6Zn9DY (accessed February 26, 2015).
*Will, The: If Only There Were No Nuclear Power* [*Yuigon: Genpatsu sae nakereba*]. 2013, Dir. Naomi Toyota and Masaya Noda, Film.
*Wind from Fukushima* [*Fukushima kara no kaze*]. 2011, Dir. Katō Tetsu. Film and DVD.
*Women of Fukushima* [*Fukushima no josei-tachi*]. 2012, Dir. Paul Johannessen, Film and web, at: https://vimeo.com/52808567 (accessed February 26, 2015).
Yagasaki, Katsuma. 2013, "Hōshasen niyoru jintai no eikyō: Naze naibuhibaku no kenkyū ga susumanakattaka?" Nagoya University. December 21, Conference Presentation.
*Zone: The Life That Did Not Exist*. 2013, Dir. Kitada Naotoshi. Film and DVD.

# 7 Gendering 'Fukushima'
## Resistance, self-responsibility, and female hysteria in Sono Sion's *Land of Hope*

*Kristina Iwata-Weickgenannt*

**Introduction**

Does 'Fukushima' resist cinematic fiction? Literally hundreds of documentary films have been produced in the wake of 3.11 and screened at international film festivals and movie theaters around the globe. In contrast, fictionalized accounts of the calamity—and in particular, of nuclear disaster—remain a rarity. Few of the existing feature films are openly critical of the socio-political structures that led to the disaster, the way it was dealt with by the authorities, or even nuclear power itself; instead the focus tends to be on the human drama involved with losing one's ancestral home, as in documentary film director Kubota Nao's feature film debut *Ieji* (*Homeland*, 2014). Although touching on sensitive issues such as the radioactive contamination of farmland and the long-term dependence of evacuated farmers on government money, in stressing attachment to home, endurance, and eventual family reconciliation, *Ieji*'s mood is closer to resigned acceptance than social criticism.

Not so in Kanno Hiroshi's *Ai to kibō no machi* (A Town of Love and Hope, 2014). Written in *hiragana* only, the film calls to mind a 1959 work by Ōshima Nagisa of the same title written in *kanji*. In Ōshima's film, a young protagonist in desperate need of money takes up the deceptive business of selling his most precious possession, a trained pigeon that inevitably returns home at night, over and over again. Far from escaping poverty, however, the protagonist is pushed into even deeper despair as his counterpart, a rich girl, kills the pigeon to end his immoral business. Kanno's film, which tells the story of four generations of a Fukushima family and their seventy-year involvement with nuclear power, rests on a similar pattern of structural inequality and exploitation, describing the vicious cycle set in motion by the selling of one's soul to the devil.

Yet the film turned out to be a commercial flop, despite starring a number of veteran actors. In the Kantō area, for example, *Ai to kibō no machi* was screened at a single movie theater only, and due to the persistently low number of moviegoers, the frequency of screenings was halved (*Nikkan Gendai* 2014). In an interview, Kanno relates the difficulties he had in finding sponsors (*Tsūhan Seikatsu* n.d.). Moreover, journalists from neither the daily newspapers nor the film magazines showed any interest in the pre-screening promotional events, which led to the speculation of a deliberate boycott (*Nikkan Gendai* 2014). The scriptwriter Inoue Jun'ichi comments as follows:

> Of course, there is an incredible number of works dealing with 3.11 and nuclear power, and should the film simply be unconvincing, there's nothing much to discuss. But TEPCO is called by its real name in the film, and although this is pure speculation, I imagine that this might have interfered with the mass media's taboo on nuclear matters. However, I didn't want to make it some fictional power company but instead make sure the responsibility for the nuclear accident is very clearly located. That's also why I added a reference to article 21 of the Constitution on 'The Freedom of Expression and Prohibition of Censorship' in the film's closing credits. I'm certainly not going to give up the freedom of expression of my own accord. That's something that as an artist, I must not even think about doing.
> 
> (*Nikkan Gendai* 2014)

The question, then, is not whether 'Fukushima'—a global shorthand for events replete with drama—lends itself to fictionalization or not. Rather, the small number of productions leads one to suspect that the pervasive influence of the so-called nuclear village (*genshiryoku mura*)—an intricate network of corruption knitting together power companies, politicians, bureaucrats, the judicative, researchers, and the mass media (see Kingston 2012)—persists despite the Fukushima debacle.

Sono Sion, who was the first to tackle the 3.11 disasters in two of his films—*Himizu* (*Himizu*, January 2012) and *Land of Hope* (*Kibō no kuni*, October 2012)—also observes a disappointing preference among his fellow Japanese for inoffensive, shallow entertainment:

> Actually, I'd expect Tōhō [one of Japan's oldest and largest film production companies] to make a film on the topic. If a company of their level was to produce a film on nuclear power plants with nationwide screenings, I'm sure more people would start thinking about the problems related to nuclear power.
> 
> (*Shūkan Kinyōbi* 2012: 25)

Instead, Sono attests to contemporary Japanese cinema's inability to deliver critical analyses of social issues (*Shūkan Kinyōbi* 2012: 26). He sees the political apathy as accompanied by a tendency to stigmatize him as strange for engaging with 'Fukushima':

> The question I get asked most frequently in interviews with Japanese media is "Why did you make a film about nuclear power?" Outside Japan, I never get this question. [...] Why did I make it? That's a strange question! After all, a nuclear power plant exploded right before our eyes, so it would be way

more abnormal *not* to make a film about it. People treat me like I'm crazy, but in reality they should be asking "Why didn't anyone else produce a film on the topic?"

(*Shūkan Kinyōbi* 2012: 26)

On a different occasion, Sono goes so far as to compare the post-3.11 mood of self-restraint to wartime repression:

> Personally, I feel that we're at some kind of 'war' right now, and that as artists our way of life is currently being probed. Thinking of Takamura Mitsutarō who during WWII wrote poems glorifying the war on the one hand and the anti-war poet Kaneko Mitsuharu on the other, I wonder which side I would choose. If John Lennon whom I greatly admire was alive today, I'm sure he would sing about the earthquake and nuclear disaster as a matter of course. Before, I thought it was kind of uncool to turn social criticism into a song just like that, but now I'm convinced that we have to make ourselves heard. [...] Anyway, that's why I'm making films like *Land of Hope*, and why I'm participating in anti-nuke demos in front of the Prime Minister's Office. I'm even ready to give a speech once in a while when asked. At any rate, I don't want to become 'someone who didn't speak up' and end up regretting it later. But of course, it's grueling. I'd love to quickly return to the stupid movies I'm normally making!

(*Quick Japan* 2012: 126)

So what is it that Sono felt necessary to express even at the risk of hurting his career,[1] and despite the demonstrated lack of interest on the part of Japanese sponsors? His film *Himizu* was the first film making direct reference to 3.11. The script, based on Furuya Minoru's eponymous manga, had already been completed when disaster struck. The manga was published around a decade earlier, and is bleak from beginning to end; suicide appears as the only way out of the desperation called life. However, faced with a reality more dreadful than fiction, and feeling that "those who survived [the 3.11 tsunami] must not die" (*Quick Japan* 2012: 126), Sono completely rewrote the script to include a positive message of hope in the finale. Yet, the reception of *Himizu* was divided into two opposing camps, with the critics accusing Sono of irreverence for shooting several key scenes in one of the towns most badly hit by the tsunami, even before much of the debris was cleared away.

While in *Himizu*, the earthquake-tsunami disaster simply added another layer of devastation to the young protagonist's already catastrophic life and implicitly raised the question of the human cost of the recent calamity, in *Land of Hope* the characters' so-far harmonious, peaceful lives are all of a sudden interrupted by nuclear disaster. Realized primarily with foreign money from the UK, Taiwan, and Germany, and released only nine months after *Himizu*, *Land of Hope* was shown at numerous film festivals around the globe, winning several prizes.[2] The film represents a clear departure from Sono's usual violent slash-and-sex approach and instead deals with the psychological ordeal two farming families, the Suzukis and the Onos, have to go through after a massive earthquake and tsunami cause the nearby nuclear power plant to explode.

While the Suzukis are hastily bused to an overcrowded evacuation shelter when radiation spreads, their neighbors across the street are told not to worry, as their home was located safely outside the danger zone. However, policemen clad in eerie white protective suits—by now a familiar sight not only for Japanese audiences—fence off a significant portion of their yard. The house and cowshed sit just a few meters outside the suddenly established borderline. Already in the very beginning, the film thus exposes the ludicrousness of defining 'safety' in purely geographical terms.

The moment the stakes are hammered in the ground, the screen unexpectedly cuts to sepia, and only slowly returns to full color as the focal character of this scene, family patriarch Ono Yasuhiko (Natsuyagi Isao), starts to comprehend what has happened. Disbelieving the authorities' mantra-like claim to safety, the old man evicts his only son Yōichi (Murakami Jun) from his home of thirty years. Yōichi reluctantly leaves with his young wife Izumi (Kagurazaka Megumi) who, after learning of her pregnancy a few weeks later, urges Yōichi to evacuate even further in order to protect their unborn child.

Meanwhile, the elderly Yasuhiko resolves to stay behind with his demented wife Chieko (Ōtani Naoko) to tend to their cows, albeit knowing that their milk has become undrinkable. Upon receiving the news that the exclusion zone will soon be enlarged to include the Onos' farm, Yasuhiko shoots his own cows to spare them from the anticipated execution at a slaughterhouse. He then commits suicide together with Chieko who gives her consent during a brief moment of total mental clarity. As the symbol of their life and love, a large tree in the divided yard is set ablaze. Meanwhile, Yōichi and Izumi arrive at a beautiful beach far enough from the disaster site to make even cautious Izumi feel safe. However, their Geiger counter suddenly sets off a warning sound, indicating an increase of radiation to a dangerous level. The film thus ends in a rather dystopian way, suggesting that after a large-scale nuclear disaster, escape is ultimately impossible.

Although the plot is clearly modeled after Japan's triple disaster of March 11, 2011, the story is insistently marked as fictional. It takes place in the rural town of Ōba—an obvious reference to Futaba, the host municipality of the havocked Fukushima Daiichi Nuclear Power Plant—which is located in a fictitious prefecture called Nagashima, an easily recognizable allusion to the nuclear horrors of Hiroshima, Nagasaki, and of course Fukushima. In a similar fashion, the responsible power company's name is rendered as *Nihon Denryoku*, or Japan Power Company, echoing TEPCO's Japanese name *Tōkyō Denryoku*. This thin fictional veil over real-life events stands in contrast to the film's otherwise straightforward documentary approach. It significantly unlinks nuclear disaster from a specific location such as Fukushima, suggesting that a similar catastrophe could occur anywhere at any time. *Land of Hope*'s setting in the not-too-distant post-'Fukushima' future further encourages a reading of the film as an indictment of an industry, a government, and a society that apparently learned nothing from the most serious nuclear disaster since Chernobyl. In short, the fictional stratagem allows Sono to criticize both the authorities' deliberate downplaying of a disaster that closely resembles the real-life calamity of 3.11, and the citizens' readiness to push the dangers of radiation to the back of their minds so quickly.

Focusing on the narrative form in the cinema of disaster under consideration here, this chapter proposes a reading of *Land of Hope* as outspoken cultural critique directed at an apathetic public all too willing to turn away from discouraging realities. *Land of Hope* unmistakably labels Japan's response to 3.11/'Fukushima' as inadequate. However, I show that at the same time, this critique is clearly gendered. While Sono's reliance on a clear affirmation of traditional gender roles likely makes his anti-nuclear criticism more socially acceptable, I argue that it eventually backfires. Not only does it lead to the re-inscription of the social limitations that are placed on female protest, which is normally restricted to issues related to health and the home (Morioka 2013), but Sono's gendered depiction of responses to the disaster also entails a reproduction of masculinist (if not outright misogynist) undertones of Japan's post-'Fukushima' discourse on nuclear power. As argued below, the uncritical reproduction of topoi such as 'female hysteria' undercuts the credibility not only of a number of key characters, but ultimately also of the director's stated desire to make the audience rethink their own stance toward nuclear power. Finally, in seeking to uncover the gendered contradictions contained within the film, I contribute to the ongoing discussion of nuclear disaster/protests as reinscribing conventional gender stereotypes.

## Reading *Land of Hope* as anti-nuclear critique

### *The mobilization of traditional family values*

Mirroring the real-life events of 3.11, *Land of Hope* features a compound disaster beginning with an earthquake followed by a massive tsunami and a large-scale nuclear emergency. The destruction caused by the tsunami is massive, immediate, and discernible even to the untrained eye. It is undeniable. In contrast, the visual impact of the *nuclear* catastrophe the film is most focused on is limited. The invisibility of radiation and the absence of *immediate* casualties imply that the horror of 'Nagashima'—read 'Fukushima'[3]—is not limited to current physical devastation but includes the anticipation of significant future damage, here expressed in Izumi's ever-mounting worries about the health of her unborn child. The uncertainty and opacity surrounding what Izumi terms an "invisible war" (*mienai sensō*) inevitably open up space not only for debate but also for denial. It is this psychological dimension that *Land of Hope* sets out to explore.

The interest in individual reactions to disaster also explains why, although dealing with two families, the fate of the forcibly evacuated Suzukis is not painted in any detail. Perhaps with the exception of their son Mitsuru (Shimizu

Yutaka), the characters remain flat and do not show any development. Instead, the film zooms in on the dilemma of the Onos who, living just outside the official danger zone, are faced with the decision to believe the authorities' claim to safety and stay in their home of generations, or to follow their own warning instincts and leave their homes/lives behind.[4]

In Chapter 6, Hideaki Fujiki dwells on this dilemma, insightfully tracing the conflict to an observed post-disaster split of people's lives into two potentially opposing components. More precisely, Fujiki argues that the everyday (community) life, or *seikatsu*, becomes artificially separated from—and all too often antagonistic to—biological life (*inochi, seimei*). While *seikatsu* is associated with staying despite possible contamination, prioritizing *inochi* will eventually lead to 'voluntary' evacuation (*jishu hinan*). In other words, the nuclear disaster forced people in the irradiated areas to consider the two aspects as separate and weigh them up against each other.

*Land of Hope* explores both sides of the divide—ultimately showing that neither choice is entirely satisfactory—while developing the *seikatsu/inochi*-theme along generational lines. By associating the preservation of livelihood with old age, and linking the prioritization of life to youth/reproduction (and in particular, to motherhood), the film reproduces a key characteristic of the post-'Fukushima' anti-nuclear street protests. Until 3.11, large-scale public expressions of dissent were a rare sight in Japan, but this changed in the wake of 'Fukushima'. The worst nuclear accident since Chernobyl made the threat of nuclear contamination real far beyond Fukushima Prefecture and, as evidenced by mass protests and nuclear shutdowns around the globe, far beyond Japan. In Japan's urban centers, 'Fukushima' led to the largest string of demonstrations since the USA–Japan security treaty (ANPO) protests almost half a century earlier (Ogawa 2013). Hundreds of thousands of people from all walks of life—ranging from long-standing anti-nuke activists and unionists to subcultural hipsters and young families making their *demo debyū* (demo debut)—took to the streets to engage in a great number of often colorful public demonstrations (Manabe 2013).

Surveys corroborate that in post-'Fukushima' Japan, opposition to nuclear power ceased to be a minority position and became widespread across society (Takahashi and Masaki 2012). Nonetheless, both the public discourse on the anti-nuclear movement as well as the actual slogans voiced at demonstrations heavily relied on tropes of femininity, in particular of motherhood. Already following Chernobyl, well-educated Japanese housewives had become a major force in the anti-nuclear movement, focusing on 'women's issues' such as food safety and children's well-being (Wēru [Wöhr] 2011; Wöhr 2013). Similarly, *inochi o mamore!* (protect life) and *kodomo o mamore!* (protect our children) were clearly among the most frequently shouted slogans of the recent anti-nuke marches. That is, seemingly apolitical[5] problems were writ large while both openly political issues and a more general concern about environmental damage played but a marginal role (Morioka 2013; Holdgrün and Holthus 2014). Importantly, Wöhr points out that in concurrence with the changing role of the father as a nurturing parent, Japan saw an unprecedented number of men explicitly protesting *as fathers*, and notes that most so-called mothers' networks did in fact include men/fathers and women without children in their ranks. She argues, however, that due to the traditionally strong association of 'domestic' issues with women and motherhood, the diversity of the protesters went almost unnoticed (Wöhr 2013: 217–22). The public face of anti-nuke protests is female, and often that of a mother.

It is safe to assume that *Land of Hope*'s domesticated and depoliticized façade made its sharp anti-nuclear criticism more acceptable to many. The affirmation of established family models including the 'motherly instinct' to protect an unborn child makes Izumi's reaction an understandable if not 'natural' one. The same can be said for the absence of openly political criticism. At the same time, however, by relying on gendered modes of protection, the film reinforces the social limitations placed on female protest. Morioka poignantly describes these confines in her study of anti-nuclear activist mothers:

> Women in social protests have drawn, consciously or unconsciously, on the prevalent cultural assumption that deem women in general, and mothers in particular, to be selfless nurturers with natural protective instincts. There is, however, a significant limitation to the women's influence. Their words are heard precisely because they hold the subordinated status of housewives and mothers whose realm of influence is confined to domestic matters. As a result, they are only able to speak effectively on issues traditionally related to female roles, such as the health and safety of workers and children. [...] Ironically, the same feminine/maternal role that gives their voice a degree of authority also obliges them to limit their sphere of political participation to family related issues.
>
> (Morioka 2013: 198)

### *Trust lost, self-responsibility reigning high*

The focus on disaster victims from *outside* the mandatory evacuation zone enables Sono to dwell on one of the most sensitive issues of post-3.11 Japanese reality, namely the deterioration of public trust in government institutions. Following the meltdowns at Fukushima I, all people living within a 20 km radius of the havocked power plant were forcibly evacuated. In addition, tens of thousands—among them an over-proportionally high number of young women and children—relocated 'voluntarily' based on their own judgments and, in most cases, without being entitled to any substantial amount of compensation.[6] This mass exodus is but one visible expression of the dramatic loss of confidence in the authorities' disaster management.

Several types of trust have been distinguished in sociological research. Trust in individuals, or 'social trust,' tends to increase during and shortly after disasters, thanks to the solidarity commonly found among those affected by a calamity. In comparison, trust in abstract systems—so-called 'institutional trust'—is greatly influenced by the quality of public disaster management (Hommerich 2012: 48–49). Hommerich notes that in post-3.11 Japan, "[i]nstead of creating stability and helping disaster victims to cope, the governmental conduct seems to have resulted in increasing anxiety, uncertainty and distrust, especially among those who need support most urgently" (Hommerich 2012: 53). According to her representative survey, the post-3.11 credibility crisis was aggravated by the government's and TEPCO's disastrous information policy regarding the nuclear catastrophe, as well as by post-'Fukushima' disclosures regarding the corruption of the so-called nuclear village (Hommerich 2012: 53–54).

*Land of Hope* critically refers to post-3.11 blunders such as the withholding of vital information and haphazard evacuation measures, and points to the omnipresence of media propaganda. As in the case of a public seminar on the Fukushima nuclear disaster that Izumi and Yōichi attend after leaving their Nagashima home, this critique is often quite straightforward and, importantly, refers to real-life events. The (fictional) speaker blames the (real) government for failing to base disaster evacuation measures on scientific projections of the spread of radiation, claiming that this led to an unnecessary irradiation of thousands.[7] One of the greatest problems back in 2011, the presenter concludes in his talk, was the lack of reliable, independent information, leaving the people at the mercy of incompetent authorities.

Determined not to blindly believe everything she is told and as a result risk making uninformed decisions, Izumi devours whatever critical information on radiation she can get hold of. The film includes a close-up shot of a huge pile of real books published after 3.11, subtly inviting the audience to pick up a particularly easy-to-understand volume written by anti-poverty activist Amamiya Karin (2011) and signaling that in post-3.11 Japan, information is no longer scarce or too difficult to understand.

Izumi's studiousness is contrasted with a television show reminiscent of similar programs broadcast in the aftermath of 'Fukushima,' *discouraging* the viewers from using protective masks and loudly voicing their worries about radiation. In an obvious dig at the government's 2011 "Eat and Support" (*tabete ōen*) campaign promoting the consumption of agricultural produce from Northern Japan,[8] and citing the then LDP General Secretary Ishihara Nobuteru's contemptuous characterization of anti-nuclear sentiments as 'mass hysteria' (*Asahi Shimbun* 2011), the television show exhorts viewers not to get overexcited about radiation; instead, the audience is encouraged to eat local produce and keep up consumption to show their solidarity. Different from his wife, Yōichi is not immune to the program's message but silently nods in agreement. However, the program's blatantly propagandistic nature clearly makes Izumi's alertness appear as the more rational reaction at this point.

Contrary to Izumi who—like most young women and (expectant) mothers in pre-3.11 Japan—apparently has no prior knowledge about radiation, her father-in-law Yasuhiko's critical awareness goes back at least to the Chernobyl disaster of 1986. In fact, it is his far-sightedness regarding the dangers of nuclear power plants that corroborates his position as the moral authority of the film. When the earthquake strikes, his thoughts fly to the nearby Nagashima nuclear power plant that he had openly opposed from before its construction. Uninterested in clearing up the mess in his house, and suspicious of the media silence on the matter, Yasuhiko rummages for the old Geiger counter he obtained back in 1986. When Yōichi objects that there were no reports about radiation leaks in the radio news broadcast, Yasuhiko brushes him aside saying: "You're not telling me to trust the government, are you?"

According to Niklas Luhmann, trust is a mechanism that helps to reduce complexity: "By failing to trust, an individual burdens him/herself with the complexity of modern society and faces decisions for which he or she lacks adequate information and thereby increases individual risk" (Luhmann 2000 [1968]: 93). In *Land of Hope*, it is above all Yasuhiko and Izumi whose institutional trust is reduced to being close to zero, and who as a consequence face immensely difficult, lonely decisions. In a key scene, old Yasuhiko urges his whiny son to pull himself together and stop relying on others:

> Yōichi, [...] you have to live on your own. Don't you even once try to rely on the central government (*kuni*), the prefecture, the city, the village, or on the village leader, the mayor of town, or on the head of state. It's just you and your wife and your child—discuss things and then decide what to do as a family. Neither the central government nor the prefectural government nor the local authorities are on your side. [...] Run away! Running away is an expression of strength. You run away exactly because you're strong!

As this scene reveals, in *Land of Hope* the deterioration of institutional trust is directly linked to what has been called *jikosekinin*, or 'self-responsibility,' in Japanese. The term received its first close-up in 2004 after three Japanese civilians were kidnapped by a militant group in Iraq demanding the withdrawal of the Japanese military's humanitarian mission from the country. The Japanese were eventually released unharmed but met with a hostile reception upon their return. In the Japanese public perception, they had selfishly ignored the government's travel warning and thus 'got what they deserved.' As if to emphasize the dire consequences of non-compliance with social rules, the Koizumi administration (2001–2006) decided to bill the hostages for the airfare back to Japan and other costs.

*Jikosekinin* has since become a household term, more often than not linked to the stick rather than the carrot, and has been used to discourage non-conforming behavior. However, as the above scene shows, *jikosekinin* has a somewhat different nuance in *Land of Hope*. Given the complete failure of the various levels of government in the face of nuclear disaster, it is no longer reasonable for the individual to rely on state actors: in *Land of Hope*, *jikosekinin* has become a means to survive.

In the post-3.11 reality, the impression of a government abandoning its people was reinforced by a drastic and ill-communicated post-disaster elevation of acceptable radiation limits for the Fukushima Prefecture. The imposition of emergency exposure limits itself is congruent with the procedures of international radiological organizations, but the exact levels had to be determined by the Japanese government. Emergency (and other) radiological limits are directly linked to judgments about the individual acceptability of risks. Therefore, they are bound to spark controversies, as did the Japanese decision to raise the dose limit for the general public by twenty times to 20 mSv/year, a level reserved for adult occupational radiation workers before 3.11. The discussion of the safety of the chosen limits must be left to specialists. In the context of this paper, however, it is important that in Japan, specifically the lack of differentiation between dose levels for adults and (unborn) children—a demographic known to be particularly vulnerable to radiation—caused massive public outrage. Protest was not limited to concerned laypeople but included specialists such as Kosako Toshisō of Tokyo University who had been appointed Cabinet Advisor after 3.11. Kosako famously burst into tears during a press conference on April 29, 2011 in which he declared his resignation from the post, stating that as a researcher and father, he could no longer take responsibility for the 'outrageously high (*tondemonaku takai*)' limits (YouTube 2011). In the context of the government's and TEPCO's disastrous information policy, the 20 mSv/year limit clearly provoked the suspicion that the government was trying to keep evacuation costs to a minimum, prioritizing the economic aspects over the well-being of the affected population. Again, *jikosekinin* transmuted into a means for survival for many. While *Land of Hope* does not directly engage with this particular issue, the film reveals that pregnant Izumi's 'invisible war' is not only directed against radiation itself, but equally against the government. Moreover, the film shows that the psychological dimension of this war becomes more important as trust in governmental institutions erodes.

## Mental incapacity, 'female hysteria,' and a self-inflicted credibility crisis

### *Ubiquitous danger and collective denial, or the impossible desire for return to a pristine state*

*Land of Hope* touches upon a number of sensitive issues such as inappropriate government support of disaster victims and the ubiquity of media propaganda. At the same time, the film presents a clear critique of the social obliviousness surrounding nuclear disaster. In fact, apart from the Ono family, most other people (including a number of pregnant women awaiting their monthly check-up at the local hospital) appear more than ready to quickly forget their anxiety of the early days. The film presents this suppression of fear as taking place at a collective rather than an individual level, and it exposes the accompanying stigmatization of those who show overt concern. Izumi, for instance, soon becomes known as overly worried in the small town to which Izumi and Yōichi first evacuate. Possibly to release their own stress, Yōichi's new colleagues begin by poking fun at him, but soon they turn more serious, claiming that Izumi's behavior was an insult to their town. Yōichi reminds them that until just a few weeks ago, all of them had been taking precautions such as resorting to bottled water and rice from safer areas, but in vain—he is told to shut up, or leave the town. On his way back home, a frustrated Yōichi is seen yelling at children climbing on a jungle gym marked as off-limits due to high radiation.

The film does not, however, solely rely on dialogue to criticize the widespread propensity to close one's eyes before potential dangers. The social amnesia is superimposed with Yōichi's mother Chieko's dementia, an affliction that significantly worsens in the aftermath of disaster. As her life is torn apart, Chieko mentally slips back to her youth during a time when there were no nuclear power plants in Japan. She is thus genuinely surprised when she hears on the television that something as detestable as a nuclear power plant has been built nearby. The news about the explosion upsets her terribly—but a moment later she has already forgotten about it and returned to her own private world. Moreover, she falls into the habit of saying *Let's go home* all the time even though she never leaves the house. Needless to say, this phrase does not simply reflect the deterioration of her mental health, but on a metaphorical level points to the impossibility of undoing nuclear disaster. Chieko's inability to grasp the seriousness of the situation and react in an adequate way can thus be read as a critique, directed not only at the post-'Fukushima' present but extending to the whole post-war period during which a brainwashed, unconcerned public allowed dozens of nuclear power plants to be built in seismic Japan.

Chieko's dementia is also an example of the film's gendered representation of disaster response, which as I argue below at least partly subverts its critical potential. The contradictions emerging from the film's call for self-empowerment through action on the one hand, and the affirmation of traditional gender roles on the other, become particularly obvious in the film's last scene. After evacuating a second time to protect their unborn child, the couple visits a beautiful beach under a serene sky. Yōichi watches his wife from a distance, relieved to see her relax for the first time in weeks, cheerfully chatting with a young mother and her little child, presumably a projection of her future self. However, all of a sudden, the old Geiger counter they inherited from Yasuhiko gives off a warning sound. Yōichi pales as their second counter also indicates dangerously high levels of radiation. Immediately, he turns the devices off and quickly hides them from his wife. While Izumi does notice a sudden change in her husband's facial expression, she is not aware of the reason and, hugging him, insists that they will be fine because they love each other.

At first sight, this reference to the power of love as a way out of disaster appears as an ironic dig at the post-3.11 promotion of *kizuna*. *Kizuna* refers to bonds of love or friendship, and it was massively used as an appeal to collective solidarity with the disaster victims in 2011. It is important to note, however, that in *Land of Hope*, love is far from triumphant. Just as it is out of love that Yasuhiko chooses to kill his livestock, it is the strong *kizuna* between him and Chieko that makes their death a double suicide, not murder. Considering that love is linked to death and defeat rather than recovery, the film can well be read as powerful antithesis to the ubiquitous *kizuna* propaganda. The hugging scene closes with the film's title, *Land of Hope*, appearing across the scene.

### Sacrificing Izumi, sacrificing Chieko, or Yōichi's journey to manhood

However, although ironic at first sight, there is some ambiguity in the closing scene, and it is left up to the viewer to decide whether the reference to love and hope is sincere if sentimental, or sardonic to the point of cynicism. This ambiguity stems in no small part from Yōichi's silence regarding the suddenly increased radiation levels. Why does he not tell Izumi? Does he simply not want to spoil this first moment of peace she is experiencing in months? Or is it that his inclination to avert his eyes from danger wins over her efforts to protect their family? And if so, does this ending not subvert the film's most pertinent themes, namely its criticism of the prevalent head-in-the-sand mentality, and the restricted access to reliable information? The ambiguity of the last scene denies closure to a film that would no doubt lose its credibility if all conflicts were resolved at the end. However, at the same time it is difficult not to see the ending as a change of course which, to a degree, relativizes the film's potential as political critique.

Yet, the contradiction disappears if we look at the film's gendered subplot. Although no doubt revolving around a major disaster, the nuclear explosion is reduced to a mere background event if we approach *Land of Hope* from a different angle, reading it as a rather simple and straightforward coming-of-age story. In this interpretation, the young couple's hasty flight from their disaster-hit home turns into a necessary *rite de passage* on Yōichi's way to manhood, a stage that he reaches in the very moment he decides to keep the elevated radiation levels secret.

Let us look at this hidden storyline in some more detail. In the beginning of the film, 30-year-old Yōichi leads a rather easy life on his father's farm. In contrast to his wife who lovingly takes care of demented Chieko and prepares the family meals, there is no particular responsibility on the shoulders of gangly Yōichi before disaster strikes. While Izumi immediately questions the authority's claim that there is no danger a few meters outside the exclusion-zone, Yōichi is more than willing to ignore the absurdity of this claim. As a consequence, he comes across as weak, unable and unwilling to face reality—as *unmanly*. However, his eviction from his father's house signals the beginning of a maturation process, which involves becoming a father himself. It is no coincidence, therefore, that although the couple has been hoping to start a family for a long time, Izumi only gets pregnant *after* they leave Yasuhiko's house.

Different from many other fathers who have several months to prepare for parenthood, Yōichi is forced to behave as a protective father from the day he learns of his wife's pregnancy. This is because Izumi's initially somewhat diffuse concern about radioactive contamination turns into outright panic when she learns that the breast milk of a local woman she meets at the hospital was tested positive for cesium. Her mounting fears are visualized as she leaves the hospital, which for a moment appears surrounded by a blazing red inferno. Back home, Izumi tapes off the apartment to make it radiation-proof. She puts on a Tyvek suit and gas mask even inside the house and dons a bright yellow space suit when she goes outside. She pressures Yōichi to do the same, saying, "You do love your child, don't you?" Confused and embarrassed when Izumi becomes the laughing stock of town, Yōichi eventually sides with his wife and defends her against criticism.

Yet, it is not primarily because he shares Izumi's concern that Yōichi finally agrees to leave the small town to which they first evacuated. Rather, the decision can be read as another step in his transformation into a responsible (male) member of society. When Izumi's anxiety escalates, Yōichi secretly consults her doctor to find out if her concerns are justified, and whether the media are indeed purposefully spreading false information. Although this doctor appears only very briefly, I maintain that he is the film's second most important male authority next to family patriarch Ono Yasuhiko. This is because, as a male scientist connoting reason, progress, and truth, he corresponds to what Ulrike Wöhr identifies as the epitome of post-war masculinity (which replaced the previously hegemonic 'military masculinity'; Wöhr 2013: 207). On top, this doctor has apparently conducted an unspecified health survey among Fukushima children before; he thus speaks with a certain authority about nuclear matters.

Responding to Yōichi's question, the doctor states that rather than the media in general, it is the "doctors appearing on TV" who are not telling the truth. Importantly, because Japanese does not have a singular/plural distinction, the doctor's words could also be translated in the singular form. In that case, the reference to the 'lying doctor' appears as an easily recognizable stab at Dr. Yamashita Shun'ichi, one of Japan's leading authorities on radiation health. He was requested by the governor of Fukushima Prefecture to serve as a medical advisor soon after the 3.11 meltdowns and frequently appeared on television in the aftermath of 'Fukushima.' Yamashita's repeated claimed that the psychological distress caused by the meltdowns was far more harmful than the radiation itself, and his recommendation to smile and be happy in order to counter radiation's adverse effects caused a huge controversy in Japan (Brumfiel 2013; Williamson 2014).

Following the fictional doctor's statement, the camera zooms in on the visualization of what he calls the 'real data'—a graph showing three red, blue, and green upward lines. It is shown only very briefly so that the audience is unlikely to notice that the coordinate axes are not labeled. Although it contains no real information, the graph can be understood as a tool to corroborate Izumi's doctor's credibility and to differentiate him from the 'lying doctor(s)' on television.

However, having established his position as a trustworthy medical expert, Izumi's doctor then somewhat surprisingly presents a diagnosis of 'radiophobia' (*hōshanō kyōfushō*). He cautions Yōichi that in her current state, Izumi might end up not being able to give birth to her baby. Somewhat out of sync with the statement about the 'lying doctor' only moments earlier, this diagnosis seems to *affirm* Dr. Yamashita's warning of psychological distress as the real cause of health issues. More problematically, it echoes much of the post-'Fukushima' bashing of anti-nuclear activists as 'hysterical.' As mentioned, women constituted a very strong force in these protests, whether as organizers or participants speaking out as mothers. Yazawa Misaki has detailed how not only conservative politicians such as Ishihara Nobuteru mentioned earleir, but a wide range of magazines (most of which are dependent on power companies' sponsorship) belittled protesting mothers as unscientific, unsophisticated, and above all hysterical (Yazawa 2012: 62–64). According to Yazawa, men's weekly magazines such as *Shūkan Shinchō* were by far the most important but certainly not the only forum for this type of bashing. She sums up her critique with a quote from an article by Tanaka Yūko published in the August 5, 2011 edition of *Shūkan Kinyōbi*, a leftist and clearly anti-nuclear (advertisement-free) weekly magazine:

> Recently, I've been caught off guard by quite a number of men who are talking about "women and children" and in the same breath stated that "opposition to nuclear power stems from ignorance and hysteria." It was as if I had all of a sudden encountered a species I had thought extinct. Apparently, these people think of themselves as intellectuals with a solid knowledge of nuclear power. Secondly, they believe that people who oppose nuclear power without thinking about the overall picture of national energy supply are ignorant. On top of that, they are convinced that anti-nuke opposition is limited to women only and conveniently ignore that there *are* male intellectuals in the opposing camp. According to their logic, women are ignorant and hysterical to begin with, and since they themselves are overflowing with wisdom, anyone advocating a different view must be stupid.
>
> (Quoted after Yazawa 2012: 63)

This type of misogynist argument was not limited to magazines but can also readily be found in books.[9] Needless to say, woman bashing is not a prominent theme in *Land of Hope*. However, following a clearly masculinist matrix and subscribing to a hierarchical understanding of 'love,' the film does reproduce a number of the more problematic gender assumptions about anti-nuclear protests. For instance, thanks to her studiousness, Izumi has a far better understanding of the dangers of radiation than Yōichi; in fact there is not a single scene in the film where we see him reading a book. His secret consultation with her doctor reveals, however, that he remains unconvinced of the accuracy of his wife's knowledge. Yōichi needs a male scientist to take her fears seriously. Unsurprisingly, the doctor's diagnosis of 'radiophobia'—which Yōichi takes at face value despite it being delivered by a gynecologist, not a psychologist—does not make him trust her judgment any better. On the contrary, his wife now has a medical condition just like his mother. It turns out, therefore, that both of the film's key female characters are unsound of mind, while the male characters are associated with moral integrity, reason, responsibility, and maturity.

The two most important decisions that Yōichi makes in the film—first, to relocate a second time, and second, to keep the unexpected radiation alarm secret from the mentally unstable Izumi—can thus be interpreted as a protective act meant to spare his wife and unborn child from further harm. By subscribing to a hierarchical understanding of 'love' in which the male part dominates the female, Yōichi has finally become a responsible husband and father.

## Conclusion

Sono's affirmation of traditional gender roles may well have made his anti-nuclear critique more socially acceptable—after all, in the public imagination a mother's urge to protect her unborn child is only 'natural.' Equally, it can be said that the film's somewhat melodramatic nature determined the gender roles to a degree. Sono himself stated that in order to avoid confusion about which problem the film was trying to tackle, he refrained from presenting his usual dysfunctional family and made the Onos a harmonious 'Japanese' one (*Monthly Takarajima* 2012: 163). This gender-hierarchized Japanese harmony, however, not only functions at the expense of the female characters but it subverts the film's potential as anti-nuclear critique. As shown, most of the film presents a strong case against the prevalent head-in-the-sand mentality and sharply critiques the restricted access to reliable information. However, while satisfying the demands of traditional masculinity, the ending impairs the critical message developed during the first two hours of the film. In a rather paternalistic fashion, Sono here suggests that it is legitimate to hide the truth from those who might not be able to handle it (although in the case of Izumi we can probably be sure she will find out on her own in no time). While this about-turn certainly leaves the audience with open questions rather than presenting pre-formulated answers—a frequently stated maxim of Sono's work (*Monthly Takarajima* 2012: 163)—it remains paradoxical and unfortunate that the same logic may also be used to justify the government's cover-up of post-'Fukushima' truths the film spends so much time criticizing.

## Notes

1 The abrupt end of veteran Yamamoto Tarō's acting career illustrates the risk involved with anti-nuke criticism. Yamamoto was asked to leave his management company after turning activist in the wake of the 'Fukushima' disaster and has only been offered minor roles since. After a brief stint working for a company producing solar panels in 2012, Yamamoto unsuccessfully ran for a seat in the House of Representatives in the December 2012 elections. Instead, he was elected into the House of Councilors half a year later.
2 Among others, this includes the Best Actor Award at the 67th Mainichi Film Concours given to the film's lead actor, Natsuyagi Isao in the role of old man Ono Yasuhiko, the NETPAC Award at the 37th Toronto International Film Festival 2012, and the Japan Reconstruction Encouragement Film Prize 2013.
3 In order to differentiate between the geographical place and the event, the nuclear catastrophe soon came to be frequently referred to as 'Fukushima,' written in *katakana* instead of *kanji* (similar differentiations are used for the atomic bombings at Hiroshima and Nagasaki, and the Minamata disease). In the transcription, this differentiation is rendered through the use of inverted commas.
4 Later in the film, the authorities urge the Onos to 'voluntarily' leave but Yasuhiko resolves to stay.
5 Needless to say, as Ulrike Wöhr (Wēru 2011: 85) and others have pointed out, in Japan's hyper-aged society, the well-being of (future) children is anything but a non-political issue, but it is easily disguised as such and therefore more acceptable. In addition, "women's mobilization amidst 'Rise up, Japan' [also] demands some critical reflection. At the confluence of unprecedented crisis, bottom-up mobilization, and a resurgence of nationalism, women's eager participation in national affairs cannot be assumed to be entirely innocent or uncomplicated" (Koikari 2013).

6  In February 2013, 66,347 individuals had deregistered with their local resident's registration office; this number is equal to 3.28 percent of the prefecture's entire population at the time of disaster (*Fukushima Minpō* 2013). However, it is assumed that the true number of 'voluntary' evacuees is far higher as not everyone deregisters immediately.
7  On the failure to make proper use of the System for Prediction of Environmental Emergency Dose Information (SPEEDI) during the 2011 crisis, see Cleveland 2014.
8  Launched by the Ministry of Agriculture, Forestry, and Fisheries together with the Consumer Affairs Agency around six weeks after the meltdowns, this campaign encouraged people to consume agricultural produce from the disaster areas. Notably, questions of food safety were completely ignored in this campaign while solidarity with the disaster victims was writ large. Masami Yuki argues that by attaching a moral tinge to the consumption of (possibly irradiated) Tōhoku produce, open dissent became difficult; she therefore rates the campaign totalitarian (Yuki 2014: 41).
9  To give just one extreme example, Ipponmatsu Mikio in his 2012 publication unleashes a stream of lampoons and slanders directed not only at women, but equally at zainichi Koreans, *Asahi Shimbun*, critical scientists, etc.

# References

*Ai to kibō no machi.* 2014, Dir. Kanno Hiroshi. Film.
Amamiya, Karin. 2011, *14sai kara no genpatsu mondai.* Tokyo: Kawade Shobō Shinsha.
*Asahi Shimbun.* 2011, "Hangenpatsu wa 'shūdan hisuterī'—Jimin Ishihara kanjichō." June 14, at: www.asahi.com/special/10005/TKY201106140605.html (accessed August 14, 2014).
Brumfiel, Geoff. 2013, "Fukushima health-survey chief to quit post." *Nature.* February 20, at: www.nature.com/news/fukushima-health-survey-chief-to-quit-post-1.12463 (accessed June 6, 2015).
Cleveland, Kyle. 2014, "Mobilizing nuclear bias: The Fukushima nuclear crisis and the politics of uncertainty." *The Asia-Pacific Journal* Vol. 12, Issue 20, No. 1 (May 19), at: http://japanfocus.org/-Kyle-Cleveland/4116/article.html (accessed December 13, 2015).
*Fukushima Minpō.* 2013, "Ken-jinkō 6man 6345nin genshō: 195man 8054nin." March 1, at: www.minpo.jp/pub/topics/jishin2011/2013/03/post_6393.html (accessed July 15, 2013).
*Himizu.* 2012. Dir. Sono Sion. Film.
Holdgrün, Phoebe and Holthus, Barbara. 2014, "Gender and political participation in post-3/11 Japan." *DIJ Working Paper* No. 14/3, at: www.dijtokyo.org/publications//WP1403_Holdgruen_Holthus.pdf (accessed June 6, 2015).
Hommerich, Carola. 2012, "Trust and subjective well-being after the Great East Japan earthquake, tsunami and nuclear meltdown: Preliminary results." *International Journal of Japanese Sociology* 21: 46–64.
*Ieji.* 2014. Dir. Kubota Nao. Film.
Ipponmatsu, Mikio. 2012, *Kuni o horobosu hangenpatsu hisuterī—sekai kara mita nihon no sakugo.* Tokyo: Enerugī Fōramu Shinsho.
*Kibō no kuni.* 2012. Dir. Sono Sion. Film.
Kingston, Jeff. 2012, "Japan's nuclear village." *The Asia-Pacific Journal* Vol. 10, Issue 37, No. 1 (September 10), at: www.japanfocus.org/-Jeff-Kingston/3822/article.html (accessed December 13, 2015).
Koikari, Mire. 2013, "Training women for disasters: Gender, crisis management (Kiki Kanri) and post-3.11 nationalism in Japan." *The Asia-Pacific Journal* Vol. 11, Issue 26, No. 1 (July 1), at: http://japanfocus.org/-Mire-Koikari/3962/article.html (accessed December 13, 2015).

Luhmann, Niklas. 2000 [1968], *Vertrauen: Ein Mechanismus der Reduktion sozialer Komplexität*. Stuttgart: Lucius & Lucius.
Manabe, Noriko. 2013, "Music in Japanese antinuclear demonstrations: The evolution of a contentious performance model." *The Asia-Pacific Journal* Vol. 11, Issue 42, No. 3 (October 21), at: http://japanfocus.org/-Noriko-MANABE/4015/article.html (accessed December 13, 2015).
*Monthly Takarajima*, 2012, "Sono Sion intabyū." December, 161–63.
Morioka, Rika. 2013, "Mother courage. Women as activists between a passive populace and a paralyzed government," in Tom Gill, Brigitte Steger, and David H. Slater (eds), *Japan Copes with Calamity. Ethnographies of the Earthquake, Tsunami and Nuclear Disasters of March 2011*. Oxford: Peter Lang, 177–200.
*Nikkan Gendai*. 2014, "Tōden hihan de uchikiri sunzen—eiga 'Ai to kibō no machi' no junan." July 5, at: www.nikkan-gendai.com/articles/view/geino/151599/2 (accessed May 21, 2015).
Ogawa, Akihiro. 2013, "Young precariat at the forefront: Anti-nuclear rallies in post-Fukushima Japan." *Inter Asia Cultural Studies* Vol. 14, Issue 12: 317–26.
*Quick Japan*. 2012, "Sono Sion and Matsue Tetsuaki: Where's the land of hope?" October, 124–28.
*Shūkan Kinyōbi*. 2012, "Sono Sion kantoku intabyū: nihon no media no shuzai de ichiban ooi shitsumon wa 'naze genpatsu no eiga o totta no ka?'." October 19, 25–27.
Takahashi, Kōichi and Masaki, Miki. 2012, "'Higashi nihon daishinsai de nihonjin wa dō kawatta ka. '"Bōsai, enerugī, seikatsu ni kansuru seron chōsa"' kara." *NHK Broadcasting Culture Research Institute*, June, at: www.nhk.or.jp/bunken/summary/research/report/2012_06/20120603.pdf (accessed April 10, 2013).
*Tsūhan Seikatsu*. n.d., "Eiga 'Ai to kibō no machi' kantoku Kanno Hiroshi san ni intabyū," at: www.cataloghouse.co.jp/yomimono/genpatsu/kanno/ (accessed May 21, 2015).
Wēru Ururike [Wöhr, Ulrike]. 2011, "'Datsu genpatsu' no tayōsei to seijisei o kashika suru—jendā, sekushuaritī, esunishitī no kanten kara," in Takao Kikue (ed.), *Daishinsai to watashi*. Hiroshima: Hiroshima Joseigaku Kenkyūjo, 80–94.
Wöhr, Ulrike. 2013, "From Hiroshima to Fukushima: Gender in nuclear and anti-nuclear politics," in HCU 3.11 Forum (ed.), *The 3.11 Disaster as Seen from Hiroshima: A Multidisciplinary Approach*. Tokyo: Sōeisha/Sanseidō Shoten, 203–33.
Williamson, Piers. 2012, "Largest demonstrations in half a century protest the restart of Japanese nuclear power plants." *The Asia-Pacific Journal* Vol. 10, Issue 27, No. 5, (July 2), at: www.japanfocus.org/-Piers-_Williamson/3787/article.html (accessed December 13, 2015).
Williamson, Piers. 2014, "Demystifying the official discourse on childhood thyroid cancer in Fukushima." *The Asia-Pacific Journal* Vol. 12, Issue 49, No. 2, (December 8), at: http://japanfocus.org/-Piers-_Williamson/4232/article.html (accessed December 13, 2015).
Yazawa, Misaki, 2012, "'Umu sei' to genpatsu: Tsushima Yūko o tegakari ni." *'3.11' ikō no feminizumu—Datsu genpatsu to atarashii sekai e. Eds*. Shin Feminizumu Hiyō no kai. Tokyo: Ochanomizu Shobō, 57–68.
YouTube. 2011, *Kosako Toshisō naikaku kanbō sanyo jinin—20 miri shīberuto mondai* Uploaded May 3, at: www.youtube.com/watch?v=yFg2IxD7mvs (accessed June 10, 2015).
Yuki, Masami. 2014, "Post-Fukushima discourses on food and eating: Analysing political implications and literary imagination," in Lisette Gebhardt and Masami Yuki (eds), *Literature and Art after 'Fukushima'—Four Approaches*. Berlin: EB Verlag, 37–51.

# 8 Antigone in Japan
## Some responses to 3.11 at Festival/Tokyo 2012

*M. Cody Poulton*

### Theater and catastrophe

Who speaks for the dead? And if they could speak for themselves, would we be prepared to listen? How are we to commemorate them? What are the consequences when the living fail to treat the mortal remains or living memories of their loved ones with respect?[1] Questions like these have literally come to haunt the Japanese public after the immense physical destruction wrought by the Great East Japan Earthquake and Tsunami on March 11, 2011. It seemed fitting, then, that many of the productions showcased at Japan's major international theater festival, Festival/Tokyo, in 2012, referenced arguably the greatest work of dramatic literature on mourning, Sophocles' *Antigone*. Here I will focus on two productions in particular: Matsuda Masataka's (b. 1962) *Record of a Journey to Antigone* and Takayama Akira's (b. 1969) rendering of Elfriede Jelinek's (b. 1946) *Epilog?*, a work published on the occasion of the first anniversary of the earthquake and tsunami.

The psychoanalyst Maria Torok has described the forgetting of trauma as "a memory [...] buried *without a legal burial place*" (cited in Rayner 2006: 23). In short, the memory is not lost; rather, like the body of Polynices, Antigone's brother, it is not properly laid to rest, and like all unfinished business will come back to haunt us. But here I wish to stress, not so much the psychological effects of this disaster, profound as they may be, but their practical, physical, religious, and even political consequences. A body is not a metaphor, and 'laid to rest' is no better than a platitude. All who have faced the death of a loved one know that their passing tears a rent in the tissue of life, their absence making mockery of the ordinary; surely this sense is compounded manifold should we face the deaths of tens of thousands. The rituals of burial for the ancient Greeks had a similar religious significance as do those for the Japanese today and the membrane dividing the living from the dead for the Japanese is a permeable one. Governments and industries have engaged in willful acts of forgetting, but those who were directly affected by the disaster cannot so easily leave their dead unburied. Until the proper rites of burial and remembrance are enacted and continue to be re-enacted on a regular basis, the lives of the survivors can return to no semblance of normality, however well their physical needs may be taken care of.

How individuals and communities deal with the dead is not just a matter of psychological healing; it is even an issue of political urgency. In the aftermath of this disaster, many foreign commentators commended the Japanese people for their stoicism, their solidarity, their peaceful and law-abiding willingness to get down to the important work of rescue, recovery, and reconstruction. Many suggested that this reflected some national characteristic of the Japanese, an attitude imbued with a deeply Buddhist sense of resignation and recognition of life's fragility. No doubt there was some of that, but, as Rebecca Solnit (2010) noted, ad hoc organizations of the public everywhere and at all times have shown remarkable resilience in rebuilding their communities in the aftermath of overwhelming disaster. Solnit has argued that spontaneous acts of mutual aid had come to the rescue in places, like New Orleans in 2005, where governments have been seized with what she has called "elite panic." Visiting Japan's northeast a year after their disaster, she recognized a similar dynamic at work. "There is no such thing as a natural disaster," Solnit reminds us. Whatever calamity may have occurred naturally is compounded by government paralysis, incompetence, or the rush to protect property over the lives of the people. Wherever Solnit went in the *hisaichi* (the disaster zone), she encountered a deep distrust of the authorities, a common enough reaction. She noted that governments typically fear acts of insurrection at such times, but "in Japan the greater problem seems to be conformity" (Solnit 2012).

Solnit put her finger on what is perhaps the greatest threat to Japan post-3.11. Where, in particular, was the anger, which needed to be focused on the government and TEPCO, whose poorly designed Fukushima Daiichi nuclear reactor was incapable of preventing the greatest nuclear disaster since Chernobyl? The suspicion, anger, and resentment against government and big business was real and strongly felt by those who had been directly hit by the disaster, but it became quickly buried in a national rhetoric of reconstruction, with slogans like *Tsunageyō Nippon* (join together, Japan) and *Ganbarō Nippon* (never give up, Japan). It seemed cruelly ironic, in the wake of an earthquake that also caused a seismic rift in the Japanese body politic, that the word chosen to exemplify the Japanese spirit for the New Year, 2012, was *kizuna* (the ties that bind) (Iwaki 2015).

Civil liberties were curtailed in the wake of Japan's worst 'natural' disaster of the past century. The Great Kantō Earthquake of 1923 led, in its immediate aftermath, to the slaughter of more than 6,000 innocent Korean workers by vigilante groups, as well as the murder by secret police of anarchists Ōsugi Sakae and Itō Noe, and leftist playwright Hirasawa Keishichi, among others. Two years later, in 1925, political freedoms were further quashed with the passing of the Public Security Preservation Law (*Chian ijihō*), which effectively outlawed leftist political assembly. Parallels are being made today with Prime Minister Abe's State Secrets Law of 2014, his silencing of media criticism, his ongoing attempts to revise the post-war constitution and his whitewashing of Japan's war history.

Referring to Hakim Bey's notion of 'temporary autonomous zones' to describe liminal, carnivalesque spaces that are "neither revolution nor festival, in which people liberate themselves for pleasure and social reinvention," Solnit

(2010: 298) suggests that disasters can provide a place and opportunity for such spaces of freedom to be created. Can Japanese theater create 'temporary autonomous zones' for the exploration of new models of community after a disaster like Fukushima? Pace Solnit's more hopeful readings of how natural disaster can effect social and political change, such calamities have had a regrettable history in modern Japan of catalyzing powerfully conservative forces, but at the same time there is a long, popular tradition in Japan of regarding natural calamity in a messianic fashion as an augur of *yonaoshi* (correcting the world).

At the very least, the two great disasters of modern Japan were forces for radical change in Japanese. The Kantō Earthquake of 1923 gave birth to modern drama (*shingeki*) with the building of the Tsukiji Little Theatre. The bombing of Japan's major cities that precipitated the country's defeat in 1945 also spurred radical experiments in underground theater (*angura*) and dance (*butō*) that have left their mark on performing arts the world over. The Japanese of course are no strangers to disaster, and for more than 800 years (since at least the writing of Kamo no Chōmei's An Account of My Hut [*Hōjōki*] in 1212 CE), natural disaster has informed the Japanese people's sensibility and experience of life. "Disaster is a defining feature of Japan's cultural landscape, and consequently the country's general belief system has integrated the cyclicality of destruction and renewal," writes Gennifer Weisenfeld (2012: 13). Moreover, classical Greek drama has furnished us with a keyword for disaster: *catastrophe*, its original meaning (overthrow or overturning) being related to such other theatrical terms as *peripeteia* and *dénouement* (Fujii 2014: 138). We shall see that another keyword of classical tragedy, *hubris*, comes to play an important role in making sense of 3.11.

## The inability to mourn

What long-term effects will this catastrophe have on Japanese theater, and how can theater give voice to the pain specific to these circumstances? It may be too soon to tell, but it is possible here at least to sketch out some patterns that have emerged around contemporary artists' response to the disaster. One challenge soon after the disaster was the proper burial of the dead, and other related rituals that, we will see, have important connections to the origins of theater itself. In addition to the profound psychological trauma suffered by the survivors, reports flooded in from Tōhoku of hauntings and possessions by the spirits of those who had died, whose bodies had not been recovered, whose souls had not been given the proper obsequies befitting the dead. Solnit encountered a Buddhist priest in one of the areas hit by the tsunami, Kaneda Teiō, who had opened a meeting spot at his temple, which he called "Café de Monk," a play on the Japanese word *monku*, meaning 'complain.' It became a center for members of the community to express feelings that had been stunned by the disaster or stunted by efforts to forge social harmony, often at the expense of the expression of personal grief. In a subsequent report, also published in *The London Review of Books*, Richard Lloyd Parry visited Kaneda to report on the work that he was doing to provide solace to both the living and the dead. Kaneda (whose Buddhist name Teiō means, incidentally, 'a response to resignation') told Parry that the survivors had been struck dumb by the calamity. Kaneda was kept busy holding rites of exorcism for a host of people suffering from deep trauma whose source seemed not personal but collective, as if they were channeling the spirits, not only of men and women, but even of the animals that had died in the flood.

> Thousands of spirits had passed from life to death; countless others were cut loose from their moorings in the afterlife. How could they all be cared for? Who was to honour the compact between the living and the dead? In such circumstances, how could there fail to be a swarm of ghosts?
>
> (Parry 2014)

> When opinion polls put out the question: 'How religious are you?' the Japanese rank among the mostly ungodly of people in the world. It took a catastrophe for me to understand how misleading this self-assessment is. I knew about the 'household altars,' or *butsudan*, which are still seen in most homes and which the memorial tablets of the dead ancestors—the *ihai*—are displayed. [...] Offerings of flowers, incense, rice, fruit and drinks are placed before them; at the summer Festival of the Dead, families light candles and lanterns to welcome home the ancestral spirits. I had assumed that these picturesque practices were matters of symbolism and custom, attended to in the same way that people in the West will participate in a Christian funeral without any literal belief in the words of the liturgy. But in Japan spiritual beliefs are regarded less as expressions of faith than as simple common sense, so lightly and casually worn that it is easy to miss them altogether.
>
> (Parry 2014)

For the Japanese the living live with their dead, communicating with them daily. Their dead do not seem so dead as ours. But "[t]he tsunami did appalling violence to the religion of the ancestors," Parry concludes, since the survivors have not been able to carry out proper rites for so many who have quite literally been lost (Parry 2014).[2]

## *Antigone* as Locus Classicus

> Blessed be they whose lives do not taste of evil
> But if some God shakes your house
> Ruin arrives
> Ruin does not leave
> It comes tolling over the generations
> It comes rolling the black night salt up from the
> Ocean floor
> And all your thrashed coasts groan

The Chorus here of Canadian poet and classicist Ann Carson's inspired adaptation of *Antigone*, called *ANTIGONICK*, strikes an eerie echo of the tsunami that raked Japan's northeastern coast on March 11, 2011. The last play in Sophocles' Theban trilogy (but the first to have been written), *Antigone* traces the tragedy that befalls the offspring of Oedipus. The title character is daughter to Oedipus and sister to Ismene and two brothers, Eteocles and Polynices. The two brothers were to take turns ruling over Thebes, but their rivalry sparked a civil war in which both were killed. Creon, the newly-appointed king of Thebes, rules that the body of Polynices, who had taken arms against the city, must lie, in Antigone's words, "unwept and unburied, sweet sorry meat for the little lusts of birds" (Sophocles 2010); anyone who attempts to give him a proper funeral will be put to death. Torn between the city's law against traitors and her own love for her brother, Antigone faces being buried alive by an unrepentant Creon, whose literalist devotion to the law invites not only her death, but also those of his wife Euridice and son Haimon, Antigone's fiancé.

Antigone is a profoundly compelling but also disconcerting heroine, one who has inspired numerous philosophical and literary responses over the millennia, from Hegel to Beckett, Anouilh, Brecht, and Cocteau. She sacrifices her own life, as well as those of two others close to her, for the sake of a brother who has already died, all because of an insult to his mortal remains. There is something of the fanatic about her, even while we can acknowledge her implacable logic. Matsuda Masataka, playwright of one of the works discussed below, refers to Antigone's "cool madness" (Matsuda 2012: 153). Anne Carson notes that Antigone's name means something like "against birth" or "against being born" (Carson 2013), alluding to the twisted, incestuous circumstances of her birth and those of her siblings from a father who impregnated his own mother. "I'm a strange, new, in-between thing, aren't I?" she herself admits, in Carson's rendering, "not at home with the dead, nor with the living" (Sophocles 2010). Carson remarks that Antigone is "keeping faith with a deeply other organization that lies just beneath what we see or what we say" (Carson 2013), noting that in his adaptation of the play, Brecht had the actor performing Antigone play her with a door strapped to her back. "A door may come in useful if you come to places that don't have an obvious way in, like normality, or an obvious way out, like the classic double bind" (Carson 2013). She is not an easy character to warm to. Creon accuses her of being "autonomous," a word that sounds like "free," but quite literally means "a law unto herself." (Freedom for the Greeks, in any case, meant something quite different than it does for us.) But it is her world, and not just Antigone, who is out of joint. Blind Tiresias takes Creon to task for his inhuman decree against Polynice's burial, saying, "You've made a structural mistake with life and death, my dear. You've put the living underground and kept the dead up here" (Sophocles 2010). One is inclined to think that, in her own way, Antigone has done something much the same.[3]

### Record of a Journey to Antigone

The struggle with silence's hold over us is a theme running throughout *Antigone*, and one that all Japanese theater artists have had to wrestle with in their responses to 3.11. One kind of silence at work in *Antigone* is the silence imposed on dissent by Creon. Antigone tells him that the others support her desire to give proper funeral rites to her brother, but that he has "nailed their tongues to the floor." What Antigone wishes to do and speak of has become politically taboo.

It is difficult to speak of the dead; how much harder, then, is it to attune our ears to what the dead may have to tell us. Matsuda Masataka writes in his introduction to *Record of a Journey to Antigone*, his contribution to F/T 12:

> Perhaps the language of those who have passed away is not a language we can understand. In order to translate their words, we must destroy our own mother tongue, transform it even into something that sounds like some foreign language we have never heard before, or have no recollection of ever hearing before,
>
> (Matsuda 2012: 152)

Matsuda even goes so far as to say that the telling of a story constitutes an act of violence by the letter (language itself) on the listener, betraying a deep suspicion that art has to do more with coercion than liberation.

Still, Matsuda's play (at least a significant part of it) is composed of language, in a variety of registers that are thoroughly contemporary. In the preface to her study of the Great Kantō Earthquake of 1923, Gennifer Weisenfeld notes that:

> one of the greatest changes in visual culture is the ability of individuals to contribute to the dialogue [of disaster] through handheld personal devices, ubiquitous mobile phones, and miniature video recorders, which both supplement and bypass mass media through websites such as YouTube and a host of new digital social media.
>
> (Weisenfeld 2012: xi)

The Tōhoku earthquake and tsunami is surely the most recorded disaster in world history to date, its images engraved on us to an extent that other catastrophes, like the December 26, 2004 Southeast Asian tsunami or the Haiti earthquake on January 12, 2010, both of which claimed as many as ten times the number of deaths, are not. This surfeit of voices and images is reflected in a number of performance works that have come out of the experience of 3.11.

But how to make sense of this surfeit of data? *Record of a Journey to Antigone* was a performance to be read more than seen. The first 'performance' was presented by the director in the form of a written record of a series of events said to have taken place around Tokyo and Fukushima. Some of these were recorded or reported on through Facebook, Twitter, streaming video on YouTube, and various diaries and blogs posted on the Internet by several of the characters involved in the story created by Matsuda. A 'performance text' (adjunct to the blogs and Twitterfeeds, etc.) was published in the Fall 2012 issue of *Theatre Arts*. A volume containing the performance text, as well as the other records from the dramatis personae, was available for sale at the 'still performance' at the Nishi Sugamo Arts Factory in November of the same year.

Matsuda skirts around the challenge of trying to have the dead speak to us in the central narrative thread running through his work, saving their words for terse and enigmatic tweets. Rather, his work presents a collection of young people, most of them engaged in the attempt to stage a production of *Antigone* in Fukushima, for an audience of a single blind person—a play within a play that is intended to be heard, not seen. (The blind man who is the play's ideal audience is either Tiresias, *Antigone*'s blind, androgynous oracle, or even her father Oedipus.) The story is constructed out of a number of plot lines concerning the chief characters:

1   Ōki Momoko, director of the "Patriot Theater," which is attempting to stage a production of *Antigone* in Fukushima; also Hibari Unemi, who plays Antigone, Yoshimoto Mika (Ismene), Kurume Tōki (Creon), and Rosso Jun (Haimon);
2   Ikiune Minoru, a young man working in a bookstore in Shinjuku, who himself is trying to write a version of *Antigone*, and who on numerous occasions tries to interfere with Ōki's production. Ikiune, whose name sounds like *ikiume* (buried alive) is a double, as well as rival, for Antigone and the play being created about her;
3   Someone called "I" (*watashi*), who works in a health food store, blogging about her co-worker Iroyama and Iroyama's lover Kinoshita, who is cheating on her.

This story, purported to have taken place over the course of several months, from August 2011 through to late October 2012, led up to its culmination a month later, in the live 'performance' at the Nishi Sugamo Arts Center. This was, finally, an opportunity for the audience to encounter the characters in Matsuda's play, as well as tour the exhibits on the second floor of the building, where audio recordings and printouts were displayed, providing glimpses into the experience that the *Antigone* cast had in its travels around Fukushima Prefecture.

The performance, such as it was, took place on the ground floor of the Arts Center in a large, black box space, in which audience members could circulate around members of the cast, who stood or sat illuminated by spotlights, neither saying anything nor interacting with one another. It was the task of the spectator, Matsuda told us, to "read their faces," but the majority of us didn't know the characters well enough to know what to read into or out of their faces when we encountered them. The exhibit on the second floor was somewhat more intelligible, but nonetheless fragmentary, consisting for the most part of raw data: sights and sounds of a real, physical journey to Fukushima without commentary or context. The narrative that could pull together the various strands of all this lay elsewhere in the massive volume of texts and images (hundreds of web pages and hours of video and audio feeds) published on the *Antigone* homepage or, in print form, in the thirty-two-page script.

One had to wonder: just how many people had really followed Matsuda down the twisted path of his journey to *Antigone*? To be sure, the work was incredibly intricate, but it had the quality of a school project, and I suspect that many if not most of his cast were also his students, to say nothing of the audience itself (Matsuda is professor of theater at Rikkyō University.) On his website one can actually check, for example, how many dedicated readers his blogs and tweets have had. The Twitterfeed from the dead (@shisya), for example, has sadly had only six followers and this is, to date, more than two years since the production. Of course, more came in person to see the performance and exhibition staged in November 2012 at F/T. They stood or sat and listened and watched with an air of pious silence, as Japanese audiences tend to do, but I am not sure they took much more home with them of their experience than I did. The problems of these young people that were at the center of this anti-dramatic production were, frankly, banal in comparison to the subject matter. One had the feeling that, as much as the work was a "journey to Antigone," no one really ever reached either Sophocles' play or Fukushima itself.

A native of Nagasaki, Matsuda is an alumnus of Ritsumeikan University in Kyoto. He based himself in that city and was active as a director, playwright, and teacher at Kyoto University of Art and Design until 2011, when he took up his new position at Rikkyō University in Tokyo. During the 1990s he distinguished himself as one of the leading exponents of the *Quiet Theatre* (*shizuka na engeki*) movement, together with other playwrights like Hirata Oriza (b. 1962), crafting delicate and beautifully understated studies of ordinary people finding drama in ordinary situations. Some of his works from that period are superb, especially *The Sea and Parasol* (*Umi to higasa*, 1994) and *Cape Moon* (*Tsuki no misaki*, 1997); the latter won the Kishida Kunio Drama Award for the best Japanese play that year. By the time he established his Marebito Theatre Company in 2003, however, his work had already taken a turn away from the quiet realism of his 1990s drama, toward something altogether darker and more hermetic. *Record of a Journey to Antigone* was exemplary of the course Matsuda's works have taken in the past decade, toward greater experimentation with dramatic form and demanding even greater effort on the part of the audience to make sense of. His remarks in the "performance notes" about a desire to listen to the voices of the dead, as well as the name of his company, Marebito-no-kai, hint at this major dramaturgical turn he has taken since the early 2000s. *Marebito*, meaning 'stranger' or 'guest,' is a term coined by the poet and ethnologist Orikuchi Shinobu (1887–1953) to describe Japanese actors in their archetypal form: people disguised as spirits from another world come to visit humankind, to provide entertainment and oracular messages of solace and guidance for their communities. Orikuchi believed that all originary performance in Japan was based on this principle of a communication between people of this world and spirits of the other-world, mediated by the *marebito*. Accordingly,

Matsuda's work has departed from easily apprehended, linear narratives to increasingly explore alternate realities: those of dreams and ghosts.

The reader would not be mistaken if she thought Matsuda's works sounded a little like nō. The traditional form is one that many modern playwrights, from Mishima Yukio (1925–1970) to Sakate Yōji (b. 1963) and Okada Toshiki (b. 1972), have revisited in various ways. To date, Okada has written as many as three responses to the disaster, one of which, *Ground and Floor* (*Jimen to yuka*, 2013) begins with the statement that "the stage is the place where ghosts can be seen." Nō is after all the ultimate 'haunted stage,' the supreme form for exploring the intersections between dreams and reality, life and death. Matsuda, however, has thrown away the various conventions that exist in the traditional form that allow audiences to make sense of their theatrical experience, and the language that he uses remains very much a private one that few but the playwright or the most dedicated fan can make much sense of. His message threatens to return once more to the silence of the dead. He is like Tiresias, whose oracles require a priesthood—in this case, theater critics—to interpret him, but even his interpreters are unsure of his intended meaning, and critics have never been very trustworthy priests.

## Elfriede Jelinek and Fukushima

The showcase of F/T 12 was the staging of four plays by Elfriede Jelinek, in two of which Jelinek turned her attention to the ongoing disaster in Japan. *Kein Licht* (No Light) *I* and *Kein Licht II* both made explicit reference to 3.11 and Fukushima, and were staged by two of the most innovative theater companies in Japan today, Chiten and Port B, directed respectively by Miura Motoi (b. 1973) and Takayama Akira (b. 1969).

Jelinek had taken great interest in the events unfolding in Fukushima ever since the earthquake and tsunami of March 11, 2011, and began writing *Kein Licht* soon after the catastrophe. She submitted it for performance in September 2011 at Schauspiel Köln, which had commissioned a work from her on the theme of the 'twilight of democracy.' At the same time, she posted the text on her website. Her sequel, *Epilog?*, was posted on her website on March 11, 2012, the first anniversary of the earthquake and tsunami.

Jelinek picks up on a couple of themes that Matsuda had raised in his Antigone play: blindness and the voices of the dead. The title is Jelinek's play on Goethe's last words: *mehr Licht!* (More light!) as he called for a lamp to be brought to him before he died. As such, the title can be read as an indictment of the European project of enlightenment, one which produced the atom bomb and atomic power. 'No light' is also an ironic reference to the blackout Tokyo and much of the affected region experienced after the tsunami and shutdown of the Fukushima Daiichi Nuclear Power Plant, which supplied electricity exclusively to the Kantō region where Tokyo is located. As such, the work is equally an indictment of post-war Japanese energy policies and the way economically depressed regions like Tōhoku continue to be exploited by the central government. (See the translator's postscript in Jelinek 2012.)

Jelinek trained as a musician and composer, and her works are scored like music. A sense of the musicality and rhythm of language is strong in her work, even as it demonstrates a modernist skepticism about the limits of expression and representation. Voice is privileged over vision, voice that is disembodied. All of her 'Fukushima plays' are essentially *sprechoper*, works scored for voices.

In *Kein Licht*, there are two voices, but these are not characters in the conventional sense, more ghostly presences than people, channeling the spirits of the drowned victims of the tsunami. The two voices (called A and B) in *Kein Licht* are violinists, a play on words: *Geiger* (German for 'violinist') clearly alludes to the devices used to measure radiation levels after the Fukushima meltdown. Jelinek's works are densely intertextual. Among her many sources here is a fragmentary satyr play by Sophocles, called *Ichneutai* (*The Trackers*), another reference to music. Silenus and his satyrs offer to find the herd of cattle Hermes has stolen from Apollo. The text breaks off at the point where the satyrs, having discovered the cave in which Hermes has hidden the cows, are frightened off by the sound of the lyre, an instrument which Hermes has made out of the sinew, skin, and bones of the cattle. Jelinek weaves parts of this drama into an account of Fukushima's herds of cattle and other animals, abandoned in the evacuation zone. In Miura's staging of the play, the steeply banked stage created a claustrophobic, tunnel-like effect. In the foreground, the cast (some of whom wore wetsuits) looked, in the words of one critic, "like lost souls on the banks of the rivers of the underworld" (Andrews 2012b), while a jagged line of upended, naked legs waved like seaweed in the foreground. The actors delivered the text in a jarring staccato of onomatopoeic sounds and words broken into jagged syllables, repeated and reconstituted so as to sometimes lose all semantic value. At one point, one of the dead cried, "We need an interpreter!" This was a theme running through a number of the Fukushima works.

Takayama Akira's staging of *Kein Licht II* dispensed with a cast altogether, retaining only an audio recitation of the text. Takayama has distinguished himself for creating intricate, site-specific performances and installations around the Tokyo area, often (as Matsuda had done in his *Record of a Journey to Antigone*) employing a panoply of social media to get his message out. During the 1990s Takayama had studied linguistics and theater in Germany before returning to Japan in 1999. His company, Port B, was established in 2003. The participatory, magical mystery tour quality of their productions is in part inspired by the principles of Terayama Shūji's (1935–1983) 'street theater' with works like *Knock* (1975) that used real locations around Tokyo as its stage, breaking down the barriers dividing actor from audience. At F/T 2010, Port B staged a rather prophetic work called *The Complete Manual of Evacuation—Tokyo*, which had its audiences log onto a website and fill out a questionnaire, a personality profile that, depending on the response, guided audience members to specific 'evacuation' sites around the Yamanote Line in Tokyo, including a homeless shelter and a mosque. Participants were encouraged to post their responses on Twitter. For F/T 2011, Port B staged *Referendum Project*, a specific response to 3.11. Audience members watched video interviews with Fukushima survivors and evacuees before voting in a referendum on nuclear energy. Takayama later expressed disappointment with the public response to this work, however. No particular political action resulted from the exercise of this theatrical referendum.

Jelinek's *Epilog?* seemed like a natural choice for Takayama. He had previously staged a production of Jelinek's *Clouds. Home.* in 2009. Takayama set Jelinek's play in Shinbashi, a neighborhood of downtown Tokyo that had been a hub of Japan's modernization: the country's first train station was built there in 1872 for a line linking Tokyo to Yokohama; and it was no accident that the head office of TEPCO, the utility company that had built and still (mis)manages the Fukushima Daiichi reactor, is located there. Home base for Takayama's *Kein Licht II* was the New Shinbashi Building, a relic of Japan's post-war boom years in the 1960s, now a little seedy with its assortment of restaurants, bars, coffee shops, video arcades, stalls selling DVDs, and Chinese massage parlors. Inside, audience members picked up a package of postcards, a map, and a transistor radio. From there, one walked to various sites in the Shinbashi area located on the map, such as pocket parks, apartments, offices, a show window on the street, outside a pachinko parlor, a vacant lot, an empty building site. At each location was a careful reconstruction of one of the images in the postcards, images that had been selected from among thousands of photographs taken in the Fukushima no-go zone after the meltdown: abandoned houses, their occupants' belongings left as if they had no time to pack or clean up; men in hazmat suits; evacuated villagers lining up for provisions; newscasts of the prime minister at a press conference, and so on. Takayama commented,

> Since the catastrophe, I have had many opportunities to see press photographs, but I always feel full of regret somehow. The landscape reflected there has absolutely no connection with me and yet there is a sense that it has become part of me. There is no way that I have ever entered the Fukushima exclusion zone but after one and a half years, the landscape of that place has woven itself up inside me.
>
> (Andrews 2012a)

There was a sense of another world—the Fukushima disaster zone—being superimposed on Shinbashi's oblivious nightscape. This gave an apocalyptic cast to a spectator's experience as one moved through this corner of downtown Tokyo.

At each locale, one tuned the portable radio to a particular frequency, like a museum audio guide, and listened to excerpts from Jelinek's *Epilog?*, selected and recited by high school girls from Fukushima, who had themselves been evacuated from these places and many of whose fathers no doubt had worked at the Daiichi reactor or were still involved in the clean-up. This lent an added poignancy and immediacy to the production that was not felt in other productions about the disaster, like Matsuda's *Record* or Murakawa Takuya's *Kotoba* (*Words*), works that nonetheless attempted to reach out in a semi-documentary fashion to record the testimonies of people directly affected by the disaster, the so-called *tōjisha*. The chasm that exists between the victims and survivors of the tsunami, on the one hand, and the rest of the Japanese population, who escaped relatively unscathed, is one of the difficulties artists face in portraying this tragedy. The Japanese are reticent when it comes to expressions of grief, but especially so when it comes to the suffering of others, which can be seen as an intrusion on another person's privacy and dignity. Even more so is this the case when those who are portrayed are dead. Kyōko Iwaki has written that: "After Fukushima, people preferred to be silent or to agree with others, as any thoughtless words or acts could damage the feelings of the 'superior' in the hierarchy of victimization—in this case, the sacralized deceased" (Iwaki 2015: 76). It is also the case that the Fukushima evacuees are shunned by many other Japanese, who rather wish that the refugees and their problem would just go away. The threat of nuclear contamination thus has not only ecological, but also social repercussions.

That we are quite literally listening to the voices of the victims lends this work both an artistic and ethical validity not felt so keenly in the other works I saw, but surely it was also strategic that the author of the words recited is a non-Japanese, someone with perhaps sufficient distance—and impertinence—to comment on what has happened, and continues to happen, in Fukushima. This may give those involved in the Japanese production a buffer from criticism at home about the work's message, which is unequivocal and censorious. Jelinek's *Epilog?* opens with the lines: "They say: the truth is one and we cannot let it go unsaid, but they couldn't have seen. I, who witnessed it, say this: that the words of truth have all gone unsaid." The "voice" goes on to describe how the water, "our fate" because of the tsunami was, however, not enough to cool the fuel rods that have superheated (Jelinek 2012: 65).[4] Throughout the text Jelinek contrasts the power of nature ("Of all the things we cannot fathom, nature is the greatest," Jelinek 2012: 70) with unnatural power unleashed by men. "The disaster made death an unnatural event" (Jelinek 2012: 72) and the Geiger counter, she says, is a device for measuring human arrogance (Jelinek 2012: 74).

Again, light—and its lack—form the leitmotif of this work:

> What humans can't see is far brighter than the sun. A paradox. The sun has seen something brighter than itself! But now it is dark. We couldn't sleep if it weren't. In the school gymnasiums, the town halls, the community centers, thousands of people are trying to sleep, but it doesn't go well for them.
> (Jelinek 2012: 70)

"Light enables the world to see, but the world can't see what lies beyond light, nor where the light comes from," the voice says (Jelinek 2012: 72), and later: "We had no faith in the sun, we wanted something better than the sun" (Jelinek 2012: 80).[5]

Jelinek's environmentalism is also evident in the attention she focuses on how this disaster has affected animals. (Interspersed among the text of *Epilog?* on her website are photographs of abandoned livestock, both dead and alive, in the evacuation zone.)

The world of birds, afflicted with nightmares, has woken from its dream. The wild animals have formed a line and are running the other way. The animals who had said nothing before. They didn't know. Humans have been totally wrong about the value they put on animals.

(Jelinek 2012: 70)

"This land is afflicted with a terrible disease. Only big business is healthy" (Jelinek 2012: 78). The pervasive presence of radiation in the soil, the water table, the sea, the air, seems to mock the distinction between living and 'dead' matter, the afterlife of uranium, plutonium, and cesium extending far beyond the mortality of any of the humans or animals who were affected. "Behold the dead! Cry out for them! Someone has polluted our land!" (Jelinek 2012: 85). Still, Jelinek struggles with a language that can give voice to these dead souls, expressing doubts as to how one can express, much less render into artistic form, such a catastrophe. By the same token, she struggles with silence itself, claiming "silence has died more dead than death itself" (Jelinek 2012: 72). Fujii Shintarō (2013) remarked on a conference panel on Fukushima and theater that *Kein Licht* and its sequel are built of out "the ruins of language." In the opinion of *Die Zeit*'s reviewer of *Kein Licht*, Andrea Heinz, "not only God; the subject too is dead" in Jelinek's works (Heinz 2011). The lack of a subject is compounded by the fact that the Japanese language can dispense with a subject altogether as it can usually be understood from the context. Here, only the personal pronouns *watashi*, or *watashitachi* (I, we) are used, and then only sparingly.

So who is the absent subject? The epigraph to *Epilog?* reads: "*Eine Trauernde. Sie kann machen, was sie will*" (A mourner: she will make of it what she wants). The implication here is that the voice is Antigone's. Jelinek's postscript tells us that she consulted, "many, many reports, and also Sophocles' *Antigone*" (*Viele, viele Berichte studiert. Sophokles: "Antigone" auch*). Given the densely intertextual nature of Jelinek's work, and the fact that, in this case especially, one is often working from the translation of a translation of a translation—Greek to English, to German, to Japanese—trying to trace the sources of her citations would be like attempting to find home from the trail of breadcrumbs in a tale by the Brothers Grimm. Suffice it to say that, as in *Kein Licht*, these voices—Greek, German, Japanese—rise into a chorus of the dead, indicting the living.

Takayama's installation was not only deeply moving, but also profoundly alienating. Perhaps this was no paradox: one chief impact of this disaster has been the way it has uprooted people, severed the ties that had existed between loved ones, families, communities, and the region from the nation. Yet this works against the purpose behind so much of Takayama's theater with Port B, which has been to involve spectators, immersing them into real cityscapes and ideal communities that only a theater person can create. In an interview Takayama has said, "In today's society, I think we need to develop a more deft methodology that can implant theater inside the city, one that removes the audience's feeling of isolation" (quoted from Iwaki 2011: 48–49 and Andrews 2012a). And yet, my experience of *Kein Licht II* was precisely that of being severed from physical, human contact. Audience members were furnished with the tools to visit the individual stages of this dark pilgrimage into Fukushima, but each person traveled the course alone, at his or her own pace, and the young voices reciting Jelinek's sad text deeply underscored a terrible sense of loneliness and helplessness, felt not only by the girls reciting their text, but also by its director. "I cannot propose a system for building consensus," writes Takayama about this work. "It's like I've devoted myself to the work of listening just to voices, and the more I think about it the more it seems that I'm not headed towards activism. It's like I'm standing there in a stupor" (Andrews 2012a). Fukushima rejects the very sense of harmony and consensus the Japanese seem so much to crave.

## The black box

All the works discussed here are essentially examples of post-dramatic theater. I wonder if this form does not also betray a feeling of paralysis on the part of Japanese artists today, as if they could conceive of no other way to express these events than a static one that abandons conventional devices of character, action, narrative, and dramatic resolution. Perhaps that is the only honest solution, as yet, to any artistic rendering of this disaster. To think one could find some satisfactory catharsis or explanation of this event in dramatic or emotional terms would be an insult to the victims and an act of false consciousness. At the same time, however, such an expressive mode risks having our memories of this disaster remain, in Rebecca Solnit's words, "an orphan experience, unconnected and ultimately lost" (2010: 263), if they do not become a catalyst for civic action. One critic, Eguchi Masato, summing up the immediate response to 3.11 among the offerings at F/T in November of the year of the disaster, wondered whether Japanese theater had become "autistic." The productions:

> were able to raise up novel and fairly edgy artistic ideas by means of a maelstrom of sensory impressions, but at the same time, such techniques demand a kind of YouTube communicative style that is unique to the character of Japanese society today. All said and done, the Japanese works seemed structured on principles that rejected any overarching grasp of issues or concepts.
>
> (Eguchi 2012: 108)

One of the more successful works from 2011 addressing 3.11 was Miyazawa Akio's *Total Living 1986–2011*. Characters called "The Lighthouse Keeper of Forgetting" and "The Girl of Absence" reflected on the 1986 nuclear meltdown at Chernobyl, while in contemporary times (2011), the Japanese blithely distracted themselves with ephemeral amusements and media gossip. The situation has changed little, and most of Japan seems still engaged in a willful act of collective amnesia about this and many other crises. As another pointed reminder, Miyazawa also directed Jelinek's *Prolog?* (yet another sequel to *Kein Licht*) for F/T 2013.

One understands the reluctance to shape these events into readily packageable narratives. We are, nonetheless, animals that are constantly telling stories about our lives, trying to make sense of experience, and so the first impulse after catastrophe (as John Treat [1995] noted in *Writing Ground Zero* about the literature of the atomic bomb) is to record what happened, to create documents and records of the event. At first these are subjective and autobiographical (this is where I was when x happened) and resolutely factual, because we are afraid in the face of such events of speaking any falsehoods—the stuff of documentary theater. And yet the scale of such events defies human language and challenges us epistemologically (can this be real?); so we are forced to resort to metaphysical speech to relate what has occurred. Only a mythopoeic language can attempt to trace the shape of what has happened.

An important theoretical source for Jelinek's *Kein Licht* and its sequels was René Girard's *Des Choses Cachées Depuis la Fondation du Monde* (*Things Hidden since the Foundation of the World*, 1978), a development of his idea of sacrifice as central to human culture. If a murder (Abel or Christ) served as the foundation of human social order, then surely burial as much as sacrifice must be the first concerted symbolic gesture of all human cultures and not just those of the Judeo-Christian tradition. The pacification of spirits (*chinkon*) has been widely regarded as the origin of Japanese theater. Burial of the dead is the attempt to end violence and to reconcile the living with the dead and the dead with the living. What makes *Antigone* so resonant a play for the Japanese in the context of Fukushima is the fact that so many thousands have not been given their proper burial. The production of these 'Antigonish' plays after 3.11 indicates a recognition that the country, particularly its Creon-like government, which is chiefly concerned with maintaining social and economic order over the rights of the individual and of the center's control over the periphery, has yet to come to terms with a disaster that continues to burn in the afterlife of nuclear contamination. Fukushima, symbol of an energy source that has turned into its antithesis, an unkillable source of massive toxicity, remains, together with Chernobyl, an insistent reminder of the failure of political institutions and the hubris of human technology in the face of nature's terrible power.

Yet what concerns me most about Jelinek's sad, moving, but sharply critical responses to 3.11 and Fukushima is their terrible interiority. There is certainly no light in looking straight and unremittingly into the abyss. This may be a reflection of her own agoraphobia, a symptom that seems anathema to a theater person, though she has distinguished herself as a playwright. For in her plays discussed here, there is no society, only psychology, despite or perhaps even because of her critical stance.

The Japanese have a word for Jelinek's condition: *hikikomori*, which describes a kind of youth, mostly male, who has for reasons of his own chosen to shut himself out of society. The problem has for sometime in Japan reached almost epidemic proportions, evidence of a sickness in the body politic. In the context of this disaster, however, it seems to me that, once the obsequies have been attended to, the only healthy response must be a social, even a political one: what do we make of this experience? How can we rebuild community? How can massive suffering bring people together and not terminally isolate them? The first work of theater, especially in this privatized, mediatized world we live in, must be to create public spaces, *agorai*, for the discussion of what matters most to us as human beings. Sophocles' play also tells us that we cannot remain Antigones: just as we mustn't deny the dead their rightful memorialization, neither can we permanently dwell among the shades. The generation of a sense of immense grief and isolation in these plays at F/T 12 was honest to the event it addressed, but the public still craves some kind of catharsis to suffering, however false and discredited that sentiment may yet seem. Experience has nevertheless taught us that a coherent response can never be immediate or even definitive. The events of March 11, 2011 summoned an inspired but incoherent Tiresias in Matsuda and, still better, an eloquent Antigone in Jelinek and her interpreters, like Miura and Takayama, to give voice to the victims' suffering. Perhaps for the time being, a theater faithful to 3.11 must remain funereal—as Adorno puts it, "draped in black" (Adorno 2004: 39). But so long as it does, theater's black box will also be a coffin.

## Notes

1 A recent article by Peter Eckersall (2015) covers similar thematic territory as mine, but focuses on two plays by Hirata Oriza and Okada Toshiki on nuclear contamination in Fukushima.
2 Richard Bowring, Professor of Japanese literature at Cambridge University, took issue in a letter responding to Parry's characterization of Japanese as "the cult of the ancestors" because the Japanese do not have a strong concept of family bloodlines. But the permeability of the worlds of the living and the dead for the Japanese is very real.
3 A production of *Antigone*, in a revised translation by Anne Carson and directed by Ivo Van Hove with Juliet Binoche in the title role, opened at the Barbican in London in March 2015 and followed with a European and US tour (Higgins 2015).
4 The radiance of radiation is mentioned also in Inoue Hisashi's play *Chichi to Kuraseba* (*Living with Father*, 1994), which describes the atom bomb that fell on Hiroshima as being as bright as two suns (Inoue 2014).
5 Quotations, for the most part, are taken from the Japanese translation; the original German text can be found on her website, Jelinek n.d.

## References

Adorno, Theodor. 2004, *Aesthetic Theory*. Gretel Adorno and Rolf Tiedemann (eds), newly translated, edited, and with a translator's introduction by Robert Hullot-Kentor. London: Continuum.

Andrews, William. 2012a, "Going beyond the heap of broken images: *Kein Licht II*." *Tokyo Stages* (December 10), at: https://tokyostages.wordpress.com/2012/12/10 (accessed February 26, 2015).

Andrews, William. 2012b, "The year in contemporary theatre." *Tokyo Stages* (December 31), at: https://tokyostages.wordpress.com/tag/motoi-miura (accessed February 26, 2015).

Carson, Anne. 2013, "Performing *Antigonick*." Louisiana Channel, *YouTube*. at: www.youtube.com/watch?v=BEfJKjOg3ZU (accessed March 1, 2015).

Eckersall, Peter. 2015, "Performance, mourning and the long view of nuclear space." *The Asia-Pacific Journal* Vol. 13, Issue 6, No. 2 (February 16), at: www.japanfocus.org/-Peter-Eckersall/4278 (accessed March 11, 2015).

Eguchi Masato. 2012, "Sara naru jissen to gensetsu no seisan ni mukete—kōbo puroguramu no seika to kadai," in Chiaki Sōma, Orie Kiyuna, and Sayuri Fujii (eds), *Festival/Tokyo 11: Documents*. Tokyo: Seikōsha, 107–11.

Fujii, Shintarō. 2013, *Catastrophe and Theatre*. Presentation at the International Federation of Theatre Research. Barcelona, July.

Fujii, Shintarō. 2014, "Katasutorofi to engeki." *Engeki to engekisei. Nichifutsu kokusai shimpojiumu*. Waseda daigaku. Engeki eizōgaku renkei kenkyū kyoten, 137–44.

Heinz, Andrea. 2011, "Nicht Worte noch Töne." *Die Zeit* October 6, at: www.zeit.de/2011/41/Jelinek (accessed March 1, 2015).

Higgins, Charlotte, 2015, "Death becomes her: How Juliette Binoche and Ivo van Hove remade Antigone." *The Guardian*, February 18, at: www.theguardian.com/stage/2015/feb/18/juliette-binoche-ivo-van-hove-antigone (accessed March 7, 2015).

Inoue, Hisashi. 2014, "Living with father," in J. Thomas Rimer, Mitsuya Mori, and M. Cody Poulton (eds), *The Columbia Anthology of Modern Japanese Drama*. Trans. Zeljko Cipris. New York: Columbia University Press, 471–98.

Iwaki, Kyōko. 2011, *Tokyo Theatre Today: Conversations with Eight Emerging Theatre Artists*. London and Tokyo: Hublet Publishing.

Iwaki, Kyōko. 2015, "Japanese theatre after Fukushima: Okada Toshiki's *Current Location*." *New Theatre Quarterly* Vol. 31, No. 1 (February): 70–89.

Jelinek, Elfriede. 2012, *Hikari no nai*. Translated into Japanese by Hayashi Tatsuki. (Translations of *Kein Licht, Epilog? [Kein Licht II]*, *Rechnitz: Der Würgeengel*, and *Wolken. Heim*). Tokyo: Hakusuisha.

Jelinek, Elfriede. n.d., webpage, at: www.elfriedejelinek.com (Includes German texts for *Kein Licht* and *Epilog?*) (accessed March 1, 2015).

Matsuda, Masataka. 2012, "*Antigone e no tabi* no kiroku to sono jōen: sōsaku nōto." *Shiatā Ātsu* 52 (Fall): 151–73.

Parry, Richard L. 2014, "Ghosts of the tsunami." *The London Review of Books* Vol. 36, No. 3 (February): 13–17, at: www.lrb.co.uk/v36/n03/richard-lloydparry/ghosts-of-the-tsunami (accessed February 26, 2015).

Rayner, Alice. 2006, *Ghosts: Death's Double and the Phenomena of Theatre*. Minneapolis, MN and London: University of Minnesota Press.

Solnit, Rebecca. 2010, *A Paradise Built in Hell: The Extraordinary Communities that Arise in Disaster*. New York: Penguin.

Solnit, Rebecca. 2012, "Diary." *The London Review of Books* Vol. 34, No. 9 (May 10): 35–37, at: www.lrb.co.uk/v34/n09/rebecca-solnit/diary (accessed March 1, 2015).

Sophocles. 2010, *Antigonick*. A translation by Anne Carson of *Antigone*. Toronto: McClelland & Stewart.

Treat, John W. 1995, *Writing Ground Zero: Japanese Literature and the Atom Bomb*. Chicago, IL: University of Chicago Press.

Weisenfeld, Gennifer. 2012, *Imaging Disaster: Tokyo and the Visual Culture of Japan's Great Earthquake of 1923*. Berkeley, CA: University of California Press.

# 9 Poetry in an era of nuclear power
## Three poetic responses to Fukushima

*Jeffrey Angles*

### Introduction[1]

By the time the dust had settled and the tsunami had receded on March 11, 2011, the losses were staggering. As of November 10, 2014, the Japanese National Police Agency reported that 15,891 people had been killed, 2,579 people were missing, and 6,152 people had been wounded (Keisatsuchō 2015). The government estimated that the physical damage was 16.9 trillion yen, thus making 3.11 the costliest natural disaster in human history, but Standard & Poor estimated that the even greater number of 20–50 trillion yen might be in fact a closer number (Samuels 2013: 6). In a more figurative sense, the earthquake also reverberated throughout every arena of Japanese society. Almost immediately, Japan found itself rethinking many aspects of its own culture. As the Fukushima power plant melted down, ordinary citizens found themselves questioning their usage of energy and their relationship to the natural environment. Citizens who were suspicious about the information that they were receiving from authorities began reconsidering their relationships with the government, and people everywhere began wondering if the Japanese bureaucracy was up to handling problems on such a massive scale.

The 3.11 disasters also shook up the Japanese literary world. Ōe Kenzaburō, Tsushima Yūko, Ishimure Michiko, and other prominent writers known for their involvement in social issues began to publish statements in the press and to use their influence to give shape to reconstruction efforts, environment initiatives, and anti-nuclear campaigns. It was only a matter of weeks before the novelist Shimada Masahiko founded *Revival & Survival (Fukkō Shoten)*, an online bookstore that sold copies of books signed and donated by famous writers to raise money for relief efforts. Even now, a few years afterward, this volunteer-run bookstore has also been actively working to keep the disasters alive in people's imaginations through its online web series *Words & Bonds*, which publishes reflections, stories, and essays written about the disasters by novelists, poets, photographers, and other cultural figures.[2]

Perhaps the part of the Japanese literary world where the seismic forces of the March 11 disasters were felt most strongly, however, was the poetic world. Many Japanese newspapers include regular columns that include free verse, tanka, or haiku poems, but in just the few days after 3.11, poetry began to emerge from those small columns and take a more prominent place in the news, eventually finding its way into a central position in the discourse that had started unfolding across the nation. As the Japanese population struggled to find a way to express their grief, horror, and anxiety, poets became leaders using dramatic and powerful language to document the tragedy, probe its philosophical and moral implications, and to provide momentary solace. One mid-career poet, Arai Takako (b. 1966) about whom more will be said later, wrote that in the immediate aftermath of the disasters, her friends repeatedly urged her to write, realizing that they were living through momentous times and hoping that she could somehow come to grips with their traumatic experiences through language.

> I believe, without a doubt, that people desired poetry. As the immeasurable anxiety brought about by the tsunami and nuclear accident continued to grow, I was communicating with my friends via e-mail and telephone. They spurred me on countless times, saying, "It is precisely because of this moment we are living through that you need to write poetry." I was taken off guard because I felt this was the first time that I was told this sort of thing by someone who had no connection with poetry.
>
> (Arai 2013b: 4)

Indeed, poets everywhere felt the call to respond. In fact, it would not be much of an exaggeration to say that almost every poet in Japan touched upon the disasters somewhere in their work, even if they lived far outside the areas that were directly affected.

The fact that so many poets wrote so much in response to the disasters, and the Fukushima disasters in particular, means there is a dizzying array of poetry one might examine to understand cultural reactions to the tragedies. This chapter will focus on the work of three particular poets and the ways that they responded in their writing. One is Wagō Ryōichi (b. 1968) who was in Fukushima Prefecture and wrote in real-time online about the disaster as it unfolded. The other two are Takahashi Mutsuo (b. 1937) and Arai Takako, both of whom watched the unfolding horror from afar but turned to poetry as a way to explore the complex moral, social, and even linguistic issues highlighted by the Fukushima meltdown.[3] While there is great deal of diversity in terms of stylistics, approach, and theme among even these three writers, one finds that their poetry (as well that of many other poets) performs at least four overlapping functions. First, poets used poetry as a means to document the disasters, writing about what happened and eulogizing the lives that were lost. Second, poetry served as means to search for meaning in the rubble, as writers looked for some bigger cosmic purpose in the terrifying destruction. Third, poetry became a vehicle for cultural protest. At Fukushima, it was clear that humanity was responsible at least in part for the disasters, considering when it came out that numerous post-disaster inquiries found the meltdown to have been preventable. In response to these revelations, poets turned their attention to society and the ways that mankind should change to prevent future catastrophes. Fourth, poets began to probe what I will call the 'crisis of representation' that was revealed by the disasters. As poets began to write, many realized that the intensely personal and linguistically playful ways of writing poetry that had dominated the poetic landscape before 2011 would not suffice in dealing with the enormity of the Fukushima disaster. Because the disaster had struck Japan with such directness and power, some poets felt a need to respond through poetry that was direct, powerful, and could talk concretely about issues of social importance; in other words, Fukushima forced poets to reconsider the relationship between art, representation, and lived experience. In the following discussion, one finds all four of these overlapping functions present within the work of these three writers as they try to come to grips with the Fukushima disaster.

## Wagō Ryōichi reporting from the front lines

In the first few days after 3.11, some residents of northeastern Japan who were able to access the Internet immediately began using the web as a way to inform the outside world about the devastation. Conversely, people across Japan turned to the web to find out what was happening. As the Fukushima meltdown proceeded and people found themselves less and less satisfied by the government and the Tokyo Electric Power Company's (TEPCO) handling of information, people turned to the Internet to figure out what was going on, bypassing more traditional media. Social media such as Twitter and Facebook, which had played an enormous role in the Arab Spring only one year before, as well as video-hosting sites such as YouTube and Nikovideo.jp, revealed their potential to allow communication while bypassing central authority (Liscutin 2011). The resulting explosion of Internet traffic contained both a great deal of information as well as misinformation, but what is important to note is that in the midst of this situation, there quickly emerged a number of new 'authority' figures who spoke about the disasters as they saw them. Most of these figures had been relatively little known until the earthquake, but their disaster-related writing garnered them a significant audience. The poet Wagō Ryōichi is without a doubt one of the best known of these figures. Before the earthquake, he was a mid-career poet with a half-dozen books to his name and a number of poetry prizes that made him moderately well known within the world of poetry but not within society at large. In the aftermath of the earthquake, however, his writings quickly catapulted him to a position as one of the most famous poets in the nation.

Because Wagō was a Fukushima native who had previously lived in the earthquake-ravaged city of Minamisōma and was in the nearby city of Date at the time of the disasters, in many ways he had the perfect pedigree to represent the disasters to the Japanese reading public. Fortunately, the lives of Wagō's wife and child were spared, and he was able to return home after three days in an evacuation camp. Back at home on March 16, he turned to Twitter and began writing thousands of tweets that poured out with tremendous speed. These tweets began with relatively simple statements that he was safe, but quickly they turned

Poetry in an era of nuclear power    147

to more probing observations and poetic evocations of the anxiety he and the people around him were experiencing. On March 18 at 2.05 p.m., he wrote, "I will make pebbles of poetry" (2011b: 34). In selecting the phrase *shi no tsubute* (pebbles of poetry), he invokes an image of his tweets as tiny, hard, tough granules of writing that are jumbled together but do not necessarily form a coherent whole. One can read this simple statement as a performative act that declares that his Twitter feed is not just a flat, straightforward device to convey objective information; instead, his tweets serve as a means to come to grips with the enormity of the disaster. Less than an hour later at 3.20 p.m., he wrote, "Through my words on Twitter, I have come to the resolution that I will stand in the world of the rubble," then two minutes later, he wrote, "I am powerless, useless, but even so, what I can do is write poetry, write language" (Wagō 2011b: 39).

Throughout his tweets, one senses Wagō's confusion, despair, anger, and hurt. His Twitter feed quickly gathered tens of thousands of followers, many of whom retweeted his observations and questions as a way of giving voice to their own sorrow, confusion, and anger. This sudden attention catapulted Wagō into the spotlight. In short order, *Handbook of Contemporary Poetry* (*Gendai shi techō*), Japan's foremost journal of modern, free-style poetry, put together a special issue dedicated to the earthquake, including a reprint of the Twitter feed, which they titled *Pebbles of Poetry* (*Shi no tsubute*) and contained all the tweets posted between March 16 and April 9 (Wagō 2011a).[4] Around the same time, Wagō began making a large number of news, radio, and speaking appearances— so many that the Tokyo publisher Tokuma Shoten republished his Twitter feed from March 16 to May 26 in book form (Wagō 2011b). By the end of 2011, Wagō had appeared on every major television channel in Japan, often multiple times. As a result of this extensive exposure, *Pebbles of Poetry* has become probably the most famous piece of literature in any genre yet to emerge from the disasters. In the aftermath of the earthquake, vigils and poetry readings, many of which were designed to raise money for charity, were held throughout the country. *Pebbles of Poetry* was among the most frequently read works, partly because the nature of the piece, written in Twitter-sized nuggets, made it so easy to read excerpts, and partly because the work possessed such a high degree of cultural capital, having come from the front lines of the disaster itself. The composer Niimi Tokuhide has set certain segments of the work to music, giving the songs the title *Pebble Songs* (*Tsubute songu*), and composer Itō Yasuhide also followed suit, publishing several pieces of music on Wagō's texts (Niimi 2011; Itō 2011).

In order to give his Twitter feed the feeling of poetry, Wagō uses a number of poetic elements; most obviously, certain phrases recur like rhythmic cadences throughout the work. For instance, the phrase "Radiation is falling. It is a quiet, quiet night" (*Hōshanō ga futte imasu/Shizuka na shizuka na yoru desu*) (Wagō 2011b: 11) recurs multiple times throughout the first part of *Pebbles of Poetry*, thus tying the work together. In fact, when asked to contribute one of his handwritten texts to an exhibition of 3.11-related poetry to be held at the Museum of Contemporary Japanese Poetry, Tanka, and Haiku (*Nihon Gendai Shiika Bungakukan*)[5] in Iwate Prefecture in 2012 and 2013, Wagō extracted these two sentences as his contribution. The note displayed with his calligraphy stated that the lines popped into his head when the third reactor at Fukushima exploded (Nihon Gendai Shiika Bungakukan 2012: 37). He also notes that these lines were inspired by the opening "Everyone, tonight is quiet" (*Mina-san kon'ya wa shizuka desu*) from the poem "Winter night" (*Fuyu no yoru*) by the early twentieth-century modernist poet Nakahara Chūya (1907–1937). In that poem, Nakahara had used simple, direct, colloquial language to evoke a series of sights, giving the illusion that they are unfolding right before him, much as Wagō used simple, direct, colloquial language to describe the things unfolding right before him in the disaster-ravaged, radiation-laden cities of northeastern Japan (Nakahara 1969: I, 197). As for the metaphorical significance of this line, Wagō stated, "Fukushima has still not found a way out, and still remains in the midst of a 'night' of anxiety" (Nihon Gendai Shiika Bungakukan 2012: 37). The fact that he repeats this phrase over and over again throughout *Pebbles of Poetry* drives home the point that the anxiety of the disaster and meltdown had still not receded; as of the time of writing and well afterward, it was a trauma all too real for the victims of northeastern Japan, who were still unable to extract themselves from the radiation and rubble.

The use of rhythm and repetition are elements that invite the reader to consume the collection as a whole, rather than as a series of individual, unrelated observations. Even within single tweets, he employs internal repetition; for example, one tweet originally uploaded on April 9 at 11.19 pm contains some of the most often quoted passages from *Pebbles of Poetry*.

> Give back our town, give back our village, give back our sea, give back the wind. The sound of chimes, the sound of mail arriving, the sound of something in the inbox. Give back waves, give back fish, give back love, give back the sun beating down. The sound of chimes, the sound of mail arriving, the sound of something in the inbox. Give back our joyful toasts, give back grandmothers, give back pride, give back Fukushima. The sound of chimes, the sound of mail arriving, the sound of something in the inbox.
> (Wagō 2011b: 213)

Here, his impossible yet insistent demand for a return to the pre-March past overlaps with repeated flashes from his current reality, namely a small flood of emails and Twitter messages forcing their way into his consciousness, reminding him of his inescapable situation in the present. The tension of being irreconcilably caught between nostalgic memories of a happier past and the ugly realities of the present is one that informs much of *Pebbles of Poetry*. This tension clearly resonated with a certain portion of the population, who retweeted and favorited certain passages as a way of offering solace to their own pain. One should also note the repetition, such as one sees in the passage quoted above, bears the marks of traumatic experience. Psychologists and literary critics have often noted the consistent use of repetition in literature having to do with traumatic events. Early in the history of modern psychology, Pierre Janet (1903) recognized that helplessness constitutes the core insult of traumatic experience, and healing requires the victim to recover a sense of efficacy and power; repetition involves an attempt to come to mastery through language and relived experience. Similarly, as Cathy Caruth noted in *Unclaimed Experience*, her influential rereading of Freud, one can think of trauma as a sort of wound that always comes too early to be understood; as a result, people who live through traumatic experiences relive their thoughts over and over in an attempt to make it comprehensible as a total experience (Caruth 1996: 91). One sees the psychic echoes of trauma throughout Wagō's work, especially in the use of repetitious images in those places where subjective description of events give way to more personal thoughts.

Like the thoughts of most people who have lived through the disasters, Wagō's tweets quickly move from documentary mode into meaning-making mode, asking the unanswerable question "why us?" While the majority of Wagō's sadness and is directed at the forces of nature, he also notes the fact that human institutions exacerbated the problems—government offices failed to advise local citizens of the real risks of the reactor, and organizations failed to provide aid in a timely fashion to the people who need it. Most of his protests, however, are at the generally lamentable state of affairs, and relatively little of his writing takes a direct aim at particular people or institutions, a fact that would later lead to criticism from other writers.

Although Wagō turned to Twitter to document his own traumatic experiences, certain poets began to criticize Wagō and his self-appointed position as poetic ambassador to the disaster region. One detects some implicit criticism, for instance, in a poem by the leading young haiku poet Seki Etsushi (b. 1969): "as the reactor burns/Mr. Wagō's poetry flows forth—/a cold spell" (*genpatsu moetsutsu Wagō-shi shi o nagashi iru shunkan*) (2011: 115). Seki here seems to be pointing out the irony that Wagō seemed to have no problem with his own artistic production even as Fukushima was melting down and everything around him was coming to a halt. One might even sense some bitterness toward Wagō, whose ongoing, almost automated stream of poetic production was giving him a privileged position upon the national stage. Other poets were even more directly critical of Wagō's writing, saying that it was too direct, too lacking in specificity, and that it was closer akin to journalism rather than poetry. One of the most powerful of these attacks came from the poet Morinaka Takaaki (b. 1960) who wrote at length an essay called *Catastrophe and Language* (*Katasutorofi to kotoba*) about the problems of attempting to produce poetry after a disaster so enormous. He argues that Wagō's writing, and *Pebbles of Poetry* in particular, sounds more like a collection of clichés and slogans than poetry, and in one spot, he compares Wagō's writing to the kinds of feel-good posters covered in encouraging, life-affirming slogans that one might find hanging outside of a Zen temple (Morinaka 2014b: 144). Morinaka harshly criticizes Wagō for lamenting the disasters at Fukushima but failing to criticize the industrial, governmental, and social forces that led to the meltdown, which he sees as entirely preventable. Indeed, it is true that Wagō does not engage in especially controversial or provocative statements, other than to decry the nuclear plants and the use of nuclear power in general. Morinaka cynically points out that instead of taking a strong and potentially controversial stand, Wagō merely describes the disasters, laments the destruction, and extols his strong love for his homeland, thus converting his position as the victim of a catastrophe into cultural capital, which he then uses to promote his own position as a writer.

In a book of interviews published soon after the disasters and titled *What Can Language Do?: Beyond 3.11* (*Kotoba ni nani ga dekiru no ka: 3.11 o koete*), Wagō counters the attacks of poets who thought his disaster-related work was too direct and not "poetic" enough (Sano and Wagō 2012: 41–42). He notes that he uses multiple perspectives in his Twitter work, sometimes writing from his own perspective, sometimes writing from a more universal perspective, sometimes even writing from the point of the view of the tsunami or quake itself. For instance, he sometimes shifts from his own authorial voice of the victims to the voice of the destructive forces of nature, differentiating them through the use of various different speech registers, pronouns, and levels of directness. Wagō's interviewer, Sano Shin'ichi, however, points out that what most captured the imagination of readers is the attitude behind Wagō's writing—its intensely focused eagerness to communicate through the medium of poetry. Sano comments that an enormous amount of the language before March 11 seemed to be lacking in 'power'; it suffered from an inability to convey dramatic emotion, but one of the effects of Wagō's immediate post-disaster writing was to restore language's expressive ability (Sano and Wagō 2012: 41).

Indeed, there are many passages in *Pebbles of Poetry* that suggest the need for a new form of direct and powerful expression to give voice to Japan's situation in the immediate aftermath of the disasters. Wagō does not take to task other poets directly; however, his interviews suggest that before March 11, the Japanese poetic world's tendency to engage in closed linguistic experimentation, to focus on personal exchanges between poets, and to produce difficult, often inaccessible poems led the poetic world to grow anemic and tired. The result was that poetry, and perhaps even language in general, was losing its ability to communicate and was instead devolving into an art form that was insular, unappreciated, and underutilized; given this situation, the 3.11 disasters provided a shock that could help make language and poetry relevant once again. Language, Wagō suggests, needs to be strong and powerful to deal with Japan's dire realities. In other words, he was one of the first poets to sense that 3.11 had brought about a 'crisis of representation' and poets responding to the disasters in their work needed to find a new, increasingly direct mode of representation. In fact, one finds this attitude expressed right at the beginning of *Pebbles of Poetry* when he writes, "Everywhere I go, there is nothing but tears. I want to write about this with all the ferocity of an Asura"—the powerful, demonic-looking demigods of Buddhist folklore (2011b: 10).

Wagō has published numerous other books, collections of poetry, articles, and reflections on the disasters and recovery efforts (Wagō 2011c, 2011d, 2012, and 2013). Meanwhile, he has continued to post his reflections on his Twitter feed.

Some of this work, especially the poems written after the disasters that appear in the 2013 collection *Poems on a Decommissioned Reactor* (*Hairo shihen*), use a somewhat fragmentary style and unusual typography, scattering words across the page like falling radioactive particles, but even so, they are relatively easy to read. Rather than employing the kinds of complicated, playful, and artful language one finds in the work of other poets, those poems consist primarily of strong, straightforward, anti-nuclear messages (Wagō 2013). Although this has earned him criticism from some, his straightforward style has appealed to a wide audience, including a large number of readers that are not necessarily used to reading more 'difficult' literature. For instance, the 2012 collection *Me and You, Born Here* (*Watashi to anata koko ni umarete*), a collaboration with the photographer Satō Hideaki, takes its title from this short, straightforward poem.

Me and
You
Born here
Here
We clasp hands
Here, now
One of us stands firm
Here is where
I live
    (Wagō 2012: 2)

Although this poem is written in language simple enough for even the youngest of elementary-school readers, it contains a dramatic assertion that the narrator, a native of the disaster-ravaged territory of northeastern Japan, is standing strong by his friends in the land where he was born, even in the wake of adversity. In subsequent poems, Wagō repeats the message that Tōhoku's pain is his pain, but there is hope for the region if people stand together and support one another. In this way, Wagō echoes the emphasis on *kizuna* or 'the bonds of friendship,' which became one of the most frequently repeated themes of post-3.11 popular discourse.[6] Certainly, some poets might see the simple sentiments and straightforwardness of such poems as shallow and lacking in critical efficacy; however, as his many appearances on radio and television attested, after 3.11, poetry offered ordinary people a way to feel better about their lives, relationships, and homeland, and thus had a special role to fill in a time of crisis.

## Takahashi Mutsuo on living out of balance with nature

Born in 1937, Takahashi Mutsuo is one of Japan's most active and prolific poets, well established in the poetry world thanks to the nearly one hundred volumes of poetry, prose, essays, and creative non-fiction that he has produced since the 1960s. Although Takahashi has spent most of his life far from northeastern Japan—he was born and raised in the southwestern island of Kyūshū, spent his adult life working in Tokyo, and currently lives in a seaside town near Yokohama—the 3.11 disasters sent Takahashi into a depression and poetic slump that lasted for the entire spring of 2011. He, like many throughout the country, recognized that the Fukushima meltdown represented not just a local disaster; it was a national disaster that implicated the entire population of Japan, and perhaps even the entire course of Japanese post-war development.

As the Fukushima meltdown proceeded, he found himself unable to respond to the crisis through his usual medium of poetry, even though at the same time he was increasingly questioning the directions that Japanese society had taken in recent years. In a June 2011 issue of *Handbook of Contemporary Poetry* dedicated to the disasters, however, he broke his silence with the poem *These Things Here and Now* (*Ima koko ni korera no koto o*). In a note that accompanies the poem, Takahashi writes that he sees the disasters, especially the meltdown at Fukushima, as evidence of a problematic narrative that had deep roots in the Japanese psyche.

> After Japan's defeat in World War II, there were a number of poets who drew upon T.S. Eliot's *The Waste Land*, wanting to start again, using the wasteland as a point of departure. Now, if we are to draw upon their example, and start out again from the wastelands left by the disasters of 3.11, we must recognize that the wasteland is really within ourselves. In other words, it stems from the spiritual destruction of desire and idleness that has, at some point unbeknownst to us, started growing rampant within us. Even before we were victims, we were victimizers. As long as we fail to recognize this, our words will lose their weight and circulate emptily.
> (Takahashi 2011a: 70)

Takahashi repeats his message that the earthquake revealed the spiritual emptiness of Japanese culture in his far-reaching history of Japanese poetry *Two thousand years of the poetic spirit: From Susanoo to 3.11* (*Shishin ni-sen-nen: Susanoo kara 3.11 e*), published soon afterward.

> Perhaps our own wastelands (which are not something we have borrowed) and, therefore, the true possibilities of Japanese-language poetry will take this great disaster as their starting point. The reason I say this is that the unparalleled disaster that brought about this wasteland, has as its epicenter the unbounded desire of each and every one of us in Japan. To go one step further, I suspect the roots that we need to come alive again from our contemporary wasteland can only come from a thorough awareness of the unrivaled poverty of our spirits as contemporary Japanese people.
> (Takahashi 2011b: 363)

In some ways, this rhetoric might sound at first like the nationalistic 'luxury is the enemy' rhetoric of World War II, but in Takahashi's case, the object of his criticism is a civilization that lives out of balance with nature, placing its own needs and short-lived comfort before the well-being of the environment and even the world in general.

His poem *These Things Here and Now* consists of several loosely connected stanzas that point out the human factors that led up to the Fukushima meltdown—mankind's unending desire for energy, the 'perversion' of the laws of nature in generating nuclear power, and the greed and apathy that allowed the construction of the plant to move forward (Takahashi 2011a, 2015a). Written in fairly straightforward language, Takahashi's poem compares the uranium atom to a dwarf god imprisoned and forced to work on man's behalf, so perhaps it is no surprise that when it got free, it would swell into a terrifying force and turn on humanity. Later, he describes nuclear power as a perversion of the law of nature, and he likens the atom to a murdered demon that has come back to life and is now inflicting its revenge on mankind. Takahashi expresses regret over the tragedy that has befallen Japan, but he also makes it clear that it is not simply a case of the population falling victim to some horror arising out of nowhere. If anything, he argues the Japanese population needs to recognize their own complicity in the unnatural culture that they have created. Even people who claim no involvement are not entirely innocent, since their inaction has permitted the rise of an energy-hungry culture based on comfort, immediacy, and greed.

In his view, what Japan needs now is a new ability to learn from the disaster and change its energy-hungry ways that exploit nature for their own comfort and gain. In the final stanzas, Takahashi calls upon Japan's citizens to take responsibility for their own lack of action, writing,

> We must turn our eyes to what has remained
> The mute words of the countless dead snatched by the waves
> The silence of the swelling numbers of displaced withstanding privation
> And the brilliance of the youth who have stood up from inaction
> Supporting them is none other than the silence of the dead and displaced.
>
> (Takahashi 2011a, 2015a)

He asserts that it is the moral responsibility of the population to honor the spirits of the dead and listen to the quiet suffering of the survivors; only by honoring them will the population learn the error of their ways and begin to make the changes necessary to change society and prevent similar disasters from recurring. In the last stanza, he comments that he is writing this strong poem of social protest—perhaps one of the strongest to emerge from the immediate aftermath of 3.11—not because of sense that he, as an elderly poet, necessarily knows any better than others. It is simply because as he witnesses the destruction, he feels the need to point to its root causes, to the 'truths' that that he finds in the wreckage of Fukushima. The entire poem, from the title of the poem through the final lines, suggests that he believes strongly in the ongoing relevance of the lessons of 3.11 to our ongoing lives. The disasters have not faded into the past. If anything, their lessons ought to still be very much with Japanese society.

By the end of 2011, Takahashi had returned to writing at full throttle. The poems *Since Then* (*Ano toki kara*), and *Lovers in a Time of Nuclear Energy* (*Genshiryoku jidai no koibito-tachi*), appeared in the January 2012 issue of *Handbook of Contemporary Poetry*. He has commented in private conversations that these two poems were among the works that he considers to be the greatest successes of his numerous poems about the disasters (Takahashi 2013). In fact, when asked to contribute to the 2014–2015 exhibition of disaster-related poems at the Museum of Contemporary Japanese Poetry, Tanka, and Haiku, Takahashi selected *Since Then* to represent his work (Nihon Gendai Shiika Bungakukan 2012: 50; Takahashi 2012a: 73–75; Takahashi 2015b). *Since Then* presents an allegorical description of the aftermath of the Fukushima meltdown and, like the earlier poem discussed above, attributes a big part of the problem to a failure of consciousness on the part of the Japanese people. In the poem, Takahashi notes that before the meltdown, the population's thoughts about their daily lives and the potential dangers of the reactors were kept apart by a conceptual wall that prevented them from seeing their daily life of consumption and casual energy use as connected to the nuclear threat in their own backyard. The Fukushima meltdown, however, revealed the disastrous outcome of this contradictory tendency to seek comfort while ignoring the exploitation of resources that made such comfort possible. It is essential, Takahashi believes, for humanity to recognize that the Fukushima meltdown and the destruction that it brought about were not mere accidents; they were the result of a worldview that held that people could engage in unending consumption even while ignoring the factors making that life possible. Now that the meltdown had revealed the falsehood of the myth of unproblematic, endless consumption, no one would come to save Japan's population; the responsibility to fix the problem lay with the citizens themselves.

Similarly, the allegorical poem *Lovers in a Time of Nuclear Energy*, which drew inspiration for its title from the famous novel by Gabriel García Márquez (1927–2014), builds upon the theme of nuclear power as an expression of human greed and desire; in fact, in the poem Takahashi uses the image of an endless orgy to describe the nuclear chain reaction occurring inside a nuclear plant (Takahashi 2012a: 74–75; 2015b). He imagines these orgiastic exchanges inside the reactor producing nothing but an endless stream of dead and bloody children like toxic waste; meanwhile, the number of dangerous, flame-spurting nuclear reactor towers multiplies outside. Nobody seems to notice, as all of the 'lovers' in the reactor are so devoted to the single-minded pursuit of comfort and pleasure. It is significant that in passages such as "We do not see, nor do we try to," the narrative voice identifies the orgiastic, desiring atoms using the vague, masculine pronoun "we" (*bokura*), which could refer to the male leadership of Japan or perhaps, by extension, all of Japanese society or even modern civilization as a whole. Once again, Takahashi finds that the root causes of the Fukushima disasters lie with the contemporary society and its single-minded devotion to comfort and pleasure, even while ignoring the effects of that devotion.

In anticipation of the one-year anniversary of the disasters, Kameoka Daisuke, one of the editors at *Handbook of Contemporary Poetry*, cooperated with *Asahi*

*Shimbun*, one of Japan's largest daily newspapers, to publish a series of disaster-related poems by a variety of Japan's most prominent poets, namely Tanikawa Shuntarō (b. 1931), Tsujii Takashi (b. 1927), Yoshimasu Gōzō (b. 1939), Takahashi Mutsuo, Ichimure Michiko (b. 1927), Sasaki Mikirō (b. 1947), Inaba Mayumi (b. 1950), Itō Hiromi (b. 1955), Koike Masayo (b. 1959), Wagō Ryōichi, Misumi Mizuki (b. 1981) and Minashita Kiriu (b. 1970). Of these, all but Tanikawa and Ichimure's poems were republished in the March 2012 issue of *Handbook of Contemporary Poetry*. Takahashi's contribution, titled *As for This Moment* (*Ima wa*), takes on the large and thorny subject of the relationship between language and disasters (Takahashi 2012b; Takahashi 2015c). In this work, Takahashi seems to be addressing himself, as well as all of the other authors who were struggling with the question of how to write in the face of the apocalyptic disasters of 2011. This poem shows the extent to which 3.11 was also a disaster in art and language—enormous, difficult, traumatic events that seemed to belie any attempts to express them. He begins by writing, "The first things that broke down were words," then notes that when writers tried to use language "to mend cracks and cave-ins" after the disaster, "Words did not respond" (Takahashi 2012b: 34; 2015c). In other words, Fukushima brought about not just a crisis on the ground; it brought about a crisis in representation and language as well. Indeed, it is never easy to find ways to represent destruction and trauma on such an enormous scale, but Takahashi sees this inability as symptomatic of a great, deeper problem. Language, literature, and poetry had already moved so far away from the ordinary lives of people that when poets attempted to deal with the disasters in the aftermath of the crisis, their writing did not come across as sincere or meaningful. In the continuation of the poem, however, Takahashi suggests that it is possible for this situation to change. He compares the disasters to the Big Bang, which created the world in a stupendous act of destruction, implying that the massive destruction of 3.11 can provide a creative burst of energy in which a new world of poetic representation could—and *should*—emerge.

One might read such statements as an opportunistic leveraging to mix up the poetic scene and to position a certain type of poetry—in Takahashi's case, a kind of poem that is about communication and deep philosophical reflection—at the heart of the poetic scene. In an interview that accompanied this poem in the *Asahi Shimbun*, Takahashi explains that the earthquake brought him to a realization about the dangerous relationship that mankind had developed with nature, and that the language he had been using in his pre-3.11writings did not reflect the realities of mankind's precarious position. The disasters wakened him to this fact, as well as to the fact that language needed to be sincere to make a difference. Rather than speaking irresponsibly and fill the world with empty words, he stated that it is best to think carefully and reflect before writing. Takahashi here seems to be implicitly criticizing other poets, such as Wagō Ryōichi whose flood of almost automated writing in the aftermath of the Fukushima meltdown laments the disaster but stops short of digging deeper into the desires that gave rise to it. More important than simply documenting the disasters or shouting in protest, Takahashi believes one should get to the deeper realities that have brought mankind to such a precarious situation. The role of poetry in a time of crisis, he believes, is to explore the deeper realities of mankind's situation, and rather than merely howl in protest; he chooses to find meaning in the wreckage.

## Arai Takako and the power of rewriting

Takahashi is not the only poet who used poetry as a vehicle to explore the social impact of the Fukushima meltdown. Some of the most original and startling takes on the disaster came from Arai Takako, a native of Gunma, born in 1966 who has a growing international reputation as one of Japan's most original and socially conscious young poets. Author of three collections of poetry, Arai has written extensively about the lives of the working-class women who staffed the small textile factory that her father owned in Kiryū, a town traditionally known for its weaving. She has also written in powerful ways about the economic problems that have plagued Japan during recent decades and the ways that it has affected working people, especially women. Given her history as a social poet, it is no wonder that even though Arai was living in Tokyo at the time of the disasters, she wrote about Fukushima in fresh and incisive ways.

In the first few months after 3.11, poetry vigils were held throughout the country, bringing together both new and established writers working in various genres. The result was the construction of a relatively democratic atmosphere in the literary world in which people could share their new works inspired by the disasters in the hopes of raising consciousness about the problems and money for the disaster victims. One figure in this movement was the poet and literary critic Suga Keijirō (b. 1958), who worked with the translator and essayist Nozaki Kan (b. 1959), to edit a collection of poems and prose reflections titled *Words Whispered by Candle Flames* (*Rōsoku no honō ga sasayaku kotoba*), which they published in June 2011 and sold to raise money for relief efforts. Arai Takako was a frequent participant in these public poetry vigils. She described those readings, stating,

> There was a special atmosphere in which everyone felt like they could open up to one another. There was a special, straightforward air of poetry created as the distance between peoples' hearts collapsed, along with the hierarchical relations of "superior" and "inferior."
>
> (Arai 2013b: 4)

Among the poems that Arai read aloud during these readings were a number that were eventually published in her 2013 book *Beds and Looms* (*Betto to shoki*).

One of the poems that she frequently read was a satirical and humorous poem titled '*Galapagos*' (*Garapagosu*) (Arai 2013a: 114–18; Arai 2015). The title comes from the fact that commentators sometimes compare the Japanese archipelago to the isolated group of Ecuadorian islands where change takes place at its own unique pace. Specifically, the word is frequently invoked in metaphors to describe the ways that Japanese business and economic development proceeds according to its own, local logic, cut off from the desires, needs, and practices of the rest of the world. With its playful tone and quick wit, Arai's poem helped to lighten the somber atmosphere of the vigils, and quickly became an audience favorite. The poem begins with Arai shouting in feigned exasperation at the media, which in 2011 and 2012 seemed obsessed with Japan's poor economic performance. She bombastically comments that the loves, lives, and deaths of people are frequently left out of the picture when such issues appear in the media. Instead of focusing only on big companies—the 'Incessant cellphones' and 'Microsoft monsters'—which usually occupy so much of the media coverage of business, she calls upon the media to restore the lives, loves, and deaths of ordinary people to a central position within public discourse. In one of the funniest passages in the work, she comments on the many things that the Fukushima meltdown had exposed.

>It's just been let go! Nuclear fission
>Just exposed! The the womb of the reactor dome too
>Fuel rods (*nenryōbō*), safety hats (*anzenbō*), egg cells (*ransaibō*), stinginess (*kechinbō*), thieves (*dorobō*),
>Refrigerators (*reibō*), heaters (*danbō*),
>Babies (*akanbō*), deceased (*butsunbō*), floating (*ukabō*) on the great plain of the sea, on the verge of screaming (*orabō*),
>The reactor building about to fly off (*buttobō*),
>Embankments (*teibō*), conspiracies (*inbō*), ministerial offices (*kanbō*),
>   Unbelievabō
>   Incredibō
>TEPCO
>       Puts on their Uniqlo
>       To bulwark
>       The tsunami
>
>(Arai 2013: 114–18; 2015)

As she watched the press coverage of the Fukushima meltdown, Arai was surprised that by complete coincidence, many of the vocabulary items that had started filling the news ended with the sound *bō*—*nenryōbō* (fuel rods), *anzenbō* (safety hats), *teibō* (embankments), *inbō* (conspiracies), *kanbō* (ministerial offices), and so on. Arai produces a flood of these words in rapid succession, replicating in her own particular satirical way the small tsunami of these words that washed over the Japanese press in the wake of 3.11. Although the passage quoted above inevitably evokes laughs in her public readings, it touches upon many serious themes. She has taken many of the issues that filled the headlines in the Japanese press in the year after the Fukushima meltdown and synthesized them into an organic whole: the downturn in the Japanese economy, the ongoing nuclear crisis, and even the success of the inexpensive popular clothing store Uniqlo, which is so popular that it began to look like a national uniform. In fact, in the wake of so much bad news in 2011, Uniqlo's entry into several new, major global markets in 2012 proved to be a ray of hope to the media, which seized upon it as a step forward for Japanese business and the economy. Given that situation, it is perhaps no surprise that Arai singles out Uniqlo for particular attention in this poem.

Elsewhere, Arai makes a brilliantly playful reference to the media's ongoing concern about the low national birth rate using the image of nuclear reactions. Arai notes that, given the low birth rate, Japan does not have much 'fusion' of sperm and ova; instead what the Japanese population has is mostly 'fission'—namely the breaking apart of radioactive isotopes at the meltdown at Fukushima. Arai begins to criticize the discriminatory idea, circulated in the popular media and on blogs, that young people from Fukushima who had exposure to radiation should consider using condoms rather than having unprotected sex for fear that radiation might have affected the genetic information in their reproductive organs. In fact, when asked about this poem, Arai commented that when she encountered media coverage warning Fukushima residents to use condoms, she thought, "My goodness! Fukushima has affected everything about us, even our sex lives!" (Arai 2013c). In the final stanza, she writes,

> We'll make electricity
> In our con-domes
> Is a half-life
> Good enough?

She makes a pun on the words *dōmu* (dome) and *kondōmu* (condom) to jokingly suggest that since the top has blown off the reactor at Fukushima, the population now has to use condoms, and perhaps that that friction should be the way that Japan should produce its energy. The ambiguous final question could be read in a couple of ways. The word translated here as "half-life" (*hangeki*) meaning the period which it takes a radioactive particle to lose half of its radioactivity, is written in Japanese with three characters meaning "a period of lessening by half." Although obviously inspired by the word from chemistry, Arai is using it here to ask whether or not it makes sense to have a period during which sexual pleasure is lessened or perhaps diminished by the barrier of the condom, especially in the light of the issue of Japan's low birth rate, even despite the fact that cautious conservatives might conclude a longer period of refraining from direct, procreative sexual contact might be warranted.

Arai leaves this question unresolved and hanging in the air, followed only by the single word *watashi-tachi*, meaning 'us' or 'we.' Interestingly, this word is not grammatically connected to the lines before it and thus exists in isolation from the rest of the work. The reader is left pondering the relationship between the word and the themes presented elsewhere. First of all, who is the 'us/we'? The author and her partner? Perhaps a larger pool of people—the author and her readers, wherever in Japan they might live? Perhaps the entire population of Japan? And more importantly, what is the relationship between the 'us/we' (however it may be defined) and the themes presented elsewhere in the work? How will Fukushima affect 'us'? Arai leaves those questions enticingly and provocatively open. She provides no simple solutions or answers, perhaps because no solutions or answers have yet to emerge from the wreckage of Fukushima. Indeed, the questions that she and many other poets have posed—questions about the relationship between Fukushima and daily life, between crisis, art, and lived experience—are still the subject of significant debate in Japan, even as Japan moves forward into the future.

## Notes

1 This chapter, which focuses on poetic responses to the Fukushima meltdown and nuclear crisis, is a companion piece to Angles 2014, which takes up the question of the ways that the poetic world wrote about and reflected upon the March 11, 2011 disasters more generally. So that readers may better follow the arguments in this chapter, I have placed the poems discussed in this chapter online. Please follow the links in the reference section. All poems are also available in Angles 2016.
2 This bookstore appears online at: http://fukkoshoten.com/
3 All three of the poets, whom this chapter discusses, work in genre of *gendai shi* (contemporary poetry), the style of longer, free verse that developed as Japan learned from and interacted with Western-style poetry. Readers interested in poetry in traditional forms that deal with the disaster should see Mayuzumi 2014 and Higashi Nihon daishinsai o keiken shita go-jū-go-nin no Nihonjin 2014. Both are excellent bilingual anthologies that bring together haiku and tanka on the disaster by a number of different poets.
4 I have translated two segments of this work as Wagō 2011e and 2011f. Because a significant portion of this translation is available online, I will not reproduce long extracts of this work in this chapter.
5 The museum, which was itself located in an area severely shaken by the 3.11 earthquake, has hosted three exhibitions, each of which was one-year long and has displayed manuscripts by poets writing on the disasters. The catalogs of these exhibitions form a valuable resource for anyone researching the relationship between art and catastrophe. In addition to the catalog named earlier in this note, see Nihon Gendai Shiika Bungakukan 2013 and 2014.
6 One month after 3.11, Prime Minister Kan Naoto made a statement called "*Kizuna*: The Bonds of Friendship" that expressed gratitude for the international community's show of support, and later that year, the priests of Kiyomizu Temple in Kyoto chose *kizuna* as the kanji that best represented the spirit of the year. As Samuels notes, *kizuna* was "appropriated broadly as a metaphor for social solidarity" in a time of crisis (2013: 42–43).

## References

Angles, Jeffrey. 2014, "These things here and now: Poetry in the wake of 3/11," in Roy Starrs (ed.), *When the Tsunami Came to Shore: Culture and Disaster in Japan*. Leiden: Global Oriental, 113–38.
Angles, Jeffrey. 2016. *These Things Here and Now: Poetic Responses to the March 11, 2011 Disasters*. Tokyo: Josai University Educational Corporation University Press.
Arai, Takako. 2013a, *Betto to shoki*. Tokyo: Michitani.
Arai, Takako. 2013b, "Kodama deshō ka, iie." *Ashita kara fuite kuru kaze: 2011.3.11 to shiika, sono go.* Ed. Nihon Gendai Shiika Bungakukan. Kitakami-shi: Nihon Gendai Shiika Bungakukan, 4–5.
Arai, Takako. 2013c, Personal Communication with Jeffrey Angles. March 27.

Arai, Takako. 2015, "Galapagos." Trans. Jeffrey Angles. *International Date Line*, at: http://internationaldateline.tumblr.com/post/118300523611/arai-takako-galapagos (accessed May 6, 2015).

Caruth, Cathy. 1996, *Unclaimed Experience: Trauma, Narrative, and History*. Baltimore, MD: John Hopkins University Press.

Higashi Nihon daishinsai o keiken shita go-jū-go-nin no Nihonjin (ed.). 2014, *Kawaranai sora, nakinagara, warainagara*. Trans. Laurel R. Rodd, Amy V. Heinrich, and Joan E. Ericson. Tokyo: Kōdansha.

Itō, Yasuhide. 2011, "Wagō Ryōichi 'Shi no tsubute' kakyokushū 'furusato' dai-go-kyoku 'akenai yoru wa nai.'" *YouTube*. April 27, at: www.youtube.com/watch?v=zgojFQ99HEU (accessed January 20, 2015).

Janet, Pierre. 1903, *Les Obsessions et la psychasthénie*. 2 vols. Paris: Alcan.

Keisatsuchō. 2015, *Heisei 23-nen (2011-nen) Tōhoku chihō taiseiyō oki jishin no higai jōkyō to keisatsu sochi*, at: www.npa.go.jp/archive/keibi/biki/higaijokyo.pdf (accessed April 16, 2015).

Liscutin, Nicola. 2011, "Indignez-Vous! 'Fukushima,' new media and anti-nuclear activism in Japan." *The Asia-Pacific Journal* November 21, at: http://japanfocus.org/-Nicola-Liscutin/3649 (accessed April 16, 2015).

Mayuzumi, Madoka (ed.). 2014, *So Happy to See Cherry Blossoms: Haiku from the Year of the Great Earthquake and Tsunami*. Trans. Hiroaki Sato and Nancy Sato. Winchester, VA: Red Moon Press.

Morinaka, Takaaki. 2014a, "Katasutorofī to kotoba." *Gendai shi techō* Vol. 57, No. 5 (May): 124–40.

Morinaka, Takaaki. 2014b, "Katasutorofī to kotoba." *Gendai shi techō* Vol. 57, No. 6 (June): 138–49.

Nakahara, Chūya. 1969, *Nakahara Chūya zenshū*. 6 vols. Tokyo: Kadokawa Shoten.

Nihon Gendai Shiika Bungakukan (ed.). 2012, *Mirai kara no koe ga kikoeru: 2011.3.11 to shiika (2012-nendo jōsetsu ten)*. Kitakami-shi: Nihon Gendai Shiika Bungakukan.

Nihon Gendai Shiika Bungakukan (ed.). 2013, *Ashita kara fuite kuru kaze: 2011.3.11 to shiika, sono go (2013-nendo jōsetsu ten)*. Kitakami-shi: Nihon Gendai Shiika Bungakukan.

Nihon Gendai Shiika Bungakukan (ed.). 2014, *Mirai ni tsunagu omoi: 2011.3.11 to shiika, soshite (2014-nendo jōsetsu ten)*. Kitakami-shi: Nihon Gendai Shiika Bungakukan.

Niimi, Tokuhide. 2011, "Tsubute Song 1 'Anata wa doko ni.'" *YouTube*. April 19, at: www.youtube.com/watch?v=ZWJ_wTIdPPI (accessed January 20, 2015).

Samuels, Richard J. 2013, *3.11: Disaster and Change in Japan*. Ithaca, NY: Cornell University Press.

Sano, Shin'ichi and Wagō, Ryōichi. 2012, *Kotoba ni nani ga dekiru no ka: 3/11 o koete*. Tokyo: Tokuma Shoten.

Seki, Etsushi. 2011, *Roku-jū-oku-hon no kaiten suru magatsuta bō*. Tokyo: Yūshorin.

Suga, Keijirō and Nozaki, Kan. 2011, *Rōsoku no honō ga sasayaku kotoba*. Tokyo: Keisō Shobō.

Takahashi Mutsuo. 2011a, "Ima koko ni korera no koto o." *Gendai shi techō* Vol. 54, No. 6 (June): 70–74.

Takahashi Mutsuo. 2011b, *Shishin ni-sen-nen : Susanoo kara 3.11 e*. Tokyo: Iwanami Shoten.

Takahashi Mutsuo. 2012a, "Ano toki kara/Genshiryoku jidai no koibito-tachi." *Gendai shi techō* Vol. 55, No. 1 (January): 73–75.

Takahashi Mutsuo. 2012b, "Ima wa." *Gendai shi techō* Vol. 55, No. 3 (March): 34–35.

Takahashi Mutsuo. 2013, Personal communication with Jeffrey Angles. 12 September.

Takahashi Mutsuo. 2015a, "These things here and now." Trans. Jeffrey Angles. *International Date Line*, at: http://internationaldateline.tumblr.com/post/116618556231/takahashi-mutsuo-these-things-here-and-now (accessed April 14, 2015).

Takahashi Mutsuo. 2015b, "Since then" and "Lovers in a time of nuclear energy." Trans. Jeffrey Angles. *International Date Line*, at: http://internationaldateline.tumblr.com/post/118293998531/takahashi-mutsuo-since-then-lovers-in-a-time-of-nuclear (accessed May 6, 2015).

Takahashi Mutsuo. 2015c, "Asfor this moment." Trans. Jeffrey Angles. *International Date Line*, at: http://internationaldateline.tumblr.com/post/118296553081/takahashi-mutsuo-asfor-this-moment (accessed May 6, 2015).

Wagō, Ryōichi. 2011a, "Shi no tsubute." *Gendai shi techō* Vol. 54, No. 5 (May): 37–80.

Wagō, Ryōichi. 2011b, *Shi no tsubute*. Tokyo: Tokuma Shoten.

Wagō, Ryōichi. 2011c, *Shi no kaikō*. Tokyo: Asahi Shinbun Shuppan.

Wagō, Ryōichi. 2011d, *Shi no mokurei*. Tokyo: Shinchōsha.

Wagō, Ryōichi. 2011e, "Pebbles of poetry: The Tōhoku earthquake and tsunami." Trans. Jeffrey Angles. *The Asia-Pacific Journal: Japan Focus*. July 18, at: www.japanfocus.org/-Jeffrey-Angles/3568 (accessed April 15, 2015).

Wagō, Ryōichi. 2011f, "Pebbles of Poetry 10." Trans. Jeffrey Angles. *Shisō chizu beta* 2: 224–27.

Wagō, Ryōichi. 2012, *Watashi to anata koko ni umarete*. Tokyo: Akashi Shoten.

Wagō, Ryōichi. 2013, *Hairo shihen*. Tokyo: Shichōsha.

# 10 Challenging reality with fiction

Imagining alternative readings of Japanese society in post-Fukushima theater

*Barbara Geilhorn*

## Introduction

With the emerging spatial turn in cultural studies, the particularities of the theatrical space have been the focus of increasing attention. Writing about heterotopia, Michel Foucault (1984) referred to theater as one of various counter-sites that have the potential to reflect on and challenge given norms and established positions. Theater can provide a space for temporal communities to engage in social discourse and act out alternatives. These qualities of theater become particularly clear in documentary and verbatim theater, but also in contemporary performances that invest our energies in the imagination of a better future. Highlighting the utopian potentialities of theater, Jill Dolan argues that: "[t]he affective and ideological 'doings' we see and feel demonstrated in utopian performatives also critically rehearse civic engagement that could be effective in the wider public and political realm" (Dolan 2005: 7). This chapter will discuss how these potentialities of theater can be realized in the context of the Fukushima calamity.

Recently, scholars such as Carol Martin (2010) have pointed at the re-engagement of theater with the real as indicated by the renewed interest in both addressing aspects of everyday life and in documentaries. In addition to this trend, Eckersall and Paterson detect a "turn to the slow" (Eckersall and Paterson 2011: 179) as a dramaturgical strategy to create a space for audiences' and performers' engagement with the political. What they consider slow dramaturgy:

> is a dramaturgical system of refunctioning; it makes a change to theater, changes its pace, its structure, and foregrounds its material dimensions. Finally, the refunctioning of theater is not didactic so much as dialectical and ecological, combining educative functions with uncanny experiences. [...] The role of slow dramaturgy is to bring the everyday into this new awareness and to make this a problem for our consideration.
> 
> (Eckersall and Paterson 2011: 190)

My article, which is part of a larger project on theatrical responses to 3.11,[1] will focus on an analysis of two recent plays by Okada Toshiki as prominent

*Challenging reality with fiction* 163

examples of how Tokyo theater has reacted to the Fukushima triple disaster. While *Unable to See* is a satirical piece that looks at the precarious situation from the short-term perspective, *Current Location* (*Genzaichi*) takes a more long-term view. The play addresses the issue from the position of Tokyo inhabitants experiencing the fear of nuclear threat. I will discuss how Okada explores the political potentialities of theatrical space in times of crisis and scrutinize the significance of slow dramaturgy in his attempt to engage the audiences' critical thinking. In addition, the paper argues that there has been a major turning point in Okada's work, triggered by the catastrophe.

## Okada Toshiki and his approach to theater

Okada Toshiki (b. 1973)[2] is one of the most interesting playwrights and directors of the younger generation in Japan and is also gaining a growing audience abroad. A regular guest at international art festivals,[3] his productions have a decisive impact on the image of contemporary Japanese theater abroad. Besides theater, he has also gained a reputation as novelist[4] and has published a volume of essays offering insights into his approach to making theater and his development as an artist (Okada 2013).

Okada and his theater troupe *chelfitsch*[5] are known for productions that question the interrelation of body and language, while utilizing choreography that draws on contemporary colloquial language and body movements originating from everyday life. Staging moments of everyday life in colloquial Japanese constitutes an obvious parallel between the plays of Okada Toshiki and Hirata Oriza (b. 1962),[6] who became known for a theatrical style using modern colloquial language in the 1990s (*gendai kogo engeki*) and is now a central figure in contemporary Japanese theater and a strong influence on the younger generation of theater people. While Hirata aims at freeing language on stage from the artificiality it inherited from Western theater, Okada goes one step further: He uses a kind of 'super-real' Japanese as if it were directly taken from everyday conversations among contemporary urban youth.[7] In addition, Okada broadens Hirata's concept by developing a unique body language.

In recent years, however, Okada has slowed down the tempo of his theater. While this process can be traced back to 2004, when his play *Five Days in March* (*Sangatsu no itsukakan*)[8] gained attention, it became particularly prominent in productions such as *We Are the Undamaged Others* (*Watashitachi wa mukizu na betsujin de aru*, 2010) and *The Sonic Life of a Giant Tortoise* (*Zōgame no sonikku raifu*, 2011) (Varney, Eckersall, Hudson, and Hatley 2013: 112–25). Okada's theater can be situated in a global trend in the early twenty-first century to combine the staging of the everyday with slowing down the tempo of performance as a dramaturgical strategy, as Eckersall and Paterson have argued. I will discuss the significance of slow dramaturgy for critical readings of *Current Location* later in this chapter. However, in the Japanese context, the slowing down of movements and the use of silence in Okada's recent productions are reminiscent of Ōta Shōgō's "theater of divestiture" (Boyd 2006). A leading figure in the underground theater movement (*angura*), which had its origins in the 1960s, Ōta became known for productions that were characterized by silence, slow movement, and empty space. Although Ōta's theater does not focus on the everyday, it is precisely this underlying passivity that compares with the aim of slow dramaturgy to provide a space for audiences to imaginatively engage in the search for deeper meanings.

Addressing topics such as the weariness and desperation of urban youth, Okada was invested in socially critical theater even before March 2011. For example, *Hot Pepper, Air Conditioner, and the Farewell Speech* (*Hotto peppā, kūrā, soshite owakare no aisatsu*), which premiered in October 2009 at the Hebbel Theater in Berlin, focuses on the processes of precarization and reveals the inhumanity of late capitalist society (Geilhorn 2012). Accordingly, turning to the issue of the Fukushima triple disaster can be seen as an enhancement of his interest in exploring the social and psychological conditions of people in times of crisis as well as drawing attention to deficiencies and problems in Japanese society.

## *Unable to See*

*Unable to See* (Okada 2012b),[9] which was shown at the *The World is Not Fair—The Great World's Fair 2012*[10] festival in Berlin, was among Okada's first attempts to come to terms with the Fukushima disaster. The festival featured fifteen pavilions on the site of the former airfield in Berlin Tempelhof and was implemented as a cooperation project between the Hebbel Theater and the 'raumlaborberlin' architectural collective. Okada tackles the delicate topic as an absurd farce. The pavilion that hosts the spectacle is a provisional structure made of wood and metal, reminiscent of the ruins of the damaged nuclear power plant. The audience witnesses a film team that received special permission to enter the forbidden area and their efforts to shoot a documentary on what had happened. They follow the artists on their way through the temporary construction, looking for a solution to a paradox: Although what had happened stirs up anguish and concern in faraway places such as Berlin, people's sense of danger decreases the closer they come to the nuclear reactor.

*Unable to See* is a short piece lasting about thirty minutes. The play explores the aftermath of the disaster and is characterized by strong irony and sarcasm. Okada addresses the public's short memory as well as disaster tourism. Both overreactions abroad and tendencies to push aside disturbing facts at home are held up to ridicule. The bizarre "3D dance" performed to the official theme song of the Expo '70 is not only a clever reference to the name of the Berlin festival.[11] "Progress and Harmony for Mankind" (*Jinrui no shinpo to chōwa*), the theme of the exposition, included praise of nuclear power as an advanced technology that brings about a bright future for the whole world. Okada takes such notions, which bespeak a naive faith in technology or rather governments' strategies to manipulate public opinion, to the absurd. The play culminates in the recovery of gilded fuel rods from the World's Fair's time capsule that is turned into a symbol of Japan's nuclear legacy to future generations.[12]

*Figure 10.1* *Unable to See* by Okada Toshiki (courtesy of Okada Toshiki)

In *Unable to See*, Okada uses satire as a means of social and political criticism. To this effect, the title not only refers to the invisibility of radioactivity, but it also blames the incapability of Japanese society and those responsible to recognize the dangers of nuclear power and to react appropriately. However, the play is written for a foreign audience, taking place in an informal setting in Berlin. In the German context, this rather direct form of satire is an adequate means for conveying criticism. To particularly appeal to a Japanese audience, Okada considered it more effective to take a different approach, as I will argue in my later analysis of *Current Location*.

### *Current Location (Genzaichi)*

Okada is one of several artists throughout Japan who claim that the catastrophe has given renewed purpose to their work.[13] As stated above, he was known for productions that tackle recent problems in Japanese society even before the dramatic events. However, in an article published in the German theater journal *Theater der Zeit* in 2011, he writes about his doubts regarding the necessity of the arts in society and how the catastrophe has changed his mind:

> Especially in the time directly after the earthquake catastrophe, many theater people were probably thinking the way I did: What effect can theater have now? I quite quickly came to the conclusion that for now, theater could not have any effect at all. People in the afflicted areas were in immediate need of water, food and blankets—not theater. Soon after that, something incredible happened to me. Any doubts I had about the necessity of art had almost completely vanished. Today, I am firmly convinced that art and theater are necessary for society.
>
> How did this come about? I finally came to recognize the following: Art can confront social reality with something strong. And that something is essential for society—all the more for a society in which catastrophes have occurred, like in Japan. Because if this something, an antithesis, does not exist, people will believe there was only one reality. Therefore, their thinking is limited.
>
> (Okada 2011: 19ff.)[14]

In his recent works, Okada seeks to transfer these insights onto the stage. After 'Fukushima,' the writer-director, who to date has been known for his 'super-real' theater, developed an interest in exploring the scope of fiction as 'recessive reality,' a kind of fiction that threatens reality by proposing an alternative (Okada 2011: 20).[15] Okada's reflections on fiction are reminiscent of Dolan's thoughts when writing about utopia in contemporary performance. Likewise, referring to utopian literature, the Marxist critic Frederic Jameson points out that the potential of utopia "is not to bring into focus the future that is coming to be, but rather to make us conscious precisely of the horizons or outer limits of what can be thought and imagined in our present" (Wegner 1998: 61).

In the following, I will show how Okada translates this idea into practice, taking his play *Current Location* (Okada 2014: 43–104) as an example. *Current Location* premiered at the Kanagawa Arts Theater (KAAT, *Kanagawa Geijutsu Gekijō*) in Yokohama, which is known for its innovative productions, in April 2012, and has been performed internationally.[16] The play is set in an unspecified place and time. There is a rumor going around about a big disaster destroying human civilization. Okada shows seven women and their various reactions to the situation. Naoko is convinced that the disaster will take its course. After seeing an omen in a big blue glowing cloud, she is obsessed with forebodings of a looming catastrophe. Her boyfriend's reaction is representative of her social environment: He does not want to discuss the subject, does not take her seriously, but instead only tries to calm her down. Sensitive Sana can no longer bear the prevailing tensions and anxiety in the city, and Maiko no longer knows what to accept as true. In contrast, Ayumi and Kasumi do not believe the rumors. While Ayumi pretends to be understanding when her friend Chie wants to leave the city, Kasumi tries to overcome subliminal fears by silencing Hana, who is completely alienated. *Current Location* places a special focus on the level of interpersonal relations: How do we react in the face of impending disaster, how do we deal with anxiety and uncertainty—and moreover—how do we treat others who react differently than we do? These central questions of the play are explicitly pronounced at the end of the first scene:

> VOICE: Sometimes when rumors are introduced into the world, we are forced to make a choice about whether we believe the rumor or not.
> VOICE: But there is an even greater choice we have to face, which is, once you've made a verdict about how to engage with a rumor, how do you interact with other people who have chosen to engage with it in a different way?
>
> (Okada 2012a: 2)[17]

Okada does not address the Fukushima disaster directly. However, Naoko's blue cloud will hardly escape the attention of Japanese audiences as being suggestive of the fear of radioactive fallout in a wide area around the damaged reactor, including the capital. According to Noda Manabu, an accomplished theater scholar at Meiji University, *Current Location* convincingly shows the emotions of Tokyo inhabitants and their feeling of being trapped in the metropolis after the nuclear disaster.[18] Furthermore, the paragraph cited above evokes associations of the uncertainties in the aftermath of the disaster that were not only caused by a lack of reliable information, but also by the challenge to adequately react to a highly complex situation. Thus it is reminiscent of conditions in places like Iitate, a village about 40 km from the Fukushima Daiichi Nuclear Power Plant, where the majority of villagers has been evacuated, although after a delay, only to recategorize evacuation zones to prepare for rehabitation in the following year.

In terms of its structure, *Current Location* is reminiscent of *Five Days in March* (*Sangatsu no itsukakan*) (Okada 2005), which won the renowned Kishida

Kunio Drama Award and marked a turning point in the career of Okada Toshiki and his troupe *chelfitsch*. In *Five Days in March*, Okada confronts the banalities of everyday life in Tokyo with the outbreak of the Iraq War, employing techniques of post-dramatic theater.[19] He uses a complex narrative structure to tell the simple story of a short love affair: What happens to the young couple and their lives in Shibuya, a fashionable district in the center of Tokyo, is presented several times from the various perspectives of other people the two come across or interact with during these five days. The actors change between the role of narrator, to that of one of the characters retelling the events from her or his perspective, and finally to re-enacting them. They switch between roles without prior notice or without even shifting their position on stage. The fact that the same character is represented by various actors, who also act as different characters the next time they appear on stage, adds to the complexity of the performance. The distinction between narration and display, presentation and representation becomes blurred.

Again, in *Current Location*, Okada examines the dialectic of living in a time of crisis by showing the events on stage from various perspectives. Although the narrative structure is less complex than that of *Five Days in March*, a multi-perspective approach is achieved by introducing seven female characters, who present various options for acting. Furthermore, Okada adds a play within a play. The storyline meanders along leisurely to alternatively focus on the opposing perspectives. In addition, single characters are split between contradicting feelings. This is particularly evident in the role of Kasumi. Although she rejects the rumors with ostentation, she chokes anxious Hana, a kind of alter ego to her, in an attempt to calm herself down. Okada makes a point not to offer possible solutions. Instead, he presents what people hold to be true or real as up to interpretation, as can be seen when Sana talks about her role in the play within a play scene:

> SANA: [...] There are two sisters. And I play the younger sister. The older sister is a bit more selfish. The younger sister on the other hand is more responsible.
> AYUMI: (to CHIE) Is that the story?
> CHIE: That's what she thought. People are free to interpret the characters as they like.
>
> (Okada 2012a: 5)

In this way, Okada invites audiences to draw their own conclusions from the variety of perspectives presented in the play. Besides addressing audiences in the text, dramaturgy is employed as a useful tool to achieve the same effect. *Current Location* starts with seven women appearing on stage, sitting down with their backs turned to the audience. The performers in each scene stand up and deliver their text in a distanced way. At times, the actresses step out of their role to announce the presentation of a certain event in the next scene. Like in Okada's earlier work, the emotionally convincing embodiment of characters has become

*Challenging reality with fiction* 169

obsolete. Breaking the illusion of theater is another attempt to get audiences involved on a more conscious plane. Furthermore, the production breaks the fourth wall from the very first moment: Performers become part of the audience watching the story unfold. This applies in particular to the play within the play scene, which creates alternative realities on a secondary level. In addition, Okada slows down the tempo of performance to an anti-dramatic effect. The text is delivered in a creeping manner and interrupted by pauses of silence. Physical action is reduced to a minimum. In terms of stage design, Okada employs minimal theater, hardly using any props and using simple lighting. Projections of blue skies with fluffy clouds alternate with those of the earth and other planets,[20] illustrating the illusion of peacefulness and adding to the utopian elements in the play at the same time. The music, which often plays a crucial part in Okada's productions, is reduced to spherical sounds and is another factor in slowing down the performance and creating a contemplative atmosphere.

In *Current Location*, slowness, simplification, and ambivalence open up a space for audiences' imagination.[21] Slow dramaturgy plays an essential role for Okada's indirect mode of social criticism to become effective. It is only in a second narrative level that he directly points at the precarious situation in his home country. At the same time, he modifies this reference through fictionalization. Okada makes his characters compose and act out a play that takes up central themes of *Current Location* in the form of a fairy tale with utopian elements and is situated in the fictitious country of 'Japan.' The play within a play starts with Chie narrating in a lapidary tone:

*Figure 10.2 Current Location* by Okada Toshiki (courtesy of Okada Toshiki)

CHIE: Once upon a time, there was a country called Japan. Little by little it was torn apart, and towards the end, there was a civil war that may as well have destroyed the country completely.

CHIE: Around the time the civil unrest had just begun there were two sisters who lived together. [...] The older sister was Taeko and the younger sister was Shinobu. These two sisters were very close [...]. But then, something changed. That's the story we're about to tell now.

(Okada 2012a: 7)

A small group of people is planning to leave the earth and establish 'The Village,' the utopia of a new society, causing a bitter fight between two sisters: While Taeko wants to join the group, Shinobu blames Taeko for having wanted to leave Japan for a long time, now finding a reason to do so and not caring about the people who will be left behind.

TAEKO: Hey, do you think it's crazy for me to think that we can no longer continue to live in this country?

SHINOBU: I can only tell you what I think.

SHINOBU: The way we are living now isn't any different from any kind of peaceful life anywhere else. It's not as if we hear gunshots at our doorstep. There are no land mines buried in the neighborhood. We can hang our laundry and take the bicycle out to go grocery shopping. It's not because I am part courageous or daring. There's simply no reason to be fearful.

TAEKO: I understand what you're saying. I do, but I just can't agree with you. I wonder why I can't even though I understand?

TAEKO: It's probably because I don't get attached. So I can't help but think that it's too dangerous for us to keep living here.

TAEKO: I think I'm a tedious person.

TAEKO: I don't have a deep attachment to home.

TAEKO: A normal person would have more affection towards the place she was born and raised, and think of it as home.

[...]

SHINOBU: I'm going to tell you something I've been thinking for a long time. I think that the reason you don't like Japan is not because of the war. I think you've wanted to escape Japan for a long time. Am I wrong?

TAEKO: I don't think that's something you have to accuse me of.

SHINOBU: I'm not accusing you.

TAEKO: You know, I've already begun imagining it. 'The Village' is a place where everything is beginning anew, so everyone involved in 'The Village' will have to build everything from the ground up. Nobody there will accuse me of anything, and I hope that the kind of society that is established in 'The Village' is one in which this kind of accusatory tone is not the obvious or expected response.

SHINOBU: I was right. You're just spouting off what your ideals are, and essentially you have no concern for the people here who are experiencing major change, right?

(Okada 2012a: 8ff.)

I want to point out here that both characters have telling names that bespeak their capacity to endure and that correspond to their respective attitudes. While the Japanese verb *shinobu* signifies a rather introspective kind of endurance and getting around a problem, *taeru* can be associated with a more active form of resistance.

On a secondary level, Okada calls into question the future of Japanese society. He addresses existing pressures to conform to predominant views and clear-cut standards for behavior as a fundamental problem that became particularly apparent in the immediate aftermath of the disaster. Non-compliance with the "code of *wa*," as Iwaki (2015) calls it, will be punished by social marginalization or worse, as is demonstrated in the episode cited above and is likewise symbolized by the murder of Hana. One is reminded of tendencies in post-Fukushima Japan where people are expected to not talk about the disaster in public, not even at their workplace.[22] The scenes referred to above conjure up associations of *fūhyō higai*, damage allegedly caused by baseless rumors spread about a disaster, which are a contentious issue in post-Fukushima discourse. On the one hand, rumors tend to surface when there is a lack of reliable information after the occurrence of a disaster, and reports on large areas that have become practically uninhabitable due to radiation put a significant pragmatic and emotional burden on the locals. However, allegations of *fūhyō higai* are an effective tool to silence critical voices, including self-censorship in the arts. *Current Location* points at a climate in which it is not the calamity that is perceived as a threat to society, but rather those who might point at the problem,[23] and confronts this atmosphere with the vision of an alternative society, where freedom of expression is a real option.

In the last scene of *Current Location*, which takes the form of an epilogue, the two narrative levels seem to merge, blurring the lines between fiction and reality. Okada adds to this impression by making Chie and Sana, respectively the author and the actors of the play within a play, deliver the final scene. Until the very end of the play, conflictive positions remain irreconcilably opposed. While Chie and a few other critical spirits have left on board a mysterious ship, for the majority of the villagers, including Sana, everything is back to normal.

CHIE: I couldn't understand what the people who didn't want to board the ship were thinking. Didn't they understand the obvious, that if the village was going to be destroyed, that they would be destroyed as well? Were they still thinking that the village was not going to be destroyed? Oh God forbid, had they resigned themselves to the idea that they would be destroyed with the village? But I decided not to think further along those lines. [...]

CHIE: I got on the ship and left the village.
CHIE: That's right. And now we are here. Inside the ship. Apparently, soon after we left, the village was destroyed. Or it might as well have been destroyed.
[…]
SANA: […] Everything in the village was back to normal. All the anxiety of the villagers had vanished. A feeling of happiness and health, and laughter returned to the people.
SANA: That's right. And we are now here. In the village, as before. There are people who say the village was destroyed, but that was a misguided rumor. I mean, right?

(Okada 2012a: 8–9)

The play ends with those words by Sana. Everything seems like a bad dream. The disaster never happened—or did it?

Although *Current Location* does not address the catastrophe and its aftermath directly, paradoxically, they are constantly present. In an attempt to free audiences from preconceived ideas and gridlocked positions, Okada transfers the traumatic event into a fictitious narrative and probes the idea of fiction as a challenge to reality by examining various human reactions to a pending catastrophe. Reality and fiction overlap and become increasingly blurred. What is commonly considered real is presented as mere fiction, albeit the most influential one at a certain time (Okada 2011: 20). It is precisely this overlapping of what is perceived as fiction or reality that actively encourages the audiences' engagement. Ultimately, the systematic repression of the anxiety and anguish caused by looming disaster seems as absurd as leaving the planet to escape to another world. Okada's criticism of Japanese society for silencing critical views and warning voices instead of responding actively to what is threatening human civilization can hardly go unnoticed. Besides, as a private person, Okada takes a clear position: In July 2011, only a few months after the triple disaster, he moved with his family from his home in the greater Tokyo metropolitan area to the city of Kumamoto in southern Japan to protect his children from the potential effects of radiation (Okada 2013: 23). Thus, it is likely that *Current Location* draws to some extent on Okada's own experiences as well.

*Current Location* is one of several plays in which Okada puts his critical attitude toward Japanese society on stage. However, in terms of gender roles, the play seems to merely reinforce social order. When asked what his intentions were to have all female characters, Okada explains:

To be honest, casting only females was my instinct. When I thought about a story about the change in circumstance, I imagined that it might have ended too heroic or revolutionary, if the character was male. In this respect, if I remember correctly, I imagined that female characters would be more likely to be fighting over their situations, at the level of their daily lives.

(PACT Zollverein 2012)

By portraying women as being in charge of interpersonal relationships and issues of everyday life, *Current Location* can be read as reinforcing normative gender roles, thereby sharing in the constructions of gender in a way that is central to pro-nuclear and anti-nuclear discourses alike (Wöhr 2013). However, casting women only fulfills a theatrical function, as Iwaki (2015) has shown. While this might be more effective with Japanese audiences and in line with their tendency toward rather conservative notions of gender, it also allows Okada to have numerous lines end on the particle *wa*, thus using a rather outmoded and utterly feminine language style (*joseigo*). In so doing, he makes language a tool to hint at the artificiality that keeps the fragile balance between harmony and disharmony so central to the play.

## Conclusion

In this paper I have discussed the potential of theater as a liminal space for imagining alternative realities, focusing on recent plays by Okada Toshiki. After the Fukushima disaster, his interest in exploring the political dimension of performance has gained further momentum. However, he continues to formulate his criticism in an indirect fashion, which can be considered the most appropriate strategy in a Japanese context. To be effective, Okada utilizes various techniques on the text level and through dramaturgy. While the postdramatic character of his productions, the multiperspectivity and complexity of narrative structure, and the use of slow dramaturgy is not new, he recently developed an interest in fiction. Before the calamity, Okada used to draw audiences' attention to the focal point of a play by systematically leaving it out of the narrative until it finally becomes apparent as a blank.[24] Now, he probes the potential of fiction to challenge reality with imagination. In *Current Location*, the borders between fiction and reality become increasingly blurred. What is 'true' or 'false,' 'real' or 'unreal' lies in the eye of the beholder. This marks the point of departure for the utopian potential of Okada's play to become effective. However, art cannot change the world. To borrow Herbert Marcuse's words, art can invoke "an image of the end of power, the appearance of freedom. But this is only the appearance; clearly, the fulfillment of this promise is not within the domain of art" (1979: 46).

## Notes

1 Geilhorn 2014 is an earlier version of this chapter and provides a brief overview on Japanese performance in the immediate aftermath of the disaster.
2 For further detail on Okada and studies of his plays, see Poulton 2011, Geilhorn 2012, Eckersall 2015, and Iwaki 2015.
3 Since 2007, for example, Okada has regularly participated in the Belgian Kunsten Festival des Arts (KFDA), a festival for contemporary arts that is noted for its avant-garde theater program as well.
4 His collection of two novels, *Watashitachi ni yurusareta tokubetsu na jikan no owari* (*The End of the Special Time We Were Allowed*, 2007), was awarded the Kenzaburō Ōe Prize in 2008.

5 The company's name is Okada's coinage, representing a child's mispronunciation of the English word 'selfish' (http://chelfitsch.net).
6 Hirata founded his troupe *Seinendan* in 1983 ('Group of young people'; for further information, see www.seinendan.org). Besides his activities as a playwright and director, he is the manager of Komaba Agora Theater in Tokyo and also teaches at the Center for the Study of Communication Design at Osaka University. In *Gendai kogo engeki no tame ni* (*For a Contemporary Theater in Colloquial Language*, 1995), Hirata sets the theory and background for his theater. For an easily accessible introduction, see his interview with Senda Akihiko (Hirata and Senda 2007).
7 Okada first used this kind of language for the play *Karera no kibō ni mihare* (*Be Surprised with Their Hopes*, 2001) (Okada and Soma 2010).
8 See Eckersall and Paterson (2011: 185–87) for a discussion of *Five Days in March* in the context of slow dramaturgy. Geilhorn 2012 provides another analysis of this play.
9 The play has an English title only. However, it was performed in Japanese, the German translation was read out by the dramatic adviser, Sebastian Breu. I would like to thank Okada Toshiki for providing me with the unpublished manuscript.
10 The Festival was held from June 1–24 in 2012. For the program and further details, refer to Hebbel am Ufer.
11 For more information on the Osaka World's Fair, the first in Japan, see Chappell.
12 Interestingly, Ōnbou Pelican's *Kiruannya to Uko-san* (*Kiruannya and Uko*, 2011), a documentary addressing the Fukushima calamity and a play very different in character, also employs the Osaka Expo as a means to contrast the harsh reality after the triple disaster with the naive faith in technology in general and the safety of nuclear energy in particular (see Geilhorn forthcoming).
13 Ushiro Ryūta, leader of the performance group Chim↑Pom, is another prominent example (Frontline 2011).
14 Translation by the author.
15 Okada takes a similar position in an interview with Hoshino Tomoyuki (Hoshino and Okada 2011).
16 See the website of the *chelfitsch* theater company.
17 I would like to thank Okada Toshiki for providing me with the unpublished manuscript.
18 Noda gave his view in a talk on Japanese theater after 3.11 at Meiji University on September 29, 2012.
19 The term describes forms of avant-garde theater since the 1970s that no longer strive to remain true to the text. Thus, other means of expression such as dance, lighting, or music gain in importance (see Lehmann 1999: 22–23).
20 This reflects the strong science fiction character of Okada's initial concept of the play, which was conceived under the working title *In Between Jupiter and Mars* (Okada 2013: 18).
21 Okada very consciously makes use of these effects, as he mentioned in a talk following the performance of *Ground and Floor* (*Jimen to Yuka*) in Brussels on May 23, 2013.
22 Morioka 2013 provides some insights on the silence of so many people in the afflicted areas.
23 In the political arena, this is reflected by the Act on the Protection of Specially Designated Secrets (*Tokutei Himitsu no Hogo ni Kansuru Hōritsu*), which was passed by the parliament in December 2014. The new law has been severely criticized as a blatant attack on freedom of information and free press in general. Furthermore, opponents are concerned that the law might be exploited to hide objectionable information about the damaged Fukushima nuclear reactors (Halperin and Hofsommer 2014).
24 For example, *Hot Pepper, Air Conditioner, and the Farewell Speech*.

# References

Boyd, Mari. 2006, *The Aesthetics of Quietude: Ōta Shōgo and the Theater of Divestiture.* Tokyo: Sophia University.
Chappell, Urso. n.d., "1970 Osaka." The World's Fair Museum Since 1998. *ExpoMuseum. com*, at: http://expomuseum.com/1970/ (accessed September 25, 2014).
chelfitsch. n.d., [website of the chelfitsch theater company], at: http://chelfitsch.net/index2.html (accessed December 10, 2015).
chelfitsch/Okada Toshiki. 2013, *Current Location.* DVD.
Dolan, Jill. 2005, *Utopia in Performance: Finding Hope at the Theater.* Ann Arbor, MI: University of Michigan Press.
Eckersall, Peter. 2015, "Performance, mourning and the long view of nuclear space." *The Asia-Pacific Journal* Vol. 13, Issue 6, No. 2 (February 16), at: http://japanfocus.org/-Peter-Eckersall/4278/article.html (accessed December 10, 2015).
Eckersall, Peter and Paterson, Eddie. 2011, "Slow dramaturgy: Renegotiating politics and staging the everyday." *Australasian Drama Studies* 58: 178–92.
Foucault, Michel. 1984, "Of other spaces: Utopias and heterotopias." *Architecture/ Mouvement/Continuité* (October): 1–7.
Frontline. 2011, The Atomic Artists. "Art cannot be powerless." An Interview with Ryuta Ushiro. July 26, at: www.pbs.org/wgbh/pages/frontline/the-atomic-artists/art-cannot-be-powerless (accessed December 10, 2015).
Geilhorn, Barbara. 2012, "Performing social criticism in contemporary Japanese theater: Okada Toshiki's *Hot Pepper, Air Conditioner, And the Farewell Speech* and *Five Days in March*," in Barbara Geilhorn, Eike Grossmann, Hiroko Miura, and Peter Eckersall (eds), *Enacting Culture: Historical and Contemporary Contexts of Japanese Theater.* Munich: iudicium, 251–63.
Geilhorn, Barbara. 2014, "Japanisches Theater zwischen Gesellschaftskritik und Traumaverarbeitung: Reaktionen auf die Dreifach-Katastrophe in Tōkyō und Tōhoku," in Lisette Gebhardt and Evelyn Schulz (eds), *Neue Konzepte japanischer Literatur? Nationalliteratur, literarischer Kanon und die Literaturtheorie. Referate des 15. Deutschsprachigen Japanologentags – Literatur II.* Berlin: EB Verlag, 203–22.
Geilhorn, Barbara. forthcoming, "Trauma and memory in post-Fukushima theater: Ōnobu Pelican's *Kiruannya to Uko-san*," in Marcella Mariotti, Bonaventura Ruperti, and Silvia Vesco (eds), *Rethinking Nature: Facing the Crisis in Contemporary Japan.* Venice: Edizioni Ca' Foscari.
Halperin, Morton H. and Hofsommer, Molly M. 2014, "Japan's secrecy law and international standards." *The Asia-Pacific Journal* Vol. 12, Issue 37, No. 1 (September 15), at: http://japanfocus.org/-molly_m_-hofsommer/4183/article.html (accessed December 10, 2015).
Hebbel Am Ufer. n.d., *The World Is Not Fair – Die Grosse Weltausstellung 2012*, at: www.hebbel-am-ufer.de/archiv_de/kuenstler/kuenstler_23722.html?HAU=1 (accessed July 10, 2012).
Hirata, Oriza. 1995, *Gendai kōgo engeki no tame ni.* Tokyo: Banseisha.
Hirata, Oriza and Senda, Akihiko. 2007, Artist interview. Speaking with Hirata Oriza, a new opinion leader in the world of contemporary theater (Interviewer: Akihiko Senda). *Performing Arts Network* (The Japan Foundation). March 23, at: www.performingarts.jp/E/art_interview/0703/1.html (accessed December 10, 2015).
Hoshino, Tomoyuki and Toshiki, Okada. 2011, "Genjitsu o hen'yō saseru fikushon. Hoshino Tomoyuki + Okada Toshiki." *Shinchō* Vol. 108, Issue 7: 206–17.

Iwaki, Kyoko. 2015, "Japanese Theatre after Fukushima: Okada Toshiki's Current Location." *New Theatre Quarterly* Vol. 31, Issue 1: 70–89.
Lehmann, Hans-Thies. 1999, *Postdramatisches Theater*. Frankfurt am Main: Verlag der Autoren.
Marcuse, Herbert. 1979, *The Aesthetic Dimension: Toward a Critique of Marxist Aesthetics*. Trans. Herbert Marcuse and Erica Sherover. London: Macmillan.
Martin, Carol (ed.). 2010, *The Dramaturgy of the Real on the World Stage*. New York: Palgrave Macmillan.
Morioka, Rika. 2013, "Mother Courage: Women activists between a passive populace and a paralyzed government," in Tom Gill, Brigitte Steger, and David H. Slater (eds), *Japan Copes with Calamity: Ethnographies of the Earthquake, Tsunami and Nuclear Disasters of March 2011*. Oxford: Peter Lang, 177–200.
Okada, Toshiki. 2005, *Sangatsu no itsukakan*. Tokyo: Hakusuisha.
Okada, Toshiki. 2007, *Watashitachi ni yurusareta tokubetsu na jikan no owari*. Tokyo: Shinchōsha.
Okada, Toshiki. 2010, "Hotto peppā, kūrā, soshite owakare no aisatsu." *Okada Toshiki: Enjoi awā furītaimu*. Tokyo: Hakusuisha, 7–54.
Okada, Toshiki. 2011, "Die Wirklichkeit durch Fiktion bedrohen." *Theater der Zeit* 10: 18–20.
Okada, Toshiki. 2012a, *Current Location*. Unpublished manuscript, trans. Ogawa Aya.
Okada, Toshiki. 2012b, *Unable to See*. Unpublished manuscript.
Okada, Toshiki. 2013, *Sokō. Henkei shite iku tame no engekiron*. Tokyo: Kawade Shobō Shinsha.
Okada, Toshiki. 2014, *Genzaichi*. Tokyo: Kawade Shobō Shinsha.
Okada, Toshiki and Chiaki, Soma. 2010, "Artist Interview. Insights from international activities. The latest interview with Toshiki Okada" (Interviewer: Chiaki Soma), *Performing Arts Network* (The Japan Foundation), March 26, at: www.performingarts.jp/E/art_interview/1003/1.html (accessed December 10, 2015).
PACT Zollverein. 2012, *Toshiki Okada/Chelfitsch (JP) "Current Location."* program.
Poulton, Cody. 2011, "Krapp's First Tape: Okada Toshiki's Enjoy." *TDR (The Drama Review)* Vol. 55, Issue 2: 150–57.
Varney, Denise, Eckersall, Peter, Hudson, Chris, and Hatley, Barbara 2013, *Theater and Performance in the Asia-Pacific: Regional Modernities in the Global Era*. Basingstoke: Palgrave Macmillan.
Wegner, Phillip E. 1998, "Horizons, figures, and machines: The dialectic of utopia in the work of Frederic Jameson." *Utopian Studies* Vol. 9, Issue 2: 58–74.
Wöhr, Ulrike. 2013, "From Hiroshima to Fukushima: Gender in nuclear and anti-nuclear politics," in Hiroshima Shiritsu Daigaku (ed.), Kokusai Gakubu. *Japan's 3/11 Disaster as Seen from Hiroshima: A Multidisciplinary Approach*. Tokyo: Soeisha Shoten, 203–33.

# 11 *Oishinbo*'s Fukushima elegy
## Grasping for the truth about radioactivity in a food manga

*Lorie Brau*

## Introduction

When the May 12–19, 2014 issue of the manga magazine, *Big Comic Spirits (Biggu Komikku Supirittsu)* hit newsstands on April 28, Kariya Tetsu's (author) and Hanasaki Akira's (artist) long-running food manga series *Oishinbo* stumbled into the arena of post-311 nuclear politics and panic with an episode of the story arc, *The Truth about Fukushima* (*Fukushima no shinjitsu*). The manga follows a crew of journalists who travel to Fukushima Prefecture to research the aftermath of the nuclear meltdown caused by the 3.11 earthquake and tsunami. After touring the Fukushima Daiichi Nuclear Power Plant, series protagonist Yamaoka Shirō complains of severe fatigue and develops a mysterious nosebleed. The narrative suggests that his symptoms might have been caused by exposure to radiation. This claim sparked a firestorm in the national media. Government spokesman, Suga Yoshihide, denied any possible link between nosebleeds and low levels of radiation. The manga was censured for fostering prejudice against the people of Fukushima (Takahashi and Negishi 2014). Critics also condemned Fukushima University Professor Arakida Takeru's suggestion, quoted in the manga, that he did not think it would be possible to sufficiently decontaminate the affected areas of Fukushima so that people could live there (Kariya and Hanasaki 2014: 278).

Such a comment inevitably touched a nerve in a government that had made every effort to downplay the disaster: wherever possible, the official policy emphasized decontamination and "bring[ing] back the home town (*furusato*)" (quoted in Gill 2013: 202fn), rather than resident evacuation (Nelson 2014: 358). By March 2015, about 120,000 Fukushima residents had left their homes, some of them voluntarily (*Japan Times*, March 4, 2015). Meanwhile, as of April 2014, the government had invested JPY 1.9 trillion (about US$19 billion) toward reconstruction, which included decontaminating areas by removing topsoil (Ministry of the Environment).[1]

Even more than offending the government, the manga's advice to Fukushima residents to leave because the land is too contaminated (Kariya and Hanasaki 2014: 252, 287) upset many Japanese in and out of the prefecture. Painting an image of Fukushima as unlivable was construed as harming the region's reputation and stigmatizing its people. In other words, critics said that Kariya's story constituted *fūhyō higai*, spreading false rumors that cause economic damage.[2]

In response to the controversy, the government of Fukushima prefecture sent a letter of protest to publisher Shōgakukan about the controversial episodes, refuting the manga's claims regarding deleterious health effects by citing UNSCEAR (United Nations Scientific Committee on the Effects of Atomic Radiation) and requesting that the manga base its assertions on carefully researched, unbiased, objective information.[3] Many people weighed in on the debate, from Prime Minister Abe Shinzō, who declared that it was necessary as a country to challenge such false, unfounded rumors (Hori 2014) to numerous posters to Twitter, social networking sites such as Facebook and Mixi, and videos posted on YouTube.[4] Some posts were highly critical of the manga for spreading false information, while others supported *Oishinbo* for stirring debate about the handling of the accident.

In the June 2, 2014 issue (No. 25) of *Big Comic Spirits*, Shōgakukan's editorial department responded to the many letters and complaints that they received by publishing ten pages of comments sent in by doctors, academics, scientists, writers and others, including the government of the city of Futaba, located next to the power plant. While some of the letters denounced Kariya for creating anxiety, the comment of Koide Hiroaki, a professor of nuclear engineering at Kyoto University, suggested one reason that *The Truth about Fukushima* created such a commotion. He wrote that the administration is not taking responsibility for the accident and is trying to make everyone forget it (Koide 2014: 394). The pages of comments culminated in an apology, written by *Big Comic Spirits* editor Murayama Hiroshi, to readers who had sent in complaints. In his apology, Murayama defended the magazine's decision to run the story, however, claiming that it would be a mistake to suppress the voices of people whom Kariya interviewed. He concluded with a statement of hope that the various opinions expressed about *Oishinbo* would contribute to a reasoned discussion about [Japan's] future (Murayama 2014: 400).

The *Huffington Post* (Japanese edition) commentator, psychiatrist Hori Arinobu, confessed his surprise at the reaction to the nosebleed controversy. In his view, *Oishinbo* is the "fantasy of a manga writer with a rich imagination." He wrote, "the contents were far removed from the textbook common knowledge about the effects of radiation on health" (May 19, 2014). While his assessment of Kariya's take on radiation's health effects is subject to dispute, Hori's comment raises an interesting question. How does one interpret documentary content that is embedded in a fictive graphic narrative?

To construct the story of the 'truth about Fukushima,' Kariya, Hanasaki and staff interview actual people, and illustrate their story with drawings based on photographs. The fictive characters doing the interviewing, on the other hand, are drawn in a more cartoon-like fashion. Rendered with thicker lines and such manga conventions as sweat drops, their images are more iconic. This difference in drawing style within the same picture plane emblematizes the hybrid nature of

*The Truth about Fukushima.* Shiriagari Kotobuki, winner of a Media Arts Excellency award from the Agency for Culture Affairs in February 2012 for his 3.11 manga, *Ano hi kara no manga* (Manga since 3.11), noted in an interview about the *Oishinbo* nosebleed controversy, "When manga try to deal with reality, it's complicated [...] it creates friction" (*NHK World*: 2014). *Oishinbo*'s mixing of fiction with documentary and cartoons with photo-realistic illustrations may add to this complexity.

In a post-3.11 Japan experiencing fear, mistrust, and accusations of *fūhyō higai* (spreading damaging rumors) around the issue of radioactive contamination, media coverage of a few pages about a nosebleed can eclipse the content of a work's remaining 500 or so pages. While this chapter on *The Truth about Fukushima* addresses the implications of the contentious reception of the work, it also discusses how *Oishinbo*'s rendering of the saga of the nuclear crisis harnesses the resources of the manga medium to critique the mishandling of the Fukushima accident and to mourn the serious losses that resulted.

## *Oishinbo*, grandfather of food manga

Who would have predicted that a comic book about food could generate one of the most charged Fukushima-related controversies of 2014? One of Japan's primary forms of popular discourse, manga, Japanese comics, articulate the concerns of everyday life. Almost every imaginable genre of writing, from fantasy to documentary, has been 'mangafied.' Comics about food are called *ryōri* (which means 'cooking' as well as that which is cooked, 'cuisine') or *gurume* (gourmet) *manga*. Typically, these food manga contextualize a wealth of information about food in illustrated narratives that sometimes include exciting contests and moving dramas (Suzuki 2008).

*Oishinbo*—the title is a portmanteau combining the words for delicious (*oishii*) and 'a person who likes to eat' (*kuishinbo*)—led the way in the development of the genre. It began publication in 1983 in *Big Comic Spirits*, a weekly manga magazine tailored to the *seinen*, or young men's, market. Among this magazine's current offerings, *Oishinbo* may be one of the wordiest, most serious, and most adult-oriented.[5] *Oishinbo* was the publisher Shōgakukan's second most popular series from the mid-1980s to the mid-1990s (Kinsella 2000: 82). The manga's popularity no doubt owed a great deal to Japan's bubble economy of the 1980s, which spurred a 'gourmet boom' from which the nation has yet to completely emerge, in spite of the subsequent recession. As is usual with popular manga first serialized in magazines, the episodes are published in stand-alone book format (*tankōbon*). To date, Shōgakukan has published 111 volumes of *Oishinbo*, each typically 250–300 pages long. *Oishinbo* has spawned an animated television series (1988–1993), a (live-action) television drama (1994–1999), a 'new' *Oishinbo* drama (2007–2009), a film (1996), videogames, and parodies. Viz Media has published seven thematically arranged volumes of selected episodes from *Oishinbo* in English translation.[6]

*Oishinbo* opens with a mission to create an 'ultimate menu' to celebrate the centenary of the *Tōzai Shimbun*, the fictional newspaper that is the manga's setting. The two staff members selected to head up this project are Yamaoka Shirō and a young new female employee, Kurita Yūko. While Yamaoka is at first depicted as an uncouth, lazy slob, he reveals his genius in the realm of food, taking after his father and nemesis, Kaibara Yūzan,[7] the brilliant gastronome, restaurateur, and artist who is modeled after the real life artist and epicure, Kitaōji Rosanjin (1883–1959).

In the early formula that made the manga a million seller, Yamaoka competed in numerous cooking contests, frequently humiliating rich and famous people who clung to their erroneous views about food. In addition to depicting contests, including many between Yamaoka and his imperious father, the manga features stories about "helping people through food" (Hamada 2014). A drawn-out courtship between Yamaoka and Kurita Yūko results in marriage, children, and the consequent mellowing of Yamaoka's personality. Though it begins to lessen somewhat as time passes, Yamaoka's antagonism toward his father persists throughout the series.

Yamaoka's and Kaibara's (and author, Kariya's) condemnation of the pretensions and fallacies in the food world has at times turned to a critique of Japan's agricultural practices, food culture, and even society as a whole. From early on, a number of stories have focused on environmental issues and food safety. Almost an entire volume (101) on this theme explained chemical food additives, pesticides, and the problems created by the industrialization of food. Volumes 104 and 105 treated "food and environmental problems" (Kariya and Hanasaki 2010a, 2010b). Kariya is no stranger to controversy. He has been censured before about his sometimes mistaken advice and strong biases.[8] Current events frequently find their way into his narratives. In 1993, when Japan suffered a poor rice harvest and was obliged to import rice from Thailand, *Oishinbo* confronted the culinary prejudice against Thai rice (Kariya and Hanasaki 1995: 5–92). In a piece about trade conflicts with the USA over rice imports, Kariya made a case for why rice was so important to the Japanese, yet he still condemned the use of pesticides among Japan's rice farmers (Kariya and Hanasaki 1992: 180–202).

Given his continuous engagement with social and political issues, it was natural for Kariya to take on 3.11. His first effort was a series of stories titled, *The disaster area: People who don't despair* (*Hisaichi hen: megenai hitobito*) that started publication in *Big Comic Spirits* in September 2011 and was collected into Volume 108 (Kariya and Hanasaki 2012). Two and a half months after the earthquake, Yamaoka and his journalist colleagues get permission to travel to the stricken areas to look in on former contacts from previous reporting trips (Kariya and Hanasaki 2012: 11–12). They react with shock and sorrow as they survey numerous scenes of destruction. Their trip takes them to such places as Tanesashi Kaigan in Aomori to revisit a chef whose restaurant was destroyed by the tsunami, to Omoe in Iwate to check up on a sea vegetable (*kombu* and *wakame*) producer who was starting over, and to Kesennuma north of Sendai, where they watch video of the tsunami taken by a restaurateur's son. They listen to their sources' horrifying stories of the disaster and respond with tears and words of encouragement. Volume 108 makes reference to the Fukushima nuclear accident (Kariya and Hanasaki 2012: 9–10, 71), but the focus is on the terrifying power of nature and the resilience of the survivors affected by the tsunami. Kariya's series about the after-effects of the nuclear disaster, *The Truth about Fukushima*, began publication in 2013, in Number 9 of *Big Comic Spirits*. The first eleven episodes of the series were republished as Volume 110 of *Oishinbo* in September 2013.[9] The last thirteen appeared in Volume 111 (December 2014).

Insofar as *Oishinbo* is a food manga, the journeys that the newspapermen and women make through Fukushima center on the region's famous foods, from seafood to rice and vegetables. However, while the journalists sample local cuisine, *The Truth about Fukushima* concentrates more on food production than preparation or consumption, topics that dominate most *ryōri manga* series. Regional food is deployed throughout this story to evoke nostalgia and despair over the loss of the land and its bounty as a result of the nuclear accident. For example, during a meal served by an evacuee who had run a farmhouse restaurant in Iitate, the mood darkens when the diners reflect on the fact that many of these delicious flavors made with ingredients salted away before the accident will be harder to prepare because of what is assumed will be a long period of environmental contamination. Even the steely Kaibara Yūzan sheds a tear, overcome by the thought that it would be more than ten years before these dishes could be made again with local ingredients (Kariya and Hanasaki 2013: 186).[10]

## The itinerary: *The Truth about Fukushima* as documentary

Although research in the manga is carried out by fictional characters and the content of the interviews is likely edited, Kariya noted in his blog, "The subtitle of the current *Oishinbo* is *The Truth about Fukushima* (*Fukushima no shinjitsu*). I wrote nothing but the truth" (Kariya 2014). His blog entry suggests that he intended his observations to be read as fact, as opposed to fiction. Indeed most, if not all, the people in the manga who consent to be interviewed are actual people and appear under their real names.[11]

Because of Kariya's focus on the 'truth,' it seems reasonable to assume that the timeline of the plot follows the timeline of Kariya's research trips to the prefecture. The first episode of the story is set in October of 2011. Yamaoka and colleagues request permission to report on Fukushima after the nuclear accident because "we can't clearly grasp (*tsukamu*) the condition of Fukushima." Yamaoka explains, "We want to help from the bottom of our hearts, but in order to do so, it is necessary to understand the truth about Fukushima" (Kariya and Hanasaki 2013: 8).[12] 'Grasping' is a curious, perhaps ironic metaphor. As Kariya notes in an interview, "The greatest [damage from 3.11] is from radiation. You can't see it and its effect isn't immediate. But the fact that you can't see it is absolutely terrifying" (Baba 2014). 'Grasping' the truth about Fukushima may be as elusive an endeavor as 'seeing' invisible radiation.

Nevertheless, in order to get a handle on the situation for themselves, Yamaoka and colleagues from the *Tōzai Shimbun* newspaper join with journalists from their rival publication, *Teitō Shimbun*, whose food consultant is Yamaoka's father, Kaibara Yūzan, and zigzag through Fukushima Prefecture in ten trips over the course of two years. Their stops include Haragama and Iitate in Minamisōma, Iwaki, Sōma, Kitakata, Kodaka, Funehiki, Iinomachi, Nihonmatsu, Oguni, Date City, Furudono, Tomioka, Aizu Wakamatsu and the capital, Fukushima City. They also visit the Fukushima Daiichi Nuclear Power Plant. Along with the plant, Tomioka was the only town on their itinerary that was completely within the restricted zone at the time the trips were made. The journalists also fly to Hokkaido to interview a cattle rancher who has relocated there from Fukushima and visit evacuees in Saitama prefecture, adjacent to Tokyo.

Fukushima prefecture is divided vertically into three parts: Hamadōri, the area closest to the coast, Nakadōri, the middle third, and Aizu, the westernmost third. On their first trip, in mid-November 2011, the group stops in Fukushima City (in Nakadōri) and from there travels to Matsukawaura in Sōma on the coast. There they inspect the tsunami damage to the fishing industry infrastructure (Kariya and Hanasaki 2013: 42). Further down the coast, in Iwaki, they interview fishermen who explain that they once made a good living catching abalone and sea urchin but because these creatures eat seaweed, which has been contaminated by radioactive materials released into the ocean, they can no longer sell them (Kariya and Hanasaki 2013: 69).

The group passes through Fukushima city and heads for Kitakata, in northern Aizu, to eat the local specialty, soba noodles. They then double back to Funehiki in Tamura City, located in the middle third of Fukushima, to report on *egoma* (wild sesame), an herb in the same family as *shisō* (perilla) that is grown for its oil and as an herb to flavor local dishes. They go on to cover the 'morning market' (*asaichi*) in Haragama, in Sōma City, in the Hamadōri, or coastal region. Part of the area is within the 20 km evacuation zone that was established by the government on March 12, 2011, so most of the produce at the market comes from elsewhere. This first trip acquaints the group and the manga's readers with the nature of the physical damage caused by the tsunami, but also the unseen damage caused by the release of radioactive waste into the ocean. As in many other episodes of *Oishinbo*, the narrative includes descriptions of local foods and cooking. In this case, descriptions alternate with the characters' responses of despair to scenes of devastation.

Their second tour to Fukushima begins in May 2012 with a return to Aizu to observe the rice-planting. They go to see a farmer who, before the group began visiting Fukushima, had come to Tokyo to talk to them about how 'damage caused by rumors' had cut into his sales. The group enjoys a feast of local dishes (*furusato ryōri*) in Kitakata. They then observe volunteers rake out the weirs that channel water into the rice fields, an annual traditional chore performed voluntarily by the community (Kariya and Hanasaki 2013: 129–38). In Yamatomachi, they look in on an organic farmer, who explains that although her soybeans only registered 3.25 Becquerels[13] per kilogram, far below the legal limit of 100 per kilogram,[14] no one would buy them, so she had to use them for fertilizer for her rice fields (Kariya and Hanasaki 2013: 143). She describes the difficulty selling her rice. The locals fête the visiting journalists with a meal of such local dishes as braised carp. In spite of their precarious situation, in this episode and numerous others, the victims of the nuclear accident pull out all the stops to share their food and culture with the visitors. In so doing, they present themselves as culinary tradition bearers, something more than 'victims' of the accident.

The group travels to Iitate to the west of Minamisōma in the coastal region and interviews a farmer who has adapted to post-accident circumstances by growing vegetables in hothouses (Kariya and Hanasaki 2013: 157–65). They come upon a radiation monitoring post, which registers a rate of 3.173 μSv (microsieverts)[15] per hour, high enough to prompt them all to don face masks. They follow on to Iinomachi in the north of the middle third of the prefecture to sample the cooking of Sasaki Chieko, the restaurateur noted above, who is staying there after having been evacuated from her home in Iitate. Next they visit Kodaka in Minamisōma, which has been redesignated as a "zone in preparation for having the evacuation order lifted" (Kyōdō News, March 23, 2012, quoted in Anon 2012). There they observe measures taken by organic farmers to prevent the uptake of cesium in the rice crop, which include adding zeolite and potassium to the soil (Kariya and Hanasaki 2013: 196–200).

The group returns to Tokyo but sets out almost immediately again on their third tour in June. They head for Nihonmatsu in the middle third of the prefecture and meet with representatives of a non-profit organization promoting the 'organic village,' Fukushima Tōwa. Scientists consulting with the group on how to eliminate radiation from the soil explain their experiments (Kariya and Hanasaki 2013: 210–25). In spite of their success in dramatically reducing levels of radioactive substances in rice, these farmers, too, have not been able to sell because of damaging 'unfounded rumors' (*fūhyō higai*) (Kariya and Hanasaki 2013: 221). The journalists also meet with scientists and explore experimental fields in Date City. One senses a poignancy in the manga's presentation: despite the brave efforts of local people to return to farming and produce food for the nation, consumers' fear, caused by lack of trust in the government's safety standards, has made it difficult to find a market for their crops.

The journalists visit Oguni, part of Date City, where they learn about the local situation from members of the Association to Recover Beautiful Oguni from Radioactivity, including two Fukushima University professors who are studying methods of decontamination. These professors explain that the lack of a map illustrating areas of contamination, such as the one created in Belarus after the Chernobyl disaster, makes it difficult to track the success of decontamination efforts.

The group hears that Oguni was designated a Specific Spot Recommended for Evacuation, and households located within this area receive monthly compensation. The fact that not every household was so designated has created strife and lead to a collapse of the community (*kyōdōtai*): even the festivals aren't being held (Kariya and Hanasaki 2014: 35). Even with the efforts of the association, decontamination takes time. One of the interviewees relates that the younger generation is leaving and the elementary school has had to merge classes. Oguni is facing the danger of extinction (Kariya and Hanasaki 2014: 51).[16]

To wrap up their third tour, the group meets with Professor Fujimoto Noritsugu, a professor in the Faculty of Symbiotic Systems Science at Fukushima University in Fukushima City. Professor Fujimoto describes the high levels of radiation that he has discovered while trying to decontaminate his property. He notes that when he brought his results to the city government, he was told that nothing could be done. According to Fujimoto, because Fukushima Prefecture lacks the revenue from taxes produced by local industry, it must rely on and obey the central government, which refuses to designate these areas within Fukushima City as hot spots targeted for evacuation (Kariya and Hanasaki 2014: 55–56). Professor Fujimoto suggests moving the entire city of Fukushima to a 'New Fukushima City' in a safer area near Aizu Wakamatsu.

Toward the end of June 2012, the crew of journalists embark on their fourth trip to Fukushima. An elderly man in Kitakata (in Aizu) who is famous as a gatherer of wild mountain vegetables (*sansai*) leads them to the forest and points out numerous wild plants eaten in the region. After a feast featuring the wild greens that the old man had gathered, Kaibara Yūzan chides the journalists for their hesitation to eat them. No doubt they were worrying about the radioactive substances that they were ingesting along with the lovingly gathered greens (Kariya and Hanasaki 2014: 88).

The group returns to Fukushima University to interview Marina Kuznetsova, an economics professor from Russia, who described Fukushima as a battleground in a "small-scale nuclear war" (Kariya and Hanasaki 2014: 90). Compared to the training on what to do during a nuclear emergency that she received growing up in the Soviet Union, the Japanese were woefully unprepared. And though Professor Kuznetsova has decided to remain in Fukushima, she takes every precaution to avoid exposure to radioactivity. When she urges her students to be more careful, however, she senses that they don't want to hear it (Kariya and Hanasaki 2014: 98). Professor Kuznetsova's comment exemplifies one problem that Kariya may be trying to expose: perhaps because radiation is invisible, people want to wish away the thought of any potential danger away by ignoring it.

Another professor in the Faculty of Symbiotic Systems Science at the university, Gotō Shinobu, informs them about nuclear education in Japan and the ways that it downplays the risks of nuclear power. Professor Gotō describes the new textbook that he and his colleagues are preparing, one that also covers the ethical issues involved in nuclear energy. The professor elaborates his difficulties getting schools to adopt his revised textbook because the Ministry of Education, Culture, Sports, Science and Technology (MEXT) has requested that teachers follow the official MEXT text. MEXT has proscribed discussing the pros and cons of nuclear energy in class (Kariya and Hanasaki 2014: 124). This interview with Professor Gotō strengthens Kariya's argument that open discussion about the nuclear accident is being suppressed.

On their brief fifth visit to Fukushima, in late October 2012, the group goes to Kōriyama in the middle of the prefecture. This visit contrasts the earlier tours centered on interviews with farmers and professors. In order to "understand the feelings of the people of Namie," they watch the displaced children of this completely evacuated town about six kilometers from the Fukushima Daiichi plant dance a traditional rice planting ritual dance (Kariya and Hanasaki 2014: 127). As in the food that locals share with the visiting journalists, this performance gives Fukushima residents a chance to express the native culture of their 'hometown,' or *furusato*, a term that appears as a symbol of the lost nature, home and family in discourse about the repercussions of the nuclear accident (Suzuki 2015: 115).

In November 2012, the group embarks on their sixth Fukushima research tour, which takes them to Furudono on the southern end of Nakadōri, in the middle third of the prefecture. Ringed by mountains, Furudono did not suffer the same amount of radiation as other parts of the prefecture, but even their produce does not completely escape radioactivity. Thanks to the introduction of Furudono's mayor, the group is invited on a guided tour of Tomioka, a town close to Fukushima Daiichi that lies within a restricted area on the coast. Leaving the women behind in Furudono because of Tomioka's high radiation readings, the men suit up in protective gear for their visit. One of the town officials notes that Naraha, the town next to Tomioka, was redesignated in August 2012 as a zone in which preparations are being made to have evacuees return, in spite of the fact that infrastructure has not been restored.[17] One of their guides suggests that by encouraging earlier resettlement, the government was seeking to reduce the cost of compensation funds for evacuees (Kariya and Hanasaki 2014: 160).[18]

On their way out of town, the journalists are shaken when several cows and bulls that have turned wild, having been abandoned after the disaster, charge their van. This episode parallels media reports about the reversion of abandoned domestic animals to a feral state. The group heads north to Sōma to investigate the harvest of the experimental rice paddies. They learn that the results of 20 Becquerels per kilogram should have been low enough to allow the farmers to grow rice and sell it. However, the fields are located in a zone in which radiation levels are too high to permit residents to stay overnight. Without staying over, it would be difficult to have adequate access to the fields in order to manage irrigation (Kariya and Hanasaki 2014: 176).

Next, the group returns to Sōma's port of Haragama to update their information on the condition of the fishing industry. New boats, bought with the support of government funds, crowd the harbor. The fishermen are testing their catch for radioactivity. Though the government set an upper limit of 100 Becquerels per kilogram, one man commented that consumers wouldn't buy the fish unless it registered lower than 10 Becquerels per kilogram (Kariya and Hanasaki 2014: 182). The journalists visit the temporary housing for evacuees from Iitate, which they criticize as inadequate, then proceed to Nihonmatsu to investigate the results of another experimental farm where zeolite and potassium are added to the soil to lower radioactivity levels. Returning briefly to Tokyo, the group sets out again for Date City in December to attend a conference announcing the results of the experimental rice harvest. This episode (No. 20) consists of numerous panels of talking heads, charts, and photographs digitized as illustrations.[19] Yūko and Kaibara praise one professor's argument about the difficulty of solving the problem of damage caused by rumors (*fūhyō higai*) (Kariya and Hanasaki 2014: 217), an issue that threads through the narrative.

The journalists' eighth trip to the prefecture in April 2013 trip might be considered the climax of their research itinerary, in that they finally get permission to enter the Fukushima Daiichi Nuclear Power Plant itself on a guided tour. A small group of the newspapermen participate in this tour, stopping first at J-Village, formerly a soccer training facility that has been repurposed to serve as a base camp for nuclear workers. They note the bulletin boards covered with letters of support from people throughout the country.

For most of the nuclear plant tour the journalists remain on the bus, although they do observe the command center in the plant's "Earthquake Proof Building." On the tour, they must surrender their own cameras and are only permitted to use the plant's. Reporting to their editors on their return to Tokyo, they explain that, for security reasons, TEPCO censored almost every picture that they took. Summarizing their experience, Kaibara Yūzan proclaimed, "My first impression was that the degree of destruction is far more than I had imagined. The procedures to deal with it are all just stop-gap measures" (Kariya and Hanasaki 2014: 236).

Back in Tokyo immediately following this visit, Yamaoka complains of extreme fatigue and suffers an unusually severe nosebleed that sends him to the doctor. The doctor reassures him that the amount of radiation he might have received touring Fukushima Daiichi was not enough to cause a nosebleed (Kariya and Hanasaki 2014: 241). However, the group's next interviewees, Idogawa Katsutaka, former mayor of Futaba, a city next to the plant, and Dr. Matsui Eisuke, from the Gifu Environmental Medical Research Institute, are not at all surprised by the nosebleed. Idogawa admitted to having had numerous unexplained nosebleeds himself: "In Fukushima, there are a lot of people with the same symptoms. They just don't talk about it" (Kariya and Hanasaki 2014: 212).[20]

Yamaoka's nosebleed, illustrated in close up, became the most visible target of attacks on Kariya: in the controversy that unfolded beginning in May 2014, the term 'depiction of the nosebleed' (*hanaji byōsha*) appeared frequently in the press.[21] Because of the debate regarding the lack of scientific evidence linking low-level radiation with nosebleeds, Idogawa's statement quoted above was even revised when the *Oishinbo tankōbon* volume was published in December 2014. The book version leaves out the phrase "In Fukushima" and substitutes "Among people I know" (Kariya and Hanasaki 2014: 244). Since the episode was first published in *Big Comic Spirits*, former Mayor Idogawa has spoken out about the nosebleed issue in response to criticism of the manga, even posting a picture of himself with bloody tissues on his Facebook page (Iwakami 2014).[22] During their interview with him in the manga, a few other members of the journalist crew admit to having experienced fatigue and nosebleeds as well. Dr. Matsui explains the medical cause to the journalists. Even before his interview with Kariya and the fictional characters that represent the author, Dr. Matsui had been lecturing on why nosebleeds could result from low levels of radiation exposure (e.g., Tōyama and Okumatsu 2012). Scientist Ochiai Eiichirō wrote, "No scientifically definitive proof has been found for the cause-effect relationship in the case of nose bleeding. No serious studies have been conducted on this issue" (Ochiai 2014). In other words, because serious studies have not been carried out, one cannot discount the possibility that there *could be* a link between the two. Ochiai suggests that the controversy reveals "the desperation of the government and the industry to suppress the facts concerning the danger of radiation" (Ochiai 2014). Not only does the government want to suppress the facts, it also appears to want to repress any frank discussion of the accident's influence on health, including the sharing of personal experiences with regard to nosebleeds and other physical symptoms.

In the nosebleed episode, Idogawa describes how the government's confusing and inadequate information about developments at the nuclear power plant after the tsunami resulted in many people receiving high levels of radiation as they tried to leave the area (Kariya and Hanasaki 2014: 251). He advises people to get out of Fukushima (2014: 252). After the group's visit to evacuees' quarters in a public school in Saitama, Kaibara fumes that TEPCO and the government are not taking any responsibility for "stealing the peaceful lives" of the displaced (Kariya and Hanasaki 2014: 257). The group returns to Fukushima University (their ninth visit to the prefecture) to talk with Professor Arakida Takeru, whose assertion that it was likely impossible to sufficiently decontaminate the affected areas of Fukushima so that people could live there was cited in the press as constituting a kind of "damage through rumor." Arakida points out that people have been forced to accept an increase in the level of acceptable yearly radiation, from one millisievert a year to twenty (Kariya and Hanasaki 2014: 262). Decontamination, he asserts, is a dangerous and interminable job (2014: 264).

The last two episodes of *The Truth about Fukushima* bring the story to a more hopeful close. The journalists fly to Hokkaido to report on a young cattle rancher from Iitate who had started a business in Fukushima shortly before the accident. After studying organic methods in New Zealand, he decided to relocate to Hokkaido so that he could safely produce grass-fed beef. Inspired by the positive outlook of this young family, two *Oishinbo* characters, photographer Takikawa Tatsuko and writer Nakaguchi Shinsuke, who had been hesitating to tie the knot out of fear of a radioactive future, announce that they will marry (Kariya and Hanasaki 2014: 275).

The journalists end their Fukushima mission in Aizu, where they celebrate with a feast reconstructed from Edo period (1600–1867) documents, and prepared by a food historian who has researched banquet menus that were served in the Aizu domain to the shogun's travelling inspectors. Such a menu seems fitting for journalists who have traveled the prefecture of Fukushima to inspect and report on local people struggling to survive amid elevated levels of radioactivity.

## Irradiated journeys

The busy itinerary described above attests to the intensity and breadth of Kariya's reporting. Readers learn a great deal from interviews with food producers and scientists about the challenges that Fukushima faces. Front and center in *The Truth about Fukushima* as polemic are the frequent references to levels of radioactivity that reflect the new reality for many Japanese living in and around Fukushima. The many radiation readings presented in the story underscore Kariya's anti-nuclear message. At the start of the first trip, as radiation readings rise when they near Fukushima City, a character named Nanba Daisuke,[23] a national politics writer for *Tōzai Shimbun*, takes a radiation reading and is shocked to learn that it is almost three times as high as the safe upper limit allowed per year, as determined by the International Commission on Radiological Protection (ICRP 2012: 32). He and Deputy Section Chief Fukui immediately put on face masks. For most of the rest of the story they do not remove them. However, only rarely do the other members of the team wear masks. Yamaoka calls Nanba and Fukui cowards, but Yamaoka's wife Yūko sticks up for them, reminding Yamaoka, "We still don't understand the effects of low-level radiation" (Kariya and Hanasaki 2013: 33).

A fairly recent addition to *Oishinbo*'s cast of characters, Nanba is a transplant from the newspaper's Osaka office. He speaks in Osaka dialect, which pegs him as 'other.' Fukui, a core member of the cast from the very first episodes, is often the butt of jokes for his short temper and his emotionality. While his outbursts usually provoke laughter, in *The Truth about Fukushima* he stands out for his tendency to break down in tears. By designating Nanba and Fukui, characters who provide some comic relief in the manga, as the most obviously radiophobic[24] of the journalists, Kariya may be seeking to avoid generating undue anxiety among people who have no other recourse but to live in a potentially hazardous environment.[25] Other members of the group carry Geiger counters as well, but it is Nanba who frequently announces elevated readings.

The issue of the deleterious effects of contamination surfaces constantly in encounters with locals. For example, while the rice farmer in Nihonmatsu is pleased with the results of his experiment in decreasing the radioactivity levels in the crop, he admits that "every time he enters the field," he feels a great deal of fear. "No one tells us about the extent of the influence of radioactivity that we receive on our skin, through open cuts, or breathing the air. But one cannot farm without touching the soil" (Kariya and Hanasaki 2014: 197).

Fear of consuming contaminated food permeates the narrative. In May 2012, when the journalists sample local cuisine in Aizu, Kaibara's perpetually set jaw almost softens into a smile as he asks his hosts to make sure to hand down to future generations the delicious homestyle (*furusato*) cuisine that he has been served. One farmer responds, "We'd like to, but with the nuclear power plant…" (Kariya and Hanasaki 2013: 126). At this feast and every meal thereafter, the worry that radioactive contamination will render these particular dishes difficult to prepare ever again, at least with local ingredients, hangs like a pall over the party.

Oishinbo's Fukushima elegy 189

During a feast of local foods in Kitakata, someone asks about the radiation level of the carp that is served. Yamaoka announces that he trusts what the people in Fukushima serve him, but that the others can make their own decisions regarding whether or not to consume food that has not been tested (Kariya and Hanasaki 2013: 148). This exchange reproduces the real-life dilemma faced by the Japanese who are left to judge for themselves the safety of a particular food (Fackler 2012). The episode describing the group's visit to Furudono includes illustrations of women preparing food and the characters' verbal descriptions of their gustatory experience as in all the feast scenes. What distinguishes this food sequence from innumerable others in over thirty years of *Oishinbo*'s serialization is that following the feast, officials from the town hall announce the radiation levels of the foods that they have eaten. In the post-3.11 world, in addition to cultural context, taste, and the cooks' love and spirit of hospitality, one must also take into account a food's potential to cause harm due to radioactivity.

**Fukushima elegy: tempering polemic with the rhetoric of loss**

While polemic perhaps leaves the strongest aftertaste in *The Truth about Fukushima*, Kariya also turns to elegy to season his message. All the characters in *The Truth about Fukushima* express their dismay over the nuclear accident and the tragedies, large and small, that it has engendered. In his declarations, Kaibara Yūzan often combines figurative and elegaic language with polemic. In reference to Minister of Economy, Trade and Industry, Hachirō Yoshio, whose remark that Minamisōma was like a city of death earned him opprobrium in the media, Kaibara exclaims, "[It's the] people who don't want to tell the truth, the people who want be vague and deceive, and mass media who help to add the final coat of paint to cover up these lies" (Kariya and Hanasaki 2013: 205).[26] In another panel, a stern-faced Kaibara, depicted against a white background ringed with dark saturated line work, declares: "How many precious things have we lost? Abundance, joy, radiance (*kagayaki*), happiness—we've completely lost things that we must not lose" (Kariya and Hanasaki 2013: 187).

Kariya often uses rhetorical questions to tacitly blame the nuclear accident (and those responsible for it) for the huge losses in Fukushima. For example, Kaibara poses such a question in his response to Yamaoka's comment about having to choose the lesser of two evils, agricultural chemicals or radiation contamination, "Who imagined a Japan like this?" He adds, "We cannot take one step toward the future unless we grasp this intensely heart-breaking reality, and drive it in so that it penetrates our flesh and bones" (Kariya and Hanasaki 2013: 146).

In one emotional outburst that may allude to the rhetoric surrounding the disaster, *Ganbare Nippon* or, alternatively, *Ganbarō Nippon*, (Let's hang in there together, Japan!) Deputy Section Chief Fukui exclaims, "Who put the village of Iitate into this state? Who can tell the people of Iitate, who have had their hopes and reasons for living stolen from them, to 'hang in there' (*ganbare*)?" (Kariya and Hanasaki 2013: 175). Wandering the deserted streets of Kodaka in

Minamisōma, Fukui cries, "Who created this town of death?" (Kariya and Hanasaki 2013: 206).

Repetition of phrases and images reinforce the impact of the 'truth' recounted in *The Truth about Fukushima*. In addition to the verb *tsukamu* (grasp), one phrase that appears repeatedly, especially at the beginning of the story, is "the truth/reality of Fukushima" (*Fukushima no shinjitsu*) and its variation, "The essence of Fukushima," (*Fukushima no honshitsu*). From the start of the journalists' investigation to grasp the truth, radioactive particles are identified as the source of the "reality of Fukushima's misery" (Kariya and Hanasaki 2013: 53). Kaibara remarks, "We have only begun to take the first steps toward understanding the truth about Fukushima. By investigating the suffering that Fukushima is now enduring, we will be able to firmly grasp the reality of Fukushima" (Kariya and Hanasaki 2013: 54). Later, he comments,

> This field too, was showered in radioactive particles as a result of the wind direction. My hair stands on end when I think that because of the wind direction, this lush landscape is lost. A hair's breadth from danger—this is the truth of Fukushima.
>
> (Kariya and Hanasaki 2013: 88)

When Kaibara equates the mandating of Minamisōma as an evacuation zone (as of spring 2011) to a loss of national territory, another character says, "This is one aspect of the truth about Fukushima" (Kariya and Hanasaki 2013: 108).[27]

The manga not only uses repetition to underscore its message through rhetoric, but also through visual images. One visual technique that enhances the impact of Fukushima's unfortunate reality is the 'visual chorus' of sad facial expressions reacting to a distressing report or another character's emotional verbal response. In the scene cited above, in which Deputy Chief Fukui exclaims, "Who put the village of Iitate into this state?," the bottom tier of the page features two panels of close-ups of Kaibara, Yamaoka, and colleagues all wearing face masks and distressed expressions (Kariya and Hanasaki 2013: 175). A 'visual chorus' echoes Kaibara's speech about all that Fukushima has lost. Kaibara's comment that even if levels of radioactivity have been decreased to zero, the environment in which the rice farmers live is not entirely safe elicits a response from the journalists, five of whom are depicted in two panels in the middle tier, with downcast expressions (Kariya and Hanasaki 2013: 225). Some of the panels featuring these visual representations of empathy and sadness follow statements made by one of the Fukushima residents, who wear a troubled expression. A downcast Mr. Takano, a middleman for rice producers in Oguni, comments, "If only it hadn't snowed..." on March 15, 2011, the day that the fourth reactor blew up and showered radioactive particles onto Oguni. The short middle tier below his close-up illustration features six journalists sadly looking down (Kariya and Hanasaki 2013: 40). The fictional characters thus absorb and reflect the tragedy of the entire situation, and express emotions that those interviewed do not usually reveal to their interlocutors. In this way, Kariya respects his informants' privacy, but he also frames their statements within his own critical and emotional message.

In addition to the 'choruses' of sad faces, the landscape itself offers up elegiac tableaux. While black-and-white computer-generated photo-realistic illustrations may not evoke the emotions in a way that a painting or a photograph can, the manga's verbal framing of these images calls attention to their emotional power. Yūko notices a bunch of flowers and a small 'one-cup' bottle of sake by the side of the road, just before a roadblock at a restricted entry zone. Yamaoka surmises that someone's grave must be in the restricted zone, or perhaps someone is remembering a loved one lost on 3.11. Deputy Section Chief Fukui comments, "The fact that the flowers are beautiful makes it even sadder," and the owner of the *Weekly Times* (*Shūkan Taimuzu*) adds, "This too is the reality of Fukushima" (Kariya and Hanasaki 2013: 109).

## The perfect peach: reconciliation and hope

*The Truth about Fukushima* should be considered, by and large, as a documentary manga: the people interviewed even appear under their real names, and Kariya, through his characters, claims to speak the 'truth.' However, woven into the manga's copious amounts of scientific data and accounts of the struggles of local farmers and fishermen is a story about the restoration of ties between the manga's estranged father and son protagonists, Kaibara and Yamaoka. This reconciliation might suggest a glimmer of hope in the Fukushima story, a possibility for Fukushima's revitalization as well.

Yamaoka never forgave his father for his mother's death: he stubbornly held to the belief that it was Kaibara Yūzan's perfectionism that made her ill. After she died, Yamaoka left home and completely cut ties with Kaibara, smashing his father's artworks as a parting gesture. He always publicly disparaged his father throughout the series. Yamaoka may not recognize it, but Kaibara's participation in culinary contests with his son throughout the series evidences a desire to train Yamaoka in the 'way' of cuisine, in the manner of Japanese practitioners of traditional performing and martial arts, for example, who pass on their knowledge to their heirs.

Kaibara's command to his son to learn about his roots is linked to the reconciliation. Calling his son by his first name, he says, "Shirō, it's about time that you learn where you came from. Besides learning the truth about Fukushima, you will learn about your roots. Do you have the courage to know your roots?" (Kariya and Hanasaki 2013: 28).

Kaibara commands such great authority that all honor his request to visit a place that might not otherwise have been included on the itinerary. At the end of the penultimate episode of Vol. 110, the group travels to Ryōzen Shrine in Date City. Yamaoka remarks, "Don't tell me that this is where my roots are!" Kaibara retorts, "No, it's where *my* roots are." (Kariya and Hanasaki 2013: 228).

Kaibara's story about his roots involves a perfect peach. The story arc breaks away from documentary to present a flashback about Kaibara's past. Coming at the beginning of Vol. 111, it provides a diversion from the dismal reports about Fukushima and rewards *Oishinbo*'s loyal readers with detailed background information on one of the manga's most important and iconic characters. At the Ryōzen Shrine in Date City, Kaibara tells Yamaoka and Yūko about how he went into retreat there as a young art student, in order to contemplate the meaning of art.

It was during this retreat that Kaibara met the girl who was to become his wife, Yamaoka Toshiko. She offered him a perfect peach as he sketched in the orchard.

Toshiko visited him at his room at the shrine and offered him another peach on a white plate crafted by an award-winning ceramicist who was a friend of her father's. Observing the peach on the plate, Kaibara suddenly became aware of the connection between a human being's aesthetic sense and the beauty of nature. Eating this perfect peach, he had an epiphany and realized his path: gastronomy and ceramics. In one panel, the young artist, standing on his knees, dramatically arches backwards. The dynamic page layout includes a variety of close-up and angled viewpoints and a slanted gutter[28] in the middle tier, a rare technique in this manga's fairly straightforward visual tyle (Kariya and Hanasaki 2014: 18).

On the shrine steps, Kaibara gives his son the white plate that was a cherished gift from his wife. In tears, Yamaoka clutches it to his chest. Yūko tells him, "Your father and mother were deeply in love … there's no reason any more for you to hate him" (Kariya and Hanasaki 2014: 24).

In the following episode, a visit to a peach orchard in nearby Oguni unites past and present. The peach farmer sings a local Bon festival folk song about the beauties of his hometown, moving even Yamaoka to tears. The lyrics, "I miss Oguni (village), I long for Oguni," appear in a speech bubble over a flashback image of Kaibara meeting Yamaoka's mother under a peach tree. This scene includes the rare sight of a weeping Yamaoka next to Yūko smiling through her tears. This visual arrangement yokes the tragedy narrated by the story as documentary with Yamaoka's personal tragedy of losing his mother at a young age. The white plate functions as a memento of the mother that Yamaoka lost years before. Yamaoka's grief over his mother's passing evokes and heightens the grief over the truth about Fukushima, both the farmers' and fishermen's loss of livelihood, and the inaccessibility of the land as mother—home and source of sustenance.

In the final episode, the father and son reconciliation narrative fuses even more with the characters' (and author's) mission to tell the truth about Fukushima. The large middle tier of the page is comprised of close-ups of Yamaoka and Kaibara facing each another. Kaibara remarks, "We are outsiders, but we must give our opinions about whether or not it's safe to live in Fukushima." Yamaoka adds, "If we didn't give our opinions, it would be like lying to the people of Fukushima, who are suffering because of the irresponsible way in which TEPCO and the country have dealt with them" (Kariya and Hanasaki 2014: 274).

Through the discovery of his roots, Yamaoka comes to understand that the tragedy of Fukushima has an impact on him and on all Japanese. At the final banquet in Aizu Yamaoka appeals to his father to affirm his newfound understanding.

Regarding what you said about my roots being in Fukushima, if the problem of the nuclear accident isn't settled and gets worse, Fukushima will be ruined. The damage won't be limited to Fukushima. All of Japan will be destroyed. Fukushima's future is Japan's future.

(Kariya and Hanasaki 2014: 286)

Pictured in a montage in the lower right hand corner of a map of Japan with the site of the Fukushima Daiichi Nuclear Power Plant marked, Yamaoka states, "The nuclear accident has made me realize how important Japan is. Protecting Japan means protecting Fukushima. If that's the case, my roots are in Fukushima" (Kariya and Hanasaki 2014: 286–87). In the top panel on page 290, Kaibara, Yūko, and Yamaoka appear in the foreground gazing out at a panorama of the mountains. Kaibara comments, "I'm grateful for Fukushima. It's the land where I met my irreplaceable wife and I set out on my new life." Yamaoka adds, "I'm grateful because it taught me a way to start living again with my father" (2014: 291). Kariya uses this story about his Kaibara and Yamaoka to intensify the spotlight on Fukushima. In reality, the parties allegedly responsible for Fukushima's contamination would likely rather divert attention away from its problems.

## Conclusion

How was it that a food manga created such a stir in the media and among government officials? In his book responding to the controversy, Kariya identified the two reasons for the uproar as: (1) the lack of evidence connecting nosebleeds to low-level radiation exposure; and (2) the charge of "damage-causing false rumor" that Fukushima was dangerous (Kariya 2015: 20). Some factions of the Japanese media and government may have seized upon Kariya's text as a pretext to silence dissent to of the official Fukushima policy. One conservative writer pointed out Kariya Tetsu's progressive views and condemned the manga as "ludicrous" and "full of misleading information" (Ishii 2014: 293). It is important to remember, however, that a good deal of anti-Kariya rhetoric arose on social media sites and the comments sections of articles on the Internet, some of it produced by Fukushima residents themselves. As with responses to the 3.11 disaster as a whole, reactions to *The Truth about Fukushima* tended to correlate with the writer's politics. As Richard Samuels wrote in *3.11: Disaster and Change in Japan*, "however complex it was, 3.11 changed few minds within Japan's chattering classes" (2013: xi).

Can a manga story change minds? The fact that the issue of *Big Comic Spirits* that contained the controversial episode sold out immediately indicates that, at least, *Oishinbo* got Japanese talking about the Fukushima problem, a problem that some might have hoped would "recede from public memory" (Samuels 2013: xi). It is difficult to say whether Kariya's particular approach, combining elegy, documentary, and polemic served his message or hampered it in any event. The complexities inherent in the *The Truth about Fukushima*'s hybrid style cannot compare to the complexities of the reality that the manga aims to depict.

## Notes

1 Gavan McCormack notes that much of this money was *mis*appropriated, and was even being used to subsidize more nuclear research (2013).
2 Concerned that the spread of inaccurate information on the Internet would raise the anxiety level of Japanese citizens, the Ministry of Internal Affairs and Communication even requested groups related to the telecommunications business to take "appropriate action." This request was criticized, as restricting communication would likely raise anxiety (Matsuda 2011). Kariya insists that his work is not untrue and thus does not aid in the spread of damaging false rumors: he claims that he was only reporting what he had experienced first-hand (Kariya 2015: 66–72).
3 The report on Fukushima is posted on their website, at: www.unscear.org/unscear/en/fukushima.html (accessed April 29, 2016). The Fukushima Prefecture's letter to the publisher is available on their website, at: www.pref.fukushima.lg.jp/sec/01010d/20140512.html (accessed April 29, 2016).
4 For example, "*Oishinbo* sōdō." Takajin no soko made itte iinkai. (The Commotion over *Oishinbo*. The 'Are you really going to say that?' Committee).
5 *Oishinbo* has continued to be published in *Big Comic Spirits* (*BCS*), where it stands out to some degree from the magazine's other serialized *manga*. Catering to its intended audience, *BCS* opens with a few glossy color pages of young women, cutely dressed or undressing provocatively. In the black and white newsprint pages that follow, *BCS* presents manga on a variety of themes and illustrated in a variety of styles. The stories serialized in No. 24, for example, included a work about a master swordsman and his love for his cat (*Tōgorō to Marosuke*), another about an illegal moneylender (*Yamikin Ushijima-kun*), and another called *Boku wa kōhī ga nomenai* (I can't drink coffee) about two supermarket employees. Unlike the main characters of *Oishinbo*, who have aged over the life of the manga, most of the protagonists in the other concurrent series are in their teens or twenties and reflect the interests of their targeted readership.
6 For example, Kariya Tetsu and Hanasaki Akira, *OISHINBO: JAPANESE CUISINE: A la Carte*, San Francisco, CA: Viz Media LLC, 2009.
7 Yamaoka left home at a young age because of his belief that Kaibara's perfectionism in the realm of food wore his mother out and resulted in her death. Yamaoka dropped his father's last name and began using his mother's maiden name.
8 Some of the controversies, such as *Oishinbo*'s dangerous advice to feed honey to children under one year of age and Kariya's criticism of Microsoft products, are detailed in Journey RP-san, "It's not only nosebleeds! Has the manga *Oishinbo* been strange lately?" ("Hanaji dake ja nai! Manga '*Oishinbo*' ga saikin okashii?") *Naver Matome*. May 31, 2014, at: http://matome.naver.jp/odai/2139878261496915001 (accessed April 26, 2015).
9 *Oishinbo* was one of numerous manga responses to the triple disaster. Some cartoonists created works based on their own experiences of the disaster, and many of them donated the proceeds to disaster relief. As of June 2014, more than thirty works on the Fukushima disaster alone had been published (*NHK World*: 2014). One of the most lauded is Shiragari Kotobuki's fantasy/humor manga, *Manga after 3.11* (*Ano hi kara no manga*), which depicts a world fifty years into the future, when such conveniences of modern life as electricity exist only in the memories of the old (Shiriagari 2011). Yamamoto Osamu, who writes the food manga, *Sobamon*, about an itinerant buckwheat noodle (soba) master, took up the issue of food safety and radiation after the disaster in his series. The manga noted that while no cesium is detected in the buckwheat flour grown in Fukushima, people are reluctant to buy it (*NHK World*: 2014). Yamamoto has also chronicled his own experience living in Fukushima after the disaster in the manga, *Nice weather today, too (Kyō mo ii tenki)* (Yamamoto 2013). Tatsuta Kazuto, who pens the manga, *One F (Ichiefu)*

(Kodansha) bases his stories on his personal experience as a contract employee working at the Fukushima Daiichi plant. Tatsuta Kazuto is a pen-name: he does not want to lose his job. Especially cartoonists taking a documentary approach must tread lightly for fear of stirring up anxiety regarding Fukushima radiation or spreading false and damaging rumors.

10 Perhaps this feeling emerges out of the notion of "*terroir*," the importance of place—for example, soil and climate—in giving foods their particular flavors.
11 While it was not comprehensive, my search of university, municipal, and organizational websites listed as affiliates the people mentioned in the manga under the same names.
12 All translations are my own, unless otherwise indicated.
13 A Becquerel is a unit used to measure the amount of radiation emitted by a radioactive material (Chandler 2011).
14 The upper limit after the accident had been 500 becquerels per kilogram but was reduced to 100 in April 2012.
15 Sieverts (Sv), millisieverts (mSv), and microsieverts (μSv) measure the effect of ionizing radiation on the body.
16 The implication is that the policy to keep people in a place where hot spots are scattered within the municipality has a negative effect on the cohesiveness of the community.
17 The government planned to lift the mandatory evacuation order for Naraha and allow residents to return as early as spring 2015 (Ito 2014).
18 It behoved the government and TEPCO to play down the radiation levels to encourage an early return and delay or reduce compensation payments to people forcefully evacuated (Gill 2013: 222).
19 These digitized photographs/illustrations predominate in the story (and much of the manga series as a whole). Proper attribution is given when newspaper or other images are used.
20 Part of Futaba is very close to the Fukushima Daiichi plant and has been completely evacuated. Areas of the town with readings of 20 mSv or less have been redesignated as zones in preparation to have the evacuation order lifted, but it mostly remains uninhabitable (*World Nuclear News* 2013).
21 For copyright reasons, the nosebleed image could unfortunately not be included here. It is, however, widely available on the Internet; see, for example, McCurry 2014.
22 In the interview, he pointed out that in 2012, representatives of the opposition party, LDP (Liberal Democratic Party) spoke before the Diet about the health policies of the Democratic Party, taking up the issue of complaints of nosebleeds suffered by Fukushima victims (Iwakami 2014).
23 His last name is likely a reference to Nanba (Naniwa), an area of Osaka.
24 Two staff members on the tour who had planned to marry also demonstrate a degree of radiophobia: the accident has made them rethink their plans. Ms. Takikawa comments with a worried expression, "I feel uneasy about whether I can create a home and have children in this situation," that is, after the accident (Kariya and Hanasaki 2013: Vol. 110, 195). Later they are reassured that food from Fukushima is safe, if tested, and feel they can have children (Vol. 110, 223).
25 The act of protecting oneself against radioactivity could be construed as insulting by those who go without, as illustrated in Sono Shion's 2012 film, *Kibō no kuni* (*Land of Hope*.) A similar accusation is made toward Kariya, who has stirred up anxiety.
26 This METI (Ministry of Economy, Trade and Industry) minister was forced to resign after his insensitive remarks and his making light of the radiation threat (Samuels 2013: 15).
27 The evacuation order for parts of Minamisōma was lifted in April 2012 (Kyōdō News 2012).
28 "Gutter" refers to the space between panels in comics terminology.

## References

Anonymous. 2012, "No-Entry zone and planned evacuation zone in Minami Soma to be abolished soon." *Tokyo Progressive*. March 25, at: www.tokyoprogressive.org/en/content/no-entry-zone-and-planned-evacuation-zone-minami-soma-be-abolished-soon (accessed April 19, 2015).

Baba, Kazuya. 2014, "'Genpatsu' Fukushima no shinjitsu—*Oishinbo* sakusha Kariya Tetsu shi ni kiku." *NichiGo Press*. January 13, at: http://nichigopress.jp/interview/【ルポ】原発問題を考える/51415/January 13, (accessed January 31, 2015).

Chandler, David. 2011, "Explained: rad, rem, sieverts, becquerels: A guide to terminology about radiation exposure." *MIT News*. March 8. at: http://newsoffice.mit.edu/2011/explained-radioactivity-0328 (accessed April 19, 2015).

Fackler, Martin. 2012, "Japanese struggle to protect their food supply." *New York Times* January 21, at: www.nytimes.com/2012/01/22/world/asia/wary-japanese-take-food-safety-into-their-own-hands.html (accessed April 19, 2015).

Fukushima Prefecture. 2014, *Shūkan biggu komikku supirittsu 'Oishinbo' ni kansuru honken no taiō in tsuite*. May 12, at: www.pref.fukushima.lg.jp/sec/01010d/20140512.html (accessed May 8, 2015).

Gill, Tom. 2013, "This spoiled soil: Place, people, and community in an irradiated village in Fukushima Prefecture," in Tom Gill, Brigitte Steger, and David H. Slater (eds), *Japan Copes with Calamity: Ethnographies of the Earthquake, Tsunami and Nuclear Disasters of March 2011*. Oxford: Peter Lang, 201–33.

Hamada, Rokurō. 2014, "*Oishinbo* ninki gurume manga ga motarashita kōzai to wa? O*Ishinbo* 30 nen no henkan." *Urepia* May 28, at: http://ure.pia.co.jp/articles/-/23224 (accessed January 26, 2015).

Hori, Arinobu. 2014, "Hanaji to Nihonteki narushishizumu." *Huffington Post* (Japanese). May 19, at: www.huffingtonpost.jp/arinobu-hori/nose-bleed_b_5350040.html (accessed January 31, 2015).

ICRP. 2012, "Report of ICRP task group 84 on initial lessons learned from the nuclear power point accident in Japan vis-à-vis the ICRP system of radiological protection." November 22, at: www.icrp.org/docs/ICRP%20TG84%20Summary%20Report.pdf (accessed January 24, 2015).

Ishii, Takaaki. 2014, "*Oishinbo hanaji dema no jitsugai*." *Gekkan WILL*, July, 292–98.

Ito, Hiroki. 2014, "State to lift evacuation order for Fukushima town next spring." *The Asahi Shimbun*, Web. May 30, at: http://ajw.asahi.com/article/0311disaster/fukushima/AJ201405300028 (accessed April 24, 2015).

Iwakami, Yasumi. 2014, "It's all 'real harm': Former Futaba mayor, Mr. Idogawa Katsutaka criticizes Minister of the Environment Ishihara's statement regarding false, damaging rumors. Iwakami Yasumi's interview with former Futaba mayor, Idogawa Katsutaka" ["Subete ga (jitsugai): Zen Futabachōcho, Idogawa Katsutaka shi, Ishihara kankyōsō no 'fūhyō higai' hatsugon o hihan: Iwakami Yasumi ni yoru zen Futabachōcho, Idogawa Katsutaka shi intābyū"]. *Independent Web Journal*. May 12, at: http://iwj.co.jp/wj/open/archives/139458 (accessed April 26, 2015).

Kariya, Tetsu. 2014, "Hanron wa saigo made omachi-kudasai." *Kariya Tetsu no kyō mo mata*. May 4, Web (blog), at: www.yomiuri.co.jp/adv/chuo/dy/research/20110602.html (accessed January 31, 2015).

Kariya, Tetsu. 2015, *Oishinbo "hanaji mondai" ni kotaeru [Responding to Oishinbo's "nosebleed problem."]*. Tokyo: Yūgensha, 2015.

Kariya, Tetsu and Hanasaki, Akira. 1992, "Nichibei kome sensō." *Oishinbo*. Vol. 36. Tokyo Shōgakukan, 91–202.

Kariya, Tetsu and Hanasaki, Akira. 1995, "Taimai no aji." *Oishinbo.* Vol. 49. Tokyo: Shōgakukan, 5–92.
Kariya, Tetsu and Hanasaki, Akira. 2010a, "Food and environmental problems" ["*Shoku to kankyō mondai*"]. *Oishinbo.* Vol. 104. Tokyo: Shōgakukan.
Kariya, Tetsu and Hanasaki, Akira. 2010b, "Food and environmental problems" continued ["*Zoku shoku to kankyō mondai*"]. *Oishinbo.* Vol. 105. Tokyo: Shōgakukan.
Kariya, Tetsu and Hanasaki, Akira. 2012, "Hisaichi hen: megenai hitobito." *Oishinbo.* Vol. 108. Tokyo: Shōgakukan.
Kariya, Tetsu and Hanasaki, Akira. 2013, "Fukushima no shinjitsu." *Oishinbo.* Vol. 110. Tokyo: Shōgakukan.
Kariya, Tetsu and Hanasaki, Akira. 2014, "Fukushima no shinjitsu." *Oishinbo.* Vol. 111. Tokyo: Shōgakukan.
Kinsella, Sharon. 2000, *Adult manga: Culture and Power in Contemporary Japanese Society.* Honolulu, HI: University of Hawaii Press.
Koide, Hiroaki. 2014, *Big Comic Spirits*, No. 25, June 2. Tokyo: Shōgakukan, 394.
Kyōdō News. 2012, "Evacuation order lifted for parts of Minamisoma." *Japan Times*, April 17, at: www.japantimes.co.jp/news/2012/04/17/national/evacuation-order-lifted-for-parts-of-minamisoma/#.Vm16qWThBQQ (accessed February 14, 2015).
Matsuda, Misa. 2011, "Rumors and 'fuhyo higai' (harmful rumors) during the ongoing disaster." *The Japan News by the Yomiuri Shimbun (Chūō Online)* June 6, at: www.yomiuri.co.jp/adv/chuo/dy/research/20110602.html (accessed April 20, 2015).
McCormack, Gavan. 2013, "Fukushima: An assessment of the quake, tsunami and nuclear meltdown." *The Asia-Pacific Journal.* March 25, at: http://japanfocus.org/events/view/178 (accessed April 19, 2015).
McCurry, Justin. 2014, "Gourmet manga stirs up storm after linking Fukushima to nosebleeds." *The Guardian.* May 22, at: www.theguardian.com/world/2014/may/22/gourmet-oishinbo-manga-link-fukushima-radiation-nosebleeds (accessed January 27, 2016).
Ministry of the Environment, Government of Japan Website. "Measures for decontamination of radioactive materials discharged by TEPCO's Fukushima Daiichi NPS Accident," at: http://josen.env.go.jp/en/ (accessed April 18, 2015).
Murayama, Hiroshi. 2014, "Henshūbu no kenkai." *Big Comic Spirits*, No. 25, June 2. Tokyo: Shōgakukan, 400.
Nelson, Craig. 2014, *The Age of Radiance: The Epic Rise and Dramatic Fall of the Atomic Era.* New York and London: Scribner.
*NHK World.* 2014, "Ima Fukushima o Egaku Koto: Mangaka-tachi no mosaku." NHK's show, *Kurōzu-up Gendai*, Broadcast June 2, at: www.dailymotion.com/video/x1y3wts_ (accessed January 25, 2015).
Ochiai, Eiichirō. 2014, "The manga 'Oishinbo' controversy: Radiation and nose bleeding in the wake of 3.11." *The Asia-Pacific Journal* Vol. 11, Issue 25, No. 4 (June 23), at: www.japanfocus.org/-Eiichiro-Ochiai/4138/article.html (accessed December 5, 2015).
"*Oishinbo*: On 'mistakes,' 'how wonderful' ... and 'The truth about Fukushima'" [*Oishinbo: 'gokai o' ya 'yoku zo'... 'fukushima no shinjitsu' ni*] 2014, *Mainichi shimbun.* May 20, at: http://mainichi.jp/select/news/20140520k0000m040092000c.html (accessed June 1, 2014).
"*Oishinbo* sōdō." 2014, *Takajin no soko made itte iinkai.* May 18, at: www.youtube.com/watch?v=d6eRlyup1Xk (accessed January 27, 2015).
Ōnishi, Motohiro. 2014, "*Oishinbo* tankōbon wa serifu shūsei: genpatsu meguri hanaji byōsha." *Asahi Shimbun* Digital Edition. December 11, at: www.asahi.com/articles/ASGDB5FLPGDBUCLV00D.html (accessed April 19, 2015).
Samuels, Richard J. 2013, *3.11: Disaster and Change in Japan.* Ithaca, NY and London: Cornell University Press.

Shiragari, Kotobuki. 2011, *Manga after 3.11* [*Ano hi kara no manga*]. Tokyo: Kadokawa.
Suzuki, Shoko. 2015, "In search of the lost *oikos*: Japan after the earthquake of 11 March 2011," in Isabel Capeloa Gil and Christoph Wulf (eds), *Hazardous Future: Disaster, Representation and the Assessment of Risk*. Berlin: Walter de Gruyter, 109–23.
Suzuki, Tomoyu. 2008, "Ryōri manga o meshiagare." *Excite Books.* April 8, at: http://web.archive.org/web/20080408145024/http://media.excite.co.jp/daily/thursday/030911/index.html (accessed April 19, 2015).
Takahashi, Naoyuki and Negishi, Takurō. 2014, "Oishinbo no byōsha ni hamon: Hibaku de hanaji ... kōgi aitsugu." *Asahi Shimbun* Digital Edition. May 12, at: www.asahi.com/articles/ASG5D4W9FG5DUGTB00C.html (accessed April 30, 2015).
Tōyama and Okumatsu. 2012, "Hōshasen naibu hibaku to Fukushima". *IWJ Independent Web Journal.* Recorded October 28, at: http://iwj.co.jp/wj/open/archives/37641 (accessed April 19, 2015).
*World Nuclear News.* 2013, "Futaba access restrictions relaxed." *World Nuclear News.* May 13, at: www.world-nuclear-news.org/RS-Futaba_access_restrictions_relaxed-1305134.html (accessed April 26, 2015).
Yamamoto, Osamu. 2013. *Nice Weather Today, Too: The Nuclear Power Plant Accident* [*Kyô mo ii tenki: Genpatsu jiko hen*]. Tokyo: Futabasha.

# 12 The politics of the senses
## Takayama Akira's atomized theatre after Fukushima

*Kyōko Iwaki*

Political apathy has been pervasive in Japan without much improvement for decades.[1] Indeed, after the Great Eastern Japan Earthquake and Tsunami followed by the Fukushima nuclear disaster, this political indifference seems to have ameliorated to a limited degree. However, the shift is significantly slim compared to the massiveness of the multivalent catastrophe in which the situation of damage is still expanding. The first anti-nuclear demonstration took place one week after the accident, when three activists called for action in front of the Tokyo Electric Power Company's (TEPCO) headquarters in Tokyo. Led by groups such as *Shirōto no ran* (*Amateur's Revolt*), the movement gained momentum on 10 April when 15,000 people gathered in Kōenji area, and later, on 11 June, around 79,000 people participated in the nationwide no-nuke action (Hirabayashi 2011). For around two years, all nuclear reactors in Japan were shutdown. However, in August 2015, Kagoshima's Sendai Nuclear Power Plant was restarted amidst massive protests.

From long before the government warranted the restart of the Sendai Nuclear Power Plant, several Japanese artists, such as the theatre director Takayama Akira (b. 1969), already questioned the effectiveness of the mass demonstration marches. After ardently attending countless demonstrations and meetings himself, Takayama concluded that organizing demonstrations in Japan today is only 'futile', as it is simply not 'functioning' (Takayama 2014a). This is not to say that Takayama is irresponsibly conforming to the apathetic political climate in order to forego the possibility of guiding the society in a better direction. Rather, what he is suggesting is that, taking into account the long lasting political inanity in Japan, citizens, especially artists, should understand that head-on confrontation is not the best way around in this country, and thus he proposes seeking viable alternatives which open up discourses for not a singular goal but rather for multitudinous outcomes.

As a matter of fact, Takayama is one of the most socially engaged theatre artists of his generation in Japan. As the leader of the theatre collective *Port B*, which he set up in 2002, he has always addressed socio-political issues that are extremely relevant to society. Moreover, unlike most Japanese companies, where the leader is both the playwright and the director, and thus undertakes the lion's share of the creativity, in this loose-knit group consisting of several scholars, artists and researchers, the core members gather and exchange opinions when a new production is launched and their abilities are required. The outcome is rarely presented in conventional theatre settings. The collective often, if not always, abandons the closed environment and thrusts their work into the grand cityscape of Tokyo, in order to challenge the concept of theatre. An emblematic example of Takayama's theatre output, which demonstrates his post-Fukushima political focus, as well as his methodological tenets, is *The Referendum Project* (*Refarendamu Purojekuto*, 2011), which was presented a mere seven months after the Fukushima catastrophe. As a preamble to the main argument developed in this chapter, the project should be briefly explained.

The title of the project is already provocative. It implies the possibility of a national referendum with regards to the continuation of nuclear reactors. In fact, a petition campaign for such a referendum was avidly taking place during the research period of this production. Taken at face value, therefore, the title suggests that Takayama aimed to encourage the first-ever national referendum. The outcome, however, was not so straightforward. It was more indirect, suggestive and subtle, as it attempted to reach beyond the broad parameters of politics in which the ultimate aim lies, almost always, in identifying all opinions as 'Yes' or 'No'. Rather than mechanically dividing people into groups by having them cast votes, Takayama set about collecting the uncertain voices of: first, the junior high school students of Tokyo and Fukushima; second, invited guest speakers at talks held during the project; and third, the audience members who attended the production (Takayama 2012: 36). There was also a fourth and invisible party, in that he intended to conjure up 'the voice of the dead', metaphorically, by visiting places that 'remind people of the deceased' (Takayama 2012: 36).

For two months in autumn 2011, this mobile project, consisting of only a small truck, visited fifteen locations around Japan. At each site, guest speakers such as poets, anthropologists, architects, critics and artists were invited to initiate a dialogue with Takayama at public halls and conference rooms. The audience was welcomed to attend the symposia in addition to watching video interviews inside the truck stationed at each venue. Inside the vehicle, around half a dozen monitors were meticulously aligned along both sides, each playing different short interviews with junior high school students. The interviews adopted Terayama Shūji's *machi-roku* – an on-the-street interview methodology that the theatre artist developed in his documentary television programme *You Are* (*Anata wa*, 1965). After watching several videos of their choice, the audience could cast a 'vote': not to decide on the question of nuclear power in Japan but to answer the same questions that the students answered, which were such everyday questions as 'What is your dream?'. Throughout the process, the floor of the bus shook whenever a new audience entered, thereby generating illusorily earthquakes. At the time of the performance, numerous aftershocks were still happening on the day-to-day basis and so, people could not discern whether the oscillations were natural or man-made – alluding to the dualistic causalities of Fukushima disaster.

The mission of this production was to foreground the voices of the above noted three parties plus the deceased. The production did not gain political

*Figure 12.1* The van used for *The Referendum Project* by Takayama Akira. Photo by Hasunuma Masahiro (courtesy of the photographer)

power in a literal sense, as the artist did not aim to, for instance, augment the anti-nuclear movements. His attempt was to speak beyond the known and the knowable of the existing politics; he avoided falling into the pitfall of compulsively urging people to render sensible words from the unfathomable. Conversely, as an artist who is not obliged to deliver simple viable solutions, Takayama fostered open ethical connections with heterogeneous voices, which, in the long run, may possibly become the basis to pit against the violent unifying power of politics. In Takayama's words, 'I define referendum as an antithesis to impulsively approaching authoritarianism' (Takayama 2012: 117).

When, after the Fukushima disaster, dramaturge Hayashi Tatsuki informed Takayama about Hans-Thies Lehmann's *Das politische Schreiben* (*Writing the Political*, 2002), Takayama noticed that he was interpreting the word 'politics' too straightforwardly. As Lehmann argues, politics in general 'cannot govern the deceased and the unborn' (Takayama 2012: 35). However, after the Fukushima catastrophe, which was a spatio-temporal disaster that not only eradicated space but also time, listening to those voices transcending a single lifespan – voices of afterlife as well as the unborn – became an imperative for Takayama. To this end, he started questioning the parameters of politics and tentatively concluded that, after Fukushima, 'perhaps the only possibility of theatre becoming political lies in *not* becoming political in the literal sense' (Takayama 2012: 35). The rhetoric of direct actions, at least for Takayama, was the idiom of activists and politicians. If laymen and artists, who were essentially not the owners of this language, hastily borrowed the idioms to speak out against the status quo, it is more than likely that their actions would eventually be subsumed by the existing political system. Also being aware of how theatre has been historically used to consolidate totalitarian unity, Takayama concluded that art, especially theatre – an art form that could persuade logically as well as emotionally – 'should avoid being political in the literal sense' and strive to speak from 'the interstices of politics' (Takayama 2012: 36).

Starting from this standpoint, this paper will first briefly explain the current socio-political climate, and argue why and to what extent the language of direct action is not the best option for artists in the post-Fukushima society. Second, on the basis of this contextual argument, the chapter will demonstrate how Takayama attempts to go beyond the political futility by developing an alternative language of the senses through his theatre production *Tokyo Heterotopia* (2013). One thing to note, throughout the chapter, is that the Fukushima catastrophe is not considered as a one-off disaster that has already finished and is in the past, but rather, as a 'host of incidents and disasters in chain reactions' still ongoing in the present (Virilio 2004: 257). Moreover, the catastrophe is not considered as an extraordinary event that erupted outside the ordinary, but rather, it is thought of as part and parcel of the everyday that continuously affects every aspect of humdrum life. For this reason, the chapter will elaborate the issues, which seem, at first glance, irrelevant to the catastrophe. However, to discuss the disaster not just on a national scale, but also on a palpable scale of neighbourhoods and streets is in effect a crucial, yet readily dismissed, aspect of post-Fukushima discussion – and, thus, should be addressed pertinently.

## Awakening the dimmed senses

With more than quadruple the amount of residents in Greater London, packed into a land just slightly smaller, the Greater Tokyo Area is by far the most populous metropolitan area in the world.[2] In proportion to its population density, the region is also oversaturated with immense number of cultural attractions, such as, to mention a few from its unfathomable list: 150,510 restaurants, 688 art galleries, 78,510 new book titles published and 24,575 theatre performances presented annually.[3] Not surprisingly, as an intuitive defence mechanism to protect oneself from the surfeit of stimuli, many citizens, in various degrees, become oblivious to, or, precisely, insensible to, the plethora of tumultuous events. As novelist Murakami Haruki succinctly suggests, post-war Tokyo is a place that has continually been hailed, 'the culture of slash-and-burn farming' (Murakami 1997). People slash plants in the cultural forest of the metropolis, unboundedly devour the capitalistic crops, and move to a virgin forest called the market to repeat the process all over; without ever even noticing the vast barren land left behind, or relishing the taste of the nutrients taken in.

Tellingly, to this day, the Asian capital of materialistic consumerism has acknowledged constant movement to resist stases: pressing citizens to produce

The politics of the senses 203

and consume – and, not stop and contemplate. In this megalopolis where 'consumerist culture [...] has been implanted through and through', it seems as though the citizens, who are sometimes pejoratively labelled as 'childish', 'superficial', or 'closed-circuit', has all at once abandoned the critical responsibility for sustaining a democratic society (Uchino 2004: 189). It was Mikhail Bahktin who claimed that carnivals are temporal events in which, for a few days a year, the norms of the everyday are subverted and thus the citizens are liberated from their day-to-day obligations. In just over seventy years, Bakhtin's assertion has, in a sense, become outdated; as, now in Tokyo, basically 'carnivals have been built-in to the everyday' (Suzuki 2012: 8). The sociologist Suzuki Kensuke asserts in his populist book *The Society is Becoming like a Carnival* (*Kānibaruka suru shakai*) that this Asian capital of materialistic consumerism is increasingly becoming carnivalesque (Suzuki 2012). Suzuki argues that, in order to attain temporal gratifications in a society where there are no clear 'motivations, objective ideals or coherent narratives to resort to', carnivals are now abruptly erupting everywhere in Tokyo without 'either historic or essential necessity' (Suzuki 2012: 8). It is not a routinely carnival that is cherished annually in the community, but rather a carnival of 'instantaneous fanaticism' lacking all social sustainability (Suzuki 2012: 138).

Whether or not the carnivals are now built-in to the everyday life of the urban dwellers in Tokyo is still disputable, as a robotic routine life is another veritable aspect of this city. Nevertheless, some of the requisites that predicate a Bakhtinian carnival do actually apply to the everyday life in Tokyo. For instance, Bakhtin claims that carnivals are 'not contemplated' (Bakhtin 1984: 122): the most profound philosophical contents are 'not clearly realized, but [...] somehow *dimly felt* by the participants' (Bakhtin 1993: 248, emphasis added). In a society where the events of yesterday, today and tomorrow rush at torrential speed, many people only instantaneously consume or, dimly perceive, the colourful stimuli and readily dismiss its depths, details and effects. To further support this argument regarding the dimming of the senses, playwright-director Hirata Oriza claims in his theoretical book, *Cities Do Not Need Festivals* (*Toshi ni shukusai wa iranai*), that today's mega cities like Tokyo arguably do not require any more festive events:

> For instance, in an agrarian society, there was the monotonous everyday life consisting of planting, mowing and harvesting. Through the repetition, people suppressed their exceeding energy and desired for an annual festival to give vent to the stress. [...] However, is the everyday of the present also monotonous? [...] We are surrounded with countless events and information; and amidst this flood, the urban dwellers are aggravated with a new type of stress. [...] Due to the bottomless stimuli of the city, we are placed on the verge of being dismembered from the decisions that derive from our own *bodily sensations*. I call this threat, and the aggravation that follows, the new 'stress of the city'.
> (Hirata 1997: 34–38, emphasis added)[4]

Hirata Oriza (b. 1962) is a playwright, director, owner of Komaba Agora Theatre, the leader of *Seinendan* (Youth group) theatre company based in Tokyo. Apart from being one of the most internationally well-known playwrights, he has also been an active voice in the politico-cultural sphere – for instance, he served an advisor to the deputy chief cabinet secretary in 2009. And, thus, when he was asked to speak on behalf of artists in front of politicians about the necessity of art festivals in Tokyo, he provided an argument as noted above. Being a Tokyoite himself, Hirata says that, in this city, 'the situation [of society] is inverted' (Hirata 1997: 38). People are not seeking for a greater carnivalesque atmosphere, but conversely, they are in search for 'a silent space that could shut out all information and just contemplate' (Hirata 1997). In the current climate of cacophony, Hirata suggests that a theatre should *not* function as a festive carnival, but rather, it should operate as a sanctuary for rituals: a place where the audiences could distance themselves from the secular world to rediscover their sensations bubbling up from their flesh. In his view, the fellow theatre makers should not increase but decrease the amount of stimuli. Hirata's hypothesis is that, 'stimulus demands a stronger stimulus', and thus, ends up in developing an endless desire for stimulation (Hirata 1997: 38). Although his argument is rather reductive, he seems to have a point to a certain extent, as now in Tokyo, the most radical stimulus is most rapidly consumed in the carnivalesque everyday.

On 29 June 2014, in Shinjuku, a middle-aged businessman committed suicide by self-immolation, in protest against the government's attempt to change the pacifist Constitution.[5] However, this political act was dismissed by most citizens and ignored by the mainstream media (Kingston 2014). Although some saw it as 'the most extraordinary act of political protest in the quarter century', the national public broadcasting organization, NHK, omitted the event in its flagship prime-time news programme (Ryan 2014). This reaction from the media was expected, because many media outlets felt obliged to refrain from covering the news to avoid encouraging further suicides, but also because, just recently, the president of the NHK, Momii Katsuto, had expressed his loyalty to the government line. He said, 'if the government says right, I won't say left' (Ryan 2014). Other than the indifference observed in the docile media, not many were prepared with a comprehensive answer to why information about the self-immolation so quickly disappeared from view and out of everyday discourse. One hypothesis was proposed after over a dozen locals, including artists, were questioned, two weeks after the event. As most interviewees responded with a confusing expression as if recalling a blurred event that happened in the faraway past, arguably, for people in Tokyo, it was one of the many carnivalesque events to be consumed and forgotten. Since the city dwellers perpetually receive an overdose of stimuli, their rusted senses were not able to perceive the magnitude of the event fully: people could only *dimly* comprehend the situation.

Four decades ago, the theatre director Terayama Shūji (1935–1983) made a prescient manifestation that 'setting dynamites in a building in the daytime to subvert the reality of the everyday, has, in effect, become "the reality of the everyday"' (Terayama 1983: 281). Today, his words resonate stronger than ever, since even an act of self-immolation cannot subvert, or even interfere, with the carnivalesque everyday life. As a matter of fact, against the backdrop of the ongoing Fukushima catastrophe, people seem to be wishing more for instantaneous gratitude as if to temporarily forget about the horrific event. In Tokyo today, the thrusting force of the carnivalesque is so strong that it instantly wipes out most radical political actions. When this logic is transposed to the theatre, the simplest conjecture is, that any direct intervention taken by an artist is most likely to fail. In point of fact, most Japanese artists are vaguely aware of this endemic social climate and thus, unlike *angura* (underground theatre) in the late-1960s, in which many theatre artists attempted to engage directly with the political revolution, current artists do not aspire to *go beyond* the status quo by developing a theatrical language analogous to an activist. Conversely, they subtly *go beneath* the everyday surface to function as, to borrow from Maria Shevtsova, an apparatus 'that picks up tremors below the surface [...] placing themselves [...] in a situation of anomie in respect of the collective mind' (Shevtsova 2009: 46). Their main task is not to provoke but to *invoke*. By activating the cognitive function that tunes in attentively to internal sensations, the artists awaken the audiences from their habitual carnivalesque dullness.

Understandably, however, when these artistic attempts were observed by an outsider, they seemed lukewarm or, moreover, simply apolitical. Takayama's words echoed like a strategic self-justification, shying away from the responsibility of igniting a national protest movement. For instance, when Matthias Lilienthal, the former director of the theatre Hebbel am Ufer, Berlin, was asked to comment on the reactions of the Japanese artists to the Fukushima nuclear catastrophe, he tersely disparaged them as 'too friendly':

> Despite the fact a catastrophe of such scale has occurred, the reaction to the event appears to be too friendly. [...] In 1950s in Germany, there was a mood in the society that strongly curbed the facticity of the Holocaust. [...] The most important thing at that moment was to constantly irritate the nerves of others, and to continue to do so, even when they did not welcome you for doing so.
>
> (Lilienthal *et al.* 2013: 57–58)

Lilienthal, who also worked as the dramaturge of late Christoph Schlingensief, known for his hyperbolic aesthetics, criticized Japanese artists. He said that if Schlingensief had been alive, he would have 'created an artwork which acknowledged to launch Super TEPCO (Tokyo Electronic Power Company)': he would have agitated the audience by suggesting that 'we should launch new nuclear plants, not even hundreds but thousands' (Lilienthal *et al.* 2013: 59). Diametrically opposing the aforementioned theory of Hirata, here, Lilienthal is proposing what could be termed as 'the dramaturgy of stimuli': a theatrical methodology that engenders more controversial stimulation to the point where people can no longer ignore it. This was the strategy that Schlingensief adopted, with inimitable intellectual sophistication, in projects such as *Bitte Liebt Österreich! (Please*

*Love Austria!*, 2000); and indeed, the performance agitated the cultivated yet mildly conservative audience of the Wiener Festwochen.

However, this does not substantiate that the same tactics will function in the deeply anaesthetic Japanese political climate. To begin with, to suggest creating hundreds of nuclear power plants would not function as irony in Japan, as, in reality, the prime minister has sold dozens of new plants to Turkey, Saudi Arabia, India and Eastern European countries after Fukushima. Moreover, taking into account that even an act of self-immolation vanished from the public discourse literally overnight, it is very unlikely that the same formula will elicit any effect. Sōma Chiaki, the former director of Festival/Tokyo, one of the most important performing arts festivals in Japan, mildly rebuts Lilienthal's opinion and claims that, although she highly respects the works by Schlingensief, in Japan after Fukushima, 'all provocative acts of an artist [analogous to Schlingensief] is somehow nullified by society' (Lilienthal *et al.* 2013: 59). According to Sōma, this was due to the nature of public consciousness in Japan: when a free-minded artist acted in a way that deliberately disrupts public morals, such an act was considered to be an outrageous *fukinshin* (indiscretion) and that person would more likely than not be 'implicitly rejected and ignored' (Lilienthal *et al.* 2013: 59). Due to the fact that a theatre artist as audacious as Schlingensief never appeared after Fukushima, it was not possible to evaluate the validity of Sōma's claim. Perhaps, as Lilienthal has rather condescendingly argued, the Japanese were only behaving in 'too friendly' a way through self-censorship, as they were more concerned with maintaining their societal status than changing the social situation. Or perhaps the dramaturgy of stimuli was indeed more harmful than beneficial to post-Fukushima society. Whatever the truth may be, against the backdrop of the post-nuclear chaos, most Japanese theatre artists opted for a 'friendlier' path and avoided further activating the already volatile society.

## Invisibly coerced harmony

*Fukinshin* was indeed a buzzword in the post-Fukushima society. In order to prevent a faux pas and irritating fellow citizens, many preferred to remain silent, or, to conform to the collective decision. Immediately after the catastrophe, for example, all four national theatres in Tokyo cancelled their shows for the whole month of March. Numerous other large- and middle-scale theatres followed the same decision.[6] According to playwright-director Noda Hideki (b. 1955), these rushed arrangements organized by big theatres 'implicitly guided the other decisions' (Noda 2011: 22). For this reason, when Noda announced that he would reopen his show *Minami e* (*To the South*), after four days of reluctant pause, partly from economic reasons – 'we theatre people are seasonal employees, so we can only eke out a living when there is a show' – some fellow colleagues accused his act as terribly *fukinshin* (Noda 2011: 22). The general logic by which the opponents stood was that, it is indubitably indiscreet to enjoy any entertainment when the afflicted are still suffering from the aftermath. Unlike the panoptic schema of Michel Foucault, even though people knew that no authority was monitoring them from far above, many Japanese, in post-Fukushima society, willingly conformed to the seemingly less indiscreet discipline to prioritize social harmony over individual liberty.

The theatre journalist Takahashi Yutaka, who closely observed the immediate post-Fukushima theatre reactions claimed that, at the time in Tokyo, there existed a strong *kūki* (literally, air or mood) that 'demanded self-restriction' to close the shows even though some theatres were devoid of any damage (Takahashi 2011: 19). More than fury, Noda felt fear. He was alarmed that this excessive homogenization of opinions, fortified by the *kūki* and self-censorship, strongly reminded him of 'the wartime thought-control operation by the military' (Noda 2011: 22). It was not a large leap for Noda to connect the post-Fukushima situation with the wartime imperialism, as, beneath the willing cancellation of critical thinking and dissent for the closure of theatres, there existed an analogous mechanism prompting social unification.[7] History proves that when Japanese undergo a state of siege, such as a war or a catastrophe, they are prone to degenerate into an *ochlos*: throng of people that Jacques Rancière terms as the multitude 'obsessed with its own unification at the expense of excluding the *demos*' (Rancière 2004: 88).

On a more pragmatic note, the tendency for social harmonization intensified immediately after the Fukushima disaster because the society was already in a tumultuous state. People intuitively prioritized the harmony-conscious ethics in a desperate attempt to sustain the barely-controlled status quo. What was considered a stable everyday life was now transformed into a chain reaction of events: meltdowns of nuclear power plants, ensuing food and water contamination, an increase of domestic refugees by rushed evacuations and mass unemployment at the relocated land. As a corollary of this fragile social condition, many strove to maintain stability, at least on a personal level. This was partially why, against the backdrop of the chaotic state, many theatre artists neglected adopting the more provocative approach – the dramaturgy of stimuli – like Schlingensief, that further enervates the vulnerable society. On the contrary, Hirata, Takayama and several eminent theatre artists commenced to seek a form of theatre that could provide a moment of contemplation. A space for silence, which, in turn, provides the audience with time to restore the order of exhausted senses by invoking their dormant attentiveness.

Additionally, what differentiates nuclear fallouts from all other disasters is, that, essentially the after-effects of the crisis are invisible, for at least few years until the radiation sicknesses appear. Even if an artist rashly attempts to reproduce or represent the catastrophic event, that effort is bound to fail, as unlike revolutions, war battles or pandemic diseases, there is simply no physical event that could be re-enacted. Consequently, due to this invisibility, all subjective views towards the nascent reality become equally valid. That is, the after-effects of the imperceptible catastrophe could be interpreted as both omnipresent and absent: some people may assume that the threat is ongoing and pervasive, whereas others may refute the idea and say that the effects are entirely negligible. Pierre Bourdieu claims 'proofs only convince the mind. Custom is the source of our strongest and most believed proofs' (Bourdieu 2000: 12). According to Bourdieu, no matter how solid the provided rationale of, for instance, a certain nuclear specialist may be, it is most likely that many would readily dismiss those facts and depend solely on their customary logic. Conforming to the norms is, in effect, the strongest proof that people believe; and, it is even more so, when the surrounding threat is invisible and thus one is capable of maintaining a relatively well-off life despite the potential danger. It is extremely less likely that in current post-Fukushima society, the citizens of the peripheral areas would enthusiastically welcome an artistic vision that tries to subvert the ostensibly peaceful society.

Up until this point, this chapter has provided three reasons why direct political interventions are less likely to function in post-Fukushima Tokyo. The first reason is *the numbing of the senses*, caused by the carnivalesque everyday life, and worsened by the chaotic state of the aftermath. The second is *the kūki of self-censorship*, which impels people to place a high value on social unity over individual voices. And the third is *the invisibility of the nuclear catastrophe*, which allows people to blindly believe in the customary logic as Bourdieu claims. Taking all this into account, a hypothesis for theatrical language that possibly could be politically effective after Fukushima can be deduced. That is, the artist should continuously try to reawaken the senses of the audience through their work, which, in turn, will shift the audiences' customary perspectives towards their self-evident facts and perceptions, however, by not violating the harmony-oriented regulation in society. In short, artists should aim to achieve internal shifts among the audience that are analogous to what Jacques Rancière calls 'le partage du sensible' (the distribution of the sensible) (Rancière 2004: 85).

## 'Revolution' through the senses

Rancière defines the distribution of the sensible as a political process in which the established framework of perception is reconfigured to induce 'a novel form of political subjectivity' (Rancière 2004: 9). What he explains through this terminology is that the aesthetics (or aísthēsis in Greek, meaning 'sensation') is neither naive nor apolitical, as it instills within people a novel vision replete with possibilities preceding any action. In this sense, Rancière propounds that aesthetics have their 'own politics, or its own meta-politics' as it could open up a new pathway for the yet-to-be-realized future (Rancière 2004: 80). Additionally, unlike most political actions in which the outcomes are measured through countable criteria, the main purpose of aesthetics does not lie in developing a collective body for achieving an unitary agenda, but rather, in 'introducing lines of fractures and disincorporations into imaginary collective bodies' by confronting 'the established framework of perception, thought, and action' (Rancière 2004: 85). Aesthetics is not about consensus, but rather about 'dissensus'; it is not about collective utopia but rather about multiple 'heterotopias' (Rancière 2004: 41). And, when these phrases are transposed to contemporary Tokyo, a politico-aesthetic action that may be more suitable is anticipated. That is, although the

Japanese may not be skilled at leading large-scale revolutions, as indeed, anti-government movements in the 1960s and 70s have practically failed; the same people are greatly adept at adopting small changes and accordingly improving their everyday life. Subsequently, the artists in Tokyo should utilize the latter ability of the people. They should not aim for radical and large-scale political revolutions united under the same slogan, but rather, work towards an inch of daily tectonic movements, by which, the accumulation of small differences would eventually change the whole picture of the state.

Terayama Shūji, an avant-garde poet and playwright who formed the *Tenjō Sajiki*[8] theatre troupe in 1967, was one of those artists who sought to accomplish this daily revolution. Terayama asserted that his company is an apparatus for achieving 'a revolution of everyday principals and reality that would not depend on politics' (Terayama 1983: 8). By politics, he does not suggest direct political interventions, such as, organizing an anti-government demonstration march. In fact, in his screenplay *The Dry Lake* (1960), he compared political protesters at that time to swine – 'People who go to protest marches are all swine' – and thus, Terayama was never forgiven by left-wing intellectuals for 'his indifference (or outright hostility) to their passionate political struggles' (Sorgenfrei 2005: 32). His coevals criticized Terayama's apolitical gesture, since many troupes at that time, such as Satō Makoto's Theatre Centre 68/71, or *Black Tent* (*Kuro tento*), called for a more direct political engagement by 'performing a theatre of revolution' (*kakumei no engeki*) (Rigley 2010: 127).

Senda Akihiko, who was one of the few Japanese critics to support Terayama, described his theatre as 'the great theatre of *kyo*' – the last Chinese character suggesting a double meaning of void and virtual (Senda 1983: 152). In order to question 'the foundational elements consisting theatre', Terayama audaciously discarded conventional theatre venues, rehearsals and sometimes even actors and scripts. By going out to the streets in his *shigaigeki* (city plays) and developing a *mise-en-scène* composed of ordinary people, he inverted the realm of the real and the virtual, in which 'reality was suspended' for a moment 'to establish, so to speak, the theatre of *kyo*' (Senda 1983: 152). Terayama always prioritized imagination over reality. He said that 'art needed to be severed from politics', and, to this end, no matter how harshly he was criticized by his contemporaries, who called for more direct political engagement, he refused to participate in politics.

Indeed, as Senda rightly calls it the theatre of *kyo*, Terayama believed that the lexicon of fiction, vision and imagination was the most powerful language of artists; if artists abandoned this asset and espoused the words of real-life politics, he or she would, accordingly, lose their power to change society. In a sense, it could be argued that perhaps Terayama was not indifferent to politics, but merely wished to speak through the language of meta-politics to achieve the revolution of everyday principles. A year before his death, he proclaimed, 'revolutions are not achieved by dynamites, but rather by subtle attentiveness' (Terayama 1982). Placed out of context, this statement may sound naive or, moreover, foolish. However, when it is adapted to current Japan, Terayama's assertion resonates strongly to the status quo. In a carnivalesque country inundated with stimuli, an artist should not exalt a radical revolution, but should seek a small and sensitive everyday 'revolution'.

## Carnival of an alienated awakening

The theatre works of Takayama Akira, which will be the main focus for the latter half of this chapter, are profoundly influenced by the theories of Terayama. Recently, when Takayama was invited to Berlin to participate in a symposium held at Hebbel am Ufer, which was part of the ten-day festival, *Japan Syndrome*, that focused on artists' reactions to the Fukushima disaster, he was questioned by one German audience, who was, in analogous manner to Lilienthal, somewhat frustrated by the mild measures taken by Japanese artists.[9] The man inquired whether there are any direct political interventions organized by local artists. After a hesitative pause, Takayama replied, 'Yes, of course', but went on to state that he is rather sceptical about these direct interventions:

> Of course, there are some underground political actions [also in Japan]. However, personally, I am sceptical about these activities. Is it really right to move towards activism? Shall we emulate Mishima Yukio, and take activist-like and terrorist-like means? [...] I think that these measures will not function in contemporary Japan, since, today, the reality that we live in is far more radical than art. Consequently, what we the artists should do is to take a distance from this radial reality, and cast a chill over the fanatic state. I think that a different kind of carnival, 'a carnival reminiscent of an alienated awakening [*Sameta kakusei no youna shukusai*]' should emerge from Japan.
>
> (Takayama 2014a)

The reason why the phrase 'a carnival reminiscent of an alienated awakening' seems rather abrupt in his speech is because Takayama is knowingly appropriating another's words: a term used by Terayama. By adopting a phrase that is a slightly different variation of what his predecessor terms as the 'collective ritual for alienated fanaticism' (*Samete kuruu tame no shūdanteki saigi*), he is trying to back-up his argument. Historically speaking, it was Terayama, who, against the backdrop of the politically fanatical late 1960s and early 1970s, assumed that theatres should not fetishize festive rituals, but rather should venture to 'demolish them' as if theatres function to accelerate the already fanatical atmosphere; it will only end in transforming theatres to shelters of illusion (Terayama 1983: 18). Terayama says that, through theatre making, all myths should be disillusioned – 'alienated and demolished' – in order to accomplish a 'collective ritual for an alienated fanaticism' (Terayama 1983: 18). In a similar vein, yet slightly differently, Takayama calls for 'a carnival reminiscent of an alienated awakening' (Takayama 2014a). Both Terayama and Takayama regard the theatre as an optimal apparatus for reconfiguring the established framework of perception.

*Figure 12.2 Tokyo Heterotopia* by Takayama Akira. Photo by Hasunuma Masahiro (courtesy of the photographer)

Through theatre, they try to dialectically approach the audience in order to achieve a revolution of the senses: 'a revolution of everyday principals and reality that would not depend on politics' (Terayama 1983: 8).

*Tokyo Heterotopia* is the artistic culmination of this everyday revolution organized by Takayama. In this production, Takayama espoused the theory of two thinkers, Terayama and Walter Benjamin. Takayama argues that, despite theoretical differences, such as their stances towards the reproduction of art works, both thinkers sought to rupture everyday routine by adopting new insights, through which a new politico-historical constellation would emerge. According to Takayama, what both thinkers thought of as a revolutionary moment emerged from acknowledging the slight shifts in everyday life, through which outmoded modalities suddenly attained new meanings. The word 'revolutionary' is metaphorical, as neither thinker aimed for direct political subversion. For Benjamin, this transformative experience suggested an instance of redemption, and he specifically called it the moment of 'messianic' revolution (Benjamin 1996: 37). It is the moment when, by the sudden flash, by which seemingly eternal images of the past are disrupted, and, also when, by contrast, the past events are reconnected from the standpoint of 'now-time' (*Jeztzeit*), the non-linear permutation of history is brought into relief (Benjamin 1999b: 463). A messianic moment is a revelatory spark, in which modernity's homogenous timescale is suddenly interrupted and, from that rupture of time, a vision of the past, present and future that sits outside of the normative time-frame becomes perceptible. In a nutshell, Takayama asserted his politico-aesthetic objective in *Tokyo Heterotopia* as follows:

> I think revolution per se will not happen in Tokyo. However, in the past, many visionary Asian revolutionaries lived here. The young Zhou Enlai [the first Premier of the People's Republic of China] stayed in Tokyo in 1917 and envisaged a revolution in his country. In 1957, the linguist Wang Yu De compiled the first ever Taiwanese dictionary whilst in Japan. Most people no longer know about these revolutionary events. So by collecting and connecting these hidden events [in *Tokyo Heterotopia*], I tried to form a *constellation*, bringing into relief an alternative history. Revolution, for me, is not about becoming bigger, louder and faster, but about becoming smaller, subtler and slower. It is about *stepping on the break* of history.
> (Takayama 2014b, emphasis added)

This brief passage succinctly suggests that the artist is citing the words of Benjamin. It was Benjamin who claimed that historians should grasp the 'constellation into which his own era has entered, along with a very specific earlier one', establishing a conception of 'the present as now-time shot through with splinters of messianic time' (Benjamin 1996: 397). By manifesting the constellation consisting of various events in the past and the present, Benjamin affirmed that a messianic image, or, a history concentrated in a single focal point, would come into being. Further, in contrast to Marx who claimed that 'revolutions are the locomotives of world history', Benjamin argued that it was otherwise: 'revolutions are an attempt by the passengers on this train – namely, the human race – to activate the emergency break' (Benjamin 1996: 402). By espousing these metaphysical doctrines, and by reinterpreting Benjamin's thoughts through his own reading, Takayama asserts that the immanent revolutionary histories in Tokyo could only be revealed when the participants, temporarily, brought their carnivalesque everyday lives to a standstill. He is not aiming for a large-scale political revolution united under a single slogan, but trying to work towards daily tectonic shifts of perceptions, which, when accumulated, may change the social fabric in the long run.

*Tokyo Heterotopia* is an attempt to suspend the conformist perceptions of the audience temporarily, and to provoke their pre-political state of emotion that could ideally lead to a new vision of history and future actions. Just like most of his so-called 'tour performances', using a promenade theatre-style performance format that the artist has been pursuing for the previous nine years, beginning with *Ippō tsūkōro: Sarutahiko eno tabi* (*One-Way Street: A Journey to Sarutahiko*, 2006), this production also took place outside of conventional theatre venues. In a slight divergence from his previous projects, though, the process of dehabituation was more extreme.

For instance, in his previous works, the tour was conducted in a group, such as *Sunshine 62* (2008), in which members of audience toured together. In *Tokyo/ Olympic* (2007), a Hato bus, a popular sightseeing bus was hired in which the audience rode on. In *Compartment City Tokyo* (2009), audiences encountered various artistic objects or performers, and they were even provided with a chance to talk with employed performers, who were various social pariahs. In all these previous productions, the audience could feel safer as they were collectively guided to see the artworks or to meet the performers at the end point. The process and the objective were clear.

In contrast, in *Tokyo Heterotopia*, the audience, or more precisely, the tour participants, was given carte blanche as to which places to visit and in what order, the means of transportation to use, and how long to take when visiting the designated venues. Thus, the response to the performance was far from unanimous, ranging from relatively positive responses ('an experience that changes your perspective of the city') to bemusement ('a peculiar contemporary art project').[10] The only thing the participants could latch on to was a small booklet and a portable radio, which were provided at the starting point of the tour. The booklet included simple maps with information on the thirteen designated places, respective appointed times, radio frequencies and short historical introductions to the sites.

When the participant visited the historical venues, they would tune the radio to the set frequency to hear a true-life narrative about Chinese, Taiwanese, Nepalese, Cambodian, Philippines and many other Asian revolutionists (or ordinary people with visions of changing society), who all once lived in Tokyo, and who strove to create small changes, or daily revolutions, in their respective communities. For instance, when visiting a grave in Shōunji, a Buddhist temple near Ikebukuro, the participants listened to a narrative of the linguist Wang Yu De, who edited the first Taiwanese dictionary in Tokyo, as he firmly believed that 'a language is the soul of people' (Suga *et al.* 2014: 206). The narratives provided were free interpretations of historical facts developed by four novelists suggesting that each story is only a single interpretations of historical events developed by four novelists; each story was only a single version of what is called 'history'. Additionally, as if to negate the authority of a written 'fact', these stories were *orally* conveyed through the radio by non-native Japanese speakers, which, through their stuttering and stammering, opened up a space to 'facilitate a sense of *interference*' in the ostensibly monadic history and ethical homogeneity (Eckersall 2013: 140).

More still, by designating eateries and restaurants serving Asian cuisine as many of the visiting sites, Takayama intended to make the experience not only aural but also sensory. That is, after arriving at the designated venues, the participants not only listened to a revolutionary story from the past, but also partook of the food that the revolutionaries had relished. When enjoying the same meatball soup (*qīngdùnshīzitóu*) as the young Zhou Enlai, the participants' senses of taste and smell would travel back a century, physically assimilating with those of the young revolutionary. However, the mind stayed in the immediate contemporary environment, maintaining a critical distance from the voices coming out of the radio, which could vanish at any moment by turning off the device. Takayama asserted: 'In order to be able to alienate the target object critically, one has to identify with it first, on a sensorial level', (Takayama 2014b). To this end, in *Tokyo Heterotopia*, epicurean bodily pleasures and rational critical functions are stimulated simultaneously, sensorially engaging the audience with the quasi-fictitious narrative of the past, yet critically disengaging them by the real-life *mise en scène* in the present. Through the calculated juxtaposition of fiction and reality, the emotional and rational, the past and the present, Takayama rattles the conformist attitude of post-Fukushima Tokyoites towards their everyday life. He requests them to question again if, in any way, the post-Fukushima society could be tolerated by the same old modalities. In this production, Takayama tries to reconfigure the audiences' worldview by developing, as Benjamin would say, new political 'constellations' from the 'now-time' (Benjamin 1999b: 463). Additionally, through this reconfiguration of the worldview, he is suggesting that similar everyday revolutions that Asian commonalties realized several decades ago, could also happen in current society. Throughout this production, the artist is acknowledging Terayama's 'revolution of everyday principals' (Terayama 1983: 8).

Needless to say, however, Takayama does not only emulate his predecessor's aesthetics. The differences between the two become palpable when the aforementioned phrases – collective ritual for an alienated fanaticism (Terayama) and, carnival reminiscent of an alienated awakening (Takayama) – are comparatively analysed. Placing the phrases side by side, it is easy to spot that whereas Terayama is focusing on the experience of the extraordinary fanaticism, the latter, by contrast, emphasizes the awakening from that fanaticism to an altered everyday view. Takayama describes this process of *alienated awakening* as follows:

> [L]et's say that you catch a fever and your temperature rises to thirty-nine degrees. Whether you are absorbed by the fever or are catabolized, many theatrical artists will claim that this condition of having a high temperature is where the theatre and drama lies. But what I am interested in is the condition when the temperature is cooling off, and when you sense that you are recovering. 'So, *this* is what people feel is normal.' You suddenly notice and appreciate every minor sensation with a fresh objectivity, even though you are the one who is experiencing it as yourself.
>
> (Iwaki 2011: 44)

While Terayama warned the audiences not to become absorbed in the rising heat of the spectacle, Takayama requests those same people to be fully attentive of the moment when the fever cools down. They are ultimately focusing on two different phrases of experience: the ascent and descent of the wave of heat. Along the same line, unlike his predecessor, Takayama does not strive to incite mayhem, such as the provocative tactics of striking and hypnotizing as practised in Terayama's 'guerilla' theatre (Terayama 1976: 341). According to Takayama, these shocking acts are no longer valid, as they are likely to be dismissed by the people 'as one of those many *misemono* (spectacles) in the everyday' (Takayama

*Figure 12.3* A Cambodian restaurant, which was one of the visiting sites of *Tokyo Heterotopia* by Takayama Akira. Photo by Hasunuma Masahiro (courtesy of the photographer)

2014b). When a theatre performance transforms into a surreal spectacle, its political power withers; it is disregarded as one of the many meaningless stimuli in the city. To put it differently, whereas Terayama believes that the power of the imagination is capable of subverting reality, Takayama avows that imagination should adapt, or even be subject to reality in order to let it implode. Moreover, Takayama thought that by adopting the style of the predecessor, the production might be considered as *fukinshin* by many post-Fukushima citizens, and thus readily be rejected. In order to circumvent these negations, Takayama tactfully developed a theatre that can no longer be noted as a theatre; he reduced the size of his production to the size of a portable radio in order to develop a theatre that can no longer be discerned as a theatre.

## Embedding atomized theatres

If one sees a burning airplane on the streets of Shinjuku today – like the performance of Terayama's *Man Powered Plane Solomon* (*Jinriki hikōki Soromon*, 1970) – it is most likely that, although it may at first attract the attention of the onlookers, it will soon be dismissed as meaningless fanatic art: just like the self-immolation act of the businessman was ignored. Spectators will be insensible to the performance, precisely because it is only a *misemono*, an illusion basically irrelevant to their lives. Being fully aware of this carnivalesque society incurring political anaesthesia, Takayama takes a different path in *Tokyo Heterotopia*. That is, he tries to hide or, moreover, 'integrate' the theatre aesthetics with the everyday functions (Takayama 2014b). Takayama explains this strategy by referring to Brecht's concept of 'Theaterchen', meaning tiny theatre or adorable theatre in German: 'Theaterchen is pregnant with possibilities precisely because they are "small, flexible and adaptable". I want to expand the possibility of theatre by diminishing or, moreover, demolishing its form' (Takayama 2014b).

Lehmann first described Theaterchen as a theatre that is 'small, flexible and adaptable' in a symposium organized at Festival/Tokyo (Lehmann *et al.* 2014: 42). Takayama was also a speaker at this symposium and immediately appropriated the term, as it strongly resonated with his own theory of 'atomization'. By atomization, he means 'physically segmentalizing theatres into minimum units' (Takayama 2014b). Diametrically opposite to Terayama who placed large, shocking spectacles in the middle of the city to attract public attention, Takayama aimed to diminish the form of theatre into a size as small as 'a smart phone application'. Through this act, he hoped that the audiences would smoothly integrate theatre into their everyday lives without even noticing the existence of the mini-theatre (Lehmann *et al.* 2014: 47). Through this atomization of theatre, Takayama aimed to reconfigure the audiences' conformist perceptions and modalities by introducing a renewed 'politics of the senses' within their everyday lives (Lehmann *et al.* 2014: 42).

This is why in *Tokyo Heterotopia*, he deliberately avoids using any actors or artistic objects. Conversely, the audiences are guided to restaurants, chapels, dormitories and other general facilities in which they will encounter, not gigantic historic monuments, but personal stories of small-scale revolutions, without ever physically leaving the everyday environment. To say more, the audiences are connected to the theatrical environment only through the provided portable radio, which is only slightly larger than the size of a smart phone. Reverting to his or her normal life amidst the performance is easily possible by simply turning off the device. The physical boundary between the ordinary and the extraordinary is abandoned to confuse the senses of the audience; and, when the audience enters a world where the everyday and the theatre are seamlessly integrated, Takayama hopes that they would gradually start mistaking the two realms. Slowly and discreetly, through the procedure of the tour performance, which includes dining at culturally different restaurants, the theatre director wishes that the audience would literally commence to *take in* the unfamiliar aesthetic principles into their everyday lives.

## Relaxed audience like a tourist

As a means of deploying the politics of the senses successfully, Takayama, additionally, attempted to involve a far more 'relaxed audience', compared to conventional theatregoers. By a 'relaxed audience', he is, of course, referring to Bertolt Brecht, who even encouraged the audiences to smoke and drink while watching his epic theatre. It was Brecht who refuted the aesthetics of Wagnerian immersive theatre by saying that when a person visits a theatre, along with their coats and hats, they hand in 'their normal behavior: the attitudes of "everyday life"' at the cloakroom (Brecht 2006: 39). Consequently, exploding the continuum of norms becomes difficult, as even before entering the auditorium, the audience have disrobed their normal attitudes (Terayama 1983: 8). For this reason, unlike Terayama, who, in direct response to Antonin Artaud, adopted a shock doctrine to increase the tension of the audience, Takayama never places the audiences in violent situations. As a matter of fact, he wants his audience to be relaxed as a 'sightseeing tourist' (Takayama 2014b). According to Takayama, the aesthetics of tourism has the ability to awaken the audience's senses, because, perhaps more than the theatre audience, tourists casually enjoy the process of encountering something unknown and unseen. In this sense, Takayama foresees that the aesthetics of tourism are abundant with possibilities for awakening the audiences' senses:

> When one compares the physical condition of a theatre audience and a sightseeing tourist, the latter is far more 'relaxed' than the former, and thus there are far more possibilities. Within the principle of the everydayness, the tourists encounter something novel, eerie and radical. And because they are relaxingly enjoying the process, the tourists are much more unguarded or, open, to novel perceptions.
>
> (Takayama 2014b)

To this end, although it sounds far-fetched, Takayama aimed to reconfigure the definition of 'tourism' through the wider frame of the theatre in *Tokyo Heterotopia*. That is, he invited the participants to his production not only as theatre audiences, but also as spatio-temporal travellers.

When thinking about the concept of the theatrical tourist, Takayama unavoidably adopted the aesthetics of Noh theatre. One of the most basic forms of Noh, especially Dream Noh (*mugen nō*), consists of a dialogue between the *waki* (the traveller), and, the *shite* (the dead, devils or spirits). When *Tokyo Heterotopia* is analysed through the lens of Dream Noh, it could be said that the participants were the *waki*, who travelled to heterogeneous sites and tuned into different spatio-temporal channels through the radio in order to evoke the voice of the *shite*, the dead. In fact, Takayama himself described the project as a form of 'spatio-temporal tourism' analogous to Noh (Takayama 2014b). Like *The Referendum Project*, the artist again encourages the post-Fukushima public to listen to the deceased. By placing the audience in a relaxed environment, and transforming them into theatrical tourists who transcend time and space, the artist introduced heterogeneous voices of past revolutionaries from 'the interstices of politics' (Takayama 2012: 36). By experiencing what Takayama calls the spatio-temporal tourism, he tries to reawaken the numbed senses and open up new perspectives, which could form the basis for fighting against the unifying power of politics.

In order to achieve this 'revolution' of the everyday principles, Takayama ambitiously declared his intention to set up more than 200 of these heterotopias in Tokyo before 2020, the year of the Tokyo Olympics (Takayama 2014b). In April 2015, Takayama introduced an iPhone application version of *Tokyo Heterotopia*, in which the sites would increase over the next five years, to militate against the united mainstream historical narrative that will be accelerated as the Olympic Games approach. However, the extent to which this intervention into the present would actually work is debatable. The concept of so-called revolution that Takayama promotes is only a metaphor or a political ideal, and seems to fall short of the burning necessity that activists feel to change the frustrating status quo. Indeed, it is important, as Takayama asserts, to listen to the yet-to-be-materialized reticent voices through his theatre of atomization when a national strategy for silencing the weak is underway. Ultimately, Takayama's work lacks the 'hypnotic beauty' of Terayama's, and the political ideology of Benjamin and Brecht's. For this reason, although Takayama's aim to reawaken the dimmed senses of the post-Fukushima public and to achieve a messianic revolution of everyday principles is conceptually clever and canonically plausible, one is tempted to suggest that it is purely theoretical.

To conclude, through the creation of multiple atomized heterotopias, the artist avoided providing a singular understanding of the ongoing Fukushima disaster; but, rather, introduced fragments and scatterings of voices that heed the danger of adopting a reductive answer. Along the same lines, by implanting the voices of the unfamiliar and the unknown in midst of the everyday environment, the artist aspired to catch the urban dwellers off guard to aptly reawaken their dimmed senses mired in the chaos of post-Fukushima society. Whether or not this approach that speaks through politics of the senses would be effective in real life politics is moot. For many, Takayama's atomized theatre may seem like an artform that is merely apolitical, naive, and even lacking a vision for direct political change. However, taking all together the socio-cultural condition of post-Fukushima community, Takayama thought that this tenacious procedure of everyday revolution, that inserts subtle ruptures to customary logics, is indeed the most efficient way to change the society, without ever being labelled as *fukinshin*. It may seem like a far too friendly reaction to the catastrophe, but realizing an inch of daily tectonic movements may perhaps be the optimal solution for changing the picture of the Japanese society in the long run.

## Notes

1 This article is a part of my PhD research which I am currently conducting. I am deeply indebted to Professor Maria Shevtsova for her corrections in bringing this article to publication and her continued support for my research.
2 'World Urbanization Prospects', *United Nations Population Division*, 10 July 2014, at: http://esa.un.org/unpd/wup/ (accessed 11 July 2014). According to the research, Tokyo is the largest city in terms of population with 37.8 million people living in the metropolitan area. Delhi and Shanghai follows with 25 million and 23 million respectively. Also, Tokyo is among only three of the high-income cities in the top ten. Osaka, Japan ranked seventh, and New York ranked ninth. See 'The Largest Urban Areas in the World', *Demographia World Urban Areas 10th Annual Edition*, 2014, at: http://demographia.com/db-worldua.pdf (accessed 11 July 2014).

3 The World Cities Culture Forum, *City Profile Tokyo*, 2014, at: www.worldcities cultureforum.com/cities/tokyo (accessed 10 July 2014).
4 All translations are made by the author unless otherwise stated.
5 On 11 November 2014, another man self-immolated himself as an act against the government at Hibiya Park, Tokyo.
6 For instance, Imperial Theatre, the Nissei Theatre, the Tokyo International Forum, Tennōzu Galaxy Theatre (will change to Tennōzu YOANI Theatre from April 2017) and the Sunshine Theatre, just to mention a few examples.
7 Hannah Arendt claimed in *The Origins of Totalitarianism* that, 'Totalitarianism is never content to rule by external means [...] totalitarianism has discovered a means of dominating and terrorizing human beings from within' (Arendt 1962: 325). Echoing Arendt's words, the post-Fukushima citizens willingly followed a unitary voice.
8 The theatre's named derived from Marcel Carné's film *Les Enfants du Paradis*, in Japanese, *Tenjō Sajiki no hitobito*. The name literally means cheap balcony seats.
9 *Japan Syndrome: Kunst und Politik nach Fukushima* was organized by Hebbel am Ufer theatre in Berlin from 20–29 May 2014. Alongside theatre performances by Okada Toshiki (*Ground and Floor*) and Murakawa Takuya (*Zeit-geber*), concerts, video screenings, lectures, installations and symposiums were presented.
10 Morimura Yasumasa expressed his mixed feeling towards the production, as he, as a visual artist, did not know whether or not to accept the production as theatre. Art producer Igarashi Taro hailed the production's astute structure which brings into relief the perspectives hidden inside the cityscape.

# References

Arendt, Hannah. 1962, *The Origins of Totalitarianism*. New York: Meridian Books.
Bakhtin, Mikhail. 1984, *Problems of Dostoevsky's Poetics*. Ed. and trans. Caryl Emerson. Minneapolis, MN: University of Minnesota Press.
Bakhtin, Mikhail. 1993, *Rabelais and His World*. Trans. Hélène Iswolsky. Bloomington, IN: Indiana University Press.
Benjamin, Walter. 1996, *Walter Benjamin Selected Writings Volume 1 1913–1926*, Marcus Bullock and Michael W. Jennings (eds). Cambridge, MA and London: Harvard University Press.
Benjamin, Walter. 1999a, *Illuminations*, Trans. Harry Zon. London: Pimlico.
Benjamin, Walter. 1999b, *The Arcades Project*. Trans. Howard Eiland and Kevin McLaughlin. Cambridge, MA and London: Belknap Press.
Bourdieu, Pierre. 2000, *Pascalian Meditations*. Trans. Richard Nice. Cambridge: Polity Press.
Brecht, Bertolt. 2006, *Brecht on Theatre: The Development of an Aesthetics*. Ed. and trans. John Willett. London: Bloomsbury.
Demographia World Urban Areas 10th Annual Edition. 2014, 'The largest urban areas in the world', at: http://demographia.com/db-worldua.pdf (accessed 11 July 2014).
Eckersall, Peter. 2013, *Performativity and Event in 1960s Japan: City, Body, Memory*. New York: Palgrave Macmillan, Kindle Edition.
Hirabayashi, Yuko. 2011, '6.11 Datsugenpatu demo 48% ga hatsu sanka netto kuchikomi 7 wari'. *Asahi Shimbun*, 19 October, at: www.asahi.com/culture/news_culture/TKY20 1110190199.html (accessed 29 November 2014).
Hirata, Oriza. 1997, *Toshi ni shukusai wa iranai*. Tokyo: Banseisha.
Iwaki, Kyoko. 2011, *Tokyo Theatre Today: Conversations with Eight Emerging Theatre Artists*. London and Tokyo: Hublet Publishing.

Kingston, Jeff. 2014, 'Shinjuku self-immolation act protests Abe's democracy hijack'. *Japan Times*, 5 July 25, at: http://www.japantimes.co.jp/opinion/2014/07/05/commentary/japan-commentary/shinjuku-self-immolation-act-protests-abes-democracy-hijack/#.V0FFF2Zb8VU (accessed 29 April 2016).

Lehmann, Hans-Thies. 2002, *Das Politische Schreiben: Essays zu Theatertexten*. Berlin: Theater der Zeit.

Lehmann, Hans-Thies, Carp, Stefanie, Okada, Toshiki, Takayama, Akira, Wetzel, Daniel and Miyazawa, Akio 2014, 'Engeki no mirai'. *F/T13 Document*. Tokyo: Festival/Tokyo Executive Committee Office.

Lilienthal, Matthias, Ōtori, Hidenaga, and Sōma, Chiaki. 2013, 'Genjitsu e no akushon: Engeki ga umidasu masatsu', interview by Suzuki Rieko, *F/T12 Document* (Tokyo: Festival/Tokyo Executive Committee Office), 55–64.

Murakami, Haruki. 1997, *Yagate Kanashiki Gaikokugo*. Tokyo: Kodansha.

Noda, Hideki. 2011, 'Naze gekijō no akari o keshite wa ikenai no ka'. *Higeki Kigeki* (June): 21–25.

Rancière, Jacques. 2004, *The Politics of Aesthetics*. New York and London: Continuum.

Rigley, Steven C. 2010, *Japanese Counterculture: The Antiestablishment Art of Terayama Shūji*. Minneapolis, MN: University of Minnesota.

Ryan, Kyla. 2014, 'NHK ignores Tokyo self-immolation'. *The Diplomat*, 1 July, at: http://thediplomat.com/2014/07/nhk-ignores-tokyo-self-immolation/ (accessed 10 July 2014).

Senda, Akihiko. 1983, 'Ōinaru kyo no engeki – Terayama Shuji ron'. *Gendaishi techō* Vol. 26, No. 12: 149–58.

Shevtsova, Maria. 2009, *Sociology of Theatre and Performance*. Verona: QuiEdit.

Sorgenfrei, Carol Fisher. 2005, *Unspeakable Acts: The Avant-Garde Theatre of Terayama Shuji and Postwar Japan*. Honolulu, HI: University of Hawaii Press.

Suga, Keijirō, Hayashi Tatsuki, Kimura Yusuke, Ono Masatsugu and Wen Yuju 2014, 'Tokushū: Tōkyō Heterotopia'. *Shinchō* (February): 186–289.

Suzuki, Kensuke. 2012, *Kānibaruka suru shakai*. Tokyo: Kodansha.

Takayama, Akira. 2008, *Dictée Forum Document: City, Community, Theatre*. Tokyo: Port B.

Takayama, Akira. 2012, 'Hajimari no taiwa: Port B Kokumin Tōhyō Purojekuto'. *Gendaishi techō special issue*. Tokyo: Shinchōsha.

Takayama, Akira. 2014a, 'Ende der Komfortzone: Kunst und Politic nach Fukushima'. *Japan Syndrome*. Hebbel am Ufer 2, Berlin. Symposium.

Takayama, Akira. 2014b, Unpublished interview with the artist.

Takahashi, Yutaka. 2011, 'Daishinsai o meguru shutoken no engeki'. *Higeki Kigeki* (June): 18–20.

Terayama, Shūji. 1976, *Meiro to shikai: waga engeki*. Tokyo: Hakusuisha.

Terayama, Shūji. 1982, *A Public Talk at Plan B. Tokyo*. YouTube at: http://youtu.be/Nk8CMcwhqjg (accessed 14 July 2014).

Terayama, Shūji. 1983, *Terayama Shūji Engeki Ronshū*. Tokyo: Kokubunsha.

The World Cities Culture Forum. 2014, *City Profile Tokyo*, at: www.worldcitiescultureforum.com/cities/tokyo (accessed 10 July 2014).

Uchino, Tadashi. 2004, 'Betraying "civility": On the notion of "artistic rigor"'. *Performing Arts* 5 (January): 189–204.

United Nations Population Division. 2014, 'World urbanization prospects', 10 July, at: http://esa.un.org/unpd/wup/ (accessed 11 July 2014).

Virilio, Paul. 2004, *The Virilio Reader*. Steve Redhead (ed.). Edinburgh: Edinburgh University Press.

# Index

Please note that numbers in **bold** denote figures.

*3.11* nuclear disaster (2011) 3, 9, 22, 41; art photography 62–7, **68**, **69**, 70; as catastrophe 60, 61, 78, 97, 105, 135, 137, 200, 201, 202, 205, 206; components 3–4; destruction/impact 3, 21, 22; fiction *see* fiction (3.11); as Japan's 9.11 3–6; post-3.11 mood of self-restraint 112; regionalization of 22; split between life and livelihood, causing 90, 92; as triple disaster (earthquake, tsunami and nuclear meltdown) 3, 9, 21, 40, 59, 71, 163; as 'unexpected' disaster 1–3; *see also* Festival/Tokyo 2012, responses to 3.11; Fukushima Prefecture

*A2-B-C* (2013) 13, 36n26, 91, 96, 101–5
Aalgaard, Scott 12
Abe, Shinzō 4, 5, 6, 34n4, 71, 81, 178; speeches to International Olympic Committee 7, 22, 34n3, 34n4; State Secrets Law (2014) 128
Abenomics (Abe Shinzō) 4, 81
*Act on the Protection of Specially Designated Secrets* (SDS) 6, 174n23
aesthetics 208; of tourism 217
affect 40, 95, 159
Agamben, Giorgio 92
*Ai to kibō no machi* (*A Town of Love and Hope*), 2014 110
Aldrich, Daniel 28
Alexander, Jeffrey 21, 22, 33
alienation 12, 49, 50
Amamiya, Karin 117
*Amateur Revolt* (*Shirōto no ran*) 3
Andrews, William 137
Angles, Jeffrey 14
ANPO (USA–Japan security treaty) 115

anthropogenic factors 58
anti-nuclear critique 114–19
anti-nuclear protests 123
*Antigone* (Sophocles) 14, 127, 130, 141, 142, 142n3; adaptation of (Carson) 131–5
ANTIGONICK 131
anxiety 14, 58, 75, 87, 117, 119, 145, 147, 148, 167, 172, 178, 188, 194n2, 195n25; about radiation 2, 78, 85, 90, 93, 103–4, 195n9; cancer/health risks 59, 78; for children 59, 103–4; uncanny 74, 86
*anzen shinwa* (safety myth) 4
Arab Spring 146
Arai, Takako 14, 145, 156–9
Arakida, Takeru 177
art photography 12, 63; dynamics of power, politics and space 70–2; of Fukushima disaster 62–7, **68**, **69**, 70; Japanese 61, 62; meaning 60; nostalgia in 58, 62, 64–5, 71; practical and theoretical considerations 60–2; subversion in 58, 60, 62, 66; variety 62
arts 9–11
*As for This Moment* (Takahashi, Mutsuo) 155
Ash, Ian Thomas 13, 36n26, 102, 107n11
*Ashes to Honey* (*Mitsubachi no haoto to chikyū no kaiten*, 2010) 96–7
atomic bomb 8, 16n9, 25, 34n9, 75
atomized theaters 199–220; embedding 215–16
Ayako, Fuji 39
Azuma, Hiroki 35n22

Bakhtin, Mikhail 203
Barthes, Roland 61
Beatles 43

## Index

becoming 43, 46, 51, 53; becoming-One 40, 41, 50, 52
Becquerel 195n13
Belarus 32, 97, 98, 183
Benjamin, Walter 211, 212, 214, 218
Bergson, Henri 40
Bey, Hakim 128
*Beyond the Cloud* (*Kiri no mukō no yonaoshi 3.11*, 2013) 93
*Big Comic Spirits* (manga magazine) 177, 178, 179, 186, 194n5
Big Data 9
Bikini Atoll, US thermonuclear device tests (1954) 77
*Bollard Syndrome* (Yoshimura, Man'ichi) 88n12
bonds (*kizuna*) 7, 35n12, 120
Bourdieu, Pierre 207–8
Bowring, Richard 142n2
Brecht, Bertolt 131, 216–17, 218
Breu, Sebastian 174n9
Brunt, Shelly 40
Burgin, Victor 60, 62
Butler Breese, Elizabeth 33
Button, Gregory 58–9

Campaign to Promote Cleanliness and Order in the Metropolitan Area 77
cancer/health risks 59, 78, 98
capitalism 44, 45, 48, 49, 50, 54n7, 55n10
Carné, Marcel 219n8
carnival: of an alienated awakening 210–15; carnivalesque everyday life 204, 205, 208, 212
Carson, Ann 130–5, 142n3
Caruth, Cathy 149
catastrophe 13, 15, 59, 61, 63; aftermath 172; of Fukushima disaster 60, 61, 78, 97, 105, 135, 137, 200, 201, 202, 205, 206; nuclear 3, 16n9, 62, 74, 90, 91, 92, 93, 94, 95, 96, 106, 107n6, 114, 117, 124n3, 205; and theatre 127–9; *see also 3.11* nuclear disaster (2011); *saigo* (after the catastrophe)
*Charm, The* (*Omajinai*) 34n11
Chernobyl 16n3, 29, 32, 35n19, 36n22, 74, 75, 97, 98, 114, 115, 117, 128, 141, 140–3
*Chernobyl Heart* (2003) 95
children, anxiety for 59, 103–4
Chinatown, Yokohama 76
*chinkon* (appeasing the dead) 11, 141
Chiten (theater company) 135
civil liberties, curtailing 128
Cochrane, Eddie 44–5

Cody Poulton, M. 14
collective representation 21
*Compartment City Tokyo* 213
compensation 2, 10, 75, 84, 85, 87n2, 100, 105, 116, 183, 185, 195n18
concentration camps 92
Consumer Affairs Agency 7
contamination: drinking water 75; food *see* food contamination; Japanese mainland 82; radiation-contaminated products 78; *see also* decontamination (*josen*); radiation exposure
*Controverses nucléaires* (2004) 95
counter-narratives 72
crisis of representation 146, 150
critical journalism 7
Cubitt, Sean 98
cultural trauma 21–2, 33
*Current Location* (*Genzaichi*) 14, 167–72

Daigo Fukuryū Maru incident 77
data generation, international 2
Date City, Fukushima Prefecture 87n7, 102, 182, 183, 185–6, 192
decontamination (*josen*) 2, 78–9, 87n7, 87n10, 177, 183–4, 187; and documentary films 92, 93, 97, 98, 100, 101, 103, 105; *see also* food contamination
deep ecology 107n5
Deleuze, Gilles 40
denuclearization, demand for 81
DiNitto, Rachel 11, 12, 34n2, 34n7
disaster returnees 28, 30
disaster zone 12
disasters: art photography 62–7, **68, 69**, 70; crisis of representation 146, 150; mapping as local 23–5; nuclear fallouts distinguished from other disasters 207–8; political dimension 58–9; socio-cultural dimension 9, 11; triple disaster of 3.11 (earthquake, tsunami and nuclear meltdown) 3, 9, 21, 40, 59, 71, 163
discrimination against Fukushima evacuees 8
documentary films, representing 3.11 90–109; mapping documentaries 92–6
documentary manga 191
documentary novels 23
Dylan, Bob 43

earthquakes 23, 24, 58; Kantō Earthquake of 1923 128, 129, 132; *see also 3.11* nuclear disaster (2011)

Index 223

Eat and Support (*tabete ōen*) 7, 8, 117
*Eating Ghost* (Sekiguchi, Ryōko) 78
Eckersall, Peter 142n1, 162, 174n8
Eguchi, Masato 140
Einstein, Albert 36n25
Elfriede Jelinek 14, 135–40
Eliot, T.S. 152
environmentalism 107n5, 138
ethnography 12
evacuation sites 136
exclusion zones 34; *see also* nuclear exclusion zones
Expo 1970 164, 174n12

Facebook 132, 146, 178
*Fahrenheit 9/11* (2004) 100
family values, traditional 114–16
"Far Shore The" (Tawada, Yōko) 79, 83, 84, 85
fascism 52
fear, collective and potential 76–9
Festival/Tokyo 2012, responses to 3.11 127–43; mourn, inability to 129–30; theatre and catastrophe 127–9
festivals 8–9; *see also* Festival/Tokyo 2012, responses to 3.11
fiction (3.11): contending narratives 21–38; documentary novels 23; experience of victim, mediating 25–7; local, mapping disaster as 23–5; refusal to take sides 32–3; Tōhoku 21, 27–8; *see also* 3.11 (2011); literature, following Fukushima
Field, Norma 106n1
fieldwork, ethnographic 12, 60
Figueroa, Pablo 12
*Five Days in March* (*Sangatsu no itsukakan*) 163, 167–8, 174n8
fixed terms 40, 41, 44
food 8, 32, 60, 103, 104, 182; Asian cuisine 213; contamination *see* food contamination; flavors/tastes 77, 78, 189, 195n10, 202, 213; of Fukushima 87n8, 185, 195n24; local/regional 77, 181, 189; magazines 77; manga *see* food manga; production 181, 183, 188; safety 17n14, 100, 115, 125n8, 180, 194n9; untested 189
food contamination 21, 75, 76, 78, 90, 97, 188, 189, 207; *see also* contamination; decontamination (*josen*)
food manga 177, 179–81, 193, 194n9
Foucault, Michel 162, 206
framing devices 23

France 4
Freud, Sigmund 149
*Friends after 3.11* (2012) 94
*fūhyo higai* (damage caused by rumors) 8, 14, 34n10
Fuji Film Photography Rescue Project 26
Fujiki, Hideaki 13
Fujiwara, Toshi 35n15
*fukinshin* (indiscretion) 206
Fukui District Court 6
Fukui Prefecture 79
*Fukushima 2011: A Record of People Exposed to Radiation* (*Fukushima 2011: Hibaku ni sarasareta hitobito no kiroku*) 94
*Fukushima: A Record of Living Creatures* (*Fukushima: Ikimono no kiroku*, 2013) 95
Fukushima City 99, 102, 103, 182, 184, 188
Fukushima Daiichi Nuclear Power Plant 21, 23, 67, 86, 87n2, 87n6, 113, 135, 177, 193
Fukushima Daiichi Nuclear Power Station 42, 53, 91, 93–4
Fukushima I incidents 1, 5, 6, 16n3, 116; *see also* 3.11 nuclear disaster (2011)
*Fukushima Never Again* (2012) 94
Fukushima Prefecture 15, 23, 42, 59, 78, 118; Date City 87n7, 102, 182, 183, 185–6, 192; *see also* 3.11 nuclear disaster (2011)
Fukushima Prefecture Radioactivity Measure Map 35n21
*Fukushima: We Won't Forget* (*Wasurenai Fukushima*, 2013) 94
Funahashi, Atsushi 93, 99
Funky Monkey Babys 39
*furusato* (home/native place) 48, 54, 177, 185, 188
Furuya, Minoru 112
Futaba District xiv, 59, 63, 93–4, 113, 178, 186, 195n20; and documentary films on 3.11 93, 94, 99, 107n4

*Ganbarō Nippon* (Hang in there, Japan!) 7, 40, 189
Geilhorn, Barbara 14–15, 173n1
*gendai shi* (contemporary poetry) 159n3
gender roles, traditional 124
Germany 5
Gerrard, Greg 107n5
ghostly spirits 11
Girard, René 141

# 224　Index

Goethe 135
Gotō, Kenji 80
Great East Japan Earthquake *see 3.11 nuclear disaster* (2011)
Greater Tokyo Area 201
Greenpeace 59
gripes 43–4
*Ground and Floor* (*Jimen to yuka*) 11
Guantanamo Bay 92
Guattari, Felix 40

Habermas, Jürgen 93
Hachirō, Yoshio 189
Haiti earthquake (2010) 58
Hakim Bey 128–9
Hamaoka Nuclear Power Plant, Shizuoka Prefecture 5
Hanasaki, Akira 190
*Handbook of Contemporary Poetry* 152, 154, 155
Harootunian, Harry 40, 44
Hayashi Kyōko 84
Hayashi, Tatsuki 201
Heinz, Andrea 139
heterotopia 162, 208, 217–18
*Hibakusha at the End of the World* (*Hibakusha: Sekai no owari ni, 2003*) 96
Hida, Shuntarō 97
Hidemichi, Kawanishi 7
*hikikomori* 141
Hirasawa, Keishichi 128
Hi-Red-Center (avant-garde artist group) 77
Hirata, Oriza 10, 142n1, 163, 203
Hirata Village 99
Hiroshima 16n9, 25, 75, 84, 113
*Hōjōki* (An Account of My Hut) 129
Hori, Arinobu 178
Hoshino, Tomoyuki 174n15
*Hot Pepper, Air Conditioner, and the Farewell Speech* (*Hotto peppā, kūrā, soshite owakare no aisatsu*) 164, 174n24
*hyōgensha* (those expressing themselves through art) 4
hysteria 114, 117, 122, 123

ICRP (International Commission on Radiological Protection) 90, 188
Idogawa, Katsutaka 59, 186, 187
*Imagination Radio* 9, 10
Imai, Tomoki 12, 60, 61, 66, **68, 69, 70**
Imawano, Kiyoshirō 43, 53, 54n5
information tsunami 2
Inoue, Jun'ichi 111, 142n4

institutional trust 116–17
International Atomic Energy Agency (IAEA) 16n3
International Commission on Radiological Protection (ICRP) 90, 92, 188
International Nuclear Event Scale (INES), 7-level 16n3
International Olympic Committee (IOC) 7, 22, 34n3
*In the Grey Zone* (2012) 101
*In the Zone* (Taguchi Randy) 11–12, 23, 33, 35n20; mapping radiation 28–30
irradiated zones 12, 33–4
Ishimure, Michiko 144
Ishinomaki (town) 23
*It Was a Lie All Along* (*Zutto uso datta*) 12
Italy 4
Itō, Noe 128
Itō, Seikō 9
Itō, Yasuhide 147
Iwai, Shunji 94
Iwaki, Kyōko 171, 214
Iwasaki, Akira 107n7
Iwata-Weickgenannt, Kristina 13, 15n1
Iwate Prefecture 23, 59, 148

Janet, Pierre 148–9
Japan: population 158; privatization 81; ranking in Reporters Without Borders' Press Freedom Index 6; unity of 11
Japan–Turkey nuclear deal (2013) 4
Japanese art photography 61, 62; *see also* art photography
Jelinek, Elfriede 74, 127, 135–40
*jishu hinan* (voluntary evacuation) 115
*John Lennon Super Live* 43
journalism, critical 7
judiciary 6

*kabe shimbun* 34n6
Kagoshima Prefecture 5, 79
Kaibara, Yūzan 186, 191
*Kakusei: The Fukushima End* (2013) 94
Kamaishi (town) 23
Kamanaka, Hitomi 13, 96–101
Kamata, Minoru 97, 98
Kameoka, Daisuke, 154–5
Kanagawa Arts Theater (KAAT) 167
Kanno, Yoshiaki 102, 110
Kantō Earthquake of 1923 128, 129, 132
Kariya, Tetsu 15, 190
*katakana* script 25
Kawakami, Hiromi 87n11
Kawanishi, Hidemichi 7

Kawauchi Village 99
*Kein Licht* (No Light) 14, 135, 136, 137, 139, 141
Kesennuma (town) 23
*Kibō no kuni* (Land of Hope) 10, 110–26
Kimura, Saeko 12–13
Kingston, Jeff 2, 4, 5
Kitakata (in Aizu) 182
*kizuna* (bonds of love and friendship) 7, 35n12, 120
Kōda, Shōsei 80
Kodama, Tatsuhiko 97, 98
*Kōhaku uta gassen* 39–40
Koide, Hiroaki 178
Koizumi, Jun'ichirō 80, 81, 82
Köln, Schauspiel 135
Kōri District 99
Kōriyama City 95
Kosako, Toshisō 119
*Kotoba (Words)* 137
Kubota, Nao 110
Kudō, Ken'ichi 28, 35n22
Kunsten Festival des Arts (KFDA) 173n3
Kuroko, Kazuo 25
Kuznetsova, Marina 184
Kyoto University of Art and Design 134
Kyūshū, southern 1

*Land of Hope* (Sono Sion) 10, 13, 110–26; reading as anti-nuclear critique 114–19
Lehmann, Hans-Thies 201
Lennon, John 43
Lilienthal, Matthias 205, 206
Liscutin, Nicola 6–7
literature, following Fukushima 74–89; collective and potential fear 76–9; radiation exposure 79–85; *see also* fiction (3.11)
Lithuania 4
*Living in Fukushima: A Story of Decontamination and Reconstruction (Fukushima ni ikiru: Josen to fukkō no monogatari*, 2013) 91, 93, 98, 99, 100, 101, 103, 105
*Lovers in a Time of Nuclear Energy* (Takahashi, Mutsuo) 154
Luhmann, Niklas 118

McCormack, Gavan 194n1
*Man Powered Plane Solomon (Jinriki hikōki soromon)* 215
*Map of Hope: The Tale of 3.11 (Kibō no chizu: 3.11 kara hajimaru monogatari*, 2012) 11–12, 23, 24, 32

Marcuse, Herbert 173
*marebito* 134
Márquez, Gabriel García 154
Marshall Islands 74
Martin, Carol 162
mass media 5, 6, 7, 24, 25, 26, 80, 90, 91, 93, 111, 132, 189
Matsuda, Masataka 14, 127, 131, 132, 133
Matsumoto, Hajime 3, 16n11
Meiji period 7
memory xv, 54n4, 67, 71, 72, 77, 164, 193; trauma 12, 127
men's weeklies 123
message songs 42, 43
milk, powdered 75
Minamata disease 16n9, 75, 85, 95, 124n3
Minamisanriku (town) 23
Minamisōma 29, 60, 87n2, 182, 183, 190, 195n27
Minamisōma City 63, 97, 146, 189
Ministry of Agriculture, Forestry and Fisheries 7
Ministry of Economy, Trade and Industry (METI) 35n21, 107n2, 195n26
Ministry of Education, Culture, Sports, Science and Technology (MEXT) 184
Ministry of Health, Labor and Welfare 16n6
Ministry of the Environment 87n10, 93, 177
Mishima, Yukio 135
Miura, Motoi 135
Miyagi Prefecture 23, 24, 59
Miyazawa, Akio 140
Momii, Katsuto 6, 204
Moore, Michael 100, 102
Morimura, Yasumasa 219n10
Morinaka, Takaaki 149
Morioka, Rika 116
mourning 11, 129–30
muon tomography 16n7
Murakami, Haruki 201
Museum of Contemporary Japanese Poetry 147
musical critique 39–57

Nagabuchi, Tsuyoshi 12, 47–52
Nagasaki 16n9, 25, 75, 84, 113
Nakaguchi, Shinsuke 187
Nakahara, Chūya 148
Namie District/town 12, 35n20, 50, 61, 63, 64–5, 98, 99, 100, 185; Shinmachi Street **64, 65, 66**
Nanba, Daisuke 188
Naoto, Kan (DPJ) *see* Kan, Naoto (DPJ)

## 226  Index

Narita International Airport 107n8
National Diet Library, Tokyo 1
National Police Agency 2, 34n1, 144
natural disasters *see* disasters
nature, living out of balance with 151–6
newspapers 34n6
NHK Broadcasting Culture Research Institute 4, 41, 72n4, 204
*Nihon Keizai Shimbun* (newspaper) 87n3, 87n4, 87n5, 87n9, 87n10
Nihonmatsu City 12
Niimi, Tokuhide 147
NISA (Nuclear and Industrial Safety Agency) 4
Nishi Sugamo Arts Center 133
Nishi Sugamo Arts Factory 133
*No Light* (Jelinek) 74
*No Man's Zone* 35n15
Noda administration 5
Noda, Hideki 206, 207
Noda, Manabu 167
Noh theatre 217
northern Japan 1; re-mapping 6–9
nosebleeds 177, 186, 187, 193, 195n22
nostalgia 11, 12, 31, 32, 35n15, 62–7, **68**, **69**, 70, 105, 181; in art photography 58, 62, 64–5, 71
Nozaki, Kan 156
NPPs *see* Nuclear Power Plants (NPPs)
Nuclear and Industrial Safety Agency (NISA) 4
nuclear exclusion zones 21, 28, 35n14
nuclear Ginza (*genpatsu Ginza*) 5
*Nuclear Nation* (*Futaba kara tōku hanarete*, 2012) 91, 93, 94, 99, 100, 101, 105, 106, 107n4
nuclear power 41; referenda 4
Nuclear Power Plants (NPPs) 5, 7, 8, 16n12, 17n16, 17n17; *see also* Fukushima Daiichi Nuclear Power Plant
nuclear reactors 6, 16, 16n3, 79; reactors I, II and III 2; reactors III and IV 16n12
nuclear victim (*hibakusha*) *see* victims, nuclear (*hibakusha*)
nuclear village (*genshiryoku mura*) 4–5, 47–52, 91, 111
nuclear weapons 34n8; *see also* atomic bomb

Ochiai, Eiichirō 187
Ochiai, Keiko 3
*Odayaka* (*Odayakana nichijō*, 2012) 106, 107n12

Ōe, Kenzaburō 3, 144
Ogawa, Shinsuke 95, 107n8, 115
Ogino, Anna 36n23
Ōi nuclear power plant 5, 16n12, 79
*Oishinbo* (food manga) 15, 179–81, 194n9
Okada, Toshiki 11, 14, 142n1, 162–4, **165**, 166, 173n3, 174n9, 174n15, 174n17, 174n21; approach to theater 163–4; *Current Location* (*Genzaichi*) 167–72; *Unable to See* 14, 164, **165**, 166
Okinawa, Japan 82
Onagawa Town, Miyagi Prefecture 1
Ōnbou, Pelican 174n12
*One* (*Hitotsu*) 12
*Ordinary Lives* (*Futsū no seikatsu*, 2013) 94
Orikuchi, Shinobu 134
Ōsugi, Sakae 128
Ōta, Shōgo 163
Ozeki, Ruth 87n1

*Pandora's Promise* (2013) 95
Parry, Richard Lloyd 129–30
Paterson, Eddie 162, 174n8
*Pebbles of Poetry* (Wagō, Ryōichi) 14, 147, 148, 149, 150
photographic effect 60–1
photography *see* art photography
photojournalism 60
Plaza for Information on Decontamination 93
Poetic Scape gallery, Naka Meguro 63
poetry 144–61; *gendai shi* (contemporary poetry) 159n3; vigils 156, 157
polemic 189–91
politics of the senses 216, 218
Port B (theater company) 135, 136, 139, 199
positionality 10, 11, 12, 13, 14
power supply systems 4
*Pray for Japan* (*Nihon e no inori: Kokoro o hitotsuni*, 2012) 93
Press Freedom Index, Reporters Without Borders 6
privatization 81
*Project Fukushima!* 8, 17n 18
*Prolog?* (Jelinek, Elfriede) 140
psychological trauma 21
Public Security Preservation Law 128
*punctum*, compared to *studium* 61

*Quiet Theatre* (*shizuka na engeki*) 134
quilt making 8–9
quotations 142n5

Index    227

radiation exposure 21, 23, 29, 31, 32, 36n26, 86, 187; invisibility of 3; irradiated areas 12, 33–4; literature, following Fukushima 75, 77, 79–85; low-level 8, 13, 98, 99, 177, 186, 187, 188, 193; *see also* contamination; decontamination (*josen*); food contamination
radiation readings 188
'radiophobia' (*hōshanō kyōfushō*) 123
Rancière, Jacques 207, 208
reactors *see* nuclear reactors
recessive reality 15, 166
Reconstruction Agency 78
reconstruction nationalism (*fukkō nashonarizumu*) 7
*Record of a Journey to Antigone* (Matsuda, Masataka) 14, 132, 134, 136, 137
recovery (*fukkō*) 12, 23, 24, 26, 27, 28, 34, 51, 63, 101, 120, 128, 150
referenda on nuclear power 4
*Referendum Project, The* 15, 200, 217
relaxed audience 216–18
Reporters Without Borders, Press Freedom Index 6
Reuters 17n13
*Revival & Survival* (online bookstore) 144
revolution of everyday principals 209, 211, 214, 218
rewriting, power of 156–9
Rikuzentakada (town) 23
Rokkasho Nuclear Fuel Reprocessing Facility 97
*Rokkasho Rhapsody (Rokkashomura rapusodi*, 2006) 96
Rolling Stones 43
Rosenbaum, Roman 15n1
rumors, damage caused by (*fūhyo higai*) 8, 14, 34n10
*ryōri manga* (food comics) 181

Safecast (citizen action group) 35n21
*saigo* (after the catastrophe) 3
Saitō, Kazuyoshi 12, 42–7
Sakamoto, Ryūichi 3
Sano, Shin'ichi 10, 150
Sasa, Genjū 107n7
Satō, Makoto 209
*Sayonara II* (short android theatre play) 10
Schlingensief, Christoph 205, 207
Schmitt, Carl 92
science fiction 14, 31, 81, 174n20
*Seconds from Disaster: Fukushima, Japan's Nuclear Nightmare* (2012) 95

Sede, Ikuo 84
Sekiguchi, Ryōko 13, 75, 76, 77, 85
self-censorship (*jishuku*) 171, 206, 207, 208
Self-Defense Forces 80
self-responsibility 118
*Semicircle Law* (photo book) 66, 67, 70
Senda, Akihiko 209
Sendai Nuclear Power Plant 79, 199
senses: dimmed, awakening 202–6; harmony, invisibly coerced 206–8; numbing of 208; politics of 216, 218; 'revolution' through 208–10
sentiment 49, 50, 51, 94, 100, 142, 151
Shevtsova, Maria 218n1
Shigematsu, Kiyoshi 9, 11–12, 21, 22–3, 33, 35n14; mapping of the local in fiction 24, 25
Shigeru, Izumiya 43
Shimada, Masahiko 144
Shiriagari, Kotobuki 179
*Shirōto no ran* (Amateur Revolt) 3
Shizuoka Prefecture 75; Hamaoka Nuclear Power Plant 5
Shōgakukan (publisher) 178, 179
*Shūkan Kinyōbi* 111
*Shūkan Shinchō* (weekly magazine) 123
Sichuan earthquake (2008) 58
*Sicko* (2007) 100
*Since Then* (Takahashi, Mutsuo) 154
*Site Fights: Divisive Facilities and Civil Society in Japan and the West* (Aldrich) 28
slow dramaturgy 162, 163, 164, 169, 173, 174n8
Smolnikova, Valentina 97
social media 9, 14, 17n18, 132, 136, 146, 193
*Society is Becoming like a Carnival, The* (*Kanibaruka suru shakai*) 203
Solnit, Rebecca 128–9, 140
Sōma, Chiaki 206
*Sonic Life of A Giant Tortoise, The* (*Zōgame no sonikku raifu*) 163
Sono, Sion 10, 13, 110–26
Sontag, Susan 61
Sophocles *see Antigone* (Sophocles)
*sōteigai* (exceeding all expectations) 1
South Asian tsunami (2004) 58
SPEEDI (System for Prediction of Environmental Emergency Dose Information) 125n7
Stallings, Robert A. 11
State Secrets Law (2014) 128

stigmatization of Fukushima evacuees 8
Stone, Robert 95
street protests 3
Street View Mapping Project (Google) 35n17
stress-related illnesses 59
*studium*, compared to *punctum* 61
subsidies, NPP-related 7
subversion 11, 12, 60, 62–7, **68, 69**, 70; in art photography 58, 60, 62, 66; political 70, 211
Suga, Keijirō 155
*Summertime Blues* (Cochrane) 44–5
*Surviving Internal Exposure* (*Naibu hibaku o ikinuku*, 2012) 13, 96–101
Suzuki, Kensuke, 203

Taguchi, Randy 21, 22–3; *In the Zone* 11–12, 23, 28–30, 33, 35n20
Taka Ishii Gallery, Roppongi 66
Takahama Nuclear Power Plant/reactors 6, 79
Takahashi, Mutsuo 14, 145, 151–6
Takahashi, Yutaka 207
Takaichi, Sanae 78
Takashi, Hosokawa 39
Takashi, Mikuriya 3, 16n10
Takayama, Akira 14, 15, 136, 137, 139, 199–220
Takeru, Arakida 187
Takikawa, Tatsuko 187
*Tale for the Time Being, A* (Ozeki, Ruth) 87n1
Tama Art University 63
Tamura City 12, 182
Tanka 147
*Taste of Fukushima, The* (*Le goût de Fukushima*, Sekiguchi, Ryōko 2012a) 77
Tawada, Yōko 13, 75, 76, 79, 81, 83–6
temporality 3, 11, 12
temporary autonomous zones 128, 129
TEPCO (Tokyo Electric Power Company) *see* Tokyo Electric Power Company (TEPCO)
Terayama, Shūji 136, 200, 204, 204–5, 209, 209–10, 214, 215, 216, 218
theater: atomized 199–220; and catastrophe 127–9; as counter-site 162; of divestiture 163; Noh theater 217; Okada's approach to 163–4, 166; post-Fukushima 162–76; *Quiet Theatre* (*shizuka na engeki*) 134
thermonuclear device tests, Bikini Atoll (1954) 77

*These Things Here and Now* (Takahashi, Mutsuo) 153
*This is not an Accident* (Sekiguchi, Ryōko) 76, 78
Three Mile Island 74
thyroid cancer 98
Tōhoku (northern Japan) 1, 7, 58; fiction 21, 22, 24, 27–8; Tohuku 17n16
*tōjisha* (affected individuals) 10
*Tōjisha shuken* (The Sovereignty of the Tōjisha) 10
Tokuma Shoten 147
Tokyo Electric Power Company (TEPCO) 4, 6–7, 16n8, 22, 32, 33, 42, 67, 91; headquarters 199; information policy, disastrous 117, 119, 146; and literature following Fukushima 83, 86, 87n2; Super TEPCO 205
*Tokyo Heterotopia* 15, 211–12, 214, 216, 217
Tokyo National Diet Library 1
Torok, Maria 127
*Total Living* (Miyazawa, Akio) 140
trauma: cultural 21–2, 33; memory 12, 127
Treat, John 141
triple disaster of 3.11 (earthquake, tsunami and nuclear meltdown) 3, 9, 21, 40, 59, 71, 163
trust, loss of 116–17, 118
*Truth about Fukushima, The* (documentary) 15, 179, 181–7, 189, 190, 193
Tsuchimoto, Noriaki 95
Tsukijii Little Theater 129
*Tsunageyō Nippon* (*join together*, Japan) 128
*Tsunami and the Cherry Blossom, The* (*Tsunami soshite sakura*, 2011) 93
tsunamis 1–2, 3, 23, 24, 58
Tsushima, Yūko 144
Turkey 4
Twitter 9, 14, 17n18, 132, 133, 134, 136, 146, 147, 148, 149, 150, 178

Ueno, Chizuko 10
*Unable to See* (Okada, Toshiki) 14, 164, **165**, 166
United Nations Scientific Committee on the Effects of Atomic Radiation (UNSCEAR) 178
United Nations University Institute for the Advanced Study of Sustainability 93
Ushiro, Ryūta 174n13
utopia 162, 166, 169, 170, 173, 208

Van Hove, Ivo 142n3
victims, nuclear (*hibakusha*) 22, 23, 25–7, 84; discrimination and stigmatization against 8; experience of, mediating 25–7; identifying 22, 75; and survivors 137–8; visitor or victim? 30–1; *see also* nuclear victim (*hibakusha*)

Wagō, Ryōichi 9–10, 14, 15n1, 145, 146–51, 155
Waits, Tom 43
Wakasa Bay 16n12
Watanabe, Toshiya 12, 60, 61, 63
*We Are the Undamaged Others* (*Watashitachi wa mukizu na betsujin de aru*) 163
Weisenfeld, Gennifer 129, 132
*Welcome to Fukushima* (*Fukushima e yōkoso*, 2013) 94
*Will, The: If Only There Were No Nuclear Power* (*Yuigon*: Genpatsu sae nakereba, 2013) 94
*Wind from Fukushima* (*Fukushima karano kaze*, 2011) 95
Wöhr, Ulrike 115–16, 124n5
*Women of Fukushima* (*Fukushima no joseitachi*, 2012) 94

*Words Whispered by Candle Flames* (poem collection) 156
World Cities Culture Forum 219n3
World Health Organization 98
World War II, Japan's defeat in 3
*Writing Ground Zero* (Treat) 141

Yamagata International Documentary Film Festival 96
Yamamoto, Osamu 194n9
Yamamoto, Tarō 124n1
Yamanote Line, Tokyo 136
Yamashita, Shun'ichi 101, 102, 107n10, 122
Yazawa, Misaki 122–3
*Yomiuri Shimbun* newspaper 16n10
*yonaoshi* (correcting the world) 129
YouTube 132, 146
Yukawa, Haruna 80
Yuki, Masami 17n14

Zelizer, Barbie 62–3
zone, use of term 31
*Zone I* 21
*Zone II* 21, 35n18
*Zone: The Life Did Not Exist* (2013) 95

# Taylor & Francis eBooks

## Helping you to choose the right eBooks for your Library

Add Routledge titles to your library's digital collection today. Taylor and Francis ebooks contains over 50,000 titles in the Humanities, Social Sciences, Behavioural Sciences, Built Environment and Law.

**Choose from a range of subject packages or create your own!**

**Benefits for you**
- Free MARC records
- COUNTER-compliant usage statistics
- Flexible purchase and pricing options
- All titles DRM-free.

**Benefits for your user**
- Off-site, anytime access via Athens or referring URL
- Print or copy pages or chapters
- Full content search
- Bookmark, highlight and annotate text
- Access to thousands of pages of quality research at the click of a button.

**REQUEST YOUR FREE INSTITUTIONAL TRIAL TODAY**

**Free Trials Available**
We offer free trials to qualifying academic, corporate and government customers.

## eCollections – Choose from over 30 subject eCollections, including:

| | |
|---|---|
| Archaeology | Language Learning |
| Architecture | Law |
| Asian Studies | Literature |
| Business & Management | Media & Communication |
| Classical Studies | Middle East Studies |
| Construction | Music |
| Creative & Media Arts | Philosophy |
| Criminology & Criminal Justice | Planning |
| Economics | Politics |
| Education | Psychology & Mental Health |
| Energy | Religion |
| Engineering | Security |
| English Language & Linguistics | Social Work |
| Environment & Sustainability | Sociology |
| Geography | Sport |
| Health Studies | Theatre & Performance |
| History | Tourism, Hospitality & Events |

For more information, pricing enquiries or to order a free trial, please contact your local sales team:
**www.tandfebooks.com/page/sales**

The home of Routledge books

**www.tandfebooks.com**